Beyond 1995

The Future of the NPT Regime

Center for National Security Studies
Los Alamos National Laboratory

ISSUES IN INTERNATIONAL SECURITY
Series Editors: Robert E. Pendley and Joseph F. Pilat

BEYOND 1995: The Future of the NPT Regime
Edited by Joseph F. Pilat and Robert E. Pendley

EUROPEAN SECURITY IN THE 1990s: Deterrence and Defense after the INF Treaty
Walter Laqueur and Leon Sloss

A Continuation Order Plan is available for this series. A continuation order will bring delivery of each new volume immediately upon publication. Volumes are billed only upon actual shipment. For further information please contact the publisher.

Beyond 1995

The Future of the NPT Regime

Edited by

Joseph F. Pilat and
Robert E. Pendley

Center for National Security Studies
Los Alamos National Laboratory
Los Alamos, New Mexico

Foreword by
Hans M. Blix

PLENUM PRESS • NEW YORK AND LONDON

Library of Congress Cataloging-in-Publication Data

Beyond 1995 : the future of the NPT regime / edited by Joseph F. Pilat
 and Robert E. Pendley.
     p.   cm. -- (Issues in international security)
   Includes bibliographical references.
   ISBN 0-306-43291-9
   1. Nuclear nonproliferation. 2. Security, International.
 I. Pilat, Joseph F. II. Pendley, Robert E. III. Series.
 JX1974.73.B49 1990
 327.1'74--dc20   89-29827
                                                              CIP

This series of books has been prepared as an account of work sponsored by the Los Alamos National Laboratory. Neither Los Alamos National Laboratory, any agency thereof, nor any of their employees makes any warranty, expressed or implied, or assumes any legal liability or responsibility for the accuracy, completeness, or usefulness of any information, apparatus, product, or process disclosed, or represents that its use would not infringe privately owned rights. Reference herein to any specific commercial product, process, or service by trade name, mark, manufacturer, or otherwise does not necessarily constitute or imply its endorsement, recommendation, or favoring by the United States Government or any agency thereof. The views and opinions of authors expressed herein do not necessarily state or reflect those of the United States Government or any agency thereof.

The Center for National Security Studies

The Center for National Security Studies (CNSS) is a studies and analysis organization of the Los Alamos National Laboratory. Drawing on the broad knowledge at Los Alamos of science and engineering relevant to national security issues, the Center's research focuses on the interaction between technology and policy and on developing insights that may improve the relationship between the development of new technology and the achievement of national policy goals.

The principal mission of the Center is to promote and conduct long-term research and analysis in the broad areas of defense policy and arms control, focusing in particular on the requirements for technology that derive from trends in national and international security policy. In addition, it helps Los Alamos management and technical staff better address national defense needs by providing insight into national security policy, strategy, and technology issues, and by assisting in Laboratory long-range planning. The Center also provides a forum for the exchange of ideas on international security issues among Laboratory personnel, government agency staffs, university faculties, and interested citizens.

To implement its programs and activities, the Center supports an interdisciplinary staff, drawing on expertise from the social sciences, including history and political science; the physical and biological sciences; engineering; and mathematics. The Center conducts an active visitor and consultant program. It encourages short- and long-term visits by experts from government and private institutions and by university faculty members.

The Center sponsors seminars, workshops, and conferences designed to bring Los Alamos personnel into contact with outside experts and to stimulate broader discussion of the relationships between technology and U.S. defense policy. The Center also acts to enhance communication between Los Alamos and other organizations, such as colleges and universities, that are studying issues of interest to the Laboratory.

v

The publications program of the Center is intended to communicate the results of studies to Laboratory personnel and to reach a wider policy analysis community in government, military, and academic circles, as well as private industry. Central to the publications program is this book series, *Issues in International Security*. The volumes in the series are based on research conducted by the Center's staff and by internationally recognized experts working with the CNSS. A primary goal of the series is to promote the reasoned analysis of international security issues, with emphasis on how these issues shape and are shaped by technological developments.

The Authors

Richard Butler, Ambassador of Australia to Thailand

Antonio Carrea, Counselor on Nuclear Affairs for the Embassy of Argentina in Austria

Lewis A. Dunn, Assistant Vice President, Science Applications International Corporation, McLean, Virginia

David Fischer, Consultant, International Atomic Energy Agency, Vienna, Austria

Ryukichi Imai, Ambassador of Japan to Mexico

Ashok Kapur, Professor of Political Science, University of Waterloo, Ontario, Canada

Munir Ahmad Khan, Chairman of the Pakistan Atomic Energy Commission, Islamabad, Pakistan

Harald Müller, Senior Fellow and Director of International Programs, Peace Research Institute, Frankfurt, Federal Republic of Germany

Robert E. Pendley, Staff Member, Center for National Security Studies, Los Alamos National Laboratory, Los Alamos, New Mexico

Joseph F. Pilat, Staff Member, Center for National Security Studies, Los Alamos National Laboratory, Los Alamos, New Mexico

Benjamin Sanders, Coordinator of the Programme for Promoting Nuclear Non-Proliferation, New York, New York

Lawrence Scheinman, Professor of International Law and Relations, Cornell University, Ithaca, New York

Mohamed I. Shaker, Ambassador of the Arab Republic of Egypt to the United Kingdom

Raju G. C. Thomas, Professor of Political Science, Marquette University, Milwaukee, Wisconsin

Foreword

There is almost universal support for the view that the world would be an even more dangerous place if there were to be more nuclear-weapon states. There would be more fingers on more triggers and, probably, a greater risk that a trigger might be pulled with incalculable consequences. It is easy to see, therefore, that there is a collective interest in avoiding the spread of nuclear weapons to further countries.

Nations do not, however, normally undertake or refrain from actions because of such a collective interest; they do so because of their individual interests. This is especially true in the field of national security. A nation perceiving that it has a real interest in developing nuclear weapons is not very likely to refrain from doing so merely because it is told such development would be bad for the world community.

If the global interest in avoiding the spread of nuclear weapons to more countries is to succeed, conditions that make it in the interest of each individual nation to renounce nuclear weapons need to be created or maintained. Fortunately, conditions have prevailed in which the vast majority of nations have seen an advantage in making legally binding nonproliferation commitments. An important rationale for many of these countries has been that these commitments would facilitate the transfer of desired civil nuclear technology. For many developing countries, which have seen neither any potential usefulness in possessing nuclear weapons nor any possibility within a foreseeable time to acquire such weapons, the advantage of assistance in acquiring various techniques for the peaceful uses of nuclear energy has probably been another rationale. For yet other countries, the potential dangers flowing from the possession of nuclear weapons—for example, the risk of becoming the target of a preemptive strike in a crisis situation—might have been a factor speaking in favor of an explicit and binding nonproliferation commitment. The assurances given by nuclear-weapon states to seek agreement on disarmament, along with the assumed high thresholds for the use of nuclear weapons, may have been enough to raise hopes among nonnuclear-weapon states that they will not face threats or the use of nuclear weapons in an armed controversy.

These factors, which have led states to make binding commitments to non-proliferation, notably through the Treaty on the Nonproliferation of Nuclear Weapons (NPT), are also the factors that will be decisive for the future of the treaty. While several of the excellent contributions to this book wisely explore the grave consequences of an unraveling of the NPT, there are, I think, some grounds for optimism.

First of all, the present international climate augurs well for a reduced reliance on force or the threat of force and for disarmament, including nuclear disarmament. With a substantial reduction of the nuclear threat perceived, there should also be a lessening of the perceived need for nuclear weapons for defense. Such a change might help not only to maintain existing binding nonproliferation pledges but might even trigger some additional pledges as well. Second, a continued facilitation of, and direct assistance in, the transfer of nuclear technologies to countries that have made binding nonproliferation commitments will be a factor favoring their continued commitment. Any risk of a discontinuation of such transfers in the event of a lapse of nonproliferation commitments, conversely, will be a factor suggesting to governments that they should not allow these commitments to expire or otherwise be terminated.

While these general rationales, hopefully, will be decisive for states' attitudes to the question of continuing the NPT beyond 1995, and may even be persuasive vis-à-vis countries that have not, so far, made binding nonproliferation commitments, special arrangements will probably be needed to obtain such commitments in some specific areas, notably the Middle East. When we have witnessed, recently, how one intractable problem area after another—Afghanistan, Cambodia, the Western Sahara, Angola, Namibia—seem to be moving toward settlement, one may perhaps dare to be optimistic also about nonproliferation and drastic disarmament. There is no lack of tasks to which the resources now spent on nuclear arms production and development could be better used.

HANS M. BLIX
Director General
International Atomic Energy Agency
Vienna, Austria

Preface

Even before the Fourth Review Conference of the Parties to the Treaty on the Nonproliferation of Nuclear Weapons (NPT) convenes in August 1990, the attention of interested government and nongovernmental experts has already been focusing on 1995. The NPT, the centerpiece of the international nonproliferation regime and the most widely adhered to arms control treaty in history, is not of indefinite duration. As provided in Article X of the treaty, "twenty-five years after the entry into force of the Treaty, a conference shall be convened to decide whether the Treaty shall continue in force indefinitely, or shall be extended for an additional fixed period or periods." The conference that will decide the future of the NPT will be held in 1995.

To address the prospects for the treaty beyond 1995, we have assembled a diverse and distinguished group of contributors. From many nations, they present differing points of view, and several have played key roles in past review conferences. The essays in the volume are oriented to the future, but they are deeply grounded in the past. And reflecting and supporting the historical approach taken by many of the contributors, documents pertinent to the history of the NPT are collected in an appendix. We believe this volume will appeal to policymakers and publics who are well versed in the history of the NPT, as well as to readers who have only recently become interested in arms control and nonproliferation issues.

In compiling the documents presented in the appendix, we acknowledge and appreciate the assistance of the United States Arms Control and Disarmament Agency and the United Nations Department for Disarmament Affairs. We also acknowledge and appreciate the dedication and contributions of Center for National Security Studies staff. Arthur Nichols, the Center's editor, established with the publisher editorial procedures and schedules, and he copyedited the volume. Molly Cernicek's contributions were substantial; she played a critical role in collecting, preparing, and organizing the documents in the appendix. The skilled assistance of Janis Dye was indispensable in preparing the manuscripts for the publisher, and Wanda Franks deserves special recognition for facilitating our communication with the contributors.

JOSEPH F. PILAT
ROBERT E. PENDLEY

Contents

9. European and Global Security in a World without the NPT 93

Harald Müller

10. The NPT and Nuclear Proliferation in East Asia: Views toward the 1990s 107

Ryukichi Imai

11. World and Regional Power Relations without the NPT 117

Ashok Kapur

12. Should India Sign the NPT? 133

Raju G. C. Thomas

13. A World without the NPT? 151
Joseph F. Pilat

Conclusions 165
Joseph F. Pilat and Robert E. Pendley

APPENDIX: Toward 1995: United Nations Documents Relating to the Establishment and Functioning of the NPT, 1959–1988 169

Introduction

Joseph F. Pilat and Robert E. Pendley

Nineteen ninety-five will be a fateful year for the Treaty on the Nonproliferation of Nuclear Weapons (NPT), which was concluded in 1968 and came into force in 1970. The NPT is not of indefinite duration. Twenty-five years after its entry into force, as provided in Article X.2 of the treaty, a conference must be convened in 1995 to decide whether it will continue indefinitely or be extended for an additional fixed period or periods of time.

Does the NPT have a future beyond 1995? The treaty, with approximately 140 parties, is the most widely adhered to arms control treaty in history and, at the Third Review Conference of NPT Parties held in Geneva in 1985, the parties reaffirmed its value by consensus. Yet, despite its widespread support, the NPT has been severely criticized ever since it was negotiated, and several important global and regional powers have refused to sign the treaty.

OBJECTIVES AND OBLIGATIONS OF THE NPT

What are the objectives of the NPT and the obligations of its parties? The fundamental objective of the treaty is to prevent the spread of nuclear weapons to states that do not possess them. The obligations of states parties to the NPT established in the first three articles of the treaty are designed to ensure the realization of this objective. Pursuant to Article I, each nuclear-weapon state (NWS) party undertakes not directly or indirectly to transfer nuclear weapons or other nuclear explosive devices or the control over such weapons or explosive devices, and not to assist, encourage, or induce any nonnuclear-weapon state (NNWS) to manufacture or otherwise acquire nuclear weapons or other nuclear explosive devices, or the control over such weapons or explosive devices. Under Article II, each NNWS party to the NPT undertakes not to receive the transfer or direct or indirect control of nuclear weapons or other nuclear explosive devices, and not to manufacture or

Joseph F. Pilat and Robert E. Pendley • Staff Members, Center for National Security Studies, Los Alamos National Laboratory, Los Alamos, New Mexico.

otherwise acquire nuclear weapons or other nuclear explosive devices and not to seek or receive any assistance in their manufacture. Article III provides that each NNWS party to the NPT is to accept international safeguards, as set forth in agreements to be negotiated with the International Atomic Energy Agency (IAEA), to be applied to all source or special fissionable material in all peaceful nuclear activities within its territory, under its jurisdiction or carried out under its control anywhere, for the purpose of verifying treaty obligations, with a view to preventing the diversion of nuclear energy from peaceful uses to nuclear weapons or other nuclear explosive devices.

Another objective of the treaty is to ensure the fullest cooperation in the peaceful uses of nuclear energy, consistent with the objective of nonproliferation. While Article III provides for strict controls over peaceful nuclear activities to assure they are not misused for proscribed military purposes, Articles IV and V provide a framework for peaceful cooperation. All the parties to the treaty undertake, in accordance with Article IV, to facilitate the fullest possible exchange of equipment, materials, and scientific and technological information for the peaceful uses of nuclear energy. Those parties to the treaty with an advanced nuclear capability are to cooperate in contributing to the further development of the applications of nuclear energy for peaceful purposes, especially in the territories of nonnuclear states parties to the treaty, with due consideration for the needs of the developing areas of the world. Article V affirms the principle that potential benefits from peaceful nuclear explosions should be made available to nonnuclear states on a nondiscriminatory basis.

A third objective of the NPT is to encourage arms control efforts in the nuclear and nonnuclear arenas. Accordingly, under Article VI, each of the parties undertakes to pursue "good faith" negotiations on effective measures relating to cessation of the nuclear arms race at an early date, to nuclear disarmament, and to achieving a treaty on general and complete disarmament under strict and effective international control. And, in this vein, Article VII states that nothing in the treaty affects the right of any group of states to conclude regional treaties in order to ensure the total absence of nuclear weapons in their respective territories.

OBJECTIONS TO THE TREATY

The NPT was in 1970 the boldest attempt in the post-World War II era to use multilateral means to balance international concerns for global security with emerging national ambitions in the nuclear area. It sought to reflect the interests of the United States and the Soviet Union in ensuring a degree of stability in their relationship and in sensitive regions; to address the desires of developed industrial nations, especially in Europe and Japan, to exploit a promising technology for commercial use and advantage; and to meet the hopes of developing nations that transfers of nuclear scientific and technological capabilities might ameliorate their desperate economic and social straits. Accordingly, the operative articles of the NPT clearly evince a desire to balance the rights, obligations, and benefits of the states parties to the treaty.

How could these balanced rights and obligations appear so repulsive to certain states that they have waged a virulent campaign against the treaty for decades? The objective of nuclear nonproliferation embodied in the treaty is trumpeted by virtually all states, even those now seeking nuclear-weapon capabilities, and constitutes a "norm" of international behavior that has virtually silenced those who would advocate the possession of nuclear weapons as a symbol of prestige. But the NPT's structure, as well as what many critics see as a failure to adequately implement its key provisions, has been criticized throughout the twenty-year history of the treaty. For nonparty states such as China, India, and Argentina, the treaty is viewed as structurally discriminatory because it distinguishes between nuclear and nonnuclear states on the basis of whether they had manufactured or exploded a nuclear weapon or other nuclear explosive device before January 1, 1967. The problem, as perceived by these critics, is that the NPT effectively freezes the status quo of "nuclear haves" and "nuclear have-nots" and provides for differing obligations on the part of each group, relegating the have-nots to permanent international inferiority.

Along with the critique of the structure of the NPT, there has been almost constant criticism of the implementation of major provisions of the treaty, especially Articles IV and VI. This critique is voiced not only by nonparties, but has appeared among parties themselves at the review conferences of 1975, 1980, and 1985.

At the first review conference, the often contentious debate addressed the manner in which the treaty's objectives were being fulfilled, focusing on the issues of nuclear disarmament, security assurances, and access to atomic energy for peaceful purposes. Dissatisfaction was expressed by the parties in each of these areas, but it was the debate over Article VI that was most disruptive. The majority of the parties present perceived the treaty primarily as an arms control effort, designed to balance the obligations and responsibilities of the nuclear and nonnuclear states, and held that the nuclear states had not adequately implemented their Article VI obligations. And, in their view, the implementation of the treaty during its first five years had unduly emphasized the obligations of the nonnuclear rather than those of the nuclear states. However, largely as a result of the efforts of the Swedish conference president, the parties were able to agree on a final declaration that reaffirmed their support for the treaty while recommending measures to improve its implementation.

At the second review conference, the most intense debate was again on the implementation of Article VI. A majority of the NNWS parties participating in the conference asserted that the nuclear states had not adequately fulfilled their obligations to negotiate effective measures to halt the nuclear arms race and achieve nuclear disarmament, and they urged the nuclear states to intensify their efforts in arms control and disarmament. The NWSs parties to the treaty—the United States, the United Kingdom, and the Soviet Union—recounted their efforts in this area, including their efforts to achieve a comprehensive ban on nuclear testing and to provide security guarantees to nonnuclear-weapon states.

But access to the peaceful use of nuclear energy was also a divisive issue in the conference debate. Developing countries criticized restrictive export policies adopted by the suppliers of nuclear material, equipment, and technology, as embodied in the Nuclear Suppliers' Group guidelines. They argued that the treaty had not assured them of access to the benefits of the peaceful atom, noting that nonparties to the treaty were able to obtain nuclear material, equipment, and technology more readily and under less stringent conditions than NPT parties. Fundamental differences could not be resolved at the review conference and an agreed final declaration could not be adopted by consensus.

In 1985 the third review conference also witnessed debate on these issues. While the Article IV debate was by no means as virulent and divisive as that of 1980, there were demands by developing nations for greater access to nuclear materials and technology and calls for a technical assistance fund to provide developing countries with the finances and technical resources necessary for nuclear power projects. Additionally, a number of parties sought measures designed to enhance protection of peaceful nuclear facilities from armed attacks. Article VI was the most acrimoniously debated issue at the review conference, with discussion centered on the lack of progress in arms control, and on the priority to be accorded to achieving a comprehensive test ban (CTB). While a compromise formulation was achieved that reflected the views of both those who looked to a CTB as the highest priority and those who accorded actual arms reductions the highest priority, the frustration and disappointment of many nonnuclear states were apparent. Reflecting these feelings, the neutral and nonaligned states participating in the conference included a declaration in the final document of the review conference noting that they had not brought to a vote three draft resolutions dealing with a CTB, a nuclear-weapon testing moratorium, and a quantitative and qualitative freeze on nuclear weapons, and referring to the conference's actions on nuclear-weapon testing issues.

FORGING THE FUTURE?

How should these controversies about the uneasy course of atomic diplomacy be judged? For the last forty years, we have witnessed a grand debate over the proper use of nuclear power and the appropriate distribution of that power. Imbuing this debate was the over-arching goal of prohibiting future uses of nuclear weapons in anger. The NPT was a specific attempt to deny that possibility, while allowing nondestructive uses of the power of the atom. But, given the contentious history of the NPT review conferences, looking to the 1990 review conference, and more particularly to the extension debate of 1995, is the NPT likely to be faced with a fundamental challenge to its existence? Will the treaty be allowed to lapse? Will states withdraw? Will the NPT be succeeded by an alternative treaty or regime? Will it be undermined, perhaps fatally, by attempts to amend its basic provisions, either out of an intention to improve it or to ensure its destruction? Or rather, can the parties build on the treaty's past successes and seek its evolutionary improvement?

The distinguished contributors to this volume, several of whom played major roles in the 1985 and earlier NPT review conferences, will provide a frame of reference for addressing these questions in the context of the review conference scheduled for 1990, and the extension conference in 1995. The authors have sought to evaluate the prospects for, and the value of, a continued multilateral nuclear-weapon nonproliferation regime, with special attention to the NPT; to assess the actual and perceived failings of the regime; and to define policy initiatives that may be required if the current multilateral approach is to be successful beyond 1995.

1

The Nonproliferation Treaty Regime

A Rereading before 1995

Mohamed I. Shaker

The 1968 Treaty on the Nonproliferation of Nuclear Weapons (NPT) stands out as the centerpiece of the nuclear nonproliferation regime. The treaty has been immensely successful, but in 1995 an extension conference will be held to determine its future duration. Hopefully, the NPT and the nonproliferation regime will endure well beyond 1995. At present, the major problem confronting the treaty regime is disarmament, particularly nuclear disarmament. This issue will be the real test of the NPT at the 1990 Review Conference of NPT parties and in 1995. To face and comprehend the future, it is useful to review the past.

THE CONCEPT OF NONPROLIFERATION

The NPT embodied the concept of nonproliferation that evolved from 1958 to 1961. This concept, as it was finally formulated by the U.N. General Assembly in its renowned Irish resolution of 1961, had two basic tenets. First, the problem of the proliferation of nuclear weapons was to be dealt with by means of an international agreement. Other measures were not overlooked or excluded; indeed, they later proved to be inescapable in order to build up a credible nonproliferation regime. Second, the international agreement envisaged had to be based on a set of obligations by the nuclear-weapon states (NWSs) and the nonnuclear-weapon states (NNWSs). The agreement was to:

Mohamed I. Shaker • Ambassador of the Arab Republic of Egypt to the United Kingdom.

- Bar independent national manufacture of nuclear weapons, but only NWSs parties to the international agreement would undertake not to manufacture nuclear weapons.
- Restrict both the flow of information necessary for the manufacture of nuclear weapons and the transfer of control over these weapons. The NWSs would refrain from transmitting nuclear-weapon information and they, along with the NNWSs, would be bound by obligations regarding control over nuclear weapons.

The concept did not envisage a situation in which nuclear weapons deployed beyond the territory of a nuclear power remained under its control.

The formulation of the nonproliferation concept of 1961 took place in an atmosphere that was dominated by the general belief that proliferation posed a statistical danger, that is, that the probability of nuclear war would rise as the number of nuclear powers increased. Concerns were also occasionally raised about the dangers of catalytic or accidental nuclear war. The great destructiveness and horrifying effects of the use of nuclear weapons in warfare, demonstrated by Hiroshima and Nagasaki, were very vivid and clearly present in the minds of those involved in formulating the nonproliferation concept at this time. These dangers are no less real today, although over forty years have passed since nuclear weapons were last used in anger.

As it appeared at the time, the nonproliferation concept had its limitations and gave rise to many problems, some of which were resolved in the process of negotiating the NPT. Other problems were either resolved in the implementation phase of the NPT or have continued to linger and still await settlement. In essence, all of these problems derived primarily from the distinction between two categories of states in the NPT—nuclear-weapon states and nonnuclear-weapon states.

The treaty-making process of the NPT was a long and a complicated one. After the formulation of the nonproliferation concept in 1961, it took almost ten years to bring the NPT into force, which was achieved on March 5, 1970. This was just the beginning of an intensive new phase of implementation. In this context, it is quite significant that in seeking to prevent the proliferation of nuclear weapons by means of an international agreement, a number of problems progressively arose during the formulation phase which had their impact on shaping the modalities and scope of the NPT beyond the initial intentions of its original coauthors. These problems were related to a variety of issues, including the peaceful uses of nuclear energy, peaceful nuclear explosions, international safeguards, arms control and disarmament, and security guarantees, not to mention security issues within the existing alliances of the time. The implementation phase has been no less rich and colorful in the variety of problems confronted.

Rather than examining in detail the two phases of treaty making and treaty implementation, in the following we will examine the different aspects of the NPT and their relevance in the present context, with special emphasis on the most important problems faced during both the negotiations and the implementation of the NPT. In reviewing the NPT and the nonproliferation regime, we shall focus on their prohibitive, promotional, and security aspects, as well as their durability.

PROHIBITIONS

The raison d'être of the NPT is the nontransfer and nonacquisition of nuclear weapons or other nuclear explosive devices. Articles I and II contain three different sets of prohibitions. First, NWSs undertake not to transfer to any recipient whatsoever nuclear weapons or other nuclear explosive devices, or the control over such weapons or explosive devices, directly or indirectly. On the other hand, NNWSs undertake not to receive from any state the transfer of nuclear weapons or other nuclear explosive devices, or the control over such weapons or explosive devices, directly or indirectly. Second, only nonnuclear states undertake not to manufacture or otherwise acquire nuclear weapons or other nuclear explosive devices. And, third, nuclear states undertake not in any way to assist, encourage, or induce any nonnuclear state to manufacture or otherwise acquire nuclear weapons or other nuclear explosive devices, or control over such weapons or explosive devices; and nonnuclear states undertake not to seek or receive any assistance in the manufacture of nuclear weapons or other nuclear explosive devices. Articles I and II of the NPT more or less embody the nonproliferation concept as formulated in 1961. The two articles were the result of lengthy negotiations between the United States and the Soviet Union, their two major coauthors.

The basic problems overcome in the process of negotiating these three sets of prohibitions involved, first, nuclear-sharing arrangements within NATO that would have allowed the establishment of multilateral or multinational nuclear forces and, second, the acquisition of nuclear explosive devices other than weapons. The first two articles of the NPT foreclosed the establishment of the Multilateral Nuclear Force (MLF) and the Atlantic Nuclear Force (ANF), schemes which would have allowed for joint ownership or control of strategic nuclear systems and, hence, would have led to the proliferation of nuclear weapons. With regard to discussions on other nuclear explosive devices, the negotiating history of the NPT demonstrates that nuclear devices used for peaceful purposes were the subject of this debate. The negotiating history of the NPT also demonstrates that there was a unanimous conviction that peaceful nuclear explosive devices were indistinguishable from nuclear weapons. However, during the NPT negotiations some states did not accept that a nonproliferation treaty should cover nuclear explosive devices other than weapons, arguing that this would curtail their right to explore a benign realm of science and technology. This has also been a point of contention and divergent interpretations in the context of the Treaty of Tlatelolco prohibiting nuclear weapons in Latin America. The introduction of Article V of the NPT, which promised the nonnuclear states that the benefits of nuclear explosives for peaceful purposes, performed under the control of the state furnishing the service, would be made available to them, was still not good enough for those states not ready to waive the right to conduct such explosions themselves.

Treaty prohibitions may require verification and, not surprisingly, the NPT's prohibitions require verification. But even before the NPT was concluded, some degree of verification was required or accepted for peaceful nuclear activities. International verification of such activities later came to be known as safeguards.

Article III of the NPT refers to and relies on the safeguards system of the International Atomic Energy Agency (IAEA), a system which had been developed by the IAEA a few years after its establishment in 1957, to verify the obligations undertaken by nonnuclear states in the NPT. Article III was the result of lengthy and elaborate negotiations, which especially took into account the preoccupations of the members of the European Atomic Energy Authority (EURATOM), an organization which was already applying safeguards in their respective territories. This was done without giving up the principle of the universal application of IAEA safeguards. However, the unique EURATOM–IAEA relationship was one of the most important problems in negotiating the text of Article III of the NPT, in formulating the NPT model safeguards agreement, and in negotiating the safeguards agreement between EURATOM, the states members of EURATOM, and the IAEA.

The formulation of Article III was just the beginning of an intensive and elaborate process toward the full implementation of the article. A few weeks after the entry into force of the NPT, a safeguards committee was established by the Board of Governors of the IAEA. This committee drafted the model safeguards agreement known and referred to as the Blue Book, or INFCIRC/153, which constitutes the basis of the safeguards applied to states parties to the NPT. The Blue Book was badly needed in view of the size, nature, and scope of the safeguard activities entrusted to the IAEA under the NPT. The IAEA safeguards system of 1965 (INFCIRC/66), as provisionally extended in 1966 and 1968, remains operational for states not adhering to the NPT. The IAEA is also responsible for the application of safeguards in the territories of states parties to the Treaty of Tlatelolco and the Treaty of Rarotonga establishing a South Pacific nuclear-weapon-free zone. It is quite significant that although the IAEA is not a party to the NPT or to the Treaties of Tlatelolco and Rarotonga, and therefore is under no obligation to fulfill any of the obligations prescribed therein, as a result of its role in implementing these treaties the IAEA emerged as a cornerstone of the nonproliferation regime.

The IAEA is continuously involved in improving safeguards techniques, in order to cope with the magnitude of its safeguards activities and the application of safeguards to new facilities. The ultimate objective of NPT safeguards is the timely or early detection of any diversions of significant quantities of nuclear material. It must be recalled that safeguards are not devised to prevent by physical action the diversion of nuclear material; the objective is to deter diversion by the risk of early detection. In view of this limited objective of NPT safeguards, the recent entry into force of the Convention on the Physical Protection of Nuclear Material is one more element bolstering the nonproliferation regime.

PROMOTIONAL ACTIVITIES

As a result of the prohibitions embodied in the NPT, and more particularly, the introduction of control on the peaceful nuclear activities of nonnuclear states, the latter expressed their fears that the treaty would hamper their full access to the knowledge and technology of the peaceful atom needed most for their future development and well-being. There were also fears that international control might turn into industrial espionage and that the treaty would place the nonnuclear states at a disadvantage vis-à-vis the nuclear states, which would be in a privileged position as the major suppliers of nuclear fuel and equipment.

It is against this background that the importance and significance of Article IV of the NPT, along with corresponding preambular paragraphs, can be appreciated. Article IV is the fruit of the NNWSs' endeavors to guarantee their inalienable right to develop peaceful nuclear capabilities. It is quite paradoxical that amid efforts to prevent the proliferation of nuclear weapons, controversy over peaceful uses of nuclear energy erupted dramatically. Of all the international or regional organizations involved in the promotion of peaceful uses of nuclear energy, the IAEA has emerged as the uncontested central organization. Its role in implementing the NPT in this domain has invigorated its existence. Although it is difficult to estimate how much of the growth and development of the various IAEA programs is attributable to the implementation of Article IV and how much is due to the normal evolution of the IAEA's work, it is apparent that the full implementation of Article IV is important to the IAEA in meeting its own statutory objectives and functions. In this respect, the enlargement of the IAEA Board of Governors in 1973 added new blood and vigor to the organization. However, international cooperation in peaceful uses of nuclear energy, whether through the IAEA or otherwise, has not always been smooth and easy.

In this context, one of the most important events was the emergence in the early 1970s of the so-called London Club of major nuclear suppliers, which introduced certain constraints and limitations on nuclear cooperation. Although the objectives of the suppliers' guidelines are the prevention of the proliferation of nuclear weapons and the elimination of commercial competition as a factor in negotiating safeguards, the guidelines were looked upon by a great number of states as restrictive and unfair, especially because the guidelines unnecessarily deny certain technologies and material to the developing countries, regardless of the principles embodied in Article IV of the NPT. In 1985, at the last NPT review conference, specific recommendations were made for removing obstacles to international cooperation in the nuclear field. The difficulties facing developing countries in obtaining finance for nuclear power programs were recognized, and several specific recommendations were addressed to the IAEA. The agency completed a study in 1987 on the promotion and financing of nuclear power programs in developing countries. This study was received with great interest and will continue to receive the attention of all those developing countries aspiring to invest in nuclear power. The protection of nuclear facilities from attacks and threats of attacks is also a thorny issue with regard to the promotion of peaceful uses of nuclear energy. This issue almost wrecked the last NPT review conference. Recent hints of the possible recurrence of such attacks demonstrate the need for renewed international actions, whether in the IAEA or outside of this organization.

In the aftermath of the 1985 review conference, attention to nuclear cooperation was concentrated on the work of the IAEA Committee on Assurances of Supply (CAS) and the preparation of the 1987 U.N. Conference to Promote International Cooperation in the Peaceful Uses of Nuclear Energy (UNCPICPUNE). Unfortunately, both failed to agree on a set of principles with regard to trade in nuclear material and equipment. The fate of CAS is still vague and unknown.

With regard to Article V of the NPT on the peaceful application of nuclear explosions, it is quite remarkable that certain basic rules of conduct have been formulated before any actual peaceful applications of such explosions were known to be imminent at the international level. Efforts to translate some of those rules into detailed guidelines or choices for the eventual implementation of Article V were promptly handled, including a commitment to international observation and the choice of the IAEA as the basic channel of supply. In general, the rules devised will remain a dead letter until the technology becomes a feasible one. Although peaceful nuclear explosions have lost their early attraction and glamor, the last review conference of the NPT in 1985 did not fail to devote some attention to the issue. The conference noted that the benefits of peaceful nuclear explosions have not been demonstrated and that no requests for such services had been received by the IAEA since the second NPT review conference in 1980.

SECURITY CONCERNS

Security is one of the most important objectives of efforts to build up and buttress a credible nonproliferation regime. Apart from the raison d'être of the NPT, which aims at achieving security through prohibitions on certain activities, security can also be achieved through arms control and disarmament, the establishment of nuclear-weapon-free zones, and security guarantees.

Security through arms control and disarmament and, more particularly, nuclear disarmament, has become one of the most important problems in the post-World War II era. The negotiations leading to the NPT, which is an arms control measure, were an opportunity to intensify and, at the same time, to assess the efforts already undertaken to halt and reverse the nuclear arms race. The result was Article VI and the corresponding preambular paragraphs of the NPT. Since the entry into force of the NPT, the implementation of Article VI and its corresponding preambular paragraphs has dominated the three NPT review conferences of 1975, 1980, and 1985. The lack of progress in the field of disarmament, along with sharp disagreements on drafting a common text at the second NPT review conference in 1980, led to the failure of the conference to issue a final declaration.

While results in this area have been achieved since the entry into force of the NPT, they have not been to the satisfaction of many NNWSs parties to the NPT. For example, the Strategic Arms Limitation Talks (SALT) I and II agreements of 1972 and 1979 were considered as instruments allowing the continuation of the nuclear arms race, and SALT II has never been ratified. Moreover, the signing of the Threshold Test Ban Treaty in 1974 signified the failure of the superpowers to agree on a comprehensive test ban, which would be an effective nonproliferation measure. In 1985, at the third NPT review conference, the delicate compromise reached on text referring to a comprehensive test ban treaty saved the conference from repeating the failure experienced by the 1980 review conference on the same issue.

The future of the NPT regime hinges upon the achievement of genuine prog-ress in disarmament and, more particularly, in nuclear disarmament, which is after all the raison d'être of Article VI of the NPT. In the 1990s, the most powerful guarantee for successful reviews and the extension of the NPT beyond its initial duration of twenty-five years would be the conclusion of concrete agreements on disarmament. The Intermediate-Range Nuclear Forces agreement of 1987 is an important step in the right direction. This agreement is now very much a part of the growing nonproliferation regime, as is the Limited Test Ban Treaty (LTBT) of 1963. The recent proposal to convene an amendment conference of the LTBT could open new avenues to strengthen the nonproliferation regime.

With regard to the establishment of nuclear-weapon-free zones, Article VII of the NPT acknowledged the right of any group of states to establish such zones to ensure the absence of nuclear weapons in their respective territories. The Tlatelolco Treaty of 1967, signed a year and a half before the conclusion of the NPT, greatly influenced the introduction of Article VII into the body of the NPT. The Treaty of Tlatelolco demonstrated advantages that could not otherwise be obtained through the mere adherence to an international agreement such as the NPT.

The obligations under Article 1 of the Treaty of Tlatelolco are broader in scope than those of Articles I and II of the NPT. The Treaty of Tlatelolco prohibits the storage, installation, and deployment of nuclear weapons on the territories of the contracting parties, whereas, under the NPT, NWSs can continue to store, install, and deploy nuclear weapons on the territories of NNWSs parties to the treaty. The recent row within NATO over nuclear weapons in Europe reminds us dramatically of the limited scope of the NPT. Moreover, under Article 1 of the Treaty of Tlatelolco, each contracting party is under the obligation to use exclusively for peaceful purposes the nuclear material and facilities which are under its jurisdiction, whereas under the NPT there is nothing to prevent a nonnuclear state party from using nuclear material for military purposes other than the production of nuclear weapons or other nuclear explosive devices, such as for submarine propulsion. The recent abortive Canadian project to acquire nuclear-powered submarines demon-strates the limits of the NPT's obligations in this area.

With regard to international safeguards, Article 16 of the Treaty of Tlatelolco allows for special inspections if a contracting party suspects that some activity prohibited by the treaty has been carried out or is about to be carried out, either within the territory of any other party or at any other place on the suspected party's behalf. Under Article III of the NPT, as well as under the procedures worked out by the IAEA for applying safeguards to the parties to the treaty, inspection is limited only to the nuclear activities declared by the party.

On the issue of nuclear guarantees, the parties to the Treaty of Tlatelolco benefit from a negative guarantee, that is, the undertaking by the nuclear states not to use or threaten to use nuclear weapons against them. This was an achievement which was not possible to realize on a universal level under the NPT. The NPT failed to deal with this issue in the manner it was dealt with by the Treaty of Tlatelolco because of a variety of reasons, all of which were basically connected with strategic conceptions of defense and deterrence. However, a way out was devised through the adoption of U.N. Security Council resolution 255 of June 9, 1968, a few days before opening the NPT for signature. The resolution basically welcomes the intention expressed by the three NWSs parties to the NPT, that they will provide or support immediate assistance, in accordance with the U.N. Charter, to any NNWS party to the NPT that is a victim of an act or an object of a threat of aggression in which nuclear weapons are used. The resolution has inherent limitations; however, its virtue lies in its attempt to emphasize the relevance in the nuclear age of certain provisions of the U.N. Charter pertaining to the preservation of peace and security. In 1985 the last NPT review conference took note of the continued determination of the NWSs parties to the NPT to honor their declarations. Ultimately, however, security guarantees can only be enhanced through a multifaceted approach including reaching a general prohibition on the use or threat of use of nuclear weapons.

Under the Treaty of Tlatelolco, the Agency for the Prohibition of Nuclear Weapons in Latin America (OPANAL) is to keep under constant review the operation of the treaty and ensure compliance with its obligations, whereas, under the NPT, periodic review conferences may be held only every five years.

Perhaps because of the benefits the Treaty of Tlatelolco offers to its parties, which are not repeated on the international level in the NPT, the concept of nuclear-weapon-free zones is gaining ground. The Rarotonga Treaty and the efforts to establish nuclear-weapon-free zones in the Middle East and Africa are just a few examples. With regard to the Middle East zone, the U.N. Secretary-General has recently been asked by the General Assembly to undertake a study on effective and verifiable measures which would facilitate the establishment of such a zone, taking into account the circumstances and characteristics of the Middle East, as well as the views and suggestions of the various parties in the region.

DURABILITY

The NPT includes, through clear and simple provisions, a number of features guaranteeing its continuity and its adaptability to changing circumstances. Such features are of great importance in view of the considerable strategic, political, economic, and technical interests of states parties to the NPT that are at stake in its implementation. The unique features of the NPT ensuring its durability are its universality of adherence, its duration, and its provisions for amendments, review conferences, and withdrawal. In our view, the provisions of the treaty in this respect are safety valves, which have to date guaranteed its survival during its initial phase and hopefully well beyond 1995.

The NPT is open to all states, and 141 states are parties to the treaty today. However, a number of nonnuclear states possessing advanced nuclear technology, the so-called threshold states, refuse to adhere to the NPT for a number of complex and diverse reasons involving principles, economics, and security. The discriminatory nature of the treaty, the prohibition of the manufacture and use of nuclear explosive devices for peaceful purposes by the nonnuclear states themselves, and the insufficiency of security guarantees have been repeatedly cited by these states as flaws in the NPT's structure. The retention of an option to develop nuclear explosive devices is quite important to these states, and they are not expected to adhere to the NPT under any circumstances unless it is radically transformed. While this is a very farfetched possibility, India has recently come up with the idea of a newly conceived nonproliferation treaty. All in all, the abstention of this group of countries from adhering to the NPT weakens the nonproliferation regime.

Review conferences have been useful in keeping the NPT alive. No withdrawals from the NPT have to date taken place, although a number of tragic circumstances have occurred that could have occasioned the use of the treaty's provisions for withdrawal. In five years, an extension conference will be held to decide on the duration of the NPT beyond 1995. So far no amendments to the NPT have been introduced, and the 1995 extension conference may or may not trigger an amendment process.

CONCLUSIONS

The NPT and the nuclear nonproliferation regime have expanded and are expected to continue to expand in many directions so long as they remain credible. In the process of building up the regime, many problems were encountered, and sometimes these problems were overcome. In the early phase of the NPT negotiations, the most important hurdle was the problem of nuclear sharing within the Atlantic Alliance. The mothballing of the MLF and the ANF opened the way for serious negotiations toward the conclusion of the NPT. A number of other problems were also overcome during the negotiations leading to the NPT, albeit not always to the complete satisfaction of all. They related to safeguards (including the issue of EURATOM safeguards), peaceful uses of nuclear energy, disarmament, and security guarantees.

During the NPT's implementation phase, the IAEA has been at the center of all activity with regard to the application of safeguards and the promotion of peaceful uses of nuclear energy. Its performance in these two domains has not been without difficulties. The agency has had to strike a delicate balance between expectations arising from its promotional activities and expectations concerning safeguards. However, these difficulties are generally manageable and have been more or less normal features in the performance of its responsibilities. The IAEA has certainly lived up to the expectations of the drafters of the NPT.

Yet, despite these good omens for the future, as I indicated, the major problem that the treaty and the nonproliferation regime face today is the achievement of disarmament, and more particularly, nuclear disarmament. This is the real test for the NPT in 1990 and, more so, in 1995, when the initial period of the NPT comes to an end. This should not belittle issues such as regional security. Regional issues were about to wreck the 1985 NPT review conference. The issue of full-scope safeguards with regard to nonparties to the NPT is no less important. The issue of defining principles of trade in nuclear material and equipment will most probably reemerge more forcefully than it did at the 1985 review conference. These problems are very real, but it can only be hoped that they can be resolved and that the NPT and the nonproliferation regime will remain vigorous in the decades ahead.

2

Avoiding the Worst of All Possible Worlds

Benjamin Sanders

What if. . . . To question what *should* and what *could* be done to maintain the nonproliferation regime if the conference that decides on the extension of the NPT is unable to agree on a significant prolongation of its life is not particularly rewarding. International politics is an area where the recognition that something *should* be done and, indeed, *could* be done, does not always mean that it *will* be done, however reasonable it would be to do it. Logically, therefore, if one raises the question, one must also discuss what will be done, or rather, since the future is uncertain, what one thinks *might* happen if no agreement is reached on a substantial extension of the treaty's duration.

But is it useful to do so? We start from the assumption that we want the treaty to stay alive and to be extended for as long as possible. On this basis, speculation as to what is likely to happen if the extension conference of 1995 fails to prolong the treaty's life by a significant period is really beside the point, if not actually self-defeating. Planning for a negative outcome of events makes sense if it can keep that outcome from being realized, can counteract it once it is in motion, or can help in taking measures that would neutralize or weaken its effects. But planning for a negative outcome also brings the risk that it is taken as an implication of accepting the event as unavoidable. Worse, if the event can be avoided, while the realization of the contingency plan is not guaranteed, publicizing its existence is apt to make the negative event more likely and at the same time jeopardize the chances of putting a meaningful alternative in its stead.

In the present case, critics of the NPT will take the existence of a contingency

Benjamin Sanders • Coordinator of the Programme for Promoting Nuclear Non-Proliferation, New York, New York.

plan or the development of an alternative (if an effective alternative could be devised) as an indication that even the treaty's supporters are accepting its impending demise, either because they recognize that it has outlived its usefulness or because they no longer believe in its viability. No doubt, forewarned is forearmed. Effective action in defense of the treaty should be encouraged. But a "What if. . . ." approach, based on the assumption—at the end of the 1980s—that the treaty may not survive 1995 and one should begin to think of some measure with which to replace it, not only endangers the treaty as such, but dooms any alternative one might think of adopting before it has even come off the drawing board.

Is there really a doubt that the treaty will be extended? Why should it not be? What is the source of the concern? Why should some supporters of the NPT be so concerned about its future?

CRITICS AND CRITICISM

Ever since its inception, the NPT has been criticized. This criticism has been directed at the treaty first for its conceptual approach and, once it had been in force for a while, for the way it was being implemented. The criticism of the treaty's approach is directed at the way it singles out the "horizontal" spread of nuclear weapons as a major threat to international peace and security, without giving sufficient attention to "vertical" proliferation—to the buildup of nuclear arsenals by the nuclear-weapon states (NWSs). As to implementation, in the view of the critics the major nuclear states do not fulfill even the modest obligations with respect to nuclear disarmament which they have assumed under the treaty. In other words, the treaty is felt to be conceptually misdirected and its implementation is seen as inadequate. Moreover, as some critics maintain, while the NPT makes provision to promote the peaceful uses of nuclear energy, supplier states that should be most helpful in this regard use the argument of nonproliferation to restrict their nuclear exports—a third category, presumably, of failed commitments.

The resentments are real. Some of the criticism appears well founded. Whether it is justified or not, it is capable of undermining support for the treaty. If it is not convincingly answered, it might eventually affect the treaty's further viability.

But there is no need for this to happen. There are ample arguments with which to counter the criticism from within that could erode adhesion to the treaty and imperil the results of the Fourth Review Conference of the Parties to the Treaty on the Nonproliferation of Nuclear Weapons in 1990 and the extension conference five years later. Further, the argument, if used properly, should help convince nonparty states that their national security would be served by adherence to the NPT and that, in fact, under contemporary circumstances, adherence reflects the present international norm and cannot be avoided without incurring international opprobrium.

There is good reason to believe that many of those who express doubts about the long-term viability of the treaty do so really because they see merit in the view that it contains more flaws than virtues. Pessimism about the future of the NPT—an attitude expressed, for instance, at the third special session of the General Assembly of the United Nations devoted to disarmament, in the summer of 1988—not only from nonaligned nations but also from delegates from several neutral and western states often seems inspired by the very criticism that is said to prompt that pessimism. In other words, among those professing concern about the existence of a negative attitude to the treaty there appear to be some who are inclined to share the arguments of its detractors or are at least sympathetic to them.

This criticism is not only largely unjustified, *but it can be clearly and publicly shown to lack justification.* It should be possible to convince a good many of the critics that the treaty is at least the best solution available in an imperfect world. And, by the same means, those who are concerned about the strength of the criticism, or profess to be, and therefore advocate joining the opposition in seeking alternatives to the treaty, may be persuaded that the negative views per se are no ground for negative action, however well intended. Advancing this view to good effect is both a difficult and an urgent task. It should be done intelligently, and soon.

The criticisms are targeted at two aspects—concept and implementation—and a response must keep that duality in mind. Both aspects have a substantive and a procedural side. Substantively, does one wish to meet the object of the criticism and if so, how? Procedurally, can one raise convincing arguments to counter the criticism? The two aspects are closely connected and must be treated together. If the criticism can be countered by persuasive argument to the point where potentially negative effects can be contained, one need no longer be concerned about the chances of the treaty surviving the extension conference. Nor will there be a need for substantive action (such as attempts to amend or replace the NPT) that by itself would endanger the treaty and weaken the nonproliferation system of which it is a cornerstone.

Criticism of the NPT concept focuses on the assumption that the treaty reflects a division of the world's states into nuclear "haves" and "have-nots" (among whom the former are free to build up their nuclear armaments and the latter—who would suffer the consequences of a nuclear war as much as its protagonists—pledge to refrain from doing so for all time). In addition, those opposed to the treaty see it largely as ineffective because one cannot combat horizontal proliferation without also curbing the vertical dimension. And there is the argument that the treaty is a hindrance to the development of nuclear energy for peaceful purposes.

ARGUMENTS OF DISCRIMINATION AND DISARMAMENT

The argument of discrimination is the strongest. It reflects resentment at the fact that the present NWSs arrogate to themselves that status for all time, while prohibiting other states from acquiring it. Conversely, it represents the attitude of many nonaligned nations, which hold that if they have forsworn the possession of nuclear weapons, the major powers should do so too. An obvious way to answer this facile argument would be by accepting that nuclear weapons are abhorrent. Their acquisition would not serve the security of the present nonnuclear-weapon states (NNWSs), and the major powers should recognize that neither their own security nor that of the world at large is served by their having nuclear weapons either. But if they feel they cannot now divest themselves of their means of nuclear warfare, the NWSs should as soon as possible start creating the conditions under which they would no longer need to rely on nuclear weapons for the defense of their security. Whatever formulation one chooses, it is obvious that the possession of nuclear weapons causes fatal risks to friend and foe alike. And if that is true for the nuclear-weapon powers, it is the more apt in the case of the non- or almost-nuclear-weapon states, which are by definition weaker in nuclear (and de facto also in conventional) terms than the states whose nuclear status is publicly recognized. This in itself is a convincing argument in favor of horizontal nonproliferation, that is, forgoing the nuclear option and making one's abstention known by accession to the NPT.

It is quite understandable that the supposedly discriminatory nature of the treaty should be difficult to digest, especially for states that might proceed relatively quickly to nuclear-weapon status if they chose to do so. Once one accepts the thought, however, that nuclear weapons pose a threat to international security and, if used, would worsen the effects of war immeasurably, even if it was impossible to halt vertical proliferation altogether—although recent events may be the forerunners of meaningful moves in that direction—putting an effective barrier in the way of horizontal spread should in itself be seen as an extraordinarily important step toward a safer world.

In truth, the treaty does not represent acceptance of a world inhabited forever by nuclear haves and have-nots. The way it refers to nuclear and nonnuclear states merely reflects a situation prevailing at the time the treaty was concluded, as it still is. It meant to contain an existing situation and, once contained, to help improve it. As the text makes amply clear, the treaty is intended as part of what should be a concerted attempt to rid the world of nuclear weapons. Putting a stop to horizontal proliferation is an essential part of that attempt.

But, as the history of the negotiations makes clear, the negotiators did not create the treaty to be a general nuclear disarmament measure. If its opponents see the NPT as a halfway measure, incapable of bringing about nuclear disarmament, one must realize that it was indeed intended only as a partial cure—a measure of nonarmament that would be one in a series of steps toward a safer international environment. The disappointment with which some profess to regard the NPT is the obvious result of the misconception that the spread of nuclear weapons to additional nations is inevitably linked with overall nuclear disarmament. It is correct to say that a number of nuclear disarmament measures would constitute powerful tools for nonproliferation. A comprehensive test ban and a prohibition of the production of nuclear material for explosive purposes are cases in point. On the other hand, the existence of an effective and worldwide nonproliferation regime is necessary for nuclear disarmament to be feasible. The NPT is, and was always meant to be, a measure of its own; it is connected with but not predicated on other measures of disarmament.

George Santayana said—and many others have expressed it in different words, without, unfortunately, much success—that those who cannot remember the past are condemned to repeat it. To those who know the history of multilateral arms limitation negotiations since World War II, and thus the genesis of NPT, it is clear that the present criticism of the treaty, the suggestions to change it, or the idea that it should be feasible to replace it with some instrument more capable of bringing about "real disarmament," are based to a large extent on ignorance or disregard of what has béen tried and achieved in the past.

The initial moves made in the United Nations and the negotiating bodies that came out of it, to deal with weapons of mass destruction, including nuclear weapons, were part of a comprehensive approach to disarmament. The course was set for "General and Complete Disarmament," a concept reflected in a joint U.S.–USSR declaration of 1961, known by the names of the principal disarmament negotiators, Valerian A. Zorin and John J. McCloy. The declaration was almost the last gasp in the all-encompassing approach that had guided arms limitation activities for fifteen years. It was soon recognized as too ambitious for its time and yielded to a preference for more modest, discrete steps which, all together, should lead eventually to the same goal. The Limited Test Ban Treaty of 1963 was one such step. The NPT was another. It reflected the link with various other elements of a comprehensive program of disarmament, but it deliberately limited itself to that which it was possible to achieve at the time.

The treaty was the hard-fought result of long and arduous debate. In the course of the negotiations in the Eighteen-Nation Disarmament Commission, neutral and nonaligned nations repeatedly called for the incorporation of other measures and proposed linking the treaty to the implementation of various steps towards nuclear disarmament. India, for one, made proposals very similar to those its prime minister would submit at the third special session of the U.N. General Assembly on disarmament, more than two decades later. These proposals called for a two-stage agreement: the first applying to the nuclear powers, who would inter alia stop producing nuclear weapons and reduce their stocks; and, once this was underway, a second stage applying to nonnuclear nations, much like the present treaty. Sweden was one of those calling for a package of measures, including a comprehensive nuclear test ban and a halt in the production of fissionable material for military purposes. The nonaligned nations generally wanted to see the treaty coupled with various arms reduction measures by the major powers and with security guarantees to nonnuclear states.

The NPT as we now know it was the result of many years of hard, protracted negotiation, during which both superpowers strongly opposed the linking of other measures to an agreement on nonproliferation. What resulted reflects the difficulties encountered in the course of the deliberations: an instrument primarily directed at the problem of horizontal proliferation, with a faint echo of its negotiating background contained in Article VI. The wish of nonaligned nations to couple the treaty to a guarantee of their security has been partly met in resolution 255, adopted by the Security Council in June 1968, shortly before the treaty was opened for signature. This "welcomes" the so-called positive guarantee given by the three depositaries— the USSR, the United Kingdom, and the United States—to come to the assistance of nonnuclear states parties to the treaty that fall victim to aggression with nuclear weapons. This concession on the part of the nuclear powers does not satisfy a majority of nonaligned states who seek "negative" guarantees, by which they would be assured that no nuclear force would be employed against them. This issue has lived on as a subject of controversy, although its importance seems to have subsided somewhat in recent years.

Even a simplified summary of the complicated history of the NPT may illustrate how difficult it was to come to any agreement at all. The text that resulted from the negotiations was the most that could be achieved under the circumstances. Those circumstances have changed somewhat since the late 1960s, but the political priorities of the protagonists in the protracted discussion have remained basically the same. There is no reason to believe that an attempt at amending or replacing the NPT would yield a more satisfactory instrument. There is every likelihood that such attempts would destroy the treaty, or at best greatly weaken it. Those who persist in the belief that it should have been possible to achieve more do not know the history of the treaty. They would be well advised to take careful note of that history before wasting time on attempts to devise new solutions to old problems. By endangering the partial solutions that are in place, such attempts inevitably aggravate the problems they are meant to solve.

A HISTORICAL REJOINDER

History itself yields the response to the dual arguments of the detractors of the treaty. Criticism of the concept that constitutes the basis of the treaty is historically inaccurate; it is understandable but ineffective. In brief, there is nothing better to be had, and what we have is a great deal better than nothing.

The "conceptual" discrimination to which critics object is not a flaw in the treaty so much as the reflection of a fundamental problem in world relations for which the treaty cannot be, is not, and has never been meant to be, the sole remedy. It certainly is part of the remedy; without a stable nuclear environment the big powers are less prone and able to take any meaningful nuclear disarmament measures. The NPT is an encouragement to them to negotiate toward nuclear disarmament.

An argument often heard from the more vocal holdout states is that the NPT is meant to disarm the unarmed. In fact, this argument has been used to criticize most of the elements of the worldwide system of nonproliferation steps and instruments usually called the nonproliferation regime. This is an oddly disingenuous argument. First, if the verb "to disarm" is correctly used, the subjects of the action obviously are not unarmed. But, in truth, the purpose is to help keep the unarmed that way. More importantly, it is a safe way to enable them to stay unarmed, because they can have confidence that their neighbors—assuming they are also parties to the treaty— are abstaining from the acquisition of nuclear weapons, and they have the means of convincing those neighbors that they are equally, atomically, harmless. The NPT is the confidence-building measure par excellence, and it is in the interest of every state that all other states should join it.

As to implementation, in particular the way in which the major powers meet their obligation under Article VI to "pursue negotiations in good faith," their actions appear to follow the letter of what history teaches us to be an essentially declaratory provision. Obviously, parties to the NPT have the right, and share the duty, to exert relentless pressure on the nuclear powers to make significant progress toward nuclear disarmament and take action to give substance to Article VI. Among the actions that deserve high priority are such genuine nonproliferation measures as a cutoff of nuclear material production for military purposes and a comprehensive test ban. But it is unproductive to pretend that the realization of these aims should be a condition for nonnuclear states to accede to the NPT or continue their adherence. This is so obviously unrealistic an argument that it looks like a pretext for the intransigent attitude some holdout states have adopted from the time the negotiations on an NPT took a course that did not coincide with their ambitions.

Another issue is the implementation of Article IV. The criticism voiced in this respect is not so much directed at the major powers as at the developed world in general. Article IV confirms the right of states to benefit from the peaceful application of nuclear energy and mandates parties, inter alia, to cooperate in contributing to the further development of the applications of nuclear energy for peaceful purposes. Pursuant to this article, states have the right to participate in "the fullest possible exchange" of the equipment, materials, and technology they need. Its wording obviously does not oblige potential suppliers always to provide full access to all items, no matter how much their possession might contribute to a weapon capability. It is often reasoned that the article reflects the rationale of the treaty, that as long as a state is party to an agreement by which all its nuclear activities are submitted to international safeguards, it is thereby entitled to any nuclear supplies it claims to need, whether they be fissionable material, equipment, facilities, or technology. This is just one interpretation; nowhere is this expressly stated. Even if it had ever been the drafters' intention that the mere fact that a state is a party to the NPT should entitle it to unlimited access to all components of the nuclear fuel cycle, no matter whether these might help it to obtain a latent weapon capability, technological developments have now convinced potential suppliers that they should not rely exclusively on the efficacy of safeguards to ensure that their nuclear exports are not misused, but should also impose restrictions on the export of items that carry particular proliferation risks. Perhaps Article IV was unduly optimistic regarding the infallibility of safeguards to provide totally watertight guarantees against misuse of any item covered. It also reflects an optimism about the importance of nuclear power for economic development which now seems to have been premature. In the end, greater realism about the role nuclear energy may play in economic development should give both would-be recipients and potential suppliers the time as well as the interest to reach a range of compromises that would ensure consumers of needed nuclear supplies under acceptable conditions and avoid undue proliferation risks. International cooperation in potentially sensitive stages of the nuclear fuel cycle—as variously proposed in the past dozen years or so—would be in the spirit of Article IV and should be energetically pursued, in the interest of peaceful nuclear development as well as of an effective nonproliferation policy.

THE NPT, NUCLEAR PROLIFERATION, PEACE, AND SECURITY

Nuclear proliferation, in whatever direction—sideways or up-and-down—poses an undeniable risk to world peace and security. The question which is greater, the risk posed by vertical or by horizontal proliferation, is moot, and one hopes it will never be answered. Both developments are cause for the most serious concern. The size and nature of the nuclear arsenals of the major powers may long have been seen as the more direct threat. But the spread of missile technology, the growing destructiveness of conventional weapons, and the increasing use of chemical warfare agents raise concern about possible nuclear responses.

Measures against both manifestations of nuclear rivalry are urgently needed. In a patient afflicted with two deadly diseases, seeking a cure for one illness without applying appropriate remedies for the other is clearly pointless. The NPT recognizes this. It provides a way to treat one malady while seeking to improve the conditions that should facilitate healing the other. The treaty sees both aspects as vital but is inevitably preoccupied with one—the horizontal trend. To conclude that it would therefore accept, or even condone, the other is unfair, untrue, and unproductive; the treaty simply concentrates its treatment on the condition for which it has the cure, without ignoring the other problem. Rejecting, curtailing, or weakening a positive measure on the ground that it does not present a universal solution is as shortsighted as it is dangerous.

One wonders, therefore, at the motivation of a state that would have the treaty replaced by an instrument of wider scope, aimed at achieving what has so far been illusory, on grounds of arguments both positive and negative. The positive argument is the promise of something better—a full-fledged nuclear disarmament treaty affecting the nuclear-weapon powers as well as nonnuclear states. We have seen how efforts to achieve this end have failed in the past. There is no reason to believe that they would be more successful now. Relinquishing the NPT for a chimaera would not only be counterproductive; it would also give the nuclear powers grounds to delay their present efforts toward nuclear disarmament. The negative argument is the obverse—the NPT stands in the way of "true" disarmament. Recent developments show the fallacy of this contention, if any proof was needed.

Some of the holdouts advocate that the treaty should be abolished altogether, as a restrictive and discriminatory measure. Restrictive it is, in the sense that it seeks to deter the spread of nuclear weapons to additional nations. There are reasons to believe that this is the real ground for the resentment, which is intensified by the isolation in which holdout states increasingly find themselves.

To sum up some of the arguments for the defense:

- the NPT is a hugely positive factor in present-day international relations;
- the NPT is the reflection of an international norm;
- the NPT is an enormously important confidence-building measure;
- the NPT is a cornerstone of the worldwide nonproliferation system;

- the NPT is the arms limitation measure most widely adhered to, the one measure of arms control in which every state can participate and in which all states have a vital stake;
- the NPT may well be the ultimate obstacle to total nuclear anarchy, the measure that keeps the world from sliding into self-destructive nuclear chaos.

Equality in nuclear matters, as perceived by the vocal holdouts, would mean full rights for all to acquire nuclear weapons. But the world-at-large sees the spread of nuclear weapons as contrary to a fundamental ethical norm which says that it is immoral for any one country to possess the means of putting all others at risk. Accordingly, to practice equality in nuclear matters what is needed is equality in abstinence. The big powers must disarm. That is the hopeful message of Article VI of the NPT. But this does not mean that the slowness with which the big powers proceed toward nuclear disarmament gives other states a valid reason to go nuclear, or that anything short of total nuclear disarmament makes the treaty a failure. Historically, as we have seen, the NPT was not intended to be a total nuclear disarmament measure and Article VI, important though it is, is not the nub of the treaty. Its implementation must be energetically promoted, but the fact that the "negotiations" toward nuclear disarmament are slow to yield results cannot be made the criterion for the success or failure of the NPT.

The treaty is effective. It is observed. The number of adherents grows steadily. It undoubtedly has shortcomings as well. What is needed, therefore, is an effort to complement it and achieve its purposes by additional measures. The time of decision whether to extend the treaty indefinitely or for a finite term is getting close. It is understandable that at this juncture the question should be raised whether the treaty has met its purposes and, if not, what might be done about it. That question is logical and necessary. The fourth conference to review the implementation of the treaty, in 1990, will yield an opportunity to consider how that implementation may be reinforced. But in so doing, it is essential to recognize the treaty's purposes in the light of its initial intentions. Neither the cause of nuclear disarmament nor non-proliferation is served by a misplaced emphasis on the former.

Oddly, that shift in emphasis seems to have accelerated at about the rate at which the major powers are moving toward nuclear disarmament. This in itself may indicate that any amendment or replacement of the treaty would be unnecessary, if not counterproductive. And—one cannot repeat it often enough—as history demonstrates, it is not likely to produce anything more attractive than the treaty we now have.

But is it really such an unattractive instrument? The continuing growth in the number of parties would make one think otherwise. The unanimous endorsement of the treaty at the 1985 review conference also points to the contrary. Approximately 140 states have already taken shelter in the treaty against a danger that would jeopardize their national security. The treaty helps protect the atomically innocent and has become a moral force of global importance. It may not persuade all holdout states to join, but it makes their position difficult. It may be unable still to capture those apparently embarked on a course of nuclear adventure, but it has delayed the pace of some and compels others to adopt postures, offer justifications, or present cover-ups which by themselves may be helpful in deterring overt breakouts from the nonproliferation system. It protects and it deters. It is too valuable to be put at risk by irresponsible tinkering.

The treaty should be understood for what it was meant to be, what it is, and what it could be. It should be better known. It should be reinforced by additional measures that would strengthen the nonproliferation system and promote nuclear disarmament. It should be supported and allowed to come to full fruition and be recognized for what it is: an arms limitation measure of inestimable value.

3

The Collapse of the NPT— What if?

Lewis A. Dunn

INTRODUCTION

With approximately 135 parties, the NPT has more adherents than any other arms control treaty and is justifiably regarded as an international success. Over the nearly two decades since it entered into force in 1970, the nonproliferation treaty has been a bulwark of efforts to contain the spread of nuclear weapons around the globe and has provided a framework within which many countries have begun to use the atom for peaceful purposes. Its injunction of nuclear disarmament has added strength and legitimacy to the many calls on the existing nuclear-weapon states (NWSs) to move swiftly and effectively to reduce their nuclear arsenals.

In 1995, the parties to the NPT must come together in a conference to determine the fate of the treaty. According to Article X of the NPT, the parties can choose by majority to extend it indefinitely or only for a limited, fixed period or periods. They lack the explicit option to let the treaty die, except through the tactic of extending it for only a nominal period of days or weeks.[1] It is a very "good bet" that the 1995 conference will extend the treaty for a significant period of time, although probably not indefinitely. History is filled, however, with good bets that did not pan out and surprises that no one expected.

What shocks or developments would make it harder to renew the nonproliferation treaty in 1995? What impact would a collapse of the treaty have on global security? What other institutions or approaches might be sought to fill the gap left by the NPT's collapse? What can be done in the next years, including before the

Lewis A. Dunn • Assistant Vice President, Science Applications International Corporation, McLean, Virginia.

1990 NPT review conference, to strengthen the treaty and its prospects for renewal in 1995? A brief examination of each of these questions helps to drive home the critical contribution of the treaty to global peace and security as well as the importance of continued efforts to ensure its extension.

SHOCKS TO THE NONPROLIFERATION TREATY

Under Article VI of the treaty, the parties are committed "to pursue negotiations in good faith on effective measures relating to cessation of the nuclear arms race at an early date and to nuclear disarmament, and on a treaty on general and complete disarmament." At the top of the list of possible shocks or developments that could significantly undermine chances for the renewal of the treaty in 1995 would be a future breakdown of U.S.–Soviet efforts to reduce their nuclear arsenals, particularly after the recent rise in public expectations about the prospects for arms control during and following the conclusion of the Intermediate-Range Nuclear Forces (INF) Treaty.

Throughout the history of the implementation of the nonproliferation treaty, and at the review conferences that have been held at five-year intervals since the treaty's entry into force in 1970, criticism of the nuclear states for not living up to their obligation has dominated the proceedings. At the First Review Conference of the Parties to the Treaty on the Nonproliferation of Nuclear Weapons (1975), only the last-moment intervention of the conference president prevented a breakdown of the conference over Article VI issues. In 1980, such a breakdown occurred. The developing countries blocked agreement on a final document as a means to signal their discontent with the lack of progress towards nuclear disarmament.

The successful 1985 NPT review conference at first glance might lead some persons to draw the conclusion that nuclear disarmament issues are less of a threat to renewal of the treaty than just suggested. Despite the lack of progress toward either nuclear-weapon reductions or limits on nuclear testing, the parties in 1985 were able to agree on a final declaration that reaffirmed the contribution of the NPT to their security and well-being. Moreover, formal speeches and informal conversations clearly revealed a growing recognition among the developing countries that the NPT did make the world more peaceful and secure. Partly for that reason, these countries resisted entreaties by nongovernmental groups to block a consensus on a final document to show displeasure with lack of progress on Article VI. Similarly, the developing countries that were parties stood up to the criticisms of the NPT by other nonaligned countries not parties to the NPT that were present as observers.

Nonetheless, criticism of the nuclear states for allegedly not meeting their obligations under Article VI was strong and sometimes bitter. The demand was repeatedly heard that the nuclear states get on with the job of reducing their nuclear arsenals, and, as seen by virtually all of the parties present, with negotiation of a comprehensive ban on nuclear testing. Moreover, the successful result of 1985 was due partly to factors that may not be present again: an upcoming U.S.–Soviet summit in November 1985 and a desire not to lessen the chances for progress at that meeting; the personal trust and relationships of key representatives; and extensive consultations and coordination over the two years preceding the conference.

For all these reasons, prudent planning should assume that in the absence of significant reductions of U.S. and Soviet nuclear weapons between now and 1995, going beyond the INF Treaty, supporters of the NPT will face an uphill fight for its renewal. Faced with the need to choose between renewal of the NPT on the grounds that it serves their security interests even without effective implementation of Article VI and nonrenewal (or renewal for a short period with conditions for further extension), the majority of developing countries that hold the balance might choose the latter.

Two critical questions, however, remain. How much progress toward the Article VI goal of "cessation of the nuclear arms race" and "nuclear disarmament" must be achieved to contain this threat to NPT renewal? In particular, must there be agreement on a ban on nuclear testing, a measure that is often claimed to be the litmus test of compliance with Article VI? On the latter question, there is likely to be a wide set of views, influenced as much by the respondent's policy preferences toward a nuclear test ban as by any "objective" assessment.

In the final hours, what is likely to matter most in the eyes of the 1995 review conference will be how much progress has been made in reducing strategic nuclear arsenals, not whether there is or is not a nuclear test ban.[2] With sufficient reductions, it would then be possible to argue that significant progress had been made in implementing all of the goals of the NPT: preventing the spread of nuclear weapons; fostering the peaceful uses of nuclear energy; and slowing the nuclear arms race. The costs of nonrenewal would be clear.

Those perceived costs, and particularly the perception that the treaty adds to the security of its parties, could be markedly affected, however, by one or more highly visible failures of the overall nonproliferation regime in the years ahead. This would be a second obstacle to NPT renewal in 1995.

The most obvious potential nonproliferation breakdown would be the emergence of several additional states possessing nuclear weapons. Where is there cause for concern?

High on all lists of potential proliferation "problem countries" are India and Pakistan.[3] Public reports of Pakistan's movement in recent years toward a weapon capability have increased pressures on India to gear up weapon activities of its own, building on its detonation of a nuclear explosive device in 1974. But an Indian nuclear "breakout" in an attempt to regain nuclear preeminence in South Asia is only one way in which additional nuclear powers might emerge.

Still elsewhere, South Africa is widely thought by many observers to have the capability to develop nuclear weapons should a decision be made to do so. In September 1987, South Africa's government announced that it was prepared for discussions about adherence to the NPT. Since then, talks have been held. If those discussions prove fruitless and external pressure on South Africa mounts, acquisition and testing of nuclear weapons could come to be viewed as a necessary prop for domestic public morale as well as a signal to the international community not to push South Africa too far.

In the Middle East, press reports in 1986 that Israel had covertly manufactured nuclear weapons focused attention once again on that country. However, as long as the conventional military balance in the region favors Israel—and none of the Arab countries or Iran acquires nuclear explosives—there would seem little reason for Israel to change its current ambiguous posture.

To take another scenario, in Latin America today both Argentina and Brazil are engaged in sensitive nuclear activities that could eventually provide access to nuclear-weapon-usable material. But both countries' leaders have also affirmed their countries' peaceful nuclear intentions and have taken steps to foster a dialogue on nuclear issues. At the same time, should suspicion grow within each country's elite about the ultimate peaceful intentions of the other country, both Argentina and Brazil, in a step-by-step process over the next decade, could slide steadily closer to decisions to acquire nuclear weapons.

The most immediate impact of a decision by one or more of these countries, or others, to become overt nuclear-weapon states would be within their particular regions. Pressures would mount on their neighbors, including those within the nonproliferation treaty, to reassess their decisions to renounce acquisition of nuclear weapons. Of greater importance for renewal of the treaty in 1995, more intangible but no less important perceptions in many countries of the effectiveness of the treaty would be undermined.

On the one hand, questions already are periodically raised by some parties and some critics about the security payoff of the NPT on the grounds that the most important problem countries are not parties to it. This overlooks the fact that the crucial problem countries of two decades ago—countries such as West Germany, Japan, Italy, Sweden, Switzerland, and others—are parties to the treaty. It also overlooks, as discussed below, the indirect impact of the NPT in reducing the freedom of action of even today's countries of nonproliferation concern. Nonetheless, were some of the current problem countries actually to become weapon states, this argument that the treaty does not deal with the "real" problems of proliferation concern would be reinforced.

On the other hand, further overt proliferation would weaken the international perception, created in good measure by the near-universal adherence to the nonproliferation treaty, that a world of dozens of nuclear powers can be avoided. As a result, some countries would begin to rethink their own nuclear restraint. This, too, would make it harder to sustain the argument that the NPT serves the parties' security.

Still other nonproliferation breakdowns that could occur include a violation of the treaty by a party, a violation of international safeguards, or withdrawal from the treaty. Such a breakdown involving an NPT party would have an even greater corrosive impact on perceptions of the treaty's contribution to international security.

A further development that would lessen the chances for renewal of the treaty in 1995 would be a marked reduction in peaceful nuclear cooperation provided to developing countries. For most of the parties to the treaty, this cooperation has very little to do with the use of nuclear power. Instead, it entails extensive assistance in the many nonpower uses of nuclear energy, from medicine to agriculture and industry. A very significant proportion of this assistance, in turn, is provided by the technical assistance programs of the International Atomic Energy Agency (IAEA). Consequently, at the 1985 NPT review conference, the IAEA was widely praised, and general satisfaction was expressed with the treaty's performance.

In the years ahead, however, the major financial supporters of the IAEA will face growing difficulties in providing significant and growing levels of technical assistance. Budget cutbacks in the United States, for example, have led to lessened U.S. financial support to the IAEA. Other developed countries are under similar constraints. At the same time, other demands on IAEA resources, both for safeguards coverage of new nuclear facilities and in the safety field, are increasing. The main result is likely to be at least no appreciable growth in the funding of technical assistance to NPT parties, and conceivably some diminution of assistance.

A breakdown of U.S.–Soviet arms control negotiations, highly visible nonproliferation breakdowns, and significant reductions of technical assistance in the peaceful uses of nuclear energy would each threaten renewal of the nonproliferation treaty in 1995. Their impact, moreover, is likely to be greatest on that great majority of developing countries which are parties to the treaty. It was these states that determined the outcome at previous review conferences—and will do so again in 1995.

More specifically, to the extent that these shocks occur, it will become considerably harder for the great majority of developing countries to support extension of the treaty. The readiness of moderates to speak up in favor of the NPT would be lessened. The arguments of more radical NPT parties opposed to the treaty as well as of the anti-NPT nonparties likely to be present on the sidelines as observers would both be buttressed. Most important, the diffuse but critical overall mood amongst the developing countries which are parties to the NPT that, on balance, the treaty is worth preserving, would be undermined.

Even in this situation, countervailing pressures and considerations could still be brought to bear, not least an all-out East–West, U.S.–Soviet diplomatic campaign for renewal.[4] Moreover, most countries probably would think long and hard about taking such a momentous step into the unknown—about "rocking the boat" so to speak—by not extending the treaty. Indeed, the magnitude of that step and the new risks it would bring become clear if the potential consequences of a collapse of the NPT are considered.

THE COLLAPSE OF THE NPT: AN INITIAL DAMAGE ASSESSMENT

Collapse of the nonproliferation treaty in 1995 would increase significantly the prospects for the further spread of nuclear weapons around the globe. Heightened perceptions of the likelihood of runaway proliferation, corrosion of the norm of nonproliferation, lessened assurance about neighboring countries' intentions, and a weakening of nuclear export controls are but some of the direct results of the treaty's breakdown. As a result, the world would become more dangerous, and all countries' security—both former parties and outside critics—would be gradually undermined.

To elaborate, one direct impact of a breakdown of the NPT in 1995 would be to change international perceptions of the likelihood of widespread nuclear proliferation. More specifically, over the nearly two decades since the NPT entered into force in 1970, perceptions held by government leaders, observers, and others about the prospects for the spread of nuclear weapons have markedly changed. In the early 1960s, it was widely expected that there would be twenty to twenty-five nuclear-weapon states by the mid-1970s. In the late 1980s, it is now widely assumed that such proliferation can be prevented. The very fact that more than 135 countries have renounced nuclear weapons by adhering to the NPT has greatly contributed to this change of perception. Particularly, if the treaty's collapse followed several highly visible nonproliferation breakdowns, there would be many fears that the earlier predictions, though premature, were correct. Such fears would be further reinforced if after a failure to renew the treaty many parties were reluctant to reaffirm otherwise their commitment not to acquire nuclear weapons.

This perception of the likelihood of more widespread proliferation could well become a self-fulfilling prophecy. Leaders of countries that had renounced nuclear weapons would now be asking whether such renunciation would be reciprocated by other countries, especially their close neighbors. At the least, some countries could be expected to hedge their bets by starting low-visibility programs to explore the steps needed to acquire nuclear weapons. In other countries that had already been weighing the pros and cons of covert pursuit of nuclear weapons, a perception that many countries might soon move toward nuclear weapons in the decades after 1995 could tip the balance for a national decision.

The erosion of the norm of nonproliferation that would also result from the collapse of the NPT would reinforce any such incentives to pursue nuclear weapons. The treaty, in effect, represents the global consensus that acquisition of nuclear weapons no longer is legitimate international behavior. It signals countries contemplating nuclear-weapon acquisition that the majority of nations would oppose such a choice.

In the past, this norm of nonproliferation has affected the decisions of potential new weapon states. Consider, for example, India. When India detonated a nuclear explosive device in 1974, it claimed it was only testing a "peaceful nuclear explosive," despite the fact that technically there is no distinction between nuclear explosives for peaceful or for military purposes. Afterwards, India did not conduct additional tests, though many observers feared it would do so. In addition, this norm of nonproliferation probably is one reason—although admittedly not the only reason—why some countries that have been widely rumored to have the capability to develop and openly deploy nuclear weapons (for instance, Israel and South Africa) have not done so. For the result would have been a hostile international reaction.

Without the treaty, there still would be other manifestations of the perceived illegitimacy of nuclear weapons. Nonetheless, the treaty, with its steady growth of new adherents, has most come to symbolize this international constraint. For that reason, its breakdown would remove an intangible but significant restraint on the further spread of nuclear weapons.

Breakdown of the NPT also would add to the prospects for proliferation by throwing the international safeguards system run by the IAEA into temporary disarray. That system is designed to provide assurance that peaceful nuclear activities are not misused for military purposes and includes on-site inspection by IAEA inspectors. However, many countries' obligations to accept IAEA safeguards and inspections are based only on their commitment under Article III of the treaty to "accept safeguards." In the absence of other backup legal mechanisms that would come into effect and provide a legal foundation for safeguards in the absence of the NPT, they could refuse to accept IAEA inspections.[5] Consequently, a collapse of the treaty would be likely to lead to some lapses of safeguards coverage until other legal mechanisms were negotiated. In some regions, the result would be heightened suspicion about neighboring countries' nuclear activities, whether, for example, in South Korea about North Korea; Israel about Egypt, Libya, or Iran; or China about Taiwan.

Similarly, the collapse of the NPT would undermine the foundations of the existing international nuclear export control regime, while at the same time removing an important legal basis for national nuclear export controls. More specifically, the most basic foundation of the international regime controlling nuclear exports is the commitment of NPT parties under Article III of the NPT to export "source or special fissionable material" or "equipment or material especially designed or prepared for the processing, use, or production of special fissionable material" to nonnuclear-weapon states (NNWSs) only under IAEA safeguards. To implement this Article III obligation, the major suppliers—with the exception of France, which is not a party to the treaty—developed and have periodically refined the so-called Zangger Committee "trigger lists" of items that they agree to control.[6] In practice, they also have extended the Article III commitment to include a readiness to refuse completely to export trigger list items to countries or activities of proliferation concern. To further implement their obligation under Article III, all of the major nuclear suppliers that are parties to the NPT have also put in place national legislation to govern their exports of nuclear materials, equipment, and technology to prevent its misuse for military purposes.

Without the NPT, a new legal foundation for international and in many cases national nuclear export controls would be needed. The NPT-derived trigger lists that have been at the heart of the process would lack international legal standing in the absence of the treaty.[7] Moreover, particularly in many European nuclear supplier states (but not in the United States), national legislation has been specifically tied to implementation of the supplier's obligations under the nonproliferation treaty. The treaty's collapse would call the status of this legislation into question.

In addition, experience with the practice of nuclear export controls suggests that, contrasted with IAEA safeguards, it could be far more difficult and time-consuming to put in place a surrogate international legal framework. But until that framework is in place, other countries may be reluctant to prevent export of an item of nonproliferation concern because it was not on an accepted, agreed trigger list and because they lacked an international legal obligation to control it. As a result, it would be easier for countries seeking nuclear weapons to acquire the needed materials, components, or technologies.

More broadly, collapse of the NPT probably would lead many suppliers to reassess the balance between the potential payoffs of tough export controls and their costs in terms of exports lost and ill will generated in bilateral relations with the recipient. Suppliers as well as recipients would be affected by the growing fear of runaway proliferation. Why pay a price, some would ask, in a "losing cause." Such pessimism also would or could make suppliers reluctant to move rapidly to put in place a new export control system. The resultant general weakening of nuclear export controls and supplier cohesion, in turn, would remove one important impediment to countries seeking nuclear weapons. As in the case of changing perceptions, a self-fulfilling prophecy could be set in motion.

Two other likely impacts of a collapse of the nonproliferation treaty should be mentioned briefly. The collapse of the NPT would lead in all probability to a marked reduction in the level of global, peaceful nuclear cooperation. Those suppliers that lacked a backup legal foundation for IAEA safeguards probably would be reluctant or unable due to domestic restrictions to transfer peaceful nuclear assistance. More generally, public concerns about the prospects for widespread proliferation easily could force governments to limit such cooperation only to their closest friends and allies, with even more stringent nonproliferation conditions.

Finally, the NPT's collapse could impede efforts by the nuclear states to reduce their nuclear arsenals. Fears of an increasingly unstable world of many nuclear powers would strengthen the hand of opponents of further reductions of nuclear weapons in both superpowers.

DAMAGE ASSESSMENT: THE VIEW FROM THE FRONT LINES

From a broad, global perspective, therefore, there are good reasons to be concerned that a failure to extend the NPT in 1995 would make more probable the further spread of nuclear weapons, thereby heightening global instability and regional insecurity. This conclusion is confirmed by brief consideration of the likely impact of the treaty's collapse on efforts to prevent the so-called problem countries from moving up the nuclear-weapon ladder.

The prospects for a future nuclear arms race between India and Pakistan depend most heavily on developments within the region. India is carefully watching Pakistan's nuclear program and weighing the risks of continued restraint. A growing perception that widespread proliferation was unavoidable would reinforce the position of those members of the Indian elite and public that argue that India should acquire nuclear weapons in response to Pakistani activities and to assert India's claim to global recognition. Erosion of the norm of nonproliferation would have a similar impact by lessening the perceived costs of overt weapon activities. In addition, a weakening of supplier cooperation in the wake of the NPT's collapse would make it easier for both Pakistan and India to increase their nuclear capabilities.

Within the Middle East, breakdown of the NPT would remove an important legal and political constraint on the several Arab countries that are party to the treaty as well as on Iran. With the safeguards system in disarray, moreover, it would be harder to monitor these countries' nuclear activities. Further, perceptions of runaway proliferation would increase pressures on some Arab governments as well as on Iran not to be "left behind." All of these developments would increase intra-Arab and Arab–Iranian suspicions, as well as adding to concerns in Israel. At the least, past experience suggests that Israel, in turn, would be prepared to act unilaterally to block nuclear developments it finds threatening. Or, were that precluded by the risk of Soviet response or by technical–military factors, Israel could decide to test and deploy nuclear weapons to assert its nuclear superiority in the region.

Still elsewhere, heightened perceptions that more widespread proliferation was unavoidable would give credence to the now muted argument in both Argentina and Brazil that prestige demands acquisition of nuclear weapons. Conversely, erosion of the norm of nonproliferation would lessen concerns in either country about a hostile international response, were it to embark on a nuclear-weapon program. Here, too, less effective supplier cooperation would remove an important constraint on acquisition of the components and materials for nuclear weapons.

The treaty's collapse would also remove political and legal constraints on a black African country such as Nigeria, which has in the past periodically debated whether to try to acquire nuclear weapons to match what it regards as South Africa's capability. As for South Africa, with the nonproliferation regime in disarray, the costs of moving further up the nuclear-weapon ladder would be reduced.

In Asia, collapse of the treaty could lead to concerns in South Korea about North Korea's nuclear program, especially if publicly announced North Korean plans for nuclear research and power development have been carried out by the mid-1990s. The result probably would then be heightened public and internal governmental pressures in Seoul to revive the types of weapon activities that South Korea began, and then stopped under U.S. pressure, in the mid-1970s. Once again, the U.S. security tie would likely be the key to the outcome.

Thus, viewed both from a broad global perspective and from the vantage point of efforts to prevent or contain potential weapon activities by specific countries, there is every reason to believe that the collapse of the NPT would heighten the prospects for more widespread proliferation of nuclear weapons. Space precludes a long discussion here of the varied reasons why such a development would threaten regional and global security.[8] Suffice it to assert that the results in all probability would range from heightened political tensions between newly nuclear countries to possibly even the actual use of nuclear weapons in one of the conflict-prone regions to which these weapons might spread. The risk of a U.S.–Soviet confrontation arising out of support for their respective allies or friends would also rise. This, too, is part of the overall damage assessment.

WHAT TO DO IF. . . ?

Notwithstanding the potential consequences of a collapse of the NPT in 1995, let us assume that the parties deadlock and do not vote to extend it. In the wake of that collapse, the United States and other supporters of the treaty at first glance would seem to face a basic choice: whether to try to create a new global nonproliferation treaty or to adopt a variety of more limited ad hoc approaches to limit the damage. Neither course of action is satisfactory.

To begin, there may not be sufficient time available to go about creating from scratch a new nonproliferation treaty. Negotiation of the original NPT took several years of intense U.S.–Soviet diplomacy, followed by another year of negotiations in the then Eighteen-Nation Disarmament Commission. But it would be important to move as rapidly as possible to find surrogate means for countries to affirm their nonproliferation commitments, thereby lessening the perception of imminent runaway proliferation and checking erosion of the norm of nonproliferation.

Efforts to negotiate a new nonproliferation treaty also would be impeded by the likely tabling of many and probably often contradictory proposals to improve on the original draft. For example, proposals could be expected to require "full-scope" safeguards as a condition of supply to nonnuclear states; to require nuclear states to accept safeguards on all their peaceful nuclear facilities; to obligate explicitly all parties (and not simply the NWSs) not to assist other countries to acquire nuclear explosives; to commit the NWSs to negotiate a ban on all nuclear testing by a certain specified date; to obligate the NWSs to separate absolutely their peaceful and military nuclear activities; and many others. Eventually, it might be possible to sort through all such proposals and come to a well-balanced set of obligations. That, too, would be very time-consuming. It is equally likely to prove impossible.

By contrast, a piecemeal approach would be less time-consuming and would not run into all of the technical difficulties of negotiating a new treaty. What measures would this more limited approach entail? An answer to that question should begin from the most damaging potential nonproliferation consequences of a collapse of the treaty itself. These were, to recall, heightened perceptions of the likelihood of runaway proliferation, corrosion of the norm of nonproliferation, a weakening of nuclear supplier cooperation and the legal foundation of international nuclear export controls, a threat to international safeguards, disruption of peaceful nuclear cooperation, and a more diffuse decline of intangible constraints on the most often-cited problem countries.

Widespread reaffirmation of countries' commitments not to acquire nuclear explosives would be an essential first step to counter perceptions of runaway proliferation and to check the corrosion of the nonproliferation norm. A coordinated East–West, U.S.–Soviet diplomatic campaign could be launched to convince other governments to make unilateral national nonproliferation statements. Comparable pledges might be made in appropriate regional forums, for instance, the European Community, the Association of Southeast Asian Nations, or the Organization of American States. It also would be possible to seek a consensus resolution in the United Nations General Assembly session that would soon follow the 1995 NPT review conference. None of these pledges or statements, however, would have a legally binding status. Moreover, some countries may be reluctant to reaffirm their prior decision not to acquire nuclear weapons, especially if a series of nonproliferation breakdowns had led up to the 1995 collapse of the NPT.

Closely related, the United States and other nonproliferation supporters could mount a diplomatic campaign to convince Argentina and Brazil to bring fully into force the Treaty of Tlatelolco, creating a nuclear-free zone in Latin America, assuming that they had not done so by then. Other Latin American neighbors of both countries could be expected to support such a step. Paradoxically, while both Argentina and Brazil are opponents of the NPT, the shock of its collapse could help to push them to take the final step to be bound by Tlatelolco. It might appear the best, and readily available, means to prevent a slide toward nuclear weapons that would serve neither country's security.

Measures also would be needed to ensure effective nuclear export controls after collapse of the nonproliferation treaty. To that end, it might be appropriate to reconvene the Nuclear Suppliers' Group (NSG), most probably for the first time since 1977.[9] An NSG meeting would provide a needed forum for the major suppliers to affirm their continued readiness to control their exports. In addition, at such a meeting it would be possible to revise the export control lists of the NSG to incorporate into the original NSG lists the items that had been added over the years to the NPT-tied trigger lists. Most important, the nuclear suppliers could use the meeting to discuss and begin to negotiate a legally binding commitment to control nuclear exports to replace that commitment which had lapsed with Article III of the NPT. For the NSG guidelines are not international legal commitments but only statements of national policy.

An additional damage-limiting step would be to move quickly to ensure that IAEA safeguards continued to be applied to peaceful nuclear activities, both to check the growth of mutual suspicions in some regions and to permit continued peaceful nuclear cooperation. Where present, legally binding backup safeguards obligations should be brought into force. Elsewhere, negotiation of new commitments would be needed. In the interim, the IAEA could declare that it would continue to carry out safeguards inspections, thereby placing the burden on a specific country to refuse entry to IAEA inspectors. For their part, the major nuclear suppliers could affirm that they would not carry out any prior commitments to provide nuclear equipment, fuel, or technology to any country that either lacked a backup safeguards obligation or refused to cooperate voluntarily with acceptance of IAEA safeguards in this interim period. The suppliers also could declare that no new commitments would be made to countries without a longer-term legal basis for continued IAEA safeguards until such countries had put that basis in place.

In the period after a possible collapse of the NPT, measures also would be in order to contain its impact on the policies of the problem countries. Stepped up intelligence collection to provide early warning of potential shifts toward nuclear-weapon acquisition would be a start. Diplomatic channels might also be used by the United States and other governments to continue to make the case with key countries for nuclear restraint.

In regard to the latter, the United States and the Soviet Union might build on their established pattern of cooperation in the nonproliferation field. To begin, they could hold an extraordinary ministerial-level meeting on nonproliferation to review the overall nonproliferation situation and to identify common or parallel steps that East and West could take to limit the damage of the NPT's collapse. In the shock following collapse of the NPT, both governments could well be prepared to take a fresh look at old problems and to consider new initiatives.

Specific steps would depend heavily, of course, on the nonproliferation "state of play" at the time. Among the possibilities could be concerted common pressure on potential new nuclear states to negotiate bilateral restraints or to put in force existing regional approaches, joint démarches to selected problem countries to stress the adverse costs of further weapon activities, and new efforts to deal with regional political differences that frequently underlie weapon programs. If the background to the treaty's collapse had been one or more highly visible nonproliferation failures, such coordinated action would be all the more in order. Moreover, even had a U.S.–Soviet arms control breakdown been a major precipitating factor of a collapse of the treaty, cooperation between the two superpowers to limit the damage still could be possible. Past experience shows both countries prepared to isolate pursuit of their common nonproliferation interests from differences over other security matters.

These types of more limited, ad hoc, damage-limiting measures would be more politically feasible and more easily put rapidly in place than would be efforts to negotiate a new NPT. But this approach also is not fully satisfactory. Collapse of the treaty would be a major international shock, and it would leave a major gap in the fabric of international order. The preceding piecemeal measures, though needed, simply provide surrogate means to fill parts of that gap. Is there no alternative to either a probably unsuccessful—and in any case too time-consuming—attempt to create a new NPT or a more restricted effort to pick up the pieces to the extent feasible?

One possibility comes to mind. If the 1995 NPT review conference votes on extension of the treaty, but a majority in favor is lacking, the three depositary governments could propose that the review conference not end but only adjourn for a three-month cooling off period. The three depositaries could also propose that at the end of the period the parties would reconvene for one day for a second up-or-down vote on the treaty. In the aftermath of an actual negative vote, it is quite likely that such a motion to revisit the issue would carry. The general tendency of multilateral diplomats not to take such far-reaching steps, as well as the very shock effect, would work in that direction. During this period, supporters of the NPT, led by the three depositaries, could mount an international campaign to muster the needed votes to continue the NPT—as is.[10]

Of course, this approach has its risks. In particular, a second failure probably would considerably increase perceptions that the overall global nonproliferation commitment had fallen apart, with runaway proliferation on the horizon and nuclear weapons now legitimate for all. But would there be a second negative vote? The answer would depend in large part on the origins of the initial result. If, as seems likely, the first negative vote included many small developing countries that were relatively indifferent to the treaty and whose positions were determined by their representatives on the spot, there would be a good chance to reverse that vote.

Besides, faced with the overall consequences of the NPT's collapse, this type of gamble could well be the "least bad alternative."

There seems little doubt, thus, that were the NPT not to be extended in 1995, its collapse would confront the United States and many other countries with a series of difficult choices. That said, it remains unlikely that the treaty would not be extended. There are also ways that the United States and others can reduce even further the chances of that outcome.

ON THE ROAD TO SUCCESS IN 1995

Some of the actions that the United States could take to support the NPT and increase the prospects for its long-term extension in 1995 are implicit in the preceding assessment. Following the agreement to eliminate U.S. and Soviet intermediate-range nuclear missiles with the successful negotiation of a U.S.–Soviet agreement to reduce significantly their strategic offensive nuclear forces would go far to demonstrate that the nuclear states had begun to contain their own weapon programs. Progress in other arms control areas, for example, chemical weapons and conventional forces, also would support Article VI. In turn, new or intensified nonproliferation initiatives can be taken to lessen the risk of a series of nonproliferation breakdowns. Efforts to maintain steady support for the IAEA's technical assistance program, though not costly in absolute terms, can pay high dividends in good will.

Turning to a different sort of measure, it will be especially important to preserve and strengthen U.S.–Soviet consultations on nuclear nonproliferation matters. For over five years, the two sides have met every six months to review issues running the gamut from problem countries to the IAEA. Support for the NPT has always been an important feature of these consultations. It will be important to invest the needed time and attention to keep this channel effective, uncluttered by polemics, and in use at the 1990 NPT review conference and beyond.

Another step to help set the tone for 1995 would be intensified efforts to bring into the treaty some key countries that have indicated a possible readiness to join. That Spain and Saudi Arabia have recently joined may augur well for some other important prospects. Niger, a uranium producer, suggested it would join. South Africa's possible adherence also should continue to be pursued vigorously.

The impact of the upcoming 1990 NPT review conference in setting the stage for 1995 also is likely to be very significant. In that regard, it may be most important that governments at the 1990 review avoid the temptation to define a set of specific disarmament or nonproliferation milestones to guide governments between 1990 and 1995. Among such milestones, for example, could be a comprehensive ban on nuclear testing; further reductions of U.S. and Soviet nuclear weapons; Israeli, Indian, and Pakistani adherence to the NPT; a nuclear-free zone in the Middle East or South Asia; or doubling IAEA technical assistance to developing countries. Designed to prod key governments to action, such calls are only likely to create excessive expectations about what may be possible between 1990 and 1995.

Like all conditions, moreover, they also will box in the participants in ways that are later likely to be regretted. In turn, to the extent that their objectives are unrealized, that will serve only to ensure that the 1995 conference begins on a contentious and divisive note.

By way of conclusion, what needs to be done between now and 1995 for the successful extension of the NPT? In 1995, there needs to be a broad consensus among the parties that the NPT has contributed to all countries' security by helping to contain the further spread of nuclear weapons; that the treaty has provided a valuable framework for promoting peaceful nuclear cooperation; and that the NPT has encouraged the two nuclear superpowers to negotiate successfully agreements that have turned the corner on the postwar expansion of their nuclear arsenals. This is the goal that all parties, nuclear and nonnuclear states, developed and developing, suppliers and recipients, should work toward in the years ahead. For there is little doubt that without the nonproliferation treaty, the world would become a more dangerous place for all.

NOTES AND REFERENCES

1. The position of the United States has been that the treaty would remain in force in the event of a failure of the 1995 review conference to take any action at all.
2. For a different view, from a long-standing advocate of a comprehensive nuclear test ban, see William Epstein, "Letter to the Editor," *Arms Control Today* (November/December, 1985).
3. For a solid review of activities of proliferation concern around the globe, see Leonard Spector, *Going Nuclear* (Cambridge, Mass.: Ballinger, 1987).
4. It is not contradictory to posit such a U.S.–Soviet diplomatic campaign in support of the NPT and to speculate about the possible impact on NPT renewal of a breakdown of U.S.–Soviet arms control talks. After the Soviets walked out of the Geneva arms control negotiations in November 1983, they continued to consult closely with the United States on the then upcoming 1985 NPT review conference. At the same time, the declining U.S.–Soviet influence over many of the NPT parties probably would reduce the impact of their parallel démarches in favor of the treaty.
5. The United States has put in place backup obligations to accept safeguards as part of its new agreements for peaceful nuclear cooperation. Many other nuclear suppliers, nonetheless, have not done so.
6. France has traditionally "associated" itself on a national basis with the commitment to control nuclear trigger list items, thereby supporting nonproliferation but standing clear of the NPT.
7. There are other "trigger lists" attached to the Nuclear Suppliers' Guidelines. However, these lists have not been updated to include new items added recently to the Zangger lists. In addition, the guidelines, unlike the NPT, lack legally binding status.
8. For a more complete discussion, see, for example, Lewis A. Dunn, *Controlling the Bomb* (New Haven: Yale University Press, 1982), pp. 69–94.
9. In the mid-1980s, the Soviets have on various occasions publicly called for reconvening the Nuclear Suppliers' Group. These calls have met with only modest support from many of the other suppliers. For that reason, it is assumed that such an NSG meeting after collapse of the NPT would be the first meeting in nearly two decades.
10. During this period, various compromises also might be sought with regard to the timing of the extension. Conceivably, a shorter extension than initially voted on could provide some countries with a reason to change their initial negative vote after the cooling-off period.

4

What Happens to Safeguards if the NPT Goes?

David Fischer

Article X of the NPT provides that in 1995 "a conference shall be convened to decide whether the treaty shall continue in force indefinitely, or shall be extended for an additional fixed period or periods." Theoretically, the period of extension could be a matter of months or even days.[1]

Actually, the most likely scenario is that the parties to the NPT, at the 1995 conference, will agree to a substantial extension of the treaty; however, this chapter will examine two scenarios, both of which presuppose that in 1995 the parties cannot agree to a substantial extension and that the treaty soon expires. A necessary, though not a sufficient, condition for the expiration of the treaty would be the failure of the United States and the Soviet Union to reverse the nuclear arms race, after raising the world's hopes that they would do so. Large numbers of nonnuclear-weapon states (NNWSs) then despair of the NPT as a means to constrain the nuclear powers and oppose any significant extension of the treaty.

In the worst-case scenario, the collapse of superpower efforts to reverse the nuclear arms race leads to a grave deterioration in the relations between Moscow and Washington. One consequence of this is a sharp decline in the long-standing superpower cooperation on nonproliferation matters. The events that had helped to cause the demise of the NPT then also prevent the superpowers from working together to soften the impact of its loss. Worsening relations between the United States and the Soviet Union make the rest of the world more insecure and, therefore, revive interest in the nuclear option.

David Fischer • Consultant, International Atomic Energy Agency, Vienna, Austria.

The second, and much less improbable, scenario assumes that despite the demise of the NPT, the United States and the Soviet Union would continue to cooperate in restraining the spread of nuclear weapons. It also assumes that the considerations that led NNWSs to accept the NPT and full-scope safeguards, chiefly to give assurance that their nuclear activities were exclusively peaceful, would also continue to apply. In other words, the second scenario assumes that the international "immune response" system would go into action to mitigate the effects of the loss of the NPT.

There are countless intermediate scenarios, for instance, a relatively short extension of the NPT or a substantial extension coupled with an exodus of disaffected states creating a category of former NPT states (whose intentions might be highly suspect).

THE COLLAPSE OF THE NPT: A WORST-CASE SCENARIO

What Safeguards Would Be Left?

Article III of the NPT requires each of its nonnuclear parties to conclude an agreement with the International Atomic Energy Agency (IAEA) so as to place all its peaceful nuclear activities under IAEA safeguards.[2] The agreement with the IAEA remains in force as long as the state is party to the treaty. In other words, if the NPT expired, all safeguards agreements concluded under it would automatically lapse.[3]

Even in the worst case this does not mean that safeguards would automatically drop away in all NPT NNWSs.[4] Four factors would maintain full safeguards coverage in many states and partial coverage in others:

- The safeguards of the European Atomic Energy Authority (EURATOM) would continue to operate in the twelve member states of the European community.[5]
- Full-scope IAEA safeguards are required by the treaty prohibiting nuclear weapons in Latin America, the Tlatelolco Treaty, and would continue to apply in all twenty-three Latin American countries that have brought the treaty into force.
- In several NPT NNWSs, "fall-back" IAEA safeguards, suspended when the state joined the NPT, would automatically reapply to plants and fuel covered by pre-NPT agreements or derived from such plants or fuel. Some supply agreements concluded with a state since it joined the NPT also provide for fall-back safeguards if the NPT should lapse.
- Non-NPT IAEA[6] safeguards would continue to give partial coverage in a number of NNWSs that have not joined the NPT.

The IAEA might also try to establish a "continuation principle," that is, a rule that all nuclear plant and material that was under IAEA safeguards when the NPT lapsed should continue to be under IAEA safeguards and that only "new" plants (i.e., those brought into operation after the NPT had lapsed) and newly mined or imported fuel should be exempt.

It is, of course, a moot question whether former NPT NNWSs would accept such an interpretation of their obligations. If they did, it would still be necessary to negotiate new agreements to cover many of the plants and much of the fuel remaining under safeguards, since the existing agreements derive their authority from the state's membership of the NPT.[7]

What would be the practical effect of these factors? Let us first look at the European Atomic Energy Authority, where the largest quantity of safeguarded nuclear fuel and the largest number of safeguarded plants are to be found.

EURATOM

In the five original EURATOM NNWSs—West Germany, Italy, Belgium, the Netherlands, and Luxembourg—IAEA safeguards would lapse on virtually all nuclear material and plants unless the IAEA succeeded in establishing the continuation principle. EURATOM's own full-scope safeguards would, of course, continue to apply. These safeguards do not, however, prohibit the manufacture of nuclear weapons. They only verify that nuclear items are being used in conformity with the purpose declared by the user or with conditions set by the supplier and accepted by EURATOM. This "conformity control," as it is called, permits France and Britain to make nuclear weapons and, in the absence of other constraints, would permit any other EURATOM state to do likewise.

The position in the five newer EURATOM NNWSs—Denmark, Ireland, Greece, Portugal, and Spain—is somewhat different. When these countries joined EURATOM, all their nuclear plants and material were already under pre-NPT IAEA safeguards. These safeguards would automatically reapply if the treaty were to lapse.

In summary, if the NPT lapsed, the Rome Treaty establishing EURATOM would permit any of the ten EURATOM NNWSs to manufacture nuclear weapons if it so decided. If any of the five original EURATOM NNWSs did so decide, it would have to make its warheads from nuclear material that is not subject to restrictions imposed by the supplier state (e.g., it would have to avoid using material of U.S. or Canadian origin which carries the tag that it may not be used for any military purpose). The five newer EURATOM NNWSs would have an additional constraint—they would be barred from using any nuclear plant or material that was in their possession in November 1987, because all such material and plant is subject to non-NPT IAEA safeguards, which would reapply if the NPT lapsed.[8]

Two of the leading EURATOM states, West Germany and Italy, are, however, barred by World War II peace settlements from directly acquiring nuclear weapons. Whether any of the others would join Britain and France in the ranks of weapon states would depend chiefly on their perceptions of security in a non-NPT world.

The Tlatelolco Treaty

The situation in Latin America is much clearer than that in Western Europe. As noted, the Tlatelolco Treaty requires each of its twenty-three full parties to conclude a full-scope safeguards agreement with the IAEA.[9]

The Tlatelolco Treaty is also "of a permanent nature" and does not face the same twenty-five-year challenge as the NPT. Unless a party to the Tlatelolco Treaty withdrew from it, its entire nuclear fuel cycle would thus remain permanently under IAEA safeguards, even if the NPT lapsed.

All of the twenty-three states that have brought the Tlatelolco Treaty into force are also parties to the NPT. Their safeguards agreements with the IAEA usually cover their NPT as well as their Tlatelolco obligations. The NPT obligations include the prohibition of so-called peaceful nuclear explosives and, thereby, incidentally eliminate a serious ambiguity in the Tlatelolco Treaty.[10]

Unfortunately, the four main absentees from the Tlatelolco Treaty include three of the states in Latin America that are most advanced in the use of nuclear technology, namely, Brazil, Argentina, and Cuba as well as Chile.[11]

The Warsaw Pact

All the Warsaw Pact NNWSs—Poland, Czechoslovakia, Hungary, East Germany, Romania, and Bulgaria—have accepted full-scope IAEA safeguards, but solely as a consequence of their ratification of the NPT. In theory, at least, each of them would be free to acquire nuclear weapons if the treaty were to lapse. But even in the worst case, it is virtually certain that the Soviet Union would ensure that none of them did any such thing.

Other Regions and Countries

Outside the three regional groupings—EURATOM, Tlatelolco, and the Warsaw Pact—we see a numerous and very diverse array of NNWSs parties to the NPT:

- In Europe: The Scandinavian countries, Austria, Switzerland, Yugoslavia, and two mini-states (the Holy See and San Marino).
- In North America: Canada.
- In the Middle East: Egypt, Turkey, Iraq, Iran, Libya, Algeria, and Morocco—each has at least a research reactor or is reported to be getting one; and Lebanon, Jordan, Tunisia, Syria, both Yemens, Bahrein, and Saudi Arabia—none of which have any nuclear plants, but Saudi Arabia may be buying one or more research reactors from West Germany.
- In Africa, including Indian Ocean states: Thirty NPT NNWSs are parties to the NPT. Only Zaire (a Triga reactor) and Gabon have any safeguardable items, although Gabon is an important producer of yellow-cake, the export of which to NNWSs must be reported to the IAEA but which is not subject to

inspection. Except perhaps for Nigeria, no other African NPT country is likely to have safeguardable plant and material in this century.

- In the rest of Asia and the Pacific: The NPT parties include Japan, the two Koreas, and Taiwan,[12] all four of which are operating or acquiring power reactors and other nuclear plants, as well as, *with two significant exceptions*, all twenty-six states stretching from Afghanistan to the Pacific.[13] The two significant *non-NPT* states are India and Pakistan. In this broad band from Afghanistan to the Pacific, seven NPT states have research reactors (Bangladesh, Indonesia, Malaysia, the Philippines, Thailand, Vietnam, and Australia).

The extent to which IAEA safeguards[14] would survive the NPT and be reapplied in countries in these five scattered groups would vary widely. Canadian plants are under IAEA safeguards only because Canada has ratified the NPT. At the other end of the spectrum, nearly all the developing countries in these regions that are operating one or more reactors acquired them from the United States under agreements that would ensure that IAEA safeguards would continue to apply.[15] Few if any of them would be technically able to manufacture a reactor or any other significant nuclear plant without help from one of the nuclear suppliers. Because the Nuclear Suppliers' Guidelines would presumably continue to be observed in one form or another even if the NPT expired, it is unlikely that during this century any of the *developing countries* in these groups would be able to acquire unsafeguarded plants.

However, the so-called newly industrialized countries (NICs), such as South Korea and Taiwan, are an exception. All nuclear plants that will be operating or under construction in Taiwan in 1995 and almost all those in South Korea will be under continuing IAEA safeguards.[16] There is, however, little doubt that Taiwan and South Korea would be capable of building their own unsafeguarded reactors and pilot reprocessing and enrichment plants without significant help from abroad. The same is true of Australia[17] and may be true of North Korea.

Japan is in a class by itself. Most nuclear plants and fuel in Japan came directly or indirectly from the United States and would continue to be under IAEA safeguards if the NPT lapsed. However, Japan has already built a small plant for enriching uranium without foreign help and is planning a much larger one as well as a large reprocessing plant, all of which are or will be subject to NPT safeguards only, which would lapse with the NPT.

The Irreversible Spread of Unsafeguarded Plants

In the worst-case scenario, Japan, South Korea, Taiwan, and possibly North Korea could take the option of building an unsafeguarded fuel cycle side-by-side with their still safeguarded plants.

In recent times, only Spain amongst the EURATOM countries has shown some interest in keeping open the nuclear option, a course reportedly recommended until recently by the Spanish Ministry of Defense.[18] Spanish signature and verification of the NPT has presently closed that option.

Sweden, Switzerland, and Yugoslavia might in due course also be tempted to build unsafeguarded "sensitive" plants—*not* to make the bomb—as a precaution in an insecure world. Romania, too, might do likewise.[19] Canada would also find it relatively easy to build an unsafeguarded fuel cycle.

As time went on, other countries in the developing world, besides the present six threshold states—Argentina, Brazil, South Africa, Israel, India, and Pakistan—would gradually acquire the infrastructure and materials they would need to make and operate unsafeguarded plants and, eventually, unsafeguarded fuel cycles. As the constraints of the NPT fell away, this course might seem very tempting to countries such as Egypt and other Arab states, Iran, Turkey and Greece, Nigeria, Indonesia and other present NPT parties in Southeast Asia, and also to non-NPT states at present under full-scope safeguards, such as Chile.

Except for the parties to the Tlatelolco and Rarotonga treaties, there would be no formal requirement anywhere in the world to accept full-scope IAEA safeguards. In this sense, the world would revert in 1995 to the position of May 1968 before the NPT was opened for signature.

From the point of view of safeguards and from many other points of view, the situation would be much worse. In 1968, only three nonnuclear states—India, Israel, and Spain—were operating unsafeguarded nuclear plants.[20] If the NPT expired, the *immediate* roster of unsafeguarded facilities would not only include those in the six threshold countries, but also the plants from which safeguards had fallen away in Japan, Sweden, Canada, and probably in South and North Korea, Indonesia and Vietnam, as well as in any other NNWS that might by 1995 be building plants without foreign help or importing them without fall-back safeguards. As far as one can now foresee, the additional[21] dangers that such a situation might promptly provoke would include a "nuclear capability" race or even a nuclear arms race between the two Koreas.[22] This, in turn, might spur Japan to take appropriate precautions.

But in short, in the worst case the emerging norm of nonproliferation would be shattered. As the world moved deeper into the twenty-first century, the roster of countries having unsafeguarded plants and the number, variety, and sensitivity of such plants would tend to grow. So too would the number of nations approaching and crossing the nuclear threshold increase as regional nuclear arms races erupted between mutually hostile states. We might then see the fears of the early 1960s turning into perilous realities.[23]

More Than the Loss of Safeguards

One must not see the loss of the NPT only through the narrow lens of safeguards. In the worst case, its demise might affect the prospects for peace in the twenty-first century.

The NPT and its associated safeguards are the world's first, and, so far, its only experiment in international on-site verification of a multilateral arms control agreement.[24] Intrusive verification of this kind is the issue on which most attempts at arms control have come to grief. If the first, most tested, and most extensive verification system should begin to unravel, this could harm the prospects for creating and successfully operating other international and perhaps even other bilateral systems of verification, such as the ones created for the Intermediate-Range Nuclear Forces (INF) Treaty and contemplated for the Strategic Arms Reduction Talks (START) and the Chemical Weapons Convention (CWC). The damage might be much reduced if, besides INF, there were more arms reduction treaties in place before 1995. But in that case there would be little danger of losing the NPT.

The loss of the NPT might also call into question the premises on which international security has evolved during the last twenty years. Since the treaty took shape, there have been far-reaching changes in relations between NATO and the Warsaw Pact countries and between China and the West (including Japan). Under the NPT, the former Axis powers have explicitly renounced nuclear weapons and have accepted the international verification of their commitment. This has helped to foster confidence and alleviate suspicion between East and West—and between East and East. It has helped to reduce the risk of war. Nonproliferation has also been one of the few issues on which the Soviet Union and the United States could cooperate, even when the Soviets went into Afghanistan and later when President Reagan described them as an "evil empire."

In the worst case, therefore, the loss of the NPT would be a major international setback, perhaps a political disaster. It might gravely damage the prospects for arms control. It might destroy one of the few enduring bases of superpower cooperation. It might revive suspicions of the nuclear intentions of the most dynamic nations of Western Europe and the Far East. The confidence and security of all states might be weakened, even for those who still formally reject the nonproliferation regime.

NONPROLIFERATION SURVIVES THE NPT: A MORE PROBABLE SCENARIO

The underlying interests of states would not change simply because the NPT expired. It would still be in the interest of all nuclear-weapon states (NWSs) and especially the superpowers to cooperate in preventing the further spread of nuclear weapons. Unless the loss of the NPT were due to a fatal collapse of international order and security, the considerations that prompted most of its leading nonnuclear states parties to accept the treaty would still remain valid. Chief among these is to provide an internationally verified assurance that their own nuclear activities are and will remain entirely peaceful. Another, which the leading nonnuclear states share with the nuclear states, is to secure the same assurances from as many other countries as possible. A third is to ensure that international nuclear commerce does not lead to proliferation. How could these assurances be obtained in the absence of the NPT?[25]

The NWSs would have to devise a procedure to reaffirm the undertaking they have given in Article I of the NPT not to help any NNWS to acquire nuclear weapons or other nuclear explosives.[26] It might be more difficult for the NWSs to find a way of giving a credible assurance that they remain committed to nuclear disarmament and to a comprehensive test ban treaty.

The NNWSs would have to devise means of reaffirming their commitments not to acquire nuclear weapons or other nuclear explosives, and to accept full-scope IAEA safeguards as well as to ensure that their exports to NNWSs were subject to appropriate IAEA safeguards. If the political will were there, the procedure could be relatively simple. It could be done by amending and extending the NPT safeguards agreements that the NNWSs have already concluded with the IAEA.[27]

It would also be necessary to reaffirm the present regime of export controls and restraints. The Nuclear Suppliers' Guidelines are not directly linked to the NPT and are followed by non-NPT countries like France and South Africa, but the "trigger list" which they incorporate was originally devised as a means of interpreting the obligations of suppliers under Article III.2 of the NPT.

Which countries are more likely to revive their NPT obligations? The two superpowers and the United Kingdom would probably take the lead and with them the Scandinavians, Canada, Australia, and the Netherlands among the Western nonnuclear states. The Soviet Union might be capable of pressing such a course—that is, amendment and extension of existing NPT agreements—upon its Warsaw Pact allies. Japan would be influenced by EURATOM's decision. Within EURATOM, it might be argued that its own twelve-nation safeguards system (including two nuclear states) provides ample assurance. However, EURATOM's chief suppliers, such as Australia, Canada, and, to some extent, the United States and the Soviet Union, could, if necessary, bring effective pressure to bear to continue IAEA safeguards. The United States and Japan could also press hard on South Korea and the Soviet Union on North Korea.

A Major Loss

But even if we assume that there would continue to be extensive safeguards coverage as well as cooperation between the superpowers, a great deal would have been lost. The most optimistic of our two scenarios assumes that most nonnuclear states continue to accept full-scope IAEA safeguards, for instance, by amending their existing agreements with the IAEA. However, the scope of these agreements is and would continue to be considerably narrower than that of the NPT itself. The agreement that each NPT NNWS concludes with the IAEA is intended to verify that the NNWS is not *diverting* nuclear material from *peaceful activities* to nuclear weapons or other nuclear explosives.[28] Such diversion is, however, only one of several paths a state may take to acquire nuclear weapons. The NPT closes every path. Moreover, the NPT, as an international treaty, is a contract by every state with every other state party. This formal *treaty commitment* would be lost. Similarly, the formal treaty commitment of the NWSs to strive for nuclear disarmament would be lost. The obligation which Article IV of the NPT places on all parties to promote cooperation in developing the peaceful uses of nuclear technology would be lost. At least some NNWSs would be likely to take the opportunity to opt out of their safeguards obligations. The temptation to slough off commitments might be strong in the Middle East and, possibly, in Southeast Asia.

The NPT parties that by 1995 had not negotiated their full-scope safeguards agreements with the IAEA, as they are required to do by Article III.1 and III.4 of the NPT, would no longer be under any obligation to do so. At the end of 1986, fifty-two NPT NNWSs had failed to complete their negotiations within the prescribed time limit.[29] Thus, none of these states would be under any nonproliferation or, as a rule, under any safeguards obligation.

Even under this comparatively optimistic scenario, the demise of the NPT would thus be likely to have very unpleasant consequences. It would be a grave setback to twenty years of efforts to restrain the spread of nuclear weapons and to reverse the nuclear arms race. It would remove the main underpinning of IAEA safeguards, and it could lead to a less predictable and more insecure world order. The nonproliferation norm would be severely weakened, if not altogether lost. To make good the loss, we should have to attempt to rebuild the international regime we have painstakingly put together since 1968—or, more accurately, since 1965.

BEYOND 1995: A NEW NONPROLIFERATION ORDER?

Would the collapse of the NPT, whatever the cause of its demise, perhaps clear the way to a new and better treaty? This seems highly improbable. The NPT was the product of the convergence of U.S. and Soviet interests at a time when the two superpowers could generally lay down the nuclear law and when détente had made it possible for them to work closely together. We may be entering another period of détente, by a different name, but the superpowers have lost much of their leverage in nuclear commerce and technology; indeed they have sustained a greater loss of their authority in the peaceful uses of nuclear energy than in most other areas.[30]

It would be far more difficult today to reconcile the conflicting agendas of the various states and groups whose agreement would be needed to launch a new treaty.[31] And even if agreement could be reached on a new text, one would still face the daunting task of negotiating new safeguards agreements with the states that one would wish to see in the new treaty. In short, the NPT is the best nonproliferation treaty that we have, or that we are likely to have.

NOTES AND REFERENCES

1. The prospects for extension of the NPT and some of the problems likely to arise before and during the 1995 conference are examined in a study by the author in chap. 11 of John Simpson, *Nuclear Nonproliferation: An Agenda for the 1990s* (Cambridge: Cambridge University Press, 1987).
2. In effect, the NPT permits nonpeaceful uses of nuclear energy, such as nuclear propulsion of submarines, but prohibits any explosive use of nuclear energy for any purpose. Obviously, international safeguards cannot be applied to military activities.
3. See paragraph 26 of the standard IAEA/NPT safeguards agreement, IAEA document INFCIRC/153.

4. At the end of December 1988, there were 136 NNWSs and 3 NWSs in the NPT.
5. Full-scope safeguards are in place in Belgium, Denmark, the Federal Republic of Germany, Greece, Ireland, Italy, Luxembourg, the Netherlands, Portugal, and Spain; partial safeguards in Britain and France.
6. See IAEA document INFCIRC/66/Rev. 2.
7. These new agreements would have to be concluded under the INFCIRC/66 safeguards system, which was drawn up in the mid-1960s before the NPT came into force. This system is still applied in *non-NPT* NNWSs. In the NPT, NNWS safeguards are applied under the NPT system (IAEA document INFCIRC/153, drawn up in 1970 and 1971), but in many NPT NNWSs, the demise of the NPT would revive earlier INFCIRC/66/Rev. 2 agreements, concluded before the NNWSs in question had joined the NPT and now "in suspense." These earlier agreements have become, in effect, fall-back agreements.
8. It would probably be correct to say that these states would be debarred from using "any plant or material *that is in their possession today*" rather than "*that was in their possession in November 1987*." However, it is possible that Spain (alone amongst this group) may have acquired plant or material since it ratified the NPT (on November 5, 1987), that is, plant or material that would not be covered by fall-back IAEA safeguards. The author believes all nuclear plants and material in the other members of the group are subject to fall-back IAEA safeguards.

   It should also be noted that even after the demise of the NPT, nuclear material *that had been derived from* plant or from other nuclear material under *non-NPT* IAEA safeguards would again fall under those safeguards. It would be a difficult task, especially in Spain with its large and varied nuclear program, to differentiate between such "IAEA contaminated" material and "new" material subject only to EURATOM safeguards.
9. The relevant clause requires an agreement with the IAEA "for the application of safeguards to its [the state's] nuclear activities." This has been interpreted as requiring the application of safeguards *to all the state's activities*. Anything less would hardly be compatible with the aim of the treaty to ensure that the Latin American region remains entirely free from nuclear weapons.
10. The ambiguity is essentially whether or not the Tlatelolco Treaty permits its parties to carry out nuclear explosions for peaceful purposes and hence to manufacture nuclear explosives for such purposes. The treaty's language can be read both ways.

    A legal purist would consider it necessary to amend the IAEA's existing agreements with the twenty-three NNWSs parties to the treaty and to the NPT so as to take account of the fact that after the demise of the latter their obligations would stem only from the Tlatelolco Treaty.
11. Partial IAEA safeguards under the non-NPT system will continue to apply in Argentina and Brazil, irrespective of what may happen to the NPT. Non-NPT IAEA safeguards now apply to *all* nuclear plants and material in Chile and Cuba. This position seems likely to continue indefinitely, at least in Cuba, whose future nuclear plants (like those it has at present) will almost certainly come from the USSR (or its European allies) or be derived from Soviet technology.
12. The Republic of China ratified the NPT while it was still recognized by the United States and the IAEA as the government of China. The IAEA Board of Governors withdrew recognition before the NPT safeguards agreement between it and the IAEA was approved. All nuclear plants and material produced in or imported into Taiwan are, however, automatically listed under the inventory of the earlier U.S.–Taiwan–IAEA safeguards agreement. It is probable that this arrangement would continue even if the NPT expired.
13. This was the case as of 31 December 1988. The figure includes the Pacific Island NNWSs.
14. Apart from some fall-back bilateral safeguards, now in suspense, the only safeguards applicable to countries in these groups are those of the IAEA.
15. Indonesia bought a second research reactor from West Germany, and Libya bought its research reactor from the USSR. The author does not know whether the relevant supply agreements provide for fall-back IAEA safeguards if the NPT should expire.
16. In Taiwan, these are the pre-NPT INFCIRC/66/Rev. 2 safeguards now being applied there; nearly all the plants in operation or under construction in South Korea were or are being supplied under "suspended" safeguards agreements with the United States or France and the IAEA that

would revive if the NPT lapsed. South Korea's agreement with Canada, under which it obtained a CANDU power reactor, would also require the application of IAEA safeguards even if the NPT lapsed.

17. As party to the recently established South Pacific Nuclear Free Zone (the Rarotonga Treaty), Australia would, however, be obliged to accept continuing full-scope safeguards even if the NPT were to expire. Australia is the only party to the Rarotonga Treaty which has any nuclear plant or material that would require the application of IAEA safeguards.

It is, of course, possible that other countries in these groups might buy unsafeguarded plants or materials from states that are not bound by the Nuclear Suppliers' Guidelines, such as Argentina, Brazil, India, or Pakistan. Such indications as we have, for instance, the declared policy of Argentina, indicate that even if they do not accept the guidelines, the new suppliers will require IAEA safeguards on their exports.

18. Paper presented at a workshop in Garmisch–Partenkirchen, May 25–27, 1987, by Dr. Kathlyn Saba, Instituto de Cuestiones Internacionales, Madrid.

19. Unlike other Warsaw Pact countries, Romania has turned to Canada rather than to the Soviet Union for its nuclear power reactors and has sought uranium supplies from South Africa; the CANDU reactors it is acquiring can be rather easily used as producers of weapon-grade plutonium.

20. At that time all plants and material in EURATOM NNWSs were not only under EURATOM safeguards, but were probably also still subject to prohibitions against any military use imposed by the United States and by other suppliers. The Soviets presumably required the return of all spent fuel from Eastern European reactors and from the research reactors that the USSR had exported to Egypt and Iraq (Bertrand Goldschmidt has described this requirement as the most effective of all safeguards). The only significant unsafeguarded plant in Spain was the Vandellos I power reactor; all spent fuel from this reactor went to France.

21. The danger of a "nuclear capability" or nuclear arms race between *non-NPT* Israel and the Arab states and between *non-NPT* India and Pakistan is with us already.

22. For a penetrating analysis of the South Korean approach toward the nuclear threshold, see Mitchell Reiss, *Without the Bomb, the Politics of Nuclear Nonproliferation* (New York: Columbia University Press, 1988), pp. 78–108. Reiss argues convincingly that the South Korean Government used the threat of "going nuclear" in order to ensure the continuing presence of U.S. conventional forces in South Korea and regarded the acquisition of the bomb only as a last resort if its threat failed. Its threat succeeded; U.S. troops remained.

23. In David Fischer and Paul Szasz, *Safeguarding the Atom*, for SIPRI (London: Taylor and Francis, 1985), p. 84, we wrote: "What was left of the nonproliferation regime would be a disparate and weakened structure, full of gaps at crucial points, having lost much of its international credibility."

24. With the U.S. Senate's ratification of the INF agreement for the elimination of medium-range nuclear missiles, we witness the first arms *reduction* agreement verified by on-site inspection. Until agreement is reached on a treaty to abolish chemical weapons, the NPT will remain the only arms control agreement verified by international controls including on-site inspection.

25. I assume that the circumstances that have led to the demise of the NPT would make it virtually impossible to negotiate a successor treaty acceptable to the NWSs and the leading NNWSs. This question is further examined below.

26. In 1967–1968, one of the main objects of this undertaking was to give assurance that the NWSs would not assist in the nuclear armament of their nonnuclear allies and specifically to signal the demise of the Multilateral Force, which had been proposed by the United States and would have been equipped with nuclear weapons and manned multinationally by NATO countries.

Provided that, in 1995, the NWSs had not changed their minds, and it seems increasingly unlikely that they would have done so, it should be relatively easy to find an appropriate means of reaffirming this undertaking. One possibility would be a resolution in the Security Council taking note of such undertakings given by the NWSs. A more formal arrangement would be a pact between the NWSs open to accession by NNWSs.

27. The main changes would have to be in:

- Paragraph 1 of the standard NPT safeguards agreement—at present this links the safeguards agreement to the undertaking given by the NNWSs in the NPT. A new "basic undertaking" would have to be devised.
- Paragraph 12—at present this terminates safeguards when a nuclear item is exported. It would have to be changed so as to prohibit exports unless the item concerned and its products would be under IAEA safeguards in the importing country. (Under Article III.2 of the NPT, this requirement applies to NWSs as well as to NNWSs. Nuclear states would also have to find a means of binding themselves to accept it.)
- Paragraph 26—at present this links the duration of the safeguards agreement to the state's membership of the NPT.

It would also be necessary to find a way of sanctioning the use, in the new agreements, of the technical procedures that are at present authorized for use in NPT agreements. None of this need present serious difficulties.

The ensuing negotiations with individual states and with EURATOM would, however, be time-consuming and would offer tempting opportunities to seek new constraints on IAEA safeguards, such as those already contained in the IAEA–EURATOM and IAEA–Japan agreements. Seven years elapsed between the beginning of negotiations between the IAEA and EURATOM and the final entry into force of the agreement!

28. Under Article III of the NPT, IAEA safeguards are applied to all nuclear material in the peaceful nuclear fuel cycle of the NNWSs concerned and for the exclusive purpose of verifying that there is no *diversion* of such material to nuclear explosive use. They are not designed (and could hardly be designed) to monitor the broader undertakings that the NNWSs are given in *Article II* of the NPT "not to *receive* . . . nuclear weapons . . . or *control* over them . . . directly or *indirectly*" (author's emphasis).

29. Most of these fifty-two states have no nuclear activities. The group includes three states that have research reactors (Vietnam, North Korea, and Colombia). It is assumed that the reactors in North Korea and Vietnam are covered by Soviet safeguards. Colombia has a binding nonproliferation commitment under the Tlatelolco Treaty and has concluded a safeguards agreement with the IAEA under that treaty.

30. One need only mention Three Mile Island and Chernobyl to illustrate this point.

31. Since the mid-1970s, no multinational initiative that has been proposed for peaceful nuclear cooperation has succeeded—the plans for regional fuel cycle centers, for international plutonium storage, and for an international nuclear fuel supply agency, and the work of the Committee on Assurances of Supply, the U.N. Conference to Promote International Cooperation in the Peaceful Uses of Nuclear Energy, etc. They bear witness to the irreconcilable clashes of interest that ultimately doomed them to failure.

5

Does the NPT Matter?

Lawrence Scheinman

As the twenty-fifth anniversary of the NPT approaches, interest grows in assessing the contribution and importance of the treaty to averting the spread of nuclear weapons beyond the five states that possessed them at the time that the treaty was opened for signature in 1968. The treaty, in Article IX.3, defines a nuclear-weapon state (NWS) as "one which has manufactured and exploded a nuclear weapon or other nuclear explosive device prior to 1 January 1967." By that definition only India, with its detonation of a nuclear device in 1974, has crossed the line. India's insistent denial that it has become a weapon state and that its 1974 test was anything more than the test of a peaceful nuclear device, reinforced by the absence of any evidence of a second nuclear test or the weaponization of its nuclear program, permits the conclusion that the number of states qualifying as NWSs under NPT criteria remains the same as it was twenty years ago.

At the same time, the capability to produce nuclear weapons has increased, and in several cases involving countries that have chosen not to join the NPT, covert proliferation is widely believed to have occurred. But no new state has overtly declared itself to have nuclear weapons, and about 140 states, including the three original NWSs signatories—the United States, the Soviet Union, and the United Kingdom—are today parties to the treaty. The two remaining NWSs, France and China, while declining to join the NPT for historical and politically idiosyncratic reasons, have as a matter of policy declared their opposition to the further spread of nuclear weapons. The small, but relevant, number of threshold states that have refused to become parties to the NPT have nevertheless publicly declaimed disinterest in nuclear weapons, anchoring their resistance to participation in the NPT in its discriminatory character, its failure adequately to promote the peaceful utiliza-

Lawrence Scheinman • Professor of International Law and Relations, Cornell University, Ithaca, New York.

tion of nuclear energy or disarmament pursuant to Articles IV and VI of the treaty, in its alleged undue intrusion on national sovereignty, or in special security interests that at the moment prevent their participation in an otherwise generally acceptable goal. There is no hard evidence of any of them having consciously assisted other countries in acquiring nuclear weapons. Indeed, Argentina and South Africa, two of the threshold states, have adopted criteria for nuclear assistance and supply commensurate with those required by many NPT parties, namely, a commitment by the recipient not to use peaceful nuclear assistance for nuclear weapons, and acceptance of international safeguards applied by the International Atomic Energy Agency (IAEA) to verify fulfillment of that undertaking.

Can the NPT be given credit for this state of affairs? Is it centrally relevant to nonproliferation? Would its demise significantly affect the prognosis for minimizing the number of states electing to arm themselves with nuclear weapons? The answer to each question is an emphatic "yes," but in each case the yes must be qualified. Qualified, because it *cannot* be said, nor should it be expected, that the NPT *alone* can or does *prevent* proliferation. The single most important factor in nonproliferation is a decision by national political authorities that acquiring nuclear weapons or retaining an option to do so is not in the national interest. That decision is based on a presumably reasoned calculation of political and security requirements and national interests, including an assessment of how nuclear weapons or the option to acquire them would or would not serve those interests. Many states that are technologically competent to pursue a weapon program have decided against doing so—in a few instances after lengthy and serious deliberation. Sweden and Switzerland are two cases in point. In each of these cases, national interest was perceived as being better served by forswearing nuclear weapons than by obtaining them or by retaining an option to decide one way or the other at a future time. And in both cases, national interest was seen as better served by making a formal commitment to this effect than by a unilateral declaration of intent.

It bears emphasis that even a formal decision against proliferation is not irrevocable if the circumstances that led a country initially to commit to nonproliferation fundamentally change. On the one hand, Article X of the NPT specifically provides that if a party decides that "extraordinary events, related to the subject matter of this Treaty, have jeopardized the supreme interests of its country," it may, upon three-months notice and with a statement of justification, withdraw from the treaty. On the other hand, the NPT as a whole is subject to review in 1995, after twenty-five years, to decide whether it shall continue in force indefinitely, or only for a designated additional period or periods of time.

Where the NPT becomes relevant is in its contribution to the shaping of political and security perceptions and to the calculation of whether the national interest is better served by forswearing or by maintaining a weapon option, or even by actually acquiring nuclear weapons. It is not alone in this. Not only is the NPT only one (if a decidedly central one) of a number of elements of the nonproliferation regime, but it also must be seen in terms of its interaction with a number of other factors that may bear significantly on decisions related to nuclear proliferation. These include regional conditions and circumstances, general international security and stability (which in turn is a function of the broad sweep of superpower relations and behavior), relations with friends and allies, and even domestic considerations. Changes in one or more of these factors can result in a situation in which a state that has by treaty renounced nuclear weapons feels compelled to reassess its posture toward nuclear proliferation. This assessment, in turn, could lead an NPT party to seek to invoke the treaty's withdrawal clause. These same factors also bear on decisions of nonparties whether to maintain the option without actually acquiring nuclear weapons or whether to exercise the option. It is not a trivial observation that in more than twenty years no state has been prepared to assert that changes in its environment have been of such a nature that its self-interest would best be served by overtly crossing the nuclear threshold. It would be difficult indeed to accept that the NPT has not been a significant factor in the weighing of such decisions.

In sum, the NPT is a necessary but not a sufficient condition for nonproliferation; it does not prevent proliferation, but is of significance to national decisions on acquiring nuclear weapons or maintaining a nuclear option. Nonproliferation might continue without the treaty, but its role in national decision-making environments is far-reaching if not decisive. Decisions are national decisions. They are based on assessments of the requirements for national security and the attainment of political goals, but the international environment, along with the efficacy of the nonproliferation regime, plays a major role in shaping the perceptions and assessments and, consequently, the decisions that are made. The NPT looms large in this context.

THE NPT AND NONPROLIFERATION

What role does the NPT play in nonproliferation? Many roles can be identified, but three are particularly important. Specifically, these are its roles as a legal barrier against the further spread of nuclear weapons; the embodiment of a norm of nonproliferation; and a confidence-building instrument reinforcing national security.

A Legal Barrier

While national political decisions against acquiring nuclear weapons constitute the first and most important restraint against proliferation, the NPT provides a means by which those political decisions can be formalized and given a legally binding basis. The NPT is an international security instrument involving a binding commitment to the international community regarding the development, production, and control of nuclear weapons and explosives. It is comprehensive in scope and subject to international verification.

It is arguable that a state may by unilateral declaration create a commitment which is internationally binding, but even if this can be sustained in law it is doubtful that it would impart the same degree of confidence as would participation in a multilateral treaty. Formalized commitments containing reciprocal obligations establish thresholds that are more difficult to cross. Revocation of a unilateral commitment, even if as binding in law as a multilateral undertaking, may be psychologically a less difficult step to take for the state contemplating revocation than stepping back from a formal multilateral arrangement with all the reciprocal commitments, obligations, and interdependencies it entails, not to speak of the domestic political hurdles involved in withdrawing from a formal multilateral undertaking that enjoys widespread international support. Furthermore, countries prepared to rely on international undertakings in shaping their own security policies and practices may feel that the assurances they seek are not adequately met in the absence of formalized and verified commitments. The NPT helps to bridge some of these gaps by providing a credible basis for building mutual confidence, leading to greater security and stability for all concerned.

A Normative Role

Of perhaps even greater importance than providing a legal basis for a formalized commitment to nonproliferation is the NPT's normative role. By norm is meant not merely the formal rule set down in the treaty, but the expected standard of conduct and the general principles and beliefs underlying the asserted rule. The NPT codifies and reflects the norm of nonproliferation—the conviction that acquiring nuclear weapons is not legitimate behavior. Its normative quality makes the NPT greater than the sum of its parts.

The strength of the norm is a function of time, support, and conduct. Demonstrating this strength is the fact that in the two decades it has been in force there have been no violations or defections by parties to the treaty; that the number of states parties to the NPT has continued to grow (from 43 original members that brought the treaty into force in 1970, to 91 parties in 1975, 121 in 1985, and about 140 by the end of 1988); and that even nonparties are affected by the treaty, to the extent that in their own policies and practices they must, and do, take into account the nonproliferation commitment of states important to them.

Discussion of the normative strength of the NPT also reveals some of its weaknesses. It does not enjoy universal participation and support. As mentioned, a number of important states—India, Pakistan, Israel, South Africa, Argentina, and Brazil—have chosen to remain outside the treaty. All of them are regarded as technologically capable of producing nuclear weapons; at least one is widely believed to have at least assembled the components for a number of nuclear weapons; and several of them have built or are building nuclear plants and facilities that are not subject to any international restrictions or verification and that could contribute to the acquisition of nuclear weapons. The NPT's normative strength also is affected by the extent to which it is perceived as fulfilling two other purposes associated with the treaty—securing progress in nuclear arms control and disarmament, and fostering wider use of nuclear energy for peaceful purposes. Although many parties to the treaty regard it as supporting their self-interest in strengthening national security and regional stability, and accept and endorse the NPT on those grounds alone, many of these states also feel strongly that national and regional security interests in the long run require positive and constructive action on the part of the nuclear states in reversing the nuclear arms race and bringing about a stable peace based on nonnuclear foundations.

On balance, it is clear that there is very substantial and widespread international support for the principle that the acquisition of nuclear weapons is not legitimate and must be avoided. The NPT embodies that norm and is regarded as an essential element in halting the spread of nuclear weapons and in contributing to national and international security. The best evidence is national behavior. Further corroboration of this view is found in the final document of the Third Review Conference of the Parties to the Treaty on the Nonproliferation of Nuclear Weapons (1985), in which the parties declared their conviction that "the Treaty is essential to international peace and security";[1] that "universal adherence to the Nonproliferation Treaty is the best way to strengthen the barriers against proliferation";[2] and that the "Treaty and the regime of nonproliferation it supports play a central role in promoting regional and international peace and security, inter alia, by helping to prevent the spread of nuclear explosives."[3]

A Confidence-Building Measure

The NPT not only serves as a means to formalize multilateral commitments regarding nuclear proliferation; it also provides for international verification of those commitments. In Article III.1, the treaty requires each nonnuclear-weapon state (NNWS) party to conclude a safeguards agreement with the IAEA "for the exclusive purpose of verification of the fulfillment of its obligations assumed under this Treaty with a view to preventing diversion of nuclear energy from peaceful uses to nuclear weapons or other nuclear explosive devices." Verification has two dimensions: on the one hand, it provides assurance to others about the nature of nuclear activity in the safeguarded state; on the other, it provides a safeguarded state a means by which to demonstrate to others its nuclear bona fides, that is, to assure neighbors and others that there is no reason for them to be concerned about the state's nuclear activities because it is committed under treaty to exclusively peaceful purposes, the integrity and fulfillment of which can be verified by objective third-party inspections. This confidence-building dimension of the NPT underscores the importance of the treaty to nonproliferation, and the manner in which the treaty helps to define security and self-interest.

Verification safeguards under the NPT are comprehensive, extending to all of the peaceful nuclear activities in a state, whether the result of external supply or of indigenous origin. Each safeguards agreement includes a legal commitment not to use safeguarded material for weapons or explosive purposes. Parties also are obligated not to export specified material or equipment unless under IAEA safeguards.

Termination of the NPT would have severe safeguards repercussions because nuclear material not covered by other safeguards arrangements—that is, not the result of a supply agreement in which the supplier required the supplied material, plant or equipment, or any material derived from the same, to remain under safeguards during its usable life—would presumably no longer be subject to verification. This would have a substantial negative effect on nonproliferation because a principal means of confirming the peaceful use of nuclear material and the associated legal commitment related to that material would be lost. While this inability to verify the use of nuclear material would not necessarily lead to a flood tide of proliferation, it clearly would have a bearing on assurances regarding nuclear activity in other states. It would also sap the vital element of confidence that effective and credible safeguards provide, and it could well contribute to increased concern and tension in a number of countries and regions. Whatever the long-term outcome, it would seem likely that in the near and medium terms, uncertainty would increase, security and stability would diminish, and the relationship of self-interest to forswearing nuclear weapons would once again come under scrutiny. That conclusion is confirmed in the following statement regarding NPT safeguards made in the final document of the Third NPT review conference in 1985:

> The Conference expresses the conviction that IAEA safeguards provide assurance that States are complying with their undertakings and assist States in demonstrating this compliance. They thereby promote further confidence among States and, being a fundamental element of the Treaty, help to strengthen their collective security. IAEA safeguards play a key role in preventing the proliferation of nuclear weapons and other nuclear explosive devices. Unsafeguarded nuclear activities in nonnuclear-weapon states pose serious proliferation dangers.[4]

CRIES OF DISCRIMINATION, CALLS FOR DISARMAMENT

Not all share this perspective on the Nonproliferation Treaty. A long-standing critic, K. Subrahmanyam, director of the Indian Institute for Defense Studies and Analysis, has argued that the NPT is nothing more than a discriminatory perversion, "a measure to legitimize the nuclear arsenals of the five nuclear weapon powers, to license further unlimited proliferation quantitatively, qualitatively and spatially and give them hegemony over the development of nuclear technology in the developing world."[5]

This rather extreme view stands in sharp contrast to that held by the great majority of states and statesmen, but it does underscore a legitimate and important problem, namely, that the NPT deals only with one dimension of proliferation—horizontal spread—and does not directly address the critical issue of vertical proliferation and the legitimacy of nuclear force. While this alerts us to a problem which if ignored could have a corrosive effect on the NPT and the broader nonproliferation regime, it should not lead to the conclusion shared by some critics that because of this gap the treaty and regime as they stand have little if any bearing on national security and international stability.

As mentioned above, there are several missions associated with the NPT, one of which is to promote progress in nuclear arms control and disarmament. The identical but separate NPT drafts tabled at the Eighteen-Nation Disarmament Conference (ENDC) by the United States and the Soviet Union in August, 1967, acknowledged in the preamble the need to achieve an end to the nuclear arms race, but did not make any specific provision to that effect in the body of the treaty. The

Soviet and American drafts called for a treaty of unlimited duration which would in effect have sanctioned indefinitely the division of the world into two classes of states—an outcome that even ardent supporters of the treaty among the NNWSs would not accept. Indeed, dissatisfaction over what was seen as a lack of balance between the obligations to be assumed by the nuclear and nonnuclear states led to further discussion in the ENDC and eventual inclusion of Article VI calling on all parties to undertake to pursue negotiations on measures regarding cessation of the nuclear arms race and on nuclear disarmament, as well as on general and complete disarmament.

Some argue that Article VI is the nuclear state quid pro quo for nonnuclear states renouncing nuclear weapons, as if the principal if not exclusive beneficiaries of the NPT are the nuclear states. This completely overlooks the fact that support for nonproliferation and participation in the treaty by the vast majority of states is the result of their concluding that their national security and political interests are better served by joining the NPT than by any other alternative; in other words, their self-interest has been the driving force.

However, even if this narrow construction is rejected, one cannot ignore the fact that for many of its parties the NPT is not an end in itself, but a means to a more stable and secure world. This inevitably engages the issue of nuclear arms control and disarmament. It is more than questionable, however, whether the fortunes of the NPT should be tied explicitly to progress in nuclear arms control rather than to judgments of the extent to which the treaty is effectively serving the national interests of the parties in international security and stability, and whether the treaty should be made the vehicle for driving nuclear disarmament. The prospects for progress in nuclear arms control are far more dependent on whether the political climate prevailing between the superpowers is propitious for movement than on whatever the NPT calls for in that field. To judge the treaty by the degree to which the "spirit" of Article VI is being fulfilled instead of on whether the NPT is effectively providing nonproliferation assurances is to fundamentally misconstrue the whole issue.

Nevertheless, it is not unreasonable to postulate that failure to make significant progress in nuclear arms control eventually will weaken support for the treaty if for no other reason than because the maintenance of the nuclear status quo would seem to confer legitimacy to nuclear weapons. In this regard it is useful to recall that in the final document of the 1985 review of the NPT, the conference reiterated:

> that the implementation of Article VI is essential to the maintenance and strengthening of the Treaty, reaffirmed the commitment of all States Parties to the implementation of this Article and called upon the States Parties to intensify their efforts to achieve fully the objectives of the Article, [and addressed] a call to the nuclear-weapon States Parties in particular to demonstrate this commitment.[6]

Other matters than progress in arms control involving the nuclear states bear on general approval of and support for the NPT, in particular the actions and behavior of the superpowers. Three points in particular deserve mention. First, it is clear that in the final analysis international security and stability are a function of relations between the superpowers. A collapse or even serious breakdown in established collective security relations between East and West would sharply increase tension and inevitably result in a deterioration of international peace and security. If superpower support for the NPT and the nonproliferation regime, which for two decades have been a point of common concern of the two, were to be one of the casualties of that breakdown, many states would be compelled to reexamine their security requirements, and some might conclude that nuclear weapons would offer a better alternative than continued abstention. Without superpower interest and support, the NPT would be less attractive, defections would become more likely, and the system would atrophy. Conversely, continued superpower global cooperation—including their commitment to nonproliferation, and especially if accompanied by measures for improving security and access to the peaceful benefits of nuclear technology— reinforces both the treaty and the regime. For its part, the NPT provides a focus for that cooperation.

The second point involves the legitimacy of nuclear force and the matter of how nuclear weapons figure in the relations between the nuclear and nonnuclear states. States linked by alliances or security commitments to the superpowers rely on the nuclear umbrellas that those relations entail; but brandishing nuclear weapons, even by veiled threats of withdrawing support, can have a severe impact on the nonnuclear states. Threatening behavior by the superpowers, precisely because they have nuclear weapons, could lead countries to conclude that only by having nuclear weapons can they ensure their own integrity and independence. The Gallois thesis that the ability to "tear off an arm" is all that is required to maintain adequate deterrence, even against a much superior nuclear foe, provides theoretical support for such a conclusion.

Analysts of India's decision to conduct its nuclear test in 1974 as well as to maintain nuclear independence outside of the NPT point to the appearance of elements of the U.S. Seventh Fleet in the Bay of Bengal during the 1971 Bangladesh crisis—including the nuclear-powered aircraft carrier *Enterprise*, which was presumed to be carrying nuclear weapons—to underscore the shock effect that even so subtle an incident could have on shaping the security perceptions and political interests of a nation.[7]

If nuclear states are perceived as predicating foreign policy behavior on their possession of nuclear weapons, such weapons will come to be seen as having political value. To the extent that states become persuaded of this value, changes in their assessment of nonproliferation cannot be ruled out, with all of the implications for the survival of the regime that this implies. Quite aside from directly or indirectly wielding nuclear weapons, if the nuclear states take lightly the risks of nuclear war, treating it as less than calamitous, or speak in terms of waging and winning limited nuclear conflicts, that too can only serve to undermine nonproliferation. It has been noted, for example, that Sweden's early exploration of nuclear weapons in the 1950s originated in assessments of their tactical and limited use, but evaporated with the emergence in the 1960s of strategic arsenals with global reach. Renewing older beliefs and concepts could rekindle interest in reviewing the value of modest nuclear assets.[8]

The third and related point also has to do with the notion of the legitimacy of nuclear weapons. In the broadest sense, it is the question of the soundness and acceptability of basing international stability on perpetual mutual nuclear deterrence. The more immediate point is that if the NPT denies the legitimacy of new nations acquiring nuclear weapons, then measures to delegitimize them more generally become relevant. On the one hand, this means reducing reliance on these weapons for security—a longer-term objective and one tied to nuclear arms control and disarmament measures. On the other, it means not rewarding new nuclear states with status or recognition of their action and, in the case of states that achieve nuclear status by violating a safeguards agreement or nonproliferation commitment, making that violation costly to them. With the exception of India, no state has been charged with having violated an undertaking or understanding regarding nuclear assistance, and there the withdrawal of support by a number of key states has hampered development of peaceful nuclear energy, though not to the point of forcing a change of policy. In the case of Pakistan, however, where efforts to acquire nuclear weapons have not been in doubt, for the past nine years nonproliferation objectives, at least and also most importantly in the United States, have had to compete with other foreign policy values. While no progress has been made in Pakistan's peaceful nuclear energy program, neither has its nuclear weap ons effort been thwarted. Cooperative strategies involving the nuclear states are important measures that need to be added to the existing effort to delegitimize nuclear weapons.

THE NPT AND NATIONAL NUCLEAR DECISION-MAKING

Studies of national decisions on acquiring nuclear weapons or acceding to the NPT or an equivalent arrangement show that in virtually every case the decision made can be explained by reference to something other than the NPT—either to domestic considerations, the impact of acquiring nuclear weapons on bilateral relations, assessments of technological limitations, political costs, or security consequences. Demonstrating a causal relationship between a nonproliferation decision and the NPT would be a tall order. But is it even necessary to do so to reach a conclusion that the NPT and, in particular, the norm of nonproliferation that it embraces weighs heavily and, in some instances even preponderantly, on national nuclear-weapon decisions?

Are the other factors mentioned above operating in a vacuum? Are they isolated factors? Is a decision not to challenge the strong nonproliferation convictions of an important ally a response only to that ally's stated policies, or does it also take into account the convictions and commitment to nonproliferation underlying that policy? And if the answer to that question is affirmative, what does that say about the impact of the international nonproliferation norm on the decision made? If a country like India is allegedly reluctant to risk important economic development assistance[9] as the price for moving toward nuclear weapons, does that not have anything to say about the effect of the nonproliferation norm on policy? If the countries providing that assistance are believed to feel so strongly about nonproliferation that they are seen to be prepared to take such severe economic action in response to proliferation that the recipient does not press the issue, do we ignore even the indirect impact of the norm on the would-be proliferator?

Israel will not become a party to the NPT except under conditions that are politically remote from the present. It has not overtly proliferated, and to be sure there are sound arguments against it doing so. One has to do with the possible effects of proliferation on U.S. policy vis-à-vis Israel. The United States has made a strong commitment to nonproliferation, making clear that, while sensitive to the existence of particular problems and situations, there are limits to its tolerance. An ally strongly dependent on U.S. security commitments would be foolish to force the United States into the position of having either to accept an overt act of proliferation, thereby raising questions about the depth of its nonproliferation commitment, or to publicly and formally distance itself from its dependent ally.[10]

In either of these cases, and in others as well, it is evident that if a country believes that its vital security interests or national integrity require the acquisition of nuclear weapons, it will make that decision. What is more interesting is the extent to which its evaluation of all the political, economic, diplomatic, and security considerations that enter such decisions are shaped, influenced, and tempered by the more general environment, and especially by its normative content. The argument presented here is that the impact is more than we might be ready to admit, but less than we might dare to hope. Neither the NPT medium, nor its normative message alone, can prevent a determined nation from acquiring nuclear weapons. In no case has it been, nor is it in the future likely to be, the decisive factor. But as part of the environment in which states operate, to which decision-makers respond, and in which decisions ultimately are taken, it plays an unquantifiable but meaningful role. It tints the lenses through which the world, both its opportunities and its restraints, are seen. In this sense, at least, the NPT has made a difference, and its demise would be felt far more profoundly than some of its critics would like to think.

NOTES AND REFERENCES

1. NPT/CONF. III/64/I, Annex 1, p. 1.
2. Ibid., p. 2.
3. Ibid.
4. Ibid., p. 3.
5. K. Subrahmanyam, *Nuclear Proliferation and International Security* (New Delhi: Lancer International, 1985–1986), p. 275.
6. NPT/CONF. III/64/I, Annex 1, p. 12.
7. See Girilal Jain, "India," in J. Goldblat, ed., *Non-Proliferation, The Why and the Wherefore* (London: Taylor and Francis, 1985), pp. 89,93; see also Mitchell Reiss, *Without the Bomb: The Politics of Nuclear Nonproliferation* (New York: Columbia University Press, 1988), pp. 226ff.
8. See Thomas B. Johansson, "Sweden's Abortive Nuclear Weapons Project," *Bulletin of the Atomic Scientists* (March 1986), p. 33.
9. See Reiss, *Without the Bomb*, pp. 238–39.
10. Admittedly, this is a two-edged sword. If Israel is sensitive to U.S. policy on nonproliferation, the United States is also aware that weakening of its support for Israeli security could alter Israeli views

on how to play its nuclear card. The same holds true for South Korea, whose nonproliferation posture is closely tied to the continued presence of U.S. troops on the peninsula. United States withdrawal could be the "extraordinary event" triggering South Korean withdrawal from the NPT. That risk enables South Korea to hold the U.S. presence hostage to its continued commitment to nonproliferation.

6

Beyond the NPT

Richard Butler

Eleven months after the June 1944 invasion of Fortress Europe at Normandy, the Western industrialized world and its allies had crushed a barbarian who had arisen from within and who had been feared to be close to making an atomic bomb. Three months later, atomic bombs were used at Hiroshima and Nagasaki. In June 1945, in San Francisco, the Conference on a United Nations settled the terms of the charter of the new organization. In August 1945, Mahatma Ghandi was released from jail and shortly thereafter was received at the Viceroy's Mansion at Delhi. The age in which we have lived—the age shaped by the Second World War, as well as by the rules of conduct laid down in the Charter of the United Nations and in the process of decolonization—has brought us two challenges of irreducible importance—the atom and development. The point of intersection of these two great challenges has been the NPT.

THE NPT, THE ATOM, AND DEVELOPMENT

Beneath its literal provisions, what the NPT involves is five essential commitments:

- acceptance of a political and moral norm against the possession of nuclear weapons;
- the obligation to eliminate existing stocks of nuclear weapons;
- international cooperation in the peaceful uses of nuclear energy;
- special assistance to developing countries;

Richard Butler • Ambassador of Australia to Thailand.

- the future development of further measures, regional and other, to ensure a world free of nuclear weapons.

By any standard this is a very far-reaching set of goals and obligations. Simply put, whether those who negotiated the treaty intended to or not, they established a framework for the overall management of the fundamental challenges posed by the atom and development.

The treaty can be seen literally as supplementing the terms of the Charter of the United Nations. The charter is, for all practical purposes, a pre-atomic age document. In addition, while it specifically called for decolonization, the results of that great movement were to follow later. Thus, it was necessary to supplement the charter in both areas. New and specific ways of addressing the problems of the atom and development, both individually and in their relationship, were required. The NPT was the response.

Under the NPT framework, the record for the management of our age has been, at best, mixed. This record has suggested that, in some respects, the framework itself is deeply flawed. The necessary condition for the NPT existing at all was U.S.–Soviet agreement on its provisions. This agreement was, in turn, greatly dependent upon Soviet apprehensions about West Germany's nuclear future. When the Soviet Union decided that a treaty on nonproliferation would neuter West Germany, in terms of nuclear-weapon development, it concluded that such a treaty was wholly desirable. Superpower unity on a nonproliferation treaty thus emerged. The shared U.S.–Soviet interest in the NPT has endured since, irrespective of how their bilateral relationship has been shaken by other events. Clearly, they calculate that a world with a fewer rather than a larger number of nuclear-weapon states (NWSs) is easier for them to manage.

This superpower condominium on the NPT has been a source of strength to the treaty in at least three main ways:

- It has restrained the United States and the Soviet Union from extending their nuclear competition to allied states, thus providing a high degree of overall nuclear arms control.
- In this fashion, it has clearly helped prevent nuclear war.
- It has contributed materially to overall stability and has ensured that the greater proportion of competition, especially between states which could become weapon states, has been in the economic and technology spheres. Key examples of this outcome have been the postwar resurgence of Germany and Japan.

But there have also been some serious negative effects:

- The U.S.–Soviet competition in nuclear weapons has been relatively unrestrained and has led to a critical situation where the power of each of their arsenals is now hideously disproportionate to any achievable national goal.
- Their actions in terms of the vertical proliferation of nuclear weapons and nuclear testing have been widely seen as directly contradictory to the purposes and undertakings established in the treaty.

- Their own behavior has jeopardized adherence to the norm against nuclear weapons.
- Their implementation of the peaceful cooperation provisions of the treaty has been poor.
- These negative developments have resulted in a relatively successful characterization of the treaty as an unequal, discriminatory arrangement and certainly in the failure of the treaty to achieve universal adherence.

Of this very mixed record one positive achievement, above all others, must be recognized. For almost half of the nuclear age, the NPT has provided relative stability in extraordinarily dynamic circumstances, the outcome of which could very likely have been chaos. President Kennedy's prediction that we would face a world of twenty or twenty-five nuclear-weapon states in the near future was sound. That it has not been fulfilled is in large measure attributable to the NPT compact. This has, in fact, been its crowning achievement and the reason why countries like Australia have continued, vigorously, to support the treaty.

A NEW INTERNATIONAL AGENDA

Despite widespread support for the NPT, the two central issues—the atom and development—need to be addressed anew if the goals of the treaty are to be fulfilled or, indeed, if the treaty is to survive. First, nuclear weapons must be progressively eliminated. The final phase will be the hardest one, but negotiated substantial reductions of nuclear arsenals, including the elimination of some whole categories of nuclear weapons, are required urgently in order to provide a more rational management of superpower relations and to secure the NPT regime and the norm against nuclear weapons it enshrines. Both of these goals are important, but the latter gets to the very core of the management of our age. Simply, the central reality is that there will be either a global reduction or an expansion of nuclear arms. There is no prospect for stasis; no middle position is possible. A deal between the "haves" and the "have-nots" was done in the NPT. If the "privileged" class do not keep their side of the deal, there will be a revolution and the whole regime will be swept away.

Second, there are the continuing claims upon the world's attention of the demand for development in the "South." This has several key aspects:

- The magnitude of those demands has increased.
- They have an important energy component, to which nuclear-generated energy can provide a good part of the answer.
- But their political aspects—regional conflicts, intrusion of major powers, revolution, dictatorships, human rights abuses, domestic instability—can often command predominant attention.
- Conventional arms transfers by developed to developing countries have become a key factor in the political situation and the continuing degraded state of the economies of so many developing countries.

- There remains the moral imperative to assist the developing countries or, more precisely, the people who form their populations.

The reality is that in the age of the atom and development our "interdependence" has come to be overshadowed by a number of truly malevolent relationships or, alternatively, bitter contrasts. Contrast the phenomenon of periodic, widespread starvation in the developing world with the agricultural support policies and the resultant food surpluses of many developed countries. Then, there is the contrast between investment in military and space research and development on the one hand, and the relative failure of attempts to find a truly viable solution to the global problem of fertility control on the other.

The negative role that arms trade and transfers have come to play in the global economy is illustrated, inter alia, by the fact that some 40 percent of the massive debt incurred by developing countries in the last ten years has been spent on arms. This cycle is truly a malevolent one. Another such malevolent relationship in North–South relations, with its resultant effects upon both the ability of some states, such as Colombia, to remain intact and the survival of whole sections of the population in developed countries, is the international narcotics trade. Incidentally, this trade also involves a significant associated weapons trade. Finally, there continues to be an urgent need to ensure that development in both the industrialized and the developing world does not take place at the cost of significant damage to the environment.

THE PROBLEMS AND PROMISE OF THE NPT

I have mentioned these central features of the current international agenda and the bitter contradictions they involve in order to move to a deeper reflection on what is involved in the NPT and in the challenge of the atom and development.

- The atom poses a root and branch challenge to political institutions and stability.
- The same is true of food supplies, population control, the arms trade, the narcotics trade, and management of the environment.
- This challenge is felt especially keenly in democracies because their relative freedom can also mean a reduced ability of the state to intervene to deal with such challenges.
- Apart from commanding an irresistible moral authority, assisting development in poorer countries serves to strengthen political institutions and stability as well as beneficial economic interdependence.
- The application of modern technologies, including nuclear technology, to the development task can assist materially and politically, but it must not lead to the proliferation of nuclear weapons because then what was being constructed would ultimately be destroyed.

This has been the promise and the problem of the NPT. It promised the constructive relationship between technology and politics and between the atom and development. That is, it promised a world from which nuclear weapons would be eliminated and in which technological cooperation for development would increasingly be the hallmark. The problem has been that those who were in a position to realize this promise failed to do so, and the gap this left has progressively widened.

It is no accident that today's proliferators—actual and potential—are those states bearing deep resentment in developmental terms, those locked into situations of heavily armed regional hostility, and, above all, those which are not parties to the NPT. It is of truly stark significance that the last point is what they all have in common. With one exception, Israel, each of the potential proliferators point to the "broken promises" of the NPT as its reason for remaining outside the regime.

Since the first revelations of modern atomic science—after the period of theoretical research at Göttingen, after Einstein and Fermi, to mention only two of those involved—and certainly following the development of nuclear weapons, there has been a wholesale and popular tendency toward obscurantism. There has been a massive division between the miniscule number of nuclear *cognoscenti* and the people as a whole, even though the latter have the vastly larger interest in how the nuclear age is managed. This situation has, perhaps, been not unlike the situation in Europe before printing in vernacular languages, where the *cognoscenti*, then the clergy, spoke Latin, and on that basis they controlled the life and death and, indeed, the eternal expectations of whole populations. Learning Latin, however, is probably harder than comprehending the basic facts of our nuclear age. The central expression of those facts given in the NPT is childishly simple:

- these are weapons of mass destruction;
- they cannot be used;
- no one should possess them;
- but their technology can be used beneficially;
- we all agree to promote development in this world because, if we do not, the incentive and the pressure to acquire nuclear weapons will be widespread and irresistible.

Some of the logic in this conception is less than impeccable. And some normative questions can be posed with telling effect. But the political reality which the NPT addressed and continues to address is accurately described in terms as simple as these.

The gaps in the strict logic can be bridged by noting that nuclear weapons do have, partly, a symbolic value. They have for four decades signified great-power status. This might answer the normative protest—"Why should pressures to acquire nuclear weapons be irresistible?" The answer lies in the sorry fact that the actions of the nuclear states in terms of cherishing and protecting their own nuclear weapons has shored up the status of being a "nuclear-weapon state." This, together with regional competition, maintains pressure toward the acquisition of nuclear weapons.

If actions to meet the challenges confronting the NPT are not taken, then it will degrade. Having offered a prescription, the implication is that the medicine might work. It might or might not. We might be too late in three or four countries, in addition to India and Israel.

BEYOND THE NPT

Whether or not the present form of the NPT collapses in 1995, but specifically if it does, it is certain that work is required on a successor regime for widespread proliferation and nuclear arms control. Any such new approach, if it is to have any chance of acceptance, will need, at the very least, the following characteristics:

- It will have to be negotiated multilaterally.
- It cannot again be the result and reflection of a superpower condominium.
- The existing nuclear powers, and the other states prepared or able to take part in the negotiations, will have to sit at the table as equal negotiating partners.
- To that end, the development and sharing of nuclear technology will have to form a major part of the negotiations.
- A greatly expanded or enhanced role for the International Atomic Energy Agency should be considered.
- The negotiations will need to produce a true fusion of means to solve the problems of both the atom and development.
- There will be no place for the trend toward unilateralism or selfishness that has increasingly characterized Western and Soviet policies in this area; those policies and that selfishness have been demonstrated to be threadbare.
- The negotiation will need to respond to the very real security concerns of states.
- This will mean that competition in conventional weapons and the level of the arms trade will need to be sharply reduced.
- Finally, greater efforts will need to be made to resolve military and nonmilitary problems on a regional basis.

In sum, what is required is nothing less than an overall reshaping of the way in which stability is maintained—nothing less than a new international economic and security order. Why is such a grandiose solution suggested? Is it possible to repair, or to overhaul, the existing machine? The existing machinery can certainly be made to work better than it has in the first twenty years of the treaty. As already indicated, this would require action on nuclear disarmament and nuclear testing (Article VI) and greatly enhanced implementation of the technical cooperation (Article IV) provisions of the NPT. In reality, however, such action would essentially represent an honoring of past promises, promises which were not kept.

In the meantime, the scene has shifted, and we are faced with a new set of problems different in magnitude and kind from those which the previous order sought to address. The new scene we confront encompasses:

- The magnitude of the problems of stability and development in the so-called Third World demands a new level of economic, technological, and political response both for intrinsic reasons and to prevent the proliferation of nuclear weapons.

- Key interrelationships—especially the negative ones, the bitter contrasts between the developing and developed worlds—must be addressed because of the severity of their impact on developed and developing countries alike.
- There is an urgent need to resolve the choice between truly substantial nuclear disarmament and the extension of a full-scale arms race into space.
- The similarly urgent need to reverse the trend of increasing militarization of the global economy should be addressed. The role that expenditures on conventional arms has come to play in the economies of both developed and developing countries needs to be halted and reversed on both economic and security grounds because regional competition in arms saps a state's wealth, breeds insecurity, and feeds pressures toward nuclear proliferation.

Such a new agenda will not be able to be dominated by a superpower condominium unless they choose to jointly fight the rest of the world. Early next century the combined populations of the United States and the Soviet Union will represent only 8 percent of a global population of 8 billion. It can be argued that this is not the point, that the United States, for example, could still hold, say, 25 percent of the world's resources and that this is what will count. Similarly, some could argue that the fate of a person in Ethiopia simply cannot be compared in importance to, say, doing what is necessary to "deal" with the Russians. Such an approach, although now traditional, would represent two grand failures. First, it will be proven intrinsically wrong, because no one is or will be immune to the current agenda of global problems we now face, including the continuing prospect of the proliferation of nuclear weapons. But the grandest failure of all would be to have preferred selfishness, to have said we cannot any longer afford to have vision. And, true vision recognizes that the challenges now confronting humanity demand a rethinking, and a reworking, of the solutions conceived in the period from 1945 to 1970. A successor to the NPT regime will need to resolve the problems of the atom and development, which continue to confront us all.

7

Proliferation of Nuclear Weapons

A Universal Concern

Antonio Carrea

INTRODUCTION

Whether the NPT survives beyond 1995 is not particularly important. What is important is nonproliferation, because the proliferation of nuclear weapons is a universal concern, a concern which is not adequately addressed by the NPT. The nonproliferation of nuclear weapons is an issue with many different facets—an issue which can be approached in many different ways. To deal with the future of nonproliferation, and the expectations which are being raised, it is useful to address the issue at three levels.

The first level could be qualified as philosophical. We are dealing with an absolute, irrational problem, for which rational solutions must be provided. In the scientific world, there are solutions to problems; scientists have quantified the chaos. In the political world, the problems are more complex; emotional reactions often prevail over logical thinking.

The second level is strategic. What are we trying to achieve? It could be considered obvious that a nonproliferation regime should, and does, deal with preventing proliferation, but this is not the case. The present nonproliferation regime, the central pillar of which is the NPT, deals only with nonproliferation. It does not deal with proliferation. This distinction may sound like a play on words, but it makes an enormous difference in what can be achieved.

Antonio Carrea • Counselor on Nuclear Affairs for the Embassy of Argentina in Austria.

The third level is tactical. What instruments are needed to verify what has been achieved? Here we are facing the same old problem of trying to find out whether any sheep are missing from the flock. We can count the heads or the legs. Both approaches should lead us to the same result, but one is more cumbersome than the other.

THE IRRATIONAL PROBLEM

For millennia, humanity has been fighting to survive plagues, famine, and great natural disasters such as floods and earthquakes—the great calamities. Wars were a lesser evil—they could kill many, but never so many as natural disasters, unless plagues or famine were the sequel. But in this century humanity has had to face the potential of a manmade calamity greater than any of these natural phenomena. Humanity has acquired the power to destroy itself. For the first time in history, a political conflict might trigger a sequence of events that could end with far worse consequences than any of the catastrophes that the world has suffered before.

A basic fear—that humanity itself will not survive a nuclear war—has been with us for more than forty years. It has been the driving force behind a wide variety of proposals, understandings, agreements, treaties, and the like, some of them aimed at avoiding the testing, placement, or use of nuclear weapons, others at preventing their proliferation. But pious, altruistic efforts of this sort, aimed at saving the world, are only the rational, or rationalized, reflections of this basic, irrational, driving force. That fear is the best adviser of the wise person, as an old adage goes, has been proven by the current status of nuclear-weapons; no nuclear weapon has been used since 1945, and the number of states which possess nuclear weapons, open or covert, has not changed for almost twenty years.

Taking into account the fact that fear, the driving force, will not be assuaged until nuclear weapons and the possibility of using them are definitively eliminated from our universe, it is reasonable to assume that "nonproliferation" will remain in fashion as we enter the next century, with its minimum aim being to preserve the status quo or, as something to be desired, to promote nuclear disarmament. An essentially irrational problem now requires rational solutions. We have been living for far too long immersed in an emotional confusion that has obscured the real problem.

THE NONPROLIFERATION TREATY

Among the many actions which have been taken in an attempt to arrive at a solution, the nonproliferation treaty stands in the foreground, if for no better reason than its popularity. For admirers of large numbers, it is wise to indulge in a short analysis of the NPT's popularity. Approximately half of the signatories to the treaty have no nuclear activities worth mentioning. Among the remaining half, where some verification effort might be required, less than half have any significant nuclear activities or capability worthy of concern as potential contributions to proliferation. Among these countries, more than half are already proliferators of one sort or another. That leaves us with just a handful of countries parties to the treaty which are worth counting as true members of a nonproliferation regime, and another handful which are outside the treaty. Considering the enormous amount of wheeling and dealing that has gone into popularizing the NPT, it is rather surprising that the minuscule number of true nonproliferators, those which have a potential capability to proliferate but do not indulge it, are more or less evenly divided between "insiders" and "outsiders."

However, despite the rather small number of true nonproliferators which adhere to the treaty, the fact of its near universality does suggest that it may be a possible element of any nonproliferation regime which emerges in the twenty-first century. However, to preserve the status quo may not be enough, particularly if we take into account the encouraging signs of relaxing tensions in certain regions— tensions which, if unabated, could have developed into a nuclear confrontation. But before considering the design of a better system, it is worth analyzing the essential elements of the present nonproliferation regime as defined in the NPT, and their intrinsic weaknesses, and attempting to find answers to some basic questions.

Article I of the NPT contains the undertaking of the nuclear-weapon states (NWSs) to preserve the status quo. It should be considered obvious that they would not be willing to break such a commitment; the sacrifice that they are being asked to make is minimal. Their commitment is in their best interests.

Article II of the treaty contains the fundamental undertaking of the so-called nonnuclear-weapon states (NNWSs). The fact that this commitment has not been fully observed to date has been, paradoxically, one of the essential conditions for success of the treaty in the 1970s and 1980s. Most of those countries which thought in the 1960s and the early 1970s that they needed nuclear weapons, and should enjoy the protection afforded by these weapons, have already "acquired" such protection through deployments by the NWSs in their territories. Now, the countries which depend upon nuclear weapons are not limited to the traditional five that have demonstrated their capability to produce weapons; there are now quite a few "nonnuclear-weapon states" which have weapons in their territories. They are the "spatial," or "geographical," proliferators.

It is clear, then, that the equation of proliferation with the production of nuclear weapons is not adequate. It ignores the fact that a production capability, or even a potential production capability, is not essential if you belong to the right political alliance. Arguments about the "double trigger," or about who controls the head and who controls the tail, have very little meaning from the point of view of nonproliferation. The fact that the weapons are there, and are meant to be used, is what really matters.

Article III is also worded as an undertaking by the NNWSs, each of which "undertakes to accept safeguards . . . in accordance with the Statute of the International Atomic Energy Agency [IAEA] and the Agency's safeguards system." The safeguards system of the agency, set out in INFCIRC/66/Rev. 2, was designed to foster international cooperation and trade as its main objective, without committing the sin of promoting the proliferation of nuclear weapons. Its purpose is to check the commitment undertaken by the recipient state, through the verification of what has been supplied, that it is not using the items supplied "in such a way as to further any military purpose." Safeguards do not have the purpose of verifying the recipient's general policy on nuclear matters; the assessment of this policy is the responsibility of the supplier.

Under this regime, practically every significant element in the fuel cycle, including equipment, facilities, and nuclear materials, could be submitted to verification at the front as well as at the back end of the fuel cycle. Having said this, it must be understood that making a fair assessment of what is "significant" is not an easy job, particularly at the front end of the fuel cycle; and the bureaucrats using or implementing the verification system would never dare to make bold decisions. The regime has been abused, and many insignificant elements of all sorts are being submitted to verification just to be "safe."

The system is cumbersome, it is true; but it has worked well for the specific purpose for which it was designed, and the agency should devote more attention to updating it, keeping in mind its true promotional purpose. It would be most unfortunate if its character were distorted. It seems self-evident that such a cumbersome verification system—designed to check specific activities of a much larger aggregate, without preconceptions about the purpose of the uses to which other parts of the aggregate are being put—could not be very useful in verifying that the totality of the aggregate is being used only for peaceful purposes.

Fortunately, as has been said, the founding fathers of the NPT decided not to use the safeguards system of the agency, in spite of the mandate to do so contained in Article III. A new safeguards system was designed for this purpose. This safeguards system, described in INFCIRC/153, is specific to the treaty, and the agency uses it only in nonnuclear states which are parties to the treaty. Most unfortunately, the designers of this specific safeguards system tried to draw on past practice and created a system which is also very cumbersome.

The frequently heard argument that the agency cannot adopt practices which discriminate between its members has hardly any value in this case. Each state should have the safeguards system it requires to verify the commitment it has undertaken, not one that fits or could be applied to somebody else. This, as has been acknowledged, is the true nondiscriminatory practice. To put it simply, the approach taken, drawing on past practice, seems to have as its objective the verification of source and special fissionable materials everywhere in the fuel cycle. This is not a simple job from the point of view of assuring nonproliferation. Is this approach fulfilling its purpose? If, in accordance with Article III, we interpret the purpose of safeguards in terms of ensuring that a state which accepts safeguards does so "with a view to preventing diversion of nuclear energy from peaceful uses to nuclear weapons," the system is reasonably fulfilling its job, whatever it costs. But is it worth it?

If we interpret the fundamental commitment undertaken by a NNWS to be that which is contained in Article III—that "each non-nuclear-weapon State Party to the Treaty undertakes to accept safeguards . . . for the exclusive purpose of verification of the fulfillment of its obligations assumed under this Treaty"—is the verification system envisaged in INFCIRC/153 verifying the undertaking contained in Article III? Unfortunately, the answer is no. The verification system has no means of knowing whether other activities, not under safeguards, are going on. The question is whether "all peaceful nuclear activities being verified" are one and the same thing as "all nuclear activities" in that state. The classical arguments of "timely detection" and "deterrence of diversion" to "clandestine activities" have little value when it is well known that this route is not the easiest or the most efficient in acquiring materials for manufacturing nuclear weapons. An "independent," weapon-oriented fuel cycle is simpler, cheaper, and safer for the proliferator; and the verification system is absolutely powerless in checking activities not under its control. The sad consequence of this fundamental weakness of the verification system envisaged in INFCIRC/153 is the false sense of security it gives us. People believe that we are checking the commitment of the state "not to receive . . . , control . . . , not to manufacture or otherwise acquire" nuclear weapons, when the verification system can only verify that what the state has declared as being peaceful activities are, in fact, being carried on for peaceful purposes. This is verification of the obvious.

Articles IV and V were added to the treaty to take care of the concerns of the lesser brothers of the nonproliferation fraternity, and by now they are a dead letter. Article IV starts with a statement of the obvious, about the "inalienable right" of all parties to the benefits of the peaceful atom, and follows with a nice collection of good wishes—"to facilitate," "the right to participate," "also cooperate," and so on. Whatever the promises and guarantees contained in Article IV, restrictive practices in international trade, unilaterally imposed by the London Club, and the perennial financial troubles of the developing world, have made them useless.

Article V was supposed to provide, to those renouncing the development of nuclear explosives for peaceful purposes, the benefits that could be accrued from their use. The IAEA established a most interesting program, with the strong support of some weapon states, to explore those benefits. Most encouraging prospects were reported, at first. But by the end of the 1970s enthusiasm was waning, and the program wound down with no definite conclusions. However ambiguous, these "conclusions" were expressed in rather strong terms of discouragement— apparently, peaceful nuclear explosions are of no use. The fact that one of the countries supporting the program has been using peaceful nuclear explosions by the dozen, according to a most reliable independent source, without reporting them to the agency under the program, does not seem to support the "experts'" assessment. In any case, Article V does not now stand a chance of being brought into practice, even if a technically sound, economically feasible, and radiologically safe project is proposed, given the pressure of environmentalist groups—whether they are right or wrong.

Article VI of the treaty, apparently, is supposed to balance the obligations imposed upon the NNWSs by Articles II and III. Together with Article III, it is one of the most amazing articles in the treaty. As we have seen, the earlier article gives us a false sense of security: a security that does not exist. Article VI goes one step further and describes a dream world of the future with a "cessation of the nuclear arms race," "nuclear disarmament," and "general and complete disarmament." It entrusts such menial tasks to "each of the Parties to the Treaty." Simply put in ordinary language, it means that nobody is responsible. The founding fathers did not dare to state plainly that the responsibility for the cessation of the nuclear arms race falls squarely on the nuclear states; they should stop producing more weapons, and nuclear disarmament can only be achieved when those same states decide to scrap their nuclear arsenals. What is more, general and complete disarmament is well beyond the purview of the treaty—although it is true that nuclear disarmament could be a step toward achievement of this goal. It goes without saying that this article will require quite a bit of reworking in any future nonproliferation regime, if the purpose is to achieve truly universal nonproliferation.

We have dealt so far with the content of the treaty itself, but mention needs to be made of what it does not contain. Surprisingly, there is no reference to inspection by challenge, that is, the right to request inspection of something which is supposedly going on, undeclared, but which should be under control. Two important prior treaties related to nuclear control and disarmament do contain such clauses—Article VI in the Antarctic Treaty and Article 16 of the Tlatelolco Treaty. The assumption that a so-called full-scope safeguards system, as the NPT safeguards system is often called, could be so efficient that there is no need for a special provision covering undeclared activities expects too much from any verification system. Furthermore, the NPT safeguards system is not full scope; it covers only those nuclear activities which a state declares to be peaceful, and activities which are not under safeguards are permitted by the treaty so long as they are not devoted to the production of nuclear explosives. But who knows whether they are or are not? If the assumption is that the assurances provided by the state are good enough to cover this loophole in the verification system, what then is the purpose of verifying those activities that the state assures us are devoted only to peaceful purposes? In fact, this loophole exists and it makes it easier for the state, if it wishes to do so, to carry on undeclared activities which are forbidden by the treaty.

From this brief analysis of the main components of the NPT, there may be a temptation to jump to the incorrect conclusion that the treaty is not worth saving. This temptation must be avoided. Rather, the purpose of this analysis was to explain some of the shortcomings and trade-offs accepted by many states, which felt that any nonproliferation regime, imperfect as it may be, was better than nothing. We have to recall the environment in which the treaty was elaborated in the late 1960s. As long as nuclear weapons exist, the argument for nonproliferation will be kept alive by the basic, irrational driving force of fear discussed earlier; and this argument must be acknowledged. Having said this, we must also be conscious of the fact that it is not the virtues of the treaty which have led to the present situation; it is the wisdom of the states which preserve the status quo and make the system work despite the shortcomings of the treaty. They are strongly motivated by the fear that a generalized nuclear arms race could be far more difficult to handle than trying to keep the present proliferators, known and unknown, in check. Altruistic motivations such as seeking to save the world are not in the minds of those concerned. What really counts is their assessment of the intention of neighboring states, whether their intent is known or only assumed.

ENEMIES OF THE SYSTEM

Before proceeding to an analysis of the possible shape of a future nonproliferation regime, its target, the potential proliferators, must be considered. In the 1960s and possibly in the early 1970s, nuclear weapons had a great appeal—they had glamor. Not only those seriously considering that nuclear weapons would give them the insurance they needed for survival, the "desperados," but others, the "status seekers," also looked to nuclear weapons.

For those in the first group, a nonproliferation regime has very little to offer. To one who is fighting for survival, the quality of the killing instrument does not make much difference — nuclear, chemical, or conventional weapons can be used. What really matters is quantity, so that one can kill as many as possible. Other political instruments should be used to keep open a path to survival for those in this category. They might then be willing to join the nonproliferation fraternity because it is in their best interests to avoid a final confrontation. The second group would be relatively easy to deal with in a future nonproliferation regime, but not under the present one. Once nuclear weapons stop being the privilege of the few and become a political burden to them, such weapons will retain very little glamor. They will become expensive and useless military antiques. Discounting confrontation between the superpowers, the possession of a nuclear arsenal has not helped to solve any of the myriad local or regional conflicts humanity has suffered in the second half of this century. There are, perhaps, two exceptions, that is, the Suez crisis (1956) and the Cuban missile crisis (1962), which were both direct confrontations between nuclear powers. For any other type of conflict, nuclear weapons have proven useless. In fact, it is unlikely that the "nuclear umbrella" some countries sought in the 1960s would be welcomed today.

There is also a third group of countries that should be the concern of any nonproliferation regime: the existing nuclear powers. To deal with them we need new instruments; the present regime has no means to tackle this problem.

A REGIME FOR THE TWENTY-FIRST CENTURY

We should look to a nonproliferation regime in the twenty-first century in which the emphasis will be put not on stopping horizontal proliferation, but on the cessation of the arms race and on nuclear disarmament. For this purpose, regional nuclear-weapon-free zone treaties can be highly satisfactory to the members of the region concerned; but they are not a substitute for a more universal nonproliferation regime for one fundamental reason. A patchwork of weapon-free zones can cover most of the world, but they cannot include the weapon states in their network by the very nature of such regional arrangements. As long as weapon states exist, they are the most relevant reason for a universal nonproliferation regime to exist—to commit them, and not only those without nuclear weapons, to nonproliferation. Bilateral or multilateral approaches on the part of weapon states are no substitute for such a commitment. They owe it to all members of the international community to stop proliferation and to achieve nuclear disarmament through an instrument of universal character.

If this basic argument is to be taken into account in shaping the nonproliferation regime of the next century, it is essential that undertakings such as those contained in Articles I and II of the NPT today should be properly complemented by a future version of Article VI which contains something more substantial than the present platitudes. The responsibility for the cessation of the arms race, and nuclear disarmament, should be placed on those who are responsible for the present situation; they should undertake more concrete commitments to stop it in a way that is compatible with the more general character of a universal treaty. If this balance of rights and obligations could be achieved—and it will not be an easy task—the immediate question would be: What about some kind of Article III? What about verification?

The analysis of Article III has shown that we are only verifying the obvious— that the peaceful nuclear activities of the state are devoted to peaceful purposes— without having the means within the verification system of knowing whether or not these are all the nuclear activities being conducted in the state. The fundamental undertaking in Article II is not being verified by the present verification system. Until now, whatever we thought, we have without knowing it been depending solely on assurances given by the state that the commitment undertaken in Article II is being fulfilled. There has been no mishap. Do we, then, really need a verification system? The answer could well be no—but it would not be easy to swallow. Agreements and treaties are supposed to be confidence builders; but mistrust is an intrinsic element of any deal, as demonstrated by the ever-present arbitration and sanctions clauses contained in any agreement of any kind. Therefore, we need to assume that some kind of verification system would be required.

Considering that the main undertaking committing an NNWS member of the NPT is contained in Article II, it follows that the undertaking in Article III is a subsidiary instrument for use in verifying the main undertaking. What we are aiming at then becomes more clear: What kind of safeguards system is needed, tailored to verify the undertaking in Article II? The verification system has no need at all to be concerned with all the elements in the aggregate, so long as it can check that the whole is not being used for the production of nuclear weapons.

A nuclear weapon, or nuclear explosive device, is made using separated plutonium or highly enriched uranium. These materials are essential; they are, therefore, the only, directly usable, materials which it is worth inspecting. There is no need to go into the argument about how pure or concentrated the material should be. It does not make much difference because a highly specialized installation is always needed. Plutonium is separated in reprocessing plants, uranium is enriched at an enrichment installation. There are very few reprocessing plants and enrichment installations in the world that can produce bulk quantities of separated weapon-usable material. There are also very few installations which can process bulk quantities of separated plutonium and meaningful quantities of highly enriched uranium. By verifying these "choke points" in any nuclear fuel cycle (i.e., reprocessing plants, enrichment plants, installations to process bulk quantities of separated plutonium or highly enriched uranium), we are devoting safeguards resources to the critical path for the production of any nuclear weapon. The nuclear materials contained in the hundreds, or even thousands, of other nuclear installations can only be utilized for weapons if they go through these choke points. To be more precise, we need to verify only the output of these specific installations. They are highly sophisticated endeavors of modern technology, and most operators will be rather reluctant to open them to the prying eyes of an international inspectorate. Probably some imagination needs to be exercised to control the output of a "black box" by more sophisticated means than present-day safeguards techniques. Then, by verification of the output from the choke points which come under the jurisdiction or control of the state concerned, the purpose of verifying the undertaking contained in Article II, the fundamental commitment, is fulfilled. This will make the verification system more specific and efficient. However, whether it would be simpler and cheaper, as might be expected, cannot be assured. These parameters are more dependent on the bureaucracy implementing the system than on the virtues of the approach.

At present, not all reprocessing, enrichment, and bulk-handling facilities are under safeguards; some of them are used for military purposes. This makes the distinction between verifying a facility and verifying its output fundamental. As long as this situation continues to exist, if the system is to work it is essential that all international transfers of separated plutonium or highly enriched uranium be declared. The verification of the undertaking in Article II, committing the NNWSs, could then be fully achieved. It does not seem difficult to achieve a commitment from those few countries which have control of the choke points to declare all international transfers, unless two or more countries having complementary capacities and the same political will get together to make a weapon. This possibility exists, and it will be very hard to check by any verification system.

This approach, the verification of output from the choke points, could also facilitate the verification of any future agreement on the cessation of the arms race as a first step toward nuclear disarmament. By controlling or stopping the supply of fresh materials to the nuclear arsenals, the attrition rate of nuclear weapons could be controlled, any recycling of weapon materials could be checked, and so on. Of course, this means that the output of all nuclear installations handling bulk quantities of separated plutonium or highly enriched uranium should be under verification, everywhere. If this could be achieved, it will be the best test of the commitment of all countries to nonproliferation. One does not need necessarily to be always a pessimist, whatever past experience has taught us about the reluctance of any social or political conglomerate to relinquish consecrated privileges voluntarily.

To design an ideal nonproliferation regime, then, is not a difficult feat of the imagination. It should

- have equal, or equivalent, rights and obligations for all member states;
- provide adequate guarantees to member states not to be threatened with nuclear weapons;

- avoid interfering with the peaceful activities of the member states.

If any verification system is associated with such an ideal regime, the system should

- concentrate its verification on the few installations in the nuclear fuel cycle that are really meaningful from the point of view of nonproliferation;
- have the means to verify undeclared installations of the type that should be under verification, if they are challenged.

Could such an ideal regime be achieved by the beginning of the twenty-first century? Even the more staunch optimists among us might feel that we are dreaming so long as nuclear weapons exist and some people think they have the right to possess them; but any future regime worthy of consideration should at least aim this high. The next step in nonproliferation should be a regime aiming at cessation of the nuclear arms race and nuclear disarmament, and not aimed at stopping nonexistent horizontal proliferation. In this regime, a nonproliferation verification system does not need to deal with the thousands of tons of indirectly usable material around the world that are useless for assembling a nuclear weapon. Only the production or transfer of directly usable material, separated plutonium or highly enriched uranium, need be submitted to verification. Only when this simplified nonproliferation verification system achieves a truly universal character—and only then—can the "promotional" verification system of the INFCIRC/66 type be dropped. There will be no need for it. Restrictive practices must stop—a pious self-assumed messianic mission to keep others from sin is no justification for measures designed effectively to choke off nuclear trade to certain countries. Moreover, until all weapons have vanished from the face of the earth, nuclear-weapon-free zones should be protected and encouraged by full guarantees that nuclear weapons will not be introduced in them, or used against their members, by third parties. Half-hearted negative guarantees are not enough. How far these commitments will be undertaken voluntarily by all states will be the yardstick of the success of the nonproliferation regime.

8

Toward a Universal Framework of Nuclear Restraint[1]

Munir Ahmad Khan

Recently, there has been a perceptible relaxation in global and regional tensions all over the world. The most noticeable sign of this "thaw" has been in the relations between the two superpowers. The leaders of the United States and the Soviet Union have publicly shared the vision of a nuclear-weapon-free globe, and the first tentative steps in the direction of nuclear disarmament have been taken. The general atmosphere is thus more conducive than ever before to evolving a new framework of nuclear restraint that ought to be nondiscriminatory in principle, universal in application, and effective in implementation. The NPT, which purportedly has nuclear restraint as its objective, has not proven itself equal to this task in its twenty-year history. The situation will be no different in 1995, when the treaty's renewal is to be considered. Disillusionment with the NPT is very real and based upon its real limitations in both structure and implementation.

DISILLUSIONMENT WITH THE NPT

By its very nature, legitimizing the possession of nuclear weapons by five states makes the nonproliferation treaty inherently discriminatory. This is why even many signatories question its moral basis. Only those states that are affluent, have a stake in the status quo, and have guaranteed assurances about their security support this treaty without reservations. The lesser-developed countries (LDCs), in general, have a negative perception of the NPT, and even those who subscribe to it feel that they have derived little benefit from it. The so-called threshold states among devel-

Munir Ahmad Khan • Chairman of the Pakistan Atomic Energy Commission, Islamabad, Pakistan.

oping countries are more vocal in their opposition to the NPT. In their view, the treaty is aimed at perpetuating the nuclear hegemony of the nuclear powers. They also resent its implied accusation of the irresponsibility of the Third World in general. They further point out that there are no checks on the nuclear-weapon states (NWSs), while the nonnuclear-weapon states (NNWSs) are effectively required to surrender part of their sovereignty in return for vague and as yet unfulfilled promises of nuclear cooperation. This unequal treatment is clearly unacceptable, and the fears and misgivings of LDCs have hardly been allayed by the subsequent behavior of major supplier states whose actions seem to be solely dictated by their respective national and ideological interests.

The NPT was supposed to be based on a quid pro quo consisting of a balance of obligations and privileges. The NNWSs parties to the NPT agreed to give up their option to acquire nuclear weapons in return for the promised fullest possible exchange of equipment, materials, and scientific and technological information for the peaceful uses of nuclear energy, including the use of peaceful applications of nuclear explosions under strict international control. The NWSs, for their part, undertook "to pursue negotiations in good faith on effective measures relating to a cessation of the nuclear arms race at an early date and to nuclear disarmament, and on a treaty on general and complete disarmament under strict and effective international control" (Article VI). But almost before the ink of the signatures had dried, there began substantive reinterpretation of the treaty to suit the interests of the superpowers and other advanced nuclear countries. The provision in Article VI calling for nuclear disarmament was relegated to the background, and primary stress was laid instead on controlling the spread of nuclear technology. Although clearly provided for in Article V of the treaty, the benefits of peaceful uses of nuclear explosions have not been generously shared with NNWSs parties, while the superpowers continue to exploit peaceful nuclear explosions for underground seismic surveys, explorations, and engineering. Even the sharing of nuclear fuel-cycle technology is done very selectively and is subject to political conditions. As a result, there have evolved categories of membership among the signatories to the NPT: first is the "inner circle," comprising a few countries of the Organization for Economic Cooperation and Development; then the second class of "trustworthy" client states; and last, the rest, for whom the NPT "bargain" is an expanding set of obligations matched by a diminishing set of privileges. The ever-changing rules of the game give the impression that, while the nuclear powers would gladly acquiesce in selective proliferation, they would be most reluctant to share peaceful nuclear technology with the needy countries of the Third World.

RATIONALE FOR NUCLEAR RESTRAINT

Despite the failures of the NPT regime, nuclear restraint is vital. Needless to say, there are many imperatives for pursuing a policy of nuclear restraint. First and foremost is the moral argument that applies to nuclear arms as well as to other weapons of mass destruction, like chemical and biological weapons. No matter how well and specifically targeted, they inevitably involve noncombatants and spread destruction indiscriminately over a large area beyond the frontiers of the belligerents. These weapons, therefore, have always aroused feelings of horror and revulsion among all humane people of the world.

Strengthening the moral argument is the more pragmatic one—nuclear weapons now serve no military purpose whatsoever. A nuclear war is inherently unwinnable, making nuclear weapons basically unusable. In a rational world, therefore, there should be no nuclear weapons anywhere. Humanity's hope lies in striving to move toward this rational state of affairs through dismantling existing nuclear weapons and ensuring that no more are made. Both of these aspects of the issue must be addressed comprehensively in order to establish an equitable, stable, and acceptable framework of nuclear nonproliferation throughout the world.

From an international political perspective, too, it would be unwise for an NNWS to cross the nuclear threshold overtly by staging a nuclear explosion. There would be no tangible gain for it on the international scene; rather, there are bound to be adverse reactions. Similarly, any addition in the nuclear arsenals of NWSs will only enhance their "overkill" capacity and have no strategic value. It is thus in the common interest of all states to exercise restraint in regard to both vertical and horizontal proliferation.

RATIONALE FOR NUCLEAR POWER

While there is a need for further restraint in the application of nuclear power for military explosive purposes, there has already been too much restraint shown by the advanced nuclear states in making the peaceful benefits of nuclear energy available to the developing world. Economically, the most attractive of the peaceful uses of nuclear energy is the generation of electric power; however, this application has been confined almost entirely to advanced countries. There are only twenty-five nuclear power plants in developing countries with a total generating capacity of around 15,000 megawatts (MW), which is less than 5 percent of the aggregate nuclear installed capacity of the world. If the present trend continues, the entire Third World will have no more than 40,000 MW nuclear by the year 2000, which is less than that in a single European country at present. The proven fossil fuel reserves of most LDCs, as well as their ability to pay for energy imports, is very limited. If they were to consume fossil fuel in the future at the same level as industrialized countries do at present, carbon dioxide emissions will increase fourfold, leading to extensive pollution and a worsening of the greenhouse effect. This imposes a serious constraint on the development of these countries, yet the economically attractive and environmentally better alternative of nuclear power is denied to them.

There are those who perceive in this order of things a new type of technological colonialism involving the transfer of valuable mineral and energy resources from the LDCs to the industrialized countries, without adequate economic compensation or the sharing of science and technology necessary for their development. As the disparity and awareness of this inequitable treatment increase in the LDCs, dismay sets in. This feeling leads to misgivings and doubts about the real nature and intent of the nonproliferation regime and, ultimately, to the repudiation of the current regime.

NUCLEAR POWER AND NONPROLIFERATION

The industrialized countries have argued for withholding nuclear technology on the basis of an alleged "link" between nuclear power and nuclear weapons. It has been variously argued that the use of nuclear power is the primary force driving proliferation, and that power reactors can be considered large-scale military production reactors with a by-product of electricity rather than benign electricity producers with a by-product of militarily unattractive plutonium. Of these, the first assertion does not stand up to the testimony of history; each of the five recognized nuclear powers had acquired nuclear weapons before embarking upon the utilization of nuclear energy for electricity generation. The second contention requires somewhat more detailed examination. If a country had nuclear power stations and a reprocessing plant, all under safeguards, it could in principle reprocess the spent fuel from the reactor to obtain reactor-grade plutonium. Such plutonium is not easily usable for weapons, and its attempted diversion from safeguards would provoke a serious international reaction. Therefore, it would be technically impractical and politically unwise for a country to follow the nuclear power route to proliferation.

It is thus clear that a link between nuclear power plants under IAEA safeguards and nuclear-weapon proliferation is highly tenuous. It is unfortunate that certain groups have used this alleged link to create a certain confusion in the minds of laymen and policymakers and thereby to discredit the use of nuclear power. Of course, for the informed leaders—both technical and nontechnical—there has never been any confusion. Sir John Hill, former Chairman of United Kingdom Atomic Energy Authority has stated: "Stopping nuclear power programmes will not make the proliferation problem go away: the problem is primarily a political one, and the least that could be said of the proposed strategy of cutting back on nuclear power is that it would prove totally irrelevant to the task at hand."[2]

Even though there is no real linkage between the proliferation of nuclear weapons and the development of nuclear power under safeguards, the industrialized countries have chosen to use the denial of nuclear power as an instrument for enforcing the nonproliferation regime. The various manifestations of the policy are well known—unilateral abrogation of international agreements, the violation of Article IV of the NPT, the Nuclear Nonproliferation Act of the United States, and the "London Club's" nuclear supply guidelines. In this whole exercise, the technical and political realities of the 1970s and 1980s, as well as the lessons of history, are ignored.

The policy of denial has not been very effective in controlling the spread of any modern technology. Embargoes may serve some economic or political purpose in the short term and introduce delays, but, in the long run, they inevitably prove to be counterproductive by providing the political motivation for countries in sensitive areas to seek nuclear autarky. This lesson, however, does not seem to have been appreciated even by those countries of the North which have themselves been victims of such denials at one time or another. The reluctance of industrialized countries to share advanced technologies has unwittingly led to the emergence of new nuclear supplier states.

WHY NATIONS WANT TO GO NUCLEAR

Embargoes and other efforts to restrain the spread of nuclear technologies have had limited effects, and they are largely irrelevant to nonproliferation because, from a purely technical point of view, the nuclear-weapon option is available to many countries, including the so-called threshold ones, regardless of the status of their peaceful nuclear energy programs. However, the exercise of this option and its translation into an actual nuclear capability, with all the perceived benefits and attendant costs, requires a conscious decision by the nation concerned. It has been perceptively observed by the American Nuclear Society's Special Committee on Nuclear Weapons and Peaceful Uses of Nuclear Energy that

> interest in nuclear weapons is more likely to arise from complex considerations of national security, rather than from technical opportunity. . . . Once a decision to acquire nuclear weapons is made, the acquisition of sufficient material is only a matter of time, available skills and resources. Nuclear weapon proliferation is thus primarily an international political issue, and the eventual solution is in the political domain rather than in the technical.[3]

Apart from security considerations, a nation may be impelled by domestic or regional compulsions to retain a nuclear option. For some governments, the pursuit of a nuclear-weapon capability may serve to surmount internal political difficulties. There are other countries that are known to represent the interests of certain advanced countries and have virtually the status of client states. In such a situation, the responsibility for enforcing restraint lies more with the concerned patrons than with the would-be proliferator. In some cases, a nation may chase the nuclear option in its desire for an illusory prestige. There is yet another incentive that applies particularly to a large state wishing to establish political hegemony and economic domination over its smaller neighbors. The nuclear weapon can be regarded as a trump card by such a country in its power game.

The nuclear ambitions of Israel and South Africa are in a class by themselves. These states are considered by their neighbors to be extensions of Western power and culture into their territory. These two states seek security by building a nuclear fortress in order to secure their survival in politically and culturally alien surroundings by dint of sheer military superiority. They have resorted, therefore, to a policy of ambivalence in regard to their nuclear capability. They neither admit nor deny the possession of nuclear arms.

It is thus seen that, while the so-called threshold states share some common ground for retaining their nuclear option, they are mostly a heterogeneous group as regards their capabilities, motives, aspirations, and intent. We, therefore, have to address both their common features and their differences and understand the specific situation of each state. The future nonproliferation arrangements must be so fair, aboveboard, and universal that these states are left with no reasonable excuse to remain outside.

STEPS TOWARD RESTRAINT BY THRESHOLD STATES

There is need for a fresh perspective on the issue with a view to evolving a framework of restraint acceptable to all, including the so-called threshold states. The nuclear states, along with the threshold states—which include those NPT nonsignatories that have acquired a nuclear capability but have not overtly exercised the nuclear option—should exercise restraint. So too should any other states that belong to the NPT but that may have incentives to go nuclear in the future. In order to persuade all of these diverse states to exercise the needed restraint, incentives are necessary. In this context, it is useful to consider global nuclear disarmament, security guarantees, the sharing of technology, nuclear-weapon-free zones, and confidence-building measures. It must be recalled that provisions for adequate guarantees against nuclear attack and the promotion of peaceful nuclear power technology were put forward during the negotiations leading to the NPT, but security guarantees were not agreed to and the transfer of peaceful nuclear technology under the NPT has not been adequately implemented. It is necessary, therefore, that whatever measures are agreed upon for the twin issues of nuclear power development and nuclear nonproliferation, an international agency must be entrusted with the task of overseeing the satisfactory implementation of international commitments and contracts, and reporting instances of noncompliance. The IAEA, whose safeguards system has functioned reliably and adequately, is an agency with the requisite experience in the delicate task of monitoring the implementation of international safeguards agreements. The IAEA, of course, would need to be suitably strengthened to perform any additional functions entrusted to it.

Global Nuclear Disarmament

Any framework of nuclear restraint must start off by recognizing that the principal proliferators are the two superpowers themselves. The stockpiles of American and Soviet nuclear warheads, even if taken separately, are sufficient to ensure global annihilation several times over. Their combined nuclear arsenals have the equivalent of four tons of TNT for each inhabitant of the Earth. The primary responsibility for nuclear restraint must, therefore, lie with the superpowers, who have to set the moral tone for other nations to follow. The first and most important element of a viable framework of restraint, then, must be the holding of serious negotiations between the superpowers aimed at reducing their nuclear arsenals and moving gradually but firmly toward total nuclear disarmament. It must be recognized that their nuclear arms race has caused wasteful diversion of human and material resources on an unprecedented scale. It is high time that at least a part of these resources is freed and made available for the development of the underprivileged four-fifths of humanity.

Security Guarantees

The nuclear states should attempt to understand the motivation for some developing countries to retain their theoretical nuclear option. As discussed earlier, the basic driving forces behind a nation's quest for nuclear weapons are its perceptions of security and national interests, as well as a sense of national pride, and we must appreciate that nation's own point of view if we are to take any effective steps to mitigate its concerns. Clearly, the smaller states of the world, particularly in regions where they are overshadowed by one or two regional powers, would have the greatest reason to feel insecure. Unless these legitimate security concerns of threshold states are met and dealt with effectively, the political and psychological incentives for them to retain a nuclear option will remain. One effective way to achieve this objective would be for the nuclear states to offer dependable guarantees against nuclear attack or blackmail to those nonnuclear states which abjure the acquisition or use of nuclear weapons through a solemn international declaration or treaty. This could be an important component of an enlightened policy aimed at inducing threshold countries to exercise nuclear restraint.

Sharing Nuclear Technology

It can hardly be overemphasized that the proliferation of nuclear weapons is essentially a political problem, which should be tackled primarily on the political plane rather than through the self-defeating policy of trying to use technical fixes. In fact, many nonnuclear states have at present more of a nuclear industrial base than did the United States in the early 1940s, and, psychologically, it is not acceptable that the right to engage in so-called sensitive technologies should be the prerogative of a few countries considered to be politically safe by the Nuclear Suppliers' Group. An LDC, like any other sovereign state, wants to be free to exercise its right to develop, under appropriate safeguards, nuclear fuel-cycle programs based upon its own needs and requirements. The overemphasis on restricting transfer of technology has actually been counterproductive because it has generated a feeling of insecurity among the "have-nots," who do not wish to remain forever dependent on others for nuclear fuel-cycle services. This feeling has led to the indigenous development of fuel-cycle facilities outside of IAEA safeguards in a number of recipient states. Another important element of a stable policy of nonproliferation, therefore, must be to facilitate, not hinder, the transfer of technology for nuclear power generation—under international safeguards—to energy-deficient developing countries.

Nuclear-Weapon-Free Zones

Along with the steps toward nuclear disarmament by all the existing nuclear powers, led by the United States and the Soviet Union, the problem of horizontal proliferation has to be addressed. The developing world shares the concern of industrialized countries over the possible emergence, overt or covert, of new nuclear states, but the issue should be viewed in the proper perspective. Developing countries, in general, do not possess the economic and technological means or the necessary trained manpower to engage in a significant nuclear-weapon program. Even for so-called threshold countries in the Third World, such a program would preempt a major fraction of available resources sorely needed for their development. Because the LDCs cannot attain a credible nuclear deterrent, possessing a few nuclear weapons will not add to their security and may in fact endanger them. Horizontal proliferation in this sense could indeed cause serious security problems, particularly in regional contexts; lead to nuclear competition between rival neighboring states in sensitive regions; and have global repercussions. This has led to several proposals for the denuclearization of different regions and the actual establishment of nuclear-free zones in Latin America and the South Pacific. These would serve as valuable building blocks for an eventual all-encompassing nonproliferation regime. The continued success of this approach requires full backing of the nonnuclear states in the regions and the active interest and support of the nuclear powers.

Confidence-Building Measures

Regional approaches to confidence building are likely to be most fruitful in strengthening and expanding the nonproliferation regime. The establishment of nuclear-weapon-free zones would be the most effective initiative in this context. The concept of a nuclear-free zone in South Asia was advocated as early as 1972, and resolutions calling for such a zone have been overwhelmingly endorsed by the United Nations General Assembly every year since 1974. In addition to such zones, the international community should lend its support to other confidence-building measures in different "hot" spots around the globe. For South Asia, Pakistan has put forward several proposals for ensuring nuclear nonproliferation in this region, calling on both sides to simultaneously accede to NPT, accept full-scope safeguards, agree to mutual inspection of each other's nuclear facilities, ban nuclear testing, and jointly renounce the acquisition or development of nuclear weapons. To date, the two countries have signed an agreement not to attack each other's nuclear facilities, which is a good omen for building mutual trust and confidence. The implementation of some of the other proposed measures would usher in an era of nuclear restraint in the region.

Resolution of Regional Political Problems

Because the motivation to go nuclear is essentially political, the desired restraint will also come through the political route. Major regional conflicts and problems may drive certain states to seek weapons of mass destruction, including chemical, biological, and nuclear armaments. This applies particularly to the Middle East, South Africa, South Asia, and Latin America. The nature of the problems are well known; the need is to find regionally acceptable solutions in which the international community can and should lend a helping hand.

CONCLUSION

It appears that the NPT as it now exists offers neither necessary nor sufficient conditions for ensuring nuclear restraint by stemming horizontal and vertical proliferation. As suggested, its many deficiencies in structure and implementation make it largely unequal to the task. The essential characteristics of a new enlightened policy against nuclear proliferation would be equality, universality, and reasonable balance between obligations and privileges. The goal of universal nuclear disarmament will be achieved only when all states recognize, of their own volition, that modern science and technology has irrevocably shrunk the globe and that the effect of weapons of mass destruction and of environmental pollution cannot be confined to national boundaries. One cannot erect impregnable barriers between nuclear haves and have-nots, rich and poor, North and South. While differences in development may remain and will be acceptable, glaring disparities can only lead to erosion of goodwill, disruption of peace, and general instability.

In the final analysis, nuclear nonproliferation is just one dimension of humanity's quest for survival. Both the problem and the solution belong to the domain of international policies—encompassing security, progress, and prosperity for all. The North's and the South's perceptions of an equitable world order are diverging. They have to come closer and realize that their survival on this planet must be together and not at the expense of each other.

NOTES AND REFERENCES

1. A version of this chapter was delivered to the 55th Pugwash Symposium on "Nonproliferation and the NPT," held in Dublin on May 5–7, 1989.
2. Karl Kaiser, "Reconciling Energy Needs and Nonproliferation," *International Affairs* 58, no. 2 (1982), pp. 339–40.
3. *Nuclear News*, August 1983.

9

European and Global Security in a World without the NPT

Harald Müller

INTRODUCTION

However important, neither nonproliferation in general, nor the NPT in particular, is an absolute value. Both serve a higher goal, namely, the prevention of nuclear war. In this context, the NPT, for all its shortcomings, is a moderately useful instrument.

What does this treaty achieve? It is certainly no panacea for the ills of the world, and it does not even prevent proliferation, as a police officer is able to prevent crime when he or she catches a burglar before the theft. What the NPT achieves is a certain degree of confidence building among its members. The confidence it creates helps to pacify some regions that might otherwise be, or soon become, trouble spots in terms of military nuclearization, such as Europe, East Asia, Southeast Asia, and parts of the Middle East. By doing so, the NPT permits states committed to nonproliferation to focus on those corners of the globe that are true proliferation trouble spots. Moreover, for NPT parties, the existence of full-scope safeguards in countries with limited respect for international legal commitments would help give warning lights whenever something might go wrong. These functions add up to a moderate yet significant contribution by the treaty to world order. It is no just order, as the treaty's opponents are quick to emphasize—the NPT certainly confirms inequality among nations. Yet order with a certain inequality is

Harald Müller • Senior Fellow and Director of International Programs with the Peace Research Institute, Frankfurt, Federal Republic of Germany.

preferable to equal anarchy for all. On this premise, the following considerations are founded.

What would the world be like without the NPT? It is useless to answer this question in the abstract. The disappearance of this arms control treaty, which has the largest number of parties of any such accord, would be a dramatic event under any circumstances. Thus, one would assume that the state of a post-NPT world depends very much on the factors and circumstances which brought the treaty down. Four such breakdown scenarios can be imagined:

- The "bang" scenario, in which one non-NPT party goes nuclear openly, causing a chain reaction within its neighborhood among NPT parties and nonparties alike.
- The "clash" scenario, in which the 1995 conference ends in a bitter rift between North and South—or between nuclear-weapon states (NWSs) and nonnuclear-weapon states (NNWSs)—most likely over Article VI issues.
- The "creep" scenario, where the 1995 conference drags on in an indefinite stalemate, causing one party after another to end its treaty commitment.
- The "abandonment" scenario, in which dramatic changes occur in one of the major alliances in the world, and in which the treaty collapses as a result of the reconsideration of these nuclear policies by key NPT parties.

The following speculations discuss the specific problems of each scenario with regard to the question of whether a new regime structure could emerge from the ruins of the old. In each case, management problems, possible solutions, and persistent difficulties will be identified. The impact of the NPT's demise on the European security and nonproliferation setting will be discussed for each scenario.[1]

BANG

The candidates for starting this scenario are obvious. They reside in South Asia (India and Pakistan), the Middle East (Israel), and South Africa. There is a possibility that Cuba might acquire a nuclear capability within five years, but the probability of this occurring appears to be quite low. Similarly, at present, there still seems to be room for some optimism concerning the South American setting. In the three cases mentioned, chain reactions may well occur.[2] The neighbors of the South Asian states are observing the present situation with apprehension. Open nuclearization might lead faithful parties of the NPT such as Bangladesh and Sri Lanka (both of which, meanwhile, are not on the best of terms with their large Indian neighbor, and are operating their first nuclear research reactor) to reconsider their membership. This move, however, could in all likelihood be prevented by some security arrangement with the United States, if Washington could muster the will.

Far more difficult to contain would be the consequences felt at the western flank of South Asia. There is growing evidence that Iran feels more and more unhappy with its NPT status.[3] An openly nuclearized neighborhood might even provide a welcome pretense for Iran to withdraw from an unloved treaty. Iraq would follow inevitably, with similar consequences for Syria and maybe even Turkey. At this point, Israel might feel induced to go nuclear openly, and, should it do so, no Egyptian government can be expected to resist firmly public pressure to cancel its NPT commitment. This could create an additional chain reaction across North Africa and, finally, through Spain and even Italy, reach Southern Europe.

Would the treaty hold in the rest of the world if six to eight significant members withdraw? Would it hold in Europe? And how would the ensuing situation be managed? First, there is no objective reason why nonproliferation commitments as such should not be continued in other parts of the world that are not immediately threatened by the emerging nuclear states. Even a broad chain reaction such as the one described—and remember that several of the countries mentioned will be far from any significant capability even five years from now—need not necessarily spill over to other parts of the world. The security of faraway states would not immediately be affected. Containment of the problem depends critically on four conditions:

- The creation of *cordons sanitaires* adjacent to the proliferation corridor which would be covered by security guarantees. The problem is, of course, to make those guarantees credible. However, because such guarantees would be given to countries with low or no nuclear capabilities (e.g., Chad), a security capability with low credibility would be preferable to a belated and hapless tumble down a very long path toward an uncertain nuclear future.
- A sharp curb on the spread of delivery vehicles would be necessary in order to contain the spread of nuclear threats geographically. It would be of great interest to have the range of delivery systems limited in order to dissuade additional nations from following the nuclear chain. In this respect, the recent agreement among seven supplier states to limit the spread of missile technology was a welcome step, though a belated one.[4]
- An early-warning and air defense belt would have to cover the nuclearized corridor in order to reassure neighboring countries against airborne attacks, if missile delivery is successfully prevented.
- In some cases, when the acquisition of nuclear weapons by "crazy states"[5] appears imminent in the course of such a chain reaction, the preventive use of limited force might be justified.

Another critical issue is whether the nuclearization of several Third World middle powers would push prestige-minded members of the international community in the same direction. The answer depends on the status of mutual arrangements between the most prestige-prone nuclear-capable states, Argentina and Brazil. If South American rapprochement proceeds toward a regional regime which satisfies either country, then such a regime may well weather the storm of the chain reaction. But even if South America remains pacified, the NPT as such would hardly withstand the shock wave. The atmosphere of doom and depression prevailing during a 1995 extension conference convened under those circumstances is vividly imaginable. Many delegations would be guided by confused instructions. Their governments would ponder the question whether the effort was still worthwhile. It may well be. Containing disaster in a geographical corridor, even a rather wide one, might still prevent the worst outcome. If the remaining trouble spots remain sheltered from outright nuclearization, the world may breathe, if not with ease, at least with a residual relief.

Two paths are conceivable. First, the remaining parties may act defiantly to the challenge and rally around the treaty with even more unity and determination. If this occurs, the NPT will be continued, perhaps even indefinitely. The second possibility is that many parties will feel that the NPT as an instrument to strengthen world order and peace had failed the test. Even a minority insisting on that position would make inadvisable for the rest any attempts to continue the treaty. If several parties defected for security reasons and another group left out of resignation, maintaining the NPT would be a hopeless, uphill battle. In this case, substitutes would be needed. The only readily available solution would be the creation of a network of neighboring nuclear-weapon-free zones which, together, would cover the former NPT area or, hopefully, even more than that. As mentioned above, the most essential condition would be the establishment of such zones immediately adjacent to the proliferation corridor, that is, in Eastern and Western Europe, Black Africa, and Southeast Asia. At first glance, such a solution appears simple. Closer analysis reveals that it is not simple at all.

First of all, the simultaneous establishment of several such zones under the stress of a breakdown of the NPT is a far cry from both the conclusion of the Tlatelolco Treaty in the calm and nonproliferation-minded atmosphere of the late sixties or the isolated event of the Rarotonga Treaty in the eighties. The parties to the several negotiations will, for all their goodwill, observe the conduct within other regions with scrutiny and critical apprehension. Unequal zonal conditions, which were permitted to prevail under the NPT, are unlikely to be acceptable in this atmosphere. And—except for zones already established—no one is likely to be concluded before the others are ready. This reduces the probability of success considerably, because the security conditions in the various regions are very different indeed.

One big stumbling block would be Black Africa. With the exception of the South African frontline states, most countries from this region are members of the nonproliferation treaty, but many are not at ease, as can be concluded from their conscious decision not to enter into safeguards agreements with the International Atomic Energy Agency (IAEA) as required by the treaty. The stubborn insistence of the minority government in South Africa to keep open a nuclear-weapon option—it is difficult to fathom against whom—is a matter of understandable concern. Attempts at supplementing the nonproliferation treaty by a nuclear-weapon-free zone in Africa have faltered because of this concern.[6] It does not appear likely that the sub-Saharan African states would commit themselves to such a zone if South Africa stays out. Indeed, there would be little political logic in doing so. Measured by their record of stubbornness and defiance, the South Africans are unlikely to give in (assuming there is no change in government). This leaves a badly needed zone in trouble.

The other stumbling block, of course, would be Western Europe. While the security of the northern tier of NATO would most probably not immediately be affected by the projected proliferation chain, there would be major problems for the South. A nuclearized North Africa would present a formidable threat to Italy and Spain. In both cases, it appears doubtful that either reaffirmation of the nuclear guarantee by the United States or the erection of a formidable air-defense system would sufficiently mitigate the concerns of those countries. One should remember that concern over Algeria was already part of the resistance on the part of the Spanish military to their country's accession to the NPT.[7] This advises strongly of the need to stop by all means the proliferation chain before it reaches the central part of North Africa. Another big problem, which would indeed be a nightmare to NATO, would be the nuclearization of Turkey as a result of proliferation in the Middle East. A nuclearized Turkey would send panic waves through Greece, with results that may well surpass the imagination.

In any event, even if those two most troublesome consequences for Europe could be borne, Western Europe may still prove to be a stumbling block for regime resurrection. One has to assume that the East–West conflict will still exist in some form, and that present security conditions, though perhaps somewhat modified, would still hold in principle. If this is the case, a European nuclear-weapon-free zone is all but ruled out. The widespread deployment of U.S. nuclear weapons in allied territories would not be particularly compatible with any common, or common sense, definition of a nuclear-weapon-free zone. Grudgingly accepted by NPT parties, this deployment pattern is not likely to be condoned under a nuclear free zone regime.[8] Yet U.S. nuclear-weapon deployments are viewed as essential by many nonnuclear allies in Europe, and their termination could have grave proliferation repercussions indeed.[9]

To sum up, the bang scenario could emerge mainly from a problem in the realm of security policy. Its main management requirements would be to confine the nonproliferation chain through

- offers of security assurances to affected neighboring states;
- limiting the spread and degree of sophistication of the proliferators' delivery systems;
- establishing substitute mutual reassurance and confidence-building measures among the remaining NNWSs that stay committed to nonproliferation if the NPT unravels under the sudden blow.

This is a demanding task. Security guarantees are hard to make credible; to do this in haste in a fluid proliferation situation could place the two superpowers in the midst of ominous regional rivalries, exacerbating rather than mitigating the security problems of regional nations. The only bright spot in the whole story is that in the foreseeable future the marginal capabilities of most states most likely would prevent the nonproliferation chain from occurring at speeds usually ascribed to chain reactions.

CLASH

Unlike the bang scenario, the clash scenario is grounded in politics rather than security. Clash is conceivable only through a cumulative process in which the well-known grievances of Third World NNWSs parties to the NPT—that is, issues related to Article IV, Article VI, South Africa, and Israel—come together. Clash would occur if a significant number of these countries withdraw from the treaty in a concerted action, not out of fear for their security or their want for a nuclear weapon, but in anger and with the intention to send a clear signal of their deepest political dissatisfaction. There would be few immediate consequences. As the defectors had no nuclear-weapon intentions, they would most likely be willing to keep IAEA safeguards on their nuclear activities if any existed. However, serious problems would remain and grow with time.

First, this move would satisfy the wishes of the most fervent opponents of the NPT, most notably India. It must be expected that India would do its utmost to dissuade former parties to the NPT from joining any new undertaking of a similar kind. Also, India and others would probably be able to enhance their effort to portray safeguards as the corollary of the same discriminatory approach which made the NPT untenable. Simultaneously, for those former parties interested in nuclear research and energy facilities, technologies, and fuel, these same NPT adversaries—as emerging suppliers—could be willing to supply nuclear goods and services under far less stringent conditions than those required by the NPT. A growth in the number of countries with partially unsafeguarded activities would then ensue. As more buyers were offered imports with fewer strings attached, the temptation to follow suit could become insuperable for traditional exporters. And even if one admits that new suppliers could offer only a limited variety of items, it is clear that their capabilities can only grow. As a consequence, the safeguards regime would suffer a slow but steady erosion.

Two cautionary remarks are in order, however. Much depends on the development of demand rather than supply. Countries are unlikely to order millions or even billions of dollars worth of nuclear items just for symbolic defiance. And it seems unlikely that demand will take off forcefully in the foreseeable future. Anyway, emerging suppliers are less capable of offering financial assistance than traditional exporters, and even the latter have failed to generate new orders around the world. However, there would be a market for smaller items such as fuel, research units, and plutonium for experimental purposes; and, if the IAEA loses track of such items, even in smaller quantities, it would be bad enough.

Yet, this event depends on the new suppliers' behavior. So far, they have not posed too difficult a problem, as their conduct has not been worse than that of some of the traditional suppliers, and in some instances it has been distinctly better. There is no genuine reason why this should change in a clash environment.[10] The question is, however, what has motivated the restraint shown thus far. If it was a lack of opportunity (because of the customer's NPT obligations), then change might occur. If the reason was a hesitation to breach norms endorsed by approximately 140 nations, then the clash scenario will also terminate restraint. However, if it was prudence out of enlightened self-interest or, alternatively, fear of sanction by some of the more powerful NPT supporters, then restraint should be upheld, provided that these supporters succeed in making their continuing commitment to nonproliferation sufficiently credible. Even in this best case, a long-term erosion of the safeguards regime is possible. But the longer delay could buy sufficient time for establishing substitute solutions.

The clash scenario is troublesome in still another respect. It could give those parties that are less than faithful to the treaty the pretense to renounce their obligation and to get rid of safeguards. It is doubtful whether they could do so legally, as most export contracts contain obligations toward the supplier which can be constructed as implying an obligation for safeguards even when the NPT falters. The political environment, however, would be far more conducive in the clash environment for, if not outrightly supportive of, defiant actions. And the diplomatic capabilities of those states trying to keep the whole situation manageable would already be strained, perhaps to a point where the appropriate attention to any mounting problems in "less than faithful" states would not be available.

To restore a unified regime under those circumstances will require unusual efforts on the part of the nuclear powers. Once disbanded, the restoration of the NPT is unlikely, and the second-best solution would again be as seamless as possible a network of nuclear-weapon-free zones. This, however, would mean strong demands by the nonnuclear states for restrictions on the deployment patterns of nuclear forces, and on nuclear testing. "Innocent nuclear passage" and the naval tradition not to declare the nuclear status of ships calling on port, trailing through territorial waters, or crossing narrow international waterways would not be tolerable any more. Under the NPT regime, countries wishing to limit this practice have little leverage. In a post-NPT situation created by clash, the nuclear states in their eagerness to establish a substitute regime would be in the position of *demandeurs*. The regional nuclear weapon free zone aspirants, be it states of the Association of Southeast Asian Nations, be it the South Pacific states or elsewhere, are capable of pressing their requests. It will then be up to the nuclear states to decide if rebuilding the regime is worth the presumed sacrifices—or to reassess how relevant present military practices are in the first place.

Western Europe would be affected only in the longer term if a worst-case scenario should be realized, that is, if the less than faithful would go nuclear. Otherwise, the European Atomic Energy Authority (EURATOM) would fully cover the relevant fuel-cycle activities in Western Europe, and arrangements would no doubt be negotiated with the uranium suppliers in order to provide for reasonable reassurances of peaceful use. It is even conceivable that the present IAEA–EURATOM verification arrangements could be very quickly renewed on a new basis, independent of the NPT. In addition, Western Europeans can be expected to join other Western countries in strong efforts to save as much of the decaying regime as possible. Strong cooperation among existing suppliers would be essential, in order to coordinate supply policies in any market that existed at the time, including incentives to potential customers to resist the temptation of a second-tier market free of restrictions. Whether the traditional suppliers can muster the necessary solidarity in the face of mounting competition is open to question, and one could only hope that Europeans would exert the necessary restraint.

CREEP

The creep scenario is distinguished from all the others by its lack of drama. The piecemeal withdrawal of parties from the NPT during an agonizing extension conference would be neither a result of a climactic political confrontation nor of pressing security needs. It would be rather the outgrowth of distress, frustration, and loss of hope after a protracted, fruitless discussion. Some countries considering withdrawal in this setting might even intend to set a signal for improving the regime. It might be a mistaken maneuver; however, it would still express a commitment to nonproliferation rather than the contrary. Most NPT parties, therefore, would stick to the treaty's principles. Many would feel, however, that after the first defections the NPT had lost its meaning and that a new instrument was needed. Whether it would be possible to create a new instrument at the global level is questionable, though. The same quarrels which prevented the conference from succeeding would be in the way of a new worldwide agreement.

The setting up of a network of solid, tenable interim arrangements would be essential. The critical task is to convince one or several of the first defectors to enter a model arrangement which would serve as an example for all the others to follow. It would also be helpful to enlist the support of this first defector to persuade followers to act in the same way. What should such arrangements look like? The first defecting state would depose a solemn unilateral declaration, either with the Secretary-General of the United Nations or with the IAEA Director-General, or with both. This declaration would state that, while not bound anymore by the NPT proper, the state was still bound by its commitments not to acquire nuclear weapons and would continue to accept on a voluntary basis safeguards according to INFCIRC/153. Once such a precedent was set, it would become far more difficult for those creeping out of the NPT regime to slide into nuclear anarchy. If this arrangement was bolstered by strong suppliers' solidarity, it should be possible to save much of the consensus on the political principle of nonproliferation that was so visible during the Third Review Conference of the Parties to the Treaty on the Nonproliferation of Nuclear Weapons (1985). To further solidify the consensus, an arrangement between suppliers and countries accepting the new arrangements, perhaps along the lines of the aborted Committee on Assurances of Supply (CAS) discussions, could be considered. Participating countries would agree on rules concerning the renegotiation of nuclear supply arrangements, and on a backup system if agreed supplies were not forthcoming. Such an arrangement would provide a valuable incentive to defectors to enter this new regime. The difficulties of finding rules upon which states can agree should not be underestimated, as CAS and the U.N. Conference to Promote International Cooperation in the Peaceful Uses of Nuclear Energy demonstrated.

This, then, is clearly a best-case scenario and critically dependent on successful efforts during the first period of the creep. If the leading defector state is not willing to compromise, the creation of a smooth transition to a substitute regime will be far more difficult. The behavior of nonparty suppliers is also critical. If they—as assumed in the clash scenario—agitate behind the scenes and try to entangle defectors one-by-one into an attractive alternative second-tier nuclear market, regime building would become seriously hampered. Lastly, the leading defectors may perceive they have considerable leverage (which indeed they may have), and demand precisely those concessions from the nuclear states and nuclear suppliers which are likely to have caused the stalemate over NPT continuation in the first place. If no change in position occurs, creep out will continue unchecked. Most likely, gray areas of nuclear activities will develop here and there; however, this process should occur very slowly as nuclear research and, even more, nuclear energy development proceed at their restricted pace in the Third World.

From the Western European point of view, the scenario is not too troublesome in the short term, provided creep is not used by neighboring states on Europe's southern fringe to precipitate unsafeguarded activities. Safeguards arrangements and nonproliferation commitments within Western Europe are not likely to change under this scenario, all other factors being equal. In the very long term, however, states would reconsider the status of their security, as the gray zones of unsafeguarded activities and, thereby, the menace of military abuse grew slowly but relentlessly.

ABANDONMENT

The most worrisome scenario is abandonment, particularly from the Western European perspective. The immediate cause would be a precipitated change of the Western alliance through a more or less hasty U.S. withdrawal. In such a disorderly transition, a Western European substitute to the U.S. nuclear guarantee would probably not be established. If the perceived threat—nuclear and conventional— was not by that time removed by the apparently fundamental changes of Soviet policy now beginning, the pressures would be strong in some Western European nonnuclear states (the same scenario can be written for East Asia) to proceed rapidly to a national nuclear capability. Article X of the NPT would be invoked legally, and even with some justification. The West German government, for instance, made it clear in the note that accompanied the deposition of its instruments of ratification of the NPT, that it regarded present alliance arrangements as an essential condition of its treaty membership.[11]

The NPT was constructed partly to generalize the West German nonproliferation commitment given to its allies in the protocol to the Paris Treaties in 1954. At least this was a pivotal Soviet interest. West German withdrawal from the NPT would explode the treaty in two different ways. First, it would suddenly enhance tension in Europe to heights unknown since the end of the Second World War. Indeed, West German nuclearization is possibly the only event which could realistically induce the Soviet Union to consider preventive war. Tensions would also rise among Western Europeans, as lack of Western European solidarity is a precondition for this scenario to unfold, and as West German nuclear weapons would be perceived as a threat by France and others. Second, with the attention and efforts of those countries capable of supporting regime management focused on the menacing situation in Europe, a nuclear-weapon aspirant elsewhere could find it easier to pursue its aims. The experience of the last ten years teaches us that a good deal of determined and relentless vigilance is needed to keep track of ongoing legal and illegal nuclear trade, as well as technology transfers and trade practices, and to improve safeguards.[12] It is hardly conceivable that this permanent attention could be kept in the abandonment scenario. The major powers would have to struggle to keep the tense situation from exploding, and the Europeans, fully occupied with preserving their most immediate and essential national security needs, would pay little attention to events elsewhere.

The new nuclear powers would not only not be available as a nonproliferation management resource any more, they would also have strong incentives for actions that would further disrupt the regime. They would make every effort to develop a minimum deterrent in the shortest period possible, for the transition period would be a time fraught with the greatest danger. Inevitably, under those circumstances they would have to withdraw from safeguards materials which were once dedicated to peaceful purposes—a breach of legal commitments which would send a second shock wave through the regime. Alternatively, they could keep their old activities under safeguards and try to acquire unsafeguarded weapon-grade material from other suppliers. If anybody was willing to export as much as a ton of separated plutonium free of safeguards—enough for a minimum deterrent of 100 to 200 warheads—this would hardly be done without some corresponding favors. At once, a second-tier market in the worst sense of all would exist.

The major management problem in this scenario, however, would be that the immediate cause of West German defection would apply simultaneously at all those places where U.S. security commitments are seen as essential to a nation's survival. Apart from Western Europe, East Asia (Japan, South Korea, Taiwan), Israel, and Pakistan would be concerned. With West Germany and perhaps Italy going nuclear, the incentives for those states, all highly capable in the nuclear field, to follow suit would be all but irresistible.

Those circumstances are hardly conducive to restoring or reconstructing any nonproliferation regime. It would also hardly be worthwhile to make the attempt. The two regions most successfully pacified by the nonproliferation treaty already would be lost, as would the two areas of most concern under present circumstances, South Asia and the Middle East. Altogether, in the abandonment scenario the main challenge would shift to the urgent task of preventing nuclear war rather than stopping further proliferation. Yet precisely in this shift lies another danger of the situation. The threat posed to the world by nuclear-armed crazy states or terrorists[13] does not diminish after abandonment any more than under any different circumstances. On the contrary, with more nuclear states and high tensions, the possibility for catalytic nuclear war would be higher than ever. Intelligence sharing between hostile powers would be necessary to cope with an increasingly confusing scene of public, gray area, and secret civilian and military nuclear trade arrangements. The danger is less that the nuclear newcomers would willfully sponsor nuclear terrorism, or provide nuclear weapons to a Khadhafi or Khomeini; rather, it is that the breakdown of broad cooperation, of established communication channels, and of the safeguards regime would create shadowy areas of international transactions which would at once pose challenges to intelligence several orders of magnitude higher than today's. At the same time, these very circumstances would offer daring nuclear desperados and mercenaries a far less risky and more promising environment to strike favorable deals. As the color of nuclear trade would turn from bright with some gray to gray with some black, management would become as troublesome in terms of intelligence as it would be with regard to politics.

CONCLUSIONS

The initial hypothesis, that the shape of the "world without the NPT" depends critically on the factors and circumstances by which the nonproliferation treaty would unravel, has proven true. Neither the degree of immediate threat nor the management needs and policy solutions can be discussed without due regard to the specific circumstances of any breakdown. Among the conceivable breakdown scenarios, abandonment is the most threatening and least tractable. This is no surprise, as it comprehends the very regions at which the NPT was aimed in the first place. Next in terms of troubles comes bang, followed by clash. Creep is the most manageable. This rank order is contingent on the degree of drama and the precise issues involved. Abandonment and bang are contingencies in which essential security interests are immediately at stake. In clash and creep, the issues are predominantly political. In all but creep, there is high drama because of the suddenness of the event.

Nuclear-weapon-free zones stand out as a quick fix for a substitute regime which could present a network of almost global reach and, in that respect, would be similar to the NPT. The creation of nuclear-weapon-free zones, however, will create serious tradeoffs between the goal of nonproliferation and the freedom of action, movement, and deployment perceived by the nuclear states as essential. This applies particularly to the United States. Most likely, the successful use of the nuclear-free zones as the principal instruments of nonproliferation policy would be contingent on substantial American concessions.

Three factors are of exceptional importance for the manageability of a post-NPT world in the first three scenarios:

- *Supplier solidarity*—Utmost discipline and improved coordination among suppliers are necessary in order to force the nuclear industry to exert restraint in a situation of growing gray-area trade.
- *Emerging supplier behavior*—One of the most damaging features possible after the NPT demise is the emergence of a split nuclear market, with fewer strings attached to deals in the second tier. While there is little evidence

today that second-tier suppliers are seeking such conditions, the case might be different if an NPT breakdown projects the image of a markedly weakened nonproliferation consensus. It is all the more important to draw suppliers who do not adhere to the agreement into an informal or formal code of conduct as soon as possible.

• *Containment of crazy states*—They are the most likely to seek to exploit gray-area situations. Concomitantly, stronger efforts at intelligence gathering, denial, and prevention must be made to minimize any chances of their going nuclear.

Economy of intelligence and diplomatic resources would be a serious problem. Far more effort must be expanded on nonproliferation in the case of the NPT's demise than today, and the availability of those resources is open to question. While the creep scenario is most benign in this respect, because one can deal with emerging contingencies one by one, clash would strain diplomatic resources considerably. Bang may push diplomacy as well as intelligence beyond the limits of the possible. Abandonment is hopeless.

Apart from the last scenario, where Western Europe would itself be the problem, the situation poses two challenges to Western Europe: first, assuring the security of the southern tier from newly emerging nuclear states; and, second, close Western European collaboration would be required in order to solve the required management tasks. The attitude of benign neglect which has dominated the nonproliferation attitude in some European countries every now and then in the past would no longer be tolerable.

A world without the NPT? As the analysis has shown, such a world is fraught with uncertainty and danger. No substitute would fulfill the functions of the treaty as well as does the NPT itself. The critics of the treaty's imperfections would do well to think through a future without it. They may well arrive at these same conclusions. We had better see to it that the NPT survives.

NOTES AND REFERENCES

1. Harald Müller, ed., *A European Nonproliferation Policy: Prospects and Problems* (Oxford: Clarendon Press, 1987).
2. The "chain reaction" possibility has been analyzed exhaustively in Lewis A. Dunn and Herman Kahn, *Trends in Nuclear Proliferation, 1975-1995: Projections, Problems and Policy Options* (New York: Hudson Institute, 1976).
3. See the chapter on Iran by Akbar Etemad in Müller, *Nonproliferation Policy*; and Leonard S. Spector, *Going Nuclear* (Cambridge, Mass.: Ballinger, 1987), pp. 170–72.
4. See Spector, *Going Nuclear*.
5. Yehezkel Dror, *Crazy States: A Counterconventional Strategic Problem* (Lexington, Mass.: D.C. Heath, 1971).
6. See the chapter by David Fischer on South Africa in Müller, *Nonproliferation Policy*.
7. Katlyn Saba, "Spain and the NPT," paper presented to the PRIF Conference on European Nonproliferation Policy, Garmisch–Partenkirchen, May 1987.
8. David Fischer and Harald Müller, *Nonproliferation Beyond the 1985 Review, CEPS Papers*, no. 26 (Brussels, 1985), pp. 23–27.

9. See the section on abandonment below for a discussion of possible repercussions.
10. See the chapters on emerging suppliers by Ram R. Subramaniam, Randy J. Rydell, and Lewis A. Dunn in Rodney W. Jones, Cesare Merlini, Joseph F. Pilat, and William C. Potter, eds., *The Nuclear Suppliers and Nonproliferation: International Policy Choices* (Lexington, Mass.: Lexington Books, 1985).
11. Alexander Petri, *Die Entstehung des NV-Vertrages. Die Rolle der Bundesrepublik Deutschland.* Ph.D. Thesis (Tübingen, 1970).
12. Leonard S. Spector, *The New Nuclear Nations* (New York: Vintage Books, 1985), chap. II.
13. Yonah Alexander and Paul Leventhal, eds., *Nuclear Terrorism, Defining the Threat* (London: Brassey's Defence Publishers, 1986).

10

The NPT and Nuclear Proliferation in East Asia

Views toward the 1990s

Ryukichi Imai

With the exception of China, none of the states of East Asia has developed nuclear weapons. Is this attributable to the NPT or to other factors? In retrospect, one can argue that there never has been a realistic combination of political, military, and technical opportunities for nuclear armament in the region, even to the minimum level implied in the NPT regime. This observation, of course, is not inconsistent with the view that in the absence of the NPT and the discouragement of proliferation the treaty inspired, things could have been different. Nevertheless, nuclear powers do not emerge ex nihilo; nations seek to possess nuclear weapons out of an urge toward world (or regional) military hegemony, in the desire to defend or deter against threats by powerful neighbors, or as a matter of prestige in a rivalry between two or more states aspiring to regional or global status. In East Asia, all of these factors were present at one time or another. However, the appearance of any one of these motivations for nuclear weapons never coincided with the capability to develop nuclear weapons in an East Asian state, except for China. Today, with the increasing level of sophistication required for nuclear arsenals that could be useful militarily, the possibility of any new or renascent nuclear aspirations in the region is minimal, and any chance of their attainment is extremely unlikely. The only exception is the case of a country or a group of countries willing to become, in effect, international terrorists with a small number of crude bombs, another luxury that does not seem possible in East Asia. In this chapter, the difficulties of developing militarily significant nuclear arsenals will be addressed, as will nuclear weapons and

Ryukichi Imai • Ambassador of Japan to Mexico.

nonproliferation developments in East Asia, both regionally and by country. Finally, a look forward to the 1990s with special attention to East Asia will be offered.

GETTING THE BOMB

The demands on emerging nuclear powers are heavy. There are a number of requirements that must be met before nuclear weapons can effectively be integrated into a national security system. It is possible that the desire to strengthen an alliance may lead a country or countries to provide its partners with nuclear weapons or the technology necessary for their sustained production. This occurred in Sino–Soviet relations during the 1950s, and it was about to occur in Europe in 1962, in the form of the Multilateral Force (MLF). Both cases proved that suspicion within an alliance can make such arrangements unworkable, primarily because of the very strict requirement to keep the command and control of nuclear weapons in a single hand. At the same time, one needs to realize that because nuclear weapons have undergone major qualitative changes throughout the decades of the atomic age, the transfer of these weapons or the technology to produce them in the 1950s and 1960s is not comparable to what would be required today if such transfers were contemplated.

For a country independently to manufacture nuclear devices, it has to have a minimum quantity of uranium highly enriched in U-235, or plutonium with a high isotopic content of Pu-239. Lower-grade materials have been proven to work, but with efficiencies that would be unacceptably low in nuclear-weapon systems capable of being integrated into a modern military force structure. Even though the technology of producing weapon-grade material, as well as the basic design of first-generation nuclear weapons, has been a matter of public knowledge for some time, the actual technical requirements for substantial and sustained bomb production are beyond the capabilities of other than advanced industrial economies. During the early 1960s, when the world woke up to the "nth power problem," one criterion often referred to was the existence of an indigenous automobile industry in addition to several years of national R&D spending at one-half percent or more of a state's gross national product. If we carefully consider these two conditions, even Japan did not qualify at that time. In other words, nuclear armament was regarded as a reflection of the combined power of science, technology, and industry in a country rather than an ability to manufacture an occasional bomb or two. What the authors of the NPT specifically desired to prohibit is not at all clear and may have differed from country to country and person to person. The NPT was itself basically more a political than a technical document, and its logic required that not a single nuclear explosive device with an avowed military purpose would be permitted. It will be recalled that peaceful nuclear explosives (PNEs) were accorded much more respect, and were believed to have much more utility, at the time the NPT was being negotiated than today.

It is important to realize that what the nuclear-weapon and nonproliferation communities had in mind at the height of the proliferation debate in the 1960s were crude devices transported by heavy bombers and in numbers far smaller than those that constitute today's existing nuclear arsenals. The negotiations leading to the Limited Test Ban Treaty (LTBT) of 1963 were based, in addition to the concern over environmental contamination, on the notion that a ban on nuclear tests would effectively curb the development and production of new and advanced weapons (which were then thought of in terms of yields in the hundreds of kilotons). And the policy decision of Sweden in the 1950s not to participate openly in any nuclear arms race was based on its assessment that any future major nuclear exchanges would bypass Scandinavia. This was a period when nuclear arsenals were very different from those in existence today—when accuracies were measured in tens of kilometers; nothing like systems with multiple, independently targetable reentry vehicles (MIRVs) were in existence; antiballistic missile systems were no more than conceptual studies; sophisticated, space-based command, control, communication, and intelligence systems were not in operation; and land-mobile SS-20s and terminally guided *Pershing* IIs were probably not even on the drawing board. Nevertheless, even at this time, vertical proliferation was making major strides.

There were strange crosscurrents in the international arena involving the manner in which nuclear weapons were being pursued and perceived. On the one hand, there was a very strong drive for more and more sophisticated weapon systems, which surpassed anything recorded in the history of military technology. This drive resulted in inventories of tremendous destructive power—power beyond the human imagination. With intercontinental ballistic missiles and other modern technologies, the requirements for waging a nuclear war became so demanding, and the pace of decision-making so rapid, that only the most modern of high-speed computers could "manage the battle." As if to counterbalance such vertical proliferation, the two largest nuclear powers started a concerted effort immediately after the conclusion of the LTBT to ensure that none other than the privileged five should emerge as a new nuclear power. One obvious concern at the time was German rearmament and the prospect of a German state with nuclear capabilities. To deal with this concern, the solution proposed by the United States and the Soviet Union was an international regime to curb horizontal proliferation.

Was the superpowers' concern justified? No state inhabiting the world of rational nuclear strategy would attempt to pose a serious military threat to the security of either of the superpowers with only a limited number of crude weapons, especially in light of the capability of the United States and the Soviet Union to launch preemptive surgical strikes, which they were said to have considered against China in the 1960s. On the other hand, the political impact of even a very small nuclear force would be enough to cause violent reactions among the possessor's neighbors and to send shock waves through the postwar system and the East–West military balance upon which it hinges. Of course, assessing the level of nuclear-weapon capabilities that would be of interest to a proliferant country is difficult, other than to say that it depends upon subjective judgments regarding the desperation of a particular state. Do, or did, they perceive threats to their national security to be so great that the possession of a limited number of nuclear explosive devices would be, or was, sufficiently convincing to themselves and outsiders to save the nation from the brink of destruction? Other than in the world of fiction, it is difficult to conceive of a situation in which a certain colonel can somehow obtain an Islamic bomb and clandestinely transport it into New York City. The supposed bomb must be for use against a direct rival in the neighborhood. It would be very interesting to analyze the extent to which India's prestige and security have actually increased because of her known capability to detonate a (peaceful) nuclear device. It has been an interesting exercise in the past to engage in assessing the security value of Israel's unannounced and untested bomb. With these general considerations on nuclear-weapon proliferation, let us now turn to East Asia.

ATOMIC WEAPONS IN EAST ASIA: HISTORICAL AND GEOPOLITICAL TRENDS

Aside from the difficulties of developing militarily significant nuclear capabilities, historical and geopolitical factors have played an important role in the limited interest concerning nuclear weapons in the East Asian region. Most of the countries in East Asia obtained their independence after the Second World War. Nuclear weapons never played a significant role in this process of decolonization, nor in the later development of these new states into nonaligned countries. For example, countries of the Association of Southeast Asian Nations have probably never felt very much involved in anything nuclear. Except for the brief period in the 1950s when President Eisenhower's Atoms for Peace program stirred up people's imaginations, and again immediately after the oil crises of the 1970s when many talked about nuclear-generated electricity as a readily available alternative to oil, most of the nations in East Asia had thought of nuclear technology only in conjunction with their interest in international nuclear disarmament negotiations.

Not only did the decolonization process conspire against nuclear arms, but so did postwar power politics. It is obvious that there have not been any parallels in Asia to the NATO–Warsaw Pact confrontation in Europe. Europe has been the center of gravity in world politics for a very long time, and the manner in which the Second World War was terminated created the grounds for the postwar division and confrontation of the blocs, in which military nuclear capabilities have played a central role. The eastern side of the Eurasian continent has been devoid of such a massive confrontation. For various reasons, the Sino–Soviet nuclear confrontation has not expanded into the rest of Asia. It was only with the advent of the intermediate-range (5,000 kilometers) SS-20s and *Backfire* bombers in the Far East that a hitherto nonexistent theater balance has emerged as an important consideration. The conclusion of the Intermediate Nuclear Forces Treaty may help to return the situation to the status quo ante.

In addition to the intermediate-range nuclear forces, which are now being eliminated, there have been other important developments in terms of the central systems of the two superpowers. With increasing capabilities by both the United States and Soviet Union to utilize the Arctic region to deploy very long-range and very accurate MIRVed submarine-launched ballistic missiles (SLBMs), the relative military balance between the European and the Pacific fronts has been gradually shifting. Today, if one looks purely at military strategy and weapon capabilities, it is doubtful whether the same heavy preoccupation with the European front will continue to be justified. However, true to the traditional confrontation scenarios developed for the central European front, involving a combination of NATO's conventional deep strikes on the Warsaw Pact's second echelon, possibilities of chemical warfare, and likely early resort to nuclear weapons, we are witnessing what might be the last version in the long history of doctrines of flexible response. Different versions of nuclear proliferation, or more accurately "control thereof," in either of the two Germanies, have often played very central roles within these confrontational versions of the East–West relationship.

In the absence of an immediate and perceived threat by the Soviet military (except its presence along the Sino–Soviet border, which, however, has been a Chinese problem), there was less immediacy and urgency for East Asian countries, including Japan, to consider developing independent and separate nuclear deterrent forces. In fact, even the United States' extended deterrent, or "nuclear umbrella," has not been openly appreciated in East Asia. One may see an example of this rather complicated psychology in Japan's three nonnuclear principles or, more recently, in the South Pacific Forum's initiative establishing a nuclear-free zone and New Zealand's approach both to port visits by nuclear-armed naval vessels and to the ANZUS treaty. While these broad trends had influence throughout East Asia, additional factors came into play in the decisions of China to "go nuclear" and of Japan, South Korea, and Taiwan to eschew nuclear weapons.

THE DIVERGENT PATHS OF JAPAN AND CHINA

After its defeat in World War II, Japan was in no position to think of major rearmament or to challenge the postwar political and military order. The devastation wrought by the war was so great that twenty years after its defeat, Japan had to be reminded by others that it no longer needed to be apologetic about its economic status or its other advantages. The idea of nuclear armament never took hold in Japan, which in 1954 made sure that no such aspiration should ever emerge from the people, or any political grouping, by legislation that only allows peaceful applications of nuclear energy and provides that civilian control will be firmly in place. Given Japan's "nuclear allergy," even if there were incentives to manufacture nuclear weaponry, it would be very difficult to recruit a sufficient number of willing weapon scientists in Japan.

Not every Japanese has been happy about this situation. It became clear toward the end of the 1960s that the scientific, technological, and industrial infrastructures for nuclear-power generation, radiation physics, the medical application of radioisotopes, and other applications of nuclear energy, had seemingly given the country the potential to produce, if it possessed the necessary raw material, half a dozen atomic bombs and probably an equal number of thermonuclear devices. To realize this potential, of course, Japan would certainly have encountered technical difficulties, not to mention the political problems of pursuing nuclear weapons.

Japan signed the NPT in 1970 but delayed its ratification until 1976, mainly on the pretext of having to work out a satisfactory and equitable deal with the International Atomic Energy Agency (IAEA) with regard to the safeguards (verification) provisions of the treaty. In fact, Japan was waiting to make sure that the conditions for its participation in the NPT regime were not inferior to those the Federal Republic of Germany (FRG) was able to attain. The FRG, being a member of EURATOM, was considered by Japan to be a very important future competitor in the international market for nuclear technology. Additionally, it actually took six years before some influential Japanese became convinced that a half-hearted interest in nuclear armament would only damage Japan's economic possibilities, especially at the height of the oil crisis. They also came to realize that a meaningful nuclear deterrent, including a submarine-launched second-strike capability and early-warning assets deployed in outer space, would require large-scale technology transfers (presumably from the United States) and some ten to twenty years lead time—assuming that Japan could bear the prohibitive costs.

Japan's geopolitical situation, defined by its high population and industrial density, definitely denied the "paper tiger" theory of nuclear weapons as preached by Chairman Mao; the only military significance of nuclear weapons would be in their value for deterrence. In the 1975–1976 Diet debate over NPT ratification, moral value judgments were raised, as were assessments that the existing nuclear-weapon states were already experiencing a fundamental transition from their early reliance on crude atom bombs to deterrent postures involving modern nuclear-war fighting systems. Japan decided that to acquire the latter capabilities independently was clearly beyond her means.

Unlike obvious concerns over the FRG, it is difficult to determine the extent to which the former allies were concerned about a possible nuclear role for Japan in any of the global confrontation scenarios then being considered. Besides, the Japanese were very serious about their determination to remain nonnuclear. These factors resulted in vastly differing concerns over the delays in ratifying the NPT by the Federal Republic on the one hand and by Japan on the other. The German delay was a complicated political issue and it was appreciated as such. Japan's delay was a minor political issue that could be left for the Japanese to work out, as Japan was told at the time in so many words by the American president, a disclosure which did not make domestic Japanese ratification efforts any easier. The domestic debate over NPT ratification in Japan revolved around the question of whether to accept the basically unequal international order recognized and sanctioned by the treaty in exchange for the benefits to be derived from enhanced regional security and the greater opportunities for expanding nuclear power as a source of energy.

In a very different situation than Japan after the war, China took a very different path. Among nuclear and near-nuclear states, the case of China is unique. With a background in industrialization (without modernization), a wealth of human resources, and military-oriented technical assistance from the Soviet Union (unlike the case of India), China had by the time of the NPT already mastered the capabilities to produce atomic, and later thermonuclear, warheads, along with missiles, various models of Mig-19 and -21 fighter-bombers, and nuclear-powered submarines with SLBM capabilities. Unlike India, China has sufficient uranium resources of its own and no immediate need for nuclear power as a source of energy because of its abundant and insufficiently developed reserves of coal, oil, and gas. As one of the authorized weapon states under Article IX of the NPT, China never had a need to cover its development of weapons by using the PNE justification. The position accorded to China by the NPT, together with China's initial and current position that the treaty is not a useful international instrument, had put China into a category of her own. At the same time, if the reports alleging that assistance may have been given by China to the Pakistani uranium enrichment project, at least at some stage in the past, were true, they might indicate a certain lack of sensitivity about the general subject of nuclear nonproliferation on China's part. While it seems obvious that deployment by the Soviet Union of so many modern MIRVed SS-20s in Asian bases must have been meant to counterbalance Chinese nuclear forces, the Soviet Union has never admitted this publicly. The importance of Chinese nuclear weapons has continued to be underplayed, in spite of China's continued atmospheric nuclear testing, at least until very recently. As well, along with the somewhat unexplainable enthusiasm by American and Western European countries regarding China's as yet very uncertain nuclear electric future, there are features of uniqueness and unreality in this aspect of the Chinese nuclear program. It is conceivable that this is exactly what the leaders of the country would like as China's nuclear image, while China, of course, has no need to worry over issues of deterrence dogma such as decoupling.

KOREA AND TAIWAN: CONCERNS DIMINISH

Through the process of independence, situations of intense rivalry have been created in three areas in East Asia, each of which led to military engagements. These areas were Korea, Taiwan, and Indo-China, a peninsula which is still in a state of flux. The patterns of competition or rivalry have been very different between the two Koreas and between Taiwan and mainland China, but the two cases have one thing in common. Both the Republic of Korea and Taiwan have settled back into economic and commercial concerns and have successfully introduced nuclear electricity into their countries in a major way. Both are primarily dependent on U.S. technology and fuel-cycle services, including both the supply of enriched uranium and the handling of spent nuclear fuel. This means that the United States has been in a strong position to exercise (and, in fact, has exercised) nonproliferation control over the two countries. The East Asian situation is now very favorable in comparison with other well-known areas of proliferation concern, including the Middle East, South Asia, Latin America, and South Africa, for which more than passing doubts seem to exist regarding clandestine weapon capabilities. Although records indicate occasional contemplation of the use of nuclear weapons in conflicts in East Asia, there is nothing to indicate that they were more than contingency plans.

The extent to which nuclear proliferation by Taiwan and South Korea may have been a real concern in the 1970s is difficult to tell. With the construction and operation of nuclear power stations and associated industries, it was obvious that the two acquired considerable nuclear capabilities, and thus proliferation potential, by the 1970s. It then became a matter of a political decision by the leadership on whether to move in the direction of obtaining the capabilities for the enrichment of uranium or the separation of plutonium, which are difficult to justify on economic grounds but are the basic ingredients of weapon production. Since both South Korea and Taiwan are and have been under full-scope safeguards by IAEA, they would have to construct small-scale clandestine production facilities for either enriching uranium or producing weapon-grade plutonium. There were occasional reports in both countries of the leadership's interest in pursuing such a path, but it is difficult to know whether they represented a well-advised and considered policy. In any event, possession of a small number of atomic bombs does not appear to be a cost-effective policy option for either South Korea or Taiwan or, for that matter, for whoever may be in charge of nuclear policies in North Korea.

INTO THE 1990s

There have been different phases of nonproliferation from the days of a few 100-kiloton bombs, to the present day, in which the arsenals of the nuclear states are vastly larger and individual weapons frequently have more destructive power. The problem of developing states that aspire to nuclear status has to be understood today as a part of this transition. As far as East Asia is concerned, the era of major worries seems to be over. This does not mean that the nonproliferation concerns of the sixties and seventies have been in vain. Rather, it is partly because of those concerns, and the awareness they created, that East Asia has arrived at its current status.

Will this situation prevail in the future? As suggested, the postwar security situation for East Asia, with the exception of China, has not favored development of independent nuclear arsenals by the states of the region. The Soviet threat to East Asia never appeared as great as it appeared in Europe, and with Mikhail Gorbachev in power the situation could improve, although this is by no means certain. Gorbachev on a number of occasions has called for a forum in the Asia–Pacific region following the style of the Conference on Security and Cooperation in Europe. In doing so, he also tried to play to the antinuclear sentiment in the region. There are many important East Asian nations with territorial problems which cannot take seriously a call for an Asian Helsinki by the Soviet Union. Antinuclear sentiments in the region are a far more complicated and benign phenomena than the reactions in Europe over INF deployment. It is not the sort of thing that the Soviet Union, with its rapidly increasing nuclear capabilities in Petropavlovsk, Vladivostok, or Chita can try to exploit. If the Soviet Union were to reverse the process and show more restraint in military activities, there may be the possibility of different initiatives for a security forum in the Asia–Pacific region.

East Asian developments will also be influenced by global economic and energy trends and by the strength of the nonproliferation regime. It will be recalled that it was the sudden burst of interest within Third World countries in the rapid expansion of nuclear power generation to replace expensive and dwindling oil supplies that opened up a very different phase of concern about nonproliferation. The numbers mentioned as the target construction level for nuclear power plants, such as 1,500 gigawatts of generating capacity by the year 2000, clearly called for an extensive use of plutonium as fuel. This was not anticipated by the original authors of the NPT, and it led to considerable confusion and concern in the late 1970s. The name of the new game was "energy security," and people were called on to compare proliferation risks to the risk of energy shortages, both of which were focused primarily on Third World countries. Many in the nonaligned movement countered by calling attention to Article VI of the NPT and accusing the nuclear-weapon states of not having realized any tangible results in nuclear disarmament.

The glut in the oil supply and the sharp fall in oil prices since the mid-1980s have somewhat relaxed the confrontation, although none of the problems have been finally resolved. And, in this light, one extreme which cannot be totally eliminated is a possible replay of the oil crisis of the 1970s. According to some well-informed calculations, it is possible that the Organization of Petroleum Exporting Countries (OPEC) in 1995 will be supplying 60 percent of the world's oil trade, while running at more than 80 percent of its production capacity. Recent sharp decreases in oil prices have cut new investment in new energy sources, so that the industrial world is depending more and more on Middle East oil for its energy consumption. This means that by 1995, OPEC may be in the driver's seat again, manipulating prices of oil at will. It is then not inconceivable that the world may be talking about a very large number of nuclear power plants, which may be beyond the capabilities of the IAEA to safeguard. Whether the IAEA will have a problem-free future in terms of safeguards implementation is not very clear. With increases in the number and scope of facilities under safeguards, the accumulation of material unaccounted for within the existing system will have to increase. There will be a need to find politically viable and technically acceptable solutions to this issue. Otherwise the chance of people crying wolf will increase.

We all know that 1995 is the year of the most crucial review conference of the NPT, at which its fate will be decided. Even if the NPT is not the most important cause of the current nonproliferation situation in East Asia, it has surely contributed to removing states of this region from the list of "problem countries," and East Asian states are now important supporters of the treaty. By the time the Third Review Conference of the Parties to the Treaty on the Nonproliferation of Nuclear Weapons met in Geneva in the summer of 1985, those countries still being suspected of clandestine weapon activities were in the Middle East, South Asia, South Africa, and possibly in Latin America. Somehow suspicion seemed to have been lifted from the countries of East Asia. For that matter the subject of nuclear proliferation itself at the review conference seemed not to excite people as much as it did during the two earlier review conferences, and this may be the reason why the third review conference had relatively smooth sailing in adopting a final document with consensus, which emphasized the continuing importance of the NPT regime.

Of course, the resumption of nuclear and space arms control talks in Geneva had an important role to play, as did the fact that many of the major East Asian countries are within the NPT, while those from regions under suspicion are outside. Nuclear nonproliferation may, in one sense, have come of age in 1985. However, the experience of 1985 is no certain portent of success in 1995. If the NPT were ever to fail, East Asia and the world would suffer greatly.

11

World and Regional Power Relations without the NPT

Ashok Kapur

INTRODUCTION

To understand the world without the NPT *after* 1995, it is first important to understand the world *without* the NPT from the 1940s to 1968, and second, the world *with* the NPT from the 1960s to 1995. In all, there are three worlds to consider. The first is the world of "pre-NPT horizontal proliferation." The nuclear programs of Israel, South Africa, India, and Argentina, among other states, commenced[1] before the NPT negotiations started and were well along before the NPT was finalized. The second concerns "proliferation during, and in the context of, the NPT regime." The third is a hypothetical world after 1995. It assumes that an already weakened NPT regime will either collapse by 1995, or that it will be kept alive through periodic review conferences which produce cosmetic consensus and paper victories in international conference diplomacy.

Horizontal nuclear proliferation and antiproliferation are the products of a milieu characterized by evolving world and regional power relations. There are two ways which are not mutually exclusive to assess proliferation and nonproliferation. In the first perspective, they are parallel trends in the post-1945 period, and are likely to remain so. Here the near-nuclear status[2] of the horizontal proliferators has continually coexisted with the NPT regime; neither directly impacts on the other. Strategic discourse by a horizontal proliferator is carried out in a framework of domestic controversies, bureaucratic politics, leadership and elite motivations, technological capacities, military requirements, and so on. The strategic and cultur-

---

Ashok Kapur • Professor of Political Science, University of Waterloo, Ontario, Canada.

al reference points are leadership and country specific.[3] In the case of the hard-core horizontal proliferators, the intranational decision process is largely immune to international pressures, because the strategic and cultural reference points of multilateral diplomacy reflect a different set of motives and vague notions of "international security." Since the quality of the "international" antiproliferation discourse is not better than the "national" proliferation discourse, coexistence between the two is easily arranged as a dialogue of the deaf on both sides. The practitioners involved in the intranational proliferation debate ignore the international nonproliferation debate because it is mostly irrelevant to their concerns. The practitioners involved in pushing nonproliferation in international circles fail to understand the national debates because they are not curious and attentive about the motives and interests of the "enemy." Here the two mental and practical worlds of proliferation and nonproliferation need not connect so long as each side stays out of the other's way. Their relationship can continue in the form of competitive coexistence.

In the second perspective, competing motives explain an active struggle between nonproliferation and ambiguous nuclear proliferation in the post-1945 period. The future of the NPT regime depends on the balance of power between two competing conceptions of security. The case histories of the horizontal proliferators and the policies of the antiproliferators reveal an enduring quality and continuity of motivation, in the first case to avoid curbs on national programs, and in the second case to create those very curbs. The public positions on both sides have crystallized. The arguments on both sides are strategic and cultural ones. Strategic because they refer to different conceptions of security; cultural because they refer to different conceptions of future destiny or past glory. The balance of power between these competing conceptions in the 1960s favored the antiproliferators, and it led to the formation of the NPT regime. But even as the legal and institutional framework of the NPT regime has grown, the permanent conflict of interest between the nuclear and near-nuclear powers has reinforced the early convictions of the horizontal proliferators in their cause of nuclear autonomy. The balance of power between the antiproliferators and the proliferators has not shifted decisively toward the latter, in the last two decades, in part because the latter do not act as a bloc in world political, military, and nuclear affairs. But erosion in the NPT regime has set in for several reasons: first, because the regime lacks an enforcement mechanism against non-NPT states as well as against the nuclear-weapon states (NWSs); second, because the institutions and legal mechanisms of the NPT regime are weak and ridden with loopholes; and third, because the proliferators are upwardly mobile in the international system and see themselves as regional powers. The future of the nonproliferation debate and the NPT regime, therefore, must be assessed in the context of a changing structure of world and regional power. The erosion may or may not lead to a breakdown of the NPT regime by 1995, but in either case it is unlikely that the incremental growth of horizontal proliferation in the main centers of regional conflict, and the growth of power capabilities as well as the ability of the regional powers to manage hostile coalitions or pressures, will allow the NPT regime to act in an intrusive way in regional diplomatic and military affairs. In other words, historically—that is, from the 1960s to the present—the NPT regime's institutional and legal framework has grown, but its authority in select and important regions has declined. Both processes—institutional growth and the decline of authority or regime decay—have been dynamic in the last two decades.

To understand these processes, we need to study world and regional nuclear relations with a set of categories other than whether states do or do not possess nuclear weapons or belong to the NPT. These latter categories come from the NPT, but they do not explain the classification scheme which actually governs interstate relations in the world today and which prevents the existence of a common basis for a discourse on nuclear and disarmament affairs. The operative classification consists of four to five tiers of powers. The first tier includes the "Big Two," the so-called international principals in nuclear and disarmament affairs. The second comprises the three lesser nuclear powers. A third tier would consist of the autonomy-seeking regional powers, including Argentina, Brazil, South Africa, Israel, India, and Iran. The moderate–pragmatic powers like Egypt, Indonesia, Canada, several West European states, Yugoslavia, and possibly Pakistan can be understood as a fourth tier; and a fifth tier, which does not count, includes the rest of the world. The public attitude and relationship to the NPT regime of these states depends on their leaderships' and elites' mental outlook, and their domestic and external compulsions. So what states say and do in the area of horizontal proliferation or nonproliferation depends on the position of the state in the international system, its relations with the great powers, its location in relation to zones of conflict, and its concept of its security and future destiny.

The evaluation of the functions of the NPT regime depends on the subjective bias of the pundit, policymaker, or analyst with respect to the state interests which are being advanced. The popular belief that the NPT and the nonproliferation objective it embodies is "good" and horizontal proliferation is "bad" (i.e., destabilizing, irresponsible) is plain humbug. It is biased and not a scientific observation. The functions of the NPT regime are finite, actor specific, and changing; they depend on the evolution of power relations and the interests of key actors in different parts of the world. In a historical perspective, the nonproliferation regime, in relation to incipient nuclear powers, was the strongest in the period from the 1940s to the 1960s, that is, before the NPT system came into being. But even then it was ineffective in controlling both vertical and horizontal proliferation at the time. At that time, the nuclear options of the present-day short list of horizontal proliferators were hidden and in-house. The NPT debate, which was highly publicized, provided the opportunity to reveal hidden nuclear options. The NPT did not create proliferation, but it did reveal proliferants by its insistence on the notion that "if you don't sign the NPT, you are automatically suspect as a proliferator." To this, the Israelis and Indians expressed gratitude to the NPT for giving them the opportunity to reveal their nuclear ambitions and capabilities. In the sense that proliferation is not simply a technical activity, but is also a political, psychological, and cultural event—that is, a refusal to accept permanent technical and military inferiority revealing a political intent—the NPT debate promoted proliferation. In this perspective, the short list of proliferation cases crystallized after the NPT regime was instituted. The intended function of the NPT was to stop or slow proliferation, but the net effect of the NPT regime was to reveal the weaknesses of the treaty and nonproliferation efforts. In other words, the NPT regime should not be equated with the cause of nonproliferation. We should assess the negative value of the NPT inasmuch as a practical effect of the treaty on the near-nuclear states that were the objects of international controls was to reinforce their commitment to the preservation and further development of these nuclear options. And we should compare the efficacy of methods of nonproliferation that focused on national policy or bilateral and alliance ties in the pre-NPT period with the multilateral and international methods of nonproliferation that emerged in the NPT period.

To understand how the relationship between the NPT regime and the horizontal proliferation process has evolved since the 1940s, and what the future holds, let us turn to a discussion of the following questions:

- What were the nuclear activities and nuclear ambitions of countries other than the five NWSs in the pre-NPT world, from the 1940s to mid-1960s? Did the NPT affect these activities in any way, whether positively or negatively?
- What was the intellectual and the international policy setting in which the NPT and the NPT regime emerged in the late 1960s? What were the functions of the NPT regime and its effects?
- What kind of an NPT regime came into being in the 1960s? What was the direction of its growth or improvement during the life of the NPT? What are now the central components of this regime?
- What kinds of myths emerged about the dangers of nuclear proliferation and, secondly, about the NPT as a barrier to proliferation? Have the myths distorted policy or scholarly analyses?
- What actions by nuclear proliferators, as well as actions against the NPT regime, have occurred during the life of the regime, from the 1960s to 1980s? Did this occur despite the NPT or as a result of the proliferation activities which started in the pre-NPT period?
- What have been the effects of the antiregime activities on the NPT regime?

On the basis of a discussion of actual developments, and not scenarios, from the 1940s to the 1980s, a scenario of the world without the NPT in the mid-1990s will be constructed.

PRE-NPT HORIZONTAL PROLIFERATION

Israel, South Africa, Argentina, Brazil, India, Pakistan, and Taiwan are estimated to be the hard-core horizontal proliferators today, in the sense that they possess nuclear arms (Israel, as suggested most recently by Vannunu's revelations to the British press in 1986), or they possess a nuclear-weapon capability (India), or they have the ambition to acquire such a capability (Brazil). Of these countries, Israel, Argentina, South Africa, and India embraced the nuclear path between the 1930s and 1950s.[4] Their nuclear programs were dual purpose, but each program had a definite political–strategic content. By contemporary definitions of proliferation, measured by kind and level of technical activity, these states were "proliferators," although it is more accurate to call them "latent" proliferators. The Beaton and Maddox estimate at the time, which was prior to the NPT, was that nuclear proliferation was not inevitable.[5] They were right, but their view was not fashionable in Western policy circles. The fashionable views were more sensational and less judicious in comparison. However, it was fashion that was germane to the formulation of policy. Buchan's introduction to *A World of Nuclear Powers?* (1966) outlined the notion of rapid proliferation once the dam burst—with the emergence of the sixth nuclear proliferator. Buchan came to two conclusions. First, he stated: "The biggest gap in the *chain reaction* of proliferation may be from the *fifth to the sixth* nuclear power. From the *sixth to the sixteenth* the progression may be rapid." And second, according to Buchan: "One thing is certain, proliferation would change the shape of the world profoundly but the kinds of agreements needed to control it will change it even more."[6]

Buchan was wrong in dramatizing the central role of the sixth state to overtly possess nuclear weapons. The assumption that the sixth nuclear power would produce a chain reaction up to the sixteenth nuclear state conveyed a deterministic overtone that seemed to parallel the views of the 1960s about falling dominoes in Indo-China. Implicit in this assumption was the notion that near-nuclear states would go nuclear just because the sixth went nuclear. Also implicit was the notion that the seventh to sixteenth near-nuclear state just wanted an excuse to explode the "bomb," and that the sixth nuclear state would provide them an excuse for doing so. Second, Buchan was wrong in hypothesizing rapid proliferation. And finally, he was wrong in assuming that nonproliferation agreements would change the shape of the world even more than would proliferation. The period from 1966 to 1989 is a test of Buchan's accuracy. He fails miserably either to explain or to predict the pattern of proliferation during the 1960s, the 1970s, and the 1980s; and he overstated the impact of nonproliferation agreements. In retrospect, Beaton and Maddox's writings reveal accuracy in analysis and maturity in judgment.

Buchan was not alone in offering fantastic scenarios. American writers enlarged and reiterated the sensational American policy views of the 1960s. Thus, Albert and Roberta Wohlstetter, Victor Gilinsky, Joseph Nye Jr., Mason Willrich, E. Lefever, Herman Kahn, L. A. Dunn, Z. Khalilzad, and Paul Jabber have often popularized notions of imminent, inevitable, and destabilizing proliferation. Their success lies in the policy impact of their work in the American context; that is, in terms of their advocacy to Washington about what ought to be done to achieve better proliferation control. Their failure lies in their unwillingness to assess the mixture of incentives and disincentives underlying proliferation in select country cases. United States academic writings on nonproliferation and proliferation are mostly U.S.-centric and ahistorical, if not antihistorical; and they are generally ignorant of actual strategic and cultural imperatives in the proliferating countries. These studies are also mostly repetitive. The subject of nonproliferation and proliferation is complex, but Washington politics respond to slogans and causes. National politicians in the United States have a tough time understanding these complex issues. When the motive is to induce political action, the tendency of several prominent U.S. scholars in this field is to simplify the issues and to recycle the conventional wisdom. This has led to bad scholarship and bad policy.

THE NPT REGIME AND PROLIFERATION, FROM THE 1970s TO 1995

The Intellectual and Policy Base of the NPT in the 1960s

The formal origins of the contemporary NPT regime lie in the early 1960s, when the NPT idea was first planted in international conference diplomacy by an Irish-sponsored U.N. resolution in 1961. The negotiations started in 1964, and the treaty was finalized in 1968 and came into effect in 1970. The NPT idea was a product of practical international circumstances. The nuclear activities of secondary powers (other than the Big Five) revealed the emergence of a second wave of nuclear proliferation in the post-1945 international system. The superpowers sensed a need to moderate their international rivalry and to shape an inter-bloc atomic power structure in the United Nations Security Council system, the presence of the principle of consensus could be utilized to accommodate the interests of the Big Five. These features characterized the historical, indeed the historic, setting in which the NPT idea crystallized into an agreed treaty.

The NPT was a major event in postwar great-power relations. The treaty revealed a consensus between the two superpowers to stabilize Cold War relations in part by an accommodation on atomic energy and nuclear proliferation questions. The NPT, in effect, embodied a superpower compromise after the failure of the United States to disarm the Soviet Union through the Baruch Plan and to prolong the U.S. atomic monopoly, and after the U.S. government rejected disarmament as a valid U.S. policy aim.[7] In the context of Cold War history, superpower cooperation in the International Atomic Energy Agency (IAEA) and on the NPT were positive events which helped stabilize bilateral relations. They revealed a commitment to East–West stability despite ideological polarity and, in effect, constituted a détente in Vienna which has never been lost since the early 1960s, despite the low-level disturbance in superpower relations in the mid-1970s as a result of Soviet expansionism in the Third World.

The treaty also revealed a consensus between the superpowers to establish a framework for a "technological condominium over international society," that is, to give legal and institutional shape to the difference between the nuclear haves and the have-nots.[8] Here we see an attempt to create an inter-bloc nuclear law[9] to rely on the disarmament of others to confirm the status quo. In agreeing to this approach, the superpowers accommodated each other's interests as well as those of the other great powers (i.e., as defined by permanent status and a veto right in the U.N. Security Council rather than by ability to actually manage world affairs). Having compromised and compensated each other's interests and prestige, the Big Five then proceeded to build legal and institutional barriers against the acquisition of nuclear weapons, and the power they bestow, by secondary (regional and middle) powers who were the likely challengers to the power and authority of the wartime powers. That the People's Republic of China denounced the NPT and accepted and benefited from its premise is a journey into hypocrisy. It revealed China's two faces in NPT affairs. It showed also the willingness of both superpowers to accommodate the strategic interests of China within the treaty, despite China's hostilities with both the United States and the Soviet Union at the time. One cannot think of a better example of the assertiveness and the validity of the classical principles of nineteenth century European diplomacy, that is, to organize compromise and compensation between the great powers and to institutionalize the great powers' right to intervene against lesser, middling countries, all in the name of world order.

In trying to curb the development of an outer ring of secondary nuclear powers which might one day individually or collectively challenge the authority of the Big Five or the Big Two, the NPT's fathers were governed by self-interest and fear of future uncertainties. Their strategy played on one of the three arguments which had governed, since the 1940s, the actions of the second ring of nuclear aspirants:

- They were reluctant to incur the heavy cost of nuclear arms.
- They did not accept the prospect of a permanent military or technological disadvantage.
- The practitioners felt no imminent strategic need to acquire nuclear arms given their threat perceptions at the time.

It is noteworthy that those who created the NPT, especially the Big Two, have repeatedly played on the first theme in international conference diplomacy, but not the second and third.

The Effects and Functions of the NPT Regime

Even though the superpowers were united in playing on the "high costs" theme and, by design, did not recognize the validity of the second and the third themes, the effects of a superpower's coordinated diplomatic intervention varied from country to country. The effects were both positive and negative. Invariably intra-elite security and economic debates on nuclear issues were stimulated.[10] National debates yield useful intelligence; here the function was intelligence acquisition. In some cases, such as West Germany and Sweden, weapon options were closed. Closed options reduced the margin of uncertainty for the long-term strategic planners in Washington and Moscow. Here the desire to enhance the superpowers' long-term military security and international political authority was in play. In some cases, hidden nuclear-weapon options became explicit or less opaque, as in Israel and India. The refusal of the holdouts was bad news for the NPT's creators, but it still offered good information. The public positions of the anti-NPT states confirmed the validity of the three arguments of a near-nuclear state referred to earlier. To the extent that the NPT created a dilemma in national decision making—as it did in India but not in Israel—ambivalence and controversy within a near-nuclear state was itself a form of nonproliferation, if ambivalence meant a refusal to make and deploy nuclear arms. Here the function of the NPT was to induce a domestic controversy in a non-NPT, near-nuclear state, and to open a line of permanent pressure against the holdouts in the future. The expectation was that a near-nuclear state might give in to such pressure whenever its political will waned. The NPT's function was psychological warfare. Beyond these functions lay a concern to create a new mandate for the IAEA. This is not an insignificant function of the NPT—without the NPT the IAEA's international position would be weak. The IAEA needs the NPT to be a viable international organization. Here the NPT's function was and remains to strengthen the IAEA and to create a godfatherly relationship between the superpowers and the IAEA.

Finally, the NPT regime's function is to regulate nuclear commerce among the nonnuclear-weapon states (NNWSs) who are parties to the NPT and to restrict the flow of sensitive nuclear materials, technology, and equipment to non-NPT states. The record of the NPT regime is mixed. South Africa was punished, and its share of the world uranium market was curtailed. India was punished for the 1974 test, and nuclear exports for its CANDU reactor were stopped. But, on the other hand, nuclear supply controls have not worked in relation to Israel and Pakistan, either because they were not seriously enforced or because of big loopholes in the trigger lists of the London Nuclear Suppliers' Group (NSG).

The NPT had a negative effect on regional powers who had embraced the nuclear path in the 1940s and who were outside the discipline of a military bloc leader. The NPT reinforced the reluctance of India, but not of Israel, to incur the high costs of a nuclear force, but the argument about costs had important side effects. It created an incentive for India to check for itself the costs of a nuclear test. This was one reason for its 1974 test. Moreover, by fanning the suspicion that the NPT's supporters wanted to deny to an outer ring of powers what was held vital for the security of the Big Five, the NPT reinforced the opposition to the treaty and its approach. The treaty produced a negative effect because it triggered national debates which created a public identification against the treaty, when no public opposition to nonproliferation had existed before in these countries. In the latter sense, national debates over the NPT helped to reinforce in-house government secret decisions to keep the weapon option alive in an ambiguous mode. In the numbers game, the NPT advocates won—approximately 140 states have accepted the treaty. However, the negative effects were revealed in a particular class of countries—those who aspired to regional or middle-power status; those who were active participants in regional disputes; those who did not like superpower intervention or super-condominium; those who were outside the discipline of military and economic groupings led by either superpower; and those who believed in national security via self-help and the selective exploitation of their links with the superpowers. In these important instances, the NPT neither aided the cause of nonproliferation nor helped strengthen security relations between the superpowers and the near-nuclear states.

The Institutional and Legal Framework of the NPT Regime

The regime has the following components:

- the NPT with approximately 140 adherents;
- the Tlatelolco Treaty with over 20 adherents, some being NPT states and some being non-NPT states;
- the South Pacific Nuclear Free Zone;
- the Nuclear Suppliers' Group, consisting mostly of NPT states;
- the IAEA;
- national nuclear export regulations.

Erosive Elements

All kinds of states—NWSs parties to the NPT (U.S., USSR, UK), NWSs which are not party to the NPT (France, China), and NNWSs parties to the NPT—swear allegiance to the NPT and the cause of nonproliferation; and NNWSs and near-nuclear states not party to the NPT also proclaim devotion to the nonproliferation cause. However, the actual practices of many states deviate significantly from their declaratory postures and poses. The significant events and trends that erode the efficacy of the NPT regime include the following:

- Implementation of Article IV of the NPT has been heavily restrictive. It has reduced credibility in the international covenant and reveals a lack of incentives for the NPT adherent.
- The Treaty of Tlatelolco rests on the principle of nonnuclearization (i.e., preventing the spread of nuclear weapons) as distinct from denuclearization (i.e., dismantling existing nuclear arsenals) on a regional basis. The treaty has not been fully implemented; instead, there are signs of latent proliferation in Argentina and Brazil. Its example has not been adopted in other crisis-prone regions. It lacks appeal as a model for other regions of conflict.
- The NSG is an exclusive group seeking denials in nuclear commerce to achieve a discriminatory supplier-managed regime. The NSG's regulations are riddled with loopholes; the group lacks an enforcement mechanism. Its activities are vulnerable to diplomatic and strategic interests which result in an application of rules or norms that is affected by politics and discrimination. The NSG lists have induced smuggling and search for autarky among non-NPT states. The NSG approach has produced short-term gain (feeling good; macho appearance; increasing popularity at home) and long-term difficulties (hardening the other side's opposition instead of changing the enemy's mind in your favor; worsening relations instead of improving them; fanning suspicions and triggering deceptions rather than confidence building).
- The IAEA is doing an excellent safeguarding job in nuclear installations that are under safeguards. It is working well where it is needed least. Its mandate does not run to military activities of NWSs—where nuclear disarmament

and controls are needed the most; and the IAEA lacks the ability and the mandate to monitor the activities of near-nuclear states. Furthermore, the IAEA has not been able to strengthen international cooperation and non-proliferation by developing various proposals for regional fuel cycle centers, spent fuel management, plutonium storage, and assurances of supply. The lack of action among NPT parties, and between NPT and non-NPT states, reveals deep and unbridgeable differences of approach and state interests that emphasize the regime's limitations and its preoccupation with damage limitation as opposed to regime development.

- National nuclear export control regulations differ; they are not universally standardized. They are also hard to enforce. Such controls depend on a number of factors: on voluntary compliance with national regulations by private firms; on the ability of customs authorities to intercept smuggling and to understand high-technology trade; and so on. Moreover, supplier states disagree among themselves about the full-scope safeguards issue, and the debate has been shelved.
- Vertical proliferation has not been curbed; Article VI of the NPT remains unfulfilled. Instead, vertical proliferation increased after the NPT came into effect. There has been no progress on a comprehensive test ban (CTB) or on security assurances. Without a CTB, the NPT is doomed.
- The Israeli attack on Iraq's safeguarded reactor raised doubts about the efficacy of the argument that IAEA safeguards created security and confidence between enemies.
- India has emerged as an example to non-NPT parties. It demonstrates, first, that autonomous nuclear development outside the NPT system is possible and, second, that the NPT is a discriminatory treaty.

These negative elements are balanced to an extent by several positive elements, that is, that a few more states have joined the NPT system; that no state has withdrawn from the treaty; that no state has tested a device after India in 1974; and that China is now in the NPT/IAEA camp.

THE WORLD WITHOUT THE NPT AFTER 1995?

The value of the NPT is debatable because the value of the objective of nonproliferation itself is debatable. The nonproliferation objective has become a sacred cow of contemporary international relations. Yet we must recognize that there is no convincing argument against proliferation, and there is no convincing argument in favor of nuclear disarmament in foreseeable circumstances.

The NPT system rests on several myths:

- *That proliferation is likely to be rapid and uncontrolled.* Actually it has been slow and controlled because of the stability in the matrix of calculations which govern the nuclear activities and nuclear policies of the near-nuclear states, among which are to avoid the high costs of nuclear arms, to avoid a regime which creates for them a permanent technological and military disadvantage, and to avoid a formal declaration of nuclear-weapon status unless their security needs makes that necessary.

- The second myth rests on the belief that proliferation is not inevitable but it is possible. The myth is that the *NPT could hold the line against proliferation.* Actually the NPT has not held the line among the hard-core proliferators.
- *That nuclear proliferation will lead to regional wars.* Actually, the evidence is that regional rivalries continue to be pursued by the use of conventional military force or by the deterrent use of military power; and regional rivals continue to seek nuclear power as a form of insurance. But this has not led to a nuclear war or to a temptation either to acquire nuclear weapons quickly or to use them quickly. Rather, regional nuclearization has been accompanied by the practice of restraint.
- *That no one can defy the superpowers.* Actually, the authority of the United States and the Soviet Union in proliferation affairs has been challenged repeatedly by U.S. allies as well as regional powers who are not bloc members.

However evident the fallacies they embody should be, such myths will continue to coexist with actual situations because policy constituencies in different countries can comfortably live with both myths and actualities.

Regional Proliferation

The world without the NPT in 1995 may be similar to the world with the NPT as far as regions of conflict are concerned. The NPT has not changed regional power relationships in the Indian subcontinent, the Persian Gulf, the Middle East, South America, and southern Africa, if we compare the world of the 1960s with that of the 1980s. For the powers in these regions, the NPT and associated topics are declaratory issues in international conference diplomacy. The NPT regime has not markedly changed regional power realities—that is, the distribution of economic and military power and the pattern of foreign policy and military alignments within the regions. From the point of view of the regional powers in these areas, NPT issues are like an empty drum which makes a lot of noise. Nuclear power is one component of national power; it is not a substitute for economic and military strength and political will. Regional issues in the 1990s are likely, as before, to be shaped by diplomatic and nonnuclear military means. For the near-nuclear states—except for Israel which is assumed to possess a large nuclear arsenal—the matrix of calculation, as indicated earlier, has been constant in the world, both in the period before the NPT was concluded and in that during the life of the NPT regime. The three factors in the matrix have functioned as the "permanently operating factors" at the political level. At the level of national technical activities, the NPT reinforced the determination to escape external technical and diplomatic intervention and to avoid the limitations of technical plateaus. Thus, we find that during the life of the NPT regime, Israel moved into H-bomb work, Pakistan gained a weapon-grade enrichment capability, India moved into dual-use activities in nuclear and space affairs, Brazil and Argentina acquired a weapon capability, and even tiny Taiwan has continually demonstrated nuclear ambitions which the United States, with all its assets in the area, has been unable totally to eliminate.

However, even if the NPT collapsed in 1995, it is not inevitable that new nuclear states will mushroom or that near-nuclear states will abandon their nuclear activities in their present ambiguous mode and seek a declared weapon status. This may happen; but then it may not. It will depend on the exact circumstances and the matrix of compulsions and calculations at the time. "Going nuclear" is a serious political act. It has never been lightly taken in any known case of actual nuclear activity—as distinct from rhetorical ambition and declarations, such as those that have emanated from Libya. If the present day regional powers are able to incrementally structure regional power relations in their favor, if the regional powers remain convinced that the superpowers are harmful influences in regional affairs, and if the present trends in the power politics in the key regions continue, then the present matrix of calculations of the near-nuclear states is likely to remain unchanged by developments in 1995.

The Superpowers and Conflict-Prone Regions

The superpowers lack new options for 1995 because their international political authority is on the decline and they have no new ideas to strengthen the nonproliferation regime. They have already revealed their hand in various international meetings, and the determined proliferator is now on guard. Furthermore, as U.S.– Pakistani, Soviet–Indian, and other relationships between the major powers and potential proliferators demonstrate, nonproliferation is a secondary issue in the cluster of issues which shape various bilateral relations; that is, economic relations, defense cooperation, and political ties take precedence over NPT and nonproliferation issues. (Even though Canadian–Indian relations suffered badly in the mid-1970s as a result of the Indian test and Canadian sanctions, since the mid-1980s the nuclear issue has disappeared from their bilateral agenda and other issues have taken center stage.) That is, there is no obvious linkage between nonproliferation and other issues. The superpowers' cooperation in nonproliferation affairs, in the form of routine bilateral consultations, is likely to continue, as before, but it is also likely to be of dubious value, as before. Institutional forces in the United States are indifferent to the issues of nonproliferation and nuclear proliferation; and they oppose important specific measures to implement the provision of the NPT. For example, the U.S. military neither cares for nonproliferation nor worries about nuclear proliferation in regions of conflict. It opposes a CTB, nuclear-weapon-free zones (as in the South Pacific), and even confidence-building agreements against attacks on nuclear facilities. (The latter bump into first-strike options and immunized nuclear facilities could become safe havens for enemy troops.)

Comprehensive Test Ban

There is now no obvious linkage between the NPT and a CTB. The chances of moving toward a CTB regime are practically nil. Given a choice between opting for a CTB or losing the NPT, a U.S. president would choose the latter. No scientific or political constituency of any weight in the American political system favors a CTB. In other words, the agreement on intermediate-range nuclear forces is not a step toward a CTB. Likewise, issues such as the increased risks of nuclear war and nuclear terrorism are likely to remain on the back burners of the agenda of the superpowers and the regional powers.

Multilateral Implications

The IAEA will probably continue to be active in safeguards work in the 1990s. However, its status as the lead member of the nonproliferation orchestra is already on a slippery downward slope. As orders for nuclear reactors continue to decline worldwide, the IAEA's role as the directorate of global nuclear energy activities is also likely to decline. It is well to remember that the primary motive of the United States in the 1950s and the 1960s, when the IAEA was created and strengthened, was to promote its nuclear sales, and safeguards were cosmetic effects in the sales campaign. This history of U.S. atomic energy policies shows that the United States does not have a permanent constituency supporting safeguards; it is a peripheral one, and it is connected to other interests. Because of the failure of NPT states to agree on additional measures, the IAEA is not likely to obtain additional non-proliferation assignments. If the NPT collapses, it will no doubt injure the IAEA's mandate and diminish its international political significance. However, this trend has already set in and it appears irreversible. Judging by the history of the record of performance of multilateral institutions that form the NPT regime—the NSG, NPT review conferences, the International Nuclear Fuel Cycle Evaluation meetings, U.N. special sessions on disarmament—past experience does not reveal any further use for multilateral approaches to nonproliferation. Multilateral meetings waste time, money, and human resources and should not be planned unless there is a prior meeting of minds about the nature of the problem and the political and technical viability of the proposed solution. None exists with respect to the definition of the strategic and cultural motives of nuclear proliferation and nonproliferation.

New Nuclear Suppliers

New nuclear suppliers, like new arms traders, are likely to eventually find ways to fit into the world market and to avoid politically motivated export controls. The interest of the West Europeans in nuclear trade as well as trade in conventional armaments is likely to continue in the 1990s. This is not worrisome, as trade is good business and capitalism is the foundation of Western civilization. In some instances, more trade may be better. For instance, if Pakistan is induced to sell its enriched uranium until it is able to use it for its civil nuclear energy program in the 1990s, that would reduce concerns about its weapon program. Here trade could obtain valuable foreign exchange for Pakistan and aid U.S. nonproliferation objectives.

Policy Actions

The most important action that national leaders can take is to relax their position on the nuclear proliferation issue and to put it on the back burner. Western political leaders should instruct in-house government experts to anticipate, monitor, and report on developments and to develop in-house teams of area experts and technical experts to examine the long-term trends and their implications for regional and world power.

The NPT should be allowed to expire peacefully, and the NPT's advocates should be allowed to retire gracefully by 1995 for having failed to deliver the goods even though they were given a big window of opportunity comprising twenty-five years of antiproliferation activity. This is comparable to the time allowed to the CIA in Iran (1953 to 1979), and it is far greater than the time for Afghanistan operations (1979 to 1988).

The most desirable outcome is a world of nuclear proliferation with two rings of power: the inner ring consists of the present-day five proliferators. The best service the U.S. government can do for world stability is to organize command, control, and communications improvement seminars for all those who must have nuclear arms so that the danger of an accidental war is minimized even further. The existence of the NPT is a freak event in modern international relations. Nonproliferation has lasted for a while because nonproliferators were able to create a mirage of future international security and a great world bargain between the nuclear haves and the have-nots. This approach rested on workable misunderstandings of the 1960s which are no longer available.

NOTES AND REFERENCES

1. For data about their overall technical activities, see L. S. Spector, *Going Nuclear* (Cambridge, Mass.: Ballinger, 1987).
2. See A. Kapur, *Pakistan's Nuclear Development* (London: Croom Helm, 1987).
3. I have repeatedly emphasized this point in my works on nuclear proliferation, but unfortunately most arms controllers in this field find it difficult to explicitly recognize the cultural dimension of the strategic behavior of states and the need to make proliferation studies history specific.
4. For origins and case histories the following sources are informative and insightful: for Israel, see L. Beaton and J. Maddox, *The Spread of Nuclear Weapons* (New York: Praeger, 1962), chap. 11; for Argentina, see J. A. Sabato, "Atomic Energy in Argentina: A Case History," *World Development*, vol. 1, no. 8 (August 1973), pp. 23–37; for South Africa, see A. R. Newby–Fraser, *Chain Reaction* (Pretoria: The Atomic Energy Board, 1979); and for India, see A. Kapur, *India's Nuclear Option* (New York: Praeger, 1979), and S. Bhatia, *India's Nuclear Bomb* (Bombay: Vikas, 1979).
5. Beaton and Maddox, *Nuclear Weapons*, p. 185.
6. A. Buchan, ed., *A World of Nuclear Powers?* (The American Assembly, 1966), pp. 9 and 11. [Author's emphasis.]

7. In 1952, disarmament was rejected as a goal. See R. Pringle and J. Spigelman, *The Nuclear Barons* (New York: Holt, Rinehart & Winston, 1981), p. 112.

8. M. Wight, *Power Politics* (New York: Penguin, 1979), p. 286.

9. E. McWhinney, "Soviet and Western International Law and the Cold War in the Era of Bipolarity," in R. A. Falk and S. H. Mendlovitz, eds., *The Strategy of World Order*, vol. 2 (New York: World Law Fund, 1966), p. 215.

10. For example, see the cases in Buchan, *Nuclear Powers*.

12

Should India Sign the NPT?

Raju G. C. Thomas

THE CURRENT CRISIS

Would India be more secure within or outside the NPT? Would Indian security interests be enhanced if, in 1995, the NPT collapsed or was replaced by a new or amended treaty structure? Should India sign the NPT or strive to undermine or destroy the treaty, or to replace it with an alternative regime that could better serve Indian interests? Such questions have always been significant, because India is one of the most outspoken critics of the NPT regime. However, the question of whether India should sign the treaty took on particular significance at the beginning of 1989 when news reports in India alleged that Pakistan had acquired and stockpiled nuclear weapons or was about to acquire such weapons. To be sure, such Indian allegations have been made periodically over the last ten years, but the problem has taken on greater urgency and credibility at the present time because the Indian reports are supplemented by those from American sources.[1] According to the American reports, the administration of President George Bush may have to discontinue its economic and military aid to Pakistan unless it can certify that Pakistan did not possess nuclear weapons. Such a certification, as required by the Pressler Amendment, would be difficult to issue based on the present evidence available to the U.S. government.[2]

Other Indian reports have claimed that China was arranging a nuclear test for Pakistan at its Lop Nor testing ground.[3] This speculation was based on the visit to China in November 1988 of Abdul Qadir Khan, one of Pakistan's chief nuclear scientists and head of the Kahuta nuclear enrichment plant. Pakistan and China had signed a nuclear cooperation agreement in 1986, and Indian news sources have

Raju G. C. Thomas • Professor of Political Science, Marquette University, Milwaukee, Wisconsin.

claimed that China had assisted the Pakistani nuclear-weapon program at Kahuta by providing the design of a tested fission bomb. Not even the return of civilian democracy under Prime Minister Benazir Bhutto has served to alleviate these fears in India.

Initial Indian suspicions and fears of Pakistan's motives had arisen from Pakistan's earlier unsuccessful efforts in the 1970s to acquire from France a reprocessing plant to be located at Chasma under the leadership of Munir Khan of the Pakistan Atomic Energy Commission. Later, in the 1980s, Pakistan's successful acquisition of a uranium enrichment facility located at Kahuta under the leadership of Abdul Qadir Khan—before it had set up a serious nuclear energy program—raised serious doubts about Pakistan's ultimate nuclear intentions.[4] While such plants may be considered legitimate needs for acquiring control of the nuclear fuel cycle and self-sufficiency in nuclear energy, they also provide a country with weapon-usable plutonium and uranium.

Perhaps Pakistan, and Abdul Qadir Khan in particular, may be deliberately feeding the Indian belief about its weapon capability in order to provoke India into taking the first step toward acquiring nuclear weapons and thereby justifying a Pakistani decision to go nuclear. On the other hand, Pakistan has pointed out that India had already tested an atomic device in 1974 and has stockpiled weapon-grade plutonium. Meanwhile, both sides claim that they do not possess nuclear weapons but are merely pursuing a peaceful nuclear energy program. Neither side believes the other.

If the government of Rajiv Gandhi believes that Pakistan has acquired the bomb, it will find it difficult not to follow suit. Through such a cycle of fears and preemptive policy responses, the seeds of horizontal nuclear proliferation have been sown on the subcontinent. The relationship between India and Pakistan at present is probably best described as a case of "mutual nuclear brinksmanship," where each side is striving or threatening to become a nuclear-weapon power to preempt the other side's ability to obtain such a capability, without actually carrying out that threat. The ability to sustain indefinitely such a precarious strategy of brinksmanship would call for considerable political dexterity on both sides. More likely, each believing that the other side has covertly stockpiled nuclear weapons—a situation of suspected mutual "bombs in the basement"—both sides would be propelled into an overt and full-fledged nuclear arms race with all its attendant adverse consequences for regional security and the international nonproliferation regime.

One thing is clear—U.S. nonproliferation policy in South Asia has not worked. Just before and during the Carter administration, a series of internal legislation was enacted to stem the proliferation tide in South Asia. In 1976 and 1977, the Symington and Glenn Amendments were added to the Foreign Assistance Act to prohibit American economic and military aid to countries attempting to acquire reprocessing and enrichment capabilities for weapons purposes. Both amendments were essentially directed at Pakistan. In 1978, Congress passed the Nuclear Nonproliferation Act (NNPA), which called on the U.S. government to withhold cooperation on peaceful nuclear programs from countries that would not allow IAEA inspections of their nuclear facilities. This act was expected to be enforced retroactively, the target clearly being the thirty-year Indo–American agreement of 1963 that had assured the supply of enriched uranium to the two General Electric light-water nuclear power reactors set up at Tarapur near Bombay. In accordance with the NNPA, a shipment of enriched uranium was withheld by the Carter administration. India claimed that the United States had violated this international agreement. The United States claimed a violation of the agreement's peaceful nuclear uses clause because American heavy water was allegedly used in the Canadian-supplied Cirus research reactor from which India had obtained the plutonium for the 1974 atomic test. Subsequently, to circumvent the NNPA and congressional pressures, and to fulfill the contractual obligations arising from the 1963 agreement, the Reagan administration allowed India to obtain the enriched uranium from France.

The Reagan administration generally took a laissez-faire approach to the pro-liferation issue in order to maintain Pakistani cooperation and goodwill in the pursuit of the U.S. policy of assisting the Afghan Mujahideen in their war against Soviet occupation forces in Afghanistan. The reward for such Pakistani cooperation was large-scale economic and military aid to Pakistan, the largest account of U.S. aid to any country after Israel and Egypt, and a U.S. policy of minimizing the seriousness of Pakistan's clandestine nuclear-weapon program. The Reagan policy succeeded enormously on the Afghan front, but it contributed heavily to the sham-bles now found in the proliferation situation in South Asia. While India had ended its efforts to acquire nuclear weapons after its 1974 test of an atomic device, Pakistan had accelerated its own nuclear-weapon program, leading to the present posture of nuclear brinksmanship.

Can the nuclear dilemmas of South Asia be resolved by an Indian decision to sign the NPT along with Pakistan? After all, Pakistan has declared on several occasions that it was prepared to sign the NPT, or to establish South Asia as a nuclear-free zone, if India would accept the same terms or arrangement India, a long-standing critic of the NPT, has constantly rejected such offers on the grounds that the nuclear proliferation issue is a global problem that includes the spread and growth of nuclear-weapon arsenals among "haves" as well as "have-nots," and that the NPT and the nuclear-free zone proposals do not resolve the problem of the nuclear threat to India posed by China, a nuclear-weapon state (NWS) and rival of India that has not signed the NPT.

INDIA'S NUCLEAR CHOICES

The question of whether India should become a nuclear-weapon power initially became a burning issue in response to the first Chinese atomic test in October 1964. That test was conducted just two years after the sudden Sino–Indian war of October–December 1962, when the Indian army was crushed by Chinese forces along their Himalayan frontiers. Thereafter, India participated in the negotiations that led up to the formulation of the 1968 nonproliferation treaty but then refused to sign because of the discriminatory clauses between the nuclear haves and have-nots. Subsequently, a second burning issue emerged as to whether India should sign the

NPT along with several other states of the East, West, and Third World blocs who have acceded to the treaty at various times over the last twenty years. With the exception of the 1974 atomic test, the Indian government's policy has been not to build bombs, but also not to sign the NPT in order to keep open its nuclear-weapon option.

A rather unusual option has also been proposed by some Indian observers that would have India become an NWS and sign the NPT as a member of the nuclear haves.[5] K. Subrahmanyam has argued, for instance, that "India should exercise its nuclear option before 1995, before the so-called Non-Proliferation Treaty is attempted to be made permanent. The two steps are not contradictory as many one-dimensional minds argue."[6] It is not clear whether such an option is permissible or feasible. After all, the other nuclear-threshold states, including Pakistan, could then do the same, making the NPT meaningless. Such ideas may be put forward "tongue-in-cheek" in India to demonstrate the absurdity of the NPT's categorization of states on the basis of whether they possess nuclear weapons.

The NPT, of course, is not the only international legal arrangement that could be adopted to curb proliferation in South Asia. In lieu of the NPT, a regional treaty could be reached that would establish South Asia as a nuclear-weapon-free zone, along the lines of the 1967 Treaty of Tlatelolco that has sought to establish Latin America as a nuclear-weapon-free zone. With the exception of Cuba, which has refused to sign the treaty until the United States vacates the Guantanamo naval base, all the states of Latin America and the five nuclear powers have signed the treaty. However, Argentina has not ratified the treaty, and Brazil and Chile have not as yet waived its "entry-into-force" requirements. Such a regional alternative would be virtually equivalent to adhering to the NPT, and it may be considered a significant step by India and Pakistan toward the global nonproliferation arrangement represented by the NPT. Opposition to a regional arrangement establishing South Asia as a nuclear-weapon-free zone appears to be less intense than opposition to the NPT but is sufficient at present to make the prospects here seem just as hopeless. Such a zone without China does not resolve some of India's basic arguments against the NPT, nor does it resolve the problem of discrimination between nuclear haves and have-nots. For these reasons, arguments for or against the NPT will be assumed to cover Tlatelolco-type regional solutions or other NPT substitutes so long as they bar the acquisition of nuclear weapons by nonnuclear states.

In present circumstances, where Pakistan is on the brink of a nuclear-weapon capability or may have already acquired it, there are then three basic options that need to be reconsidered. The first option would be the continuation of India's present policy of neither the bomb nor the NPT, which involves resisting both the internal pro-bomb and external pro-NPT lobbies. The second option of going for the bomb would involve the future management by the government of India of a two-way nuclear arms race between India and its traditional rivals, China and Pakistan. The third option of signing the NPT or an NPT-substitute would call for a significant amount of political willpower on the part of the Indian government to reverse its present policy, and to accept a calculated risk that adherence to the NPT may not curb the covert stockpiling of nuclear weapons on the Pakistani side.

Before considering each option, it should be noted that at least in the public debate in India, and with only occasional exceptions, alternative policy choices do not appear to have been fully explored either inside or outside parliament. There may have been more extensive discussions that looked at the full range of policy options within the Indian foreign and defense policy-making bureaucracies, although little is known about their deliberations. To begin with, over the years, there has grown a monolithic and unified resistance to the NPT as a worthless, if not a harmful, international treaty.[7] This attitude toward the NPT tends to span the political spectrum from left to right, among the Congress and the Janata parties (in its various split factions and political reincarnations), among the various socialist, communist, and religious parties (at least Hindu) such as the old Jan Sangh and its successors. If there is any support for the NPT, it may lie in a few pockets of intellectual institutions in some of the major cities of India.[8]

There is, however, a polarization between those who advocate that India stay with the policy of strategic ambiguity by maintaining a nuclear-weapon option, and those who advocate the bold step forward of becoming a nuclear-weapon state. In India, the first group may be labeled the "doves," and the second group the "hawks." This may seem surprising to overseas observers who perceive the Indian government's resistance to the NPT and periodic threats to go nuclear as a hawkish posture. But in a situation where the pro-treaty advocates are virtually invisible, all that the Indian government can do for the time being is to resist pressures from those who advocate the bomb. One leading Indian strategist, who has persistently advocated the bomb for India, declared at a conference in New Delhi in January 1989 that the government of India was the greatest lobby against the bomb in India.[9] Others have contended that the Indian government is doing what it does best—undertaking no action when bold action is needed. In fact, there appears to be little or no crossover between the "pro-bomb" and "pro-option" lobbies in India, each perceiving the other's position to embody inconclusive merits.[10]

The positions appear to have crystallized on both sides, with each advocating over time the same persistent and perennial arguments under changing strategic circumstances. On the other hand, even those Indian strategic analysts who strongly disagree with the pro-bomb hawks prefer to distance themselves from the NPT, either out of the conviction that it is a seriously flawed treaty, or because they feel that their credibility to argue against the bomb may be lost in a domestic political environment that is overwhelmingly hostile to the NPT. Thus, the NPT, signed by over 135 nonnuclear nations of the world, appears to have no lobby in India.

Let us now turn to each of the policy options available to the government of India.

STRATEGIC AMBIGUITY

The Indian policy of maintaining a nuclear-weapon option was perceived to be a middle strategic ground between the extremes of inaction and action. The formal renunciation of nuclear weapons by signing the NPT has been considered unacceptable because the potential threat from a nuclear China during times of crisis on the subcontinent may call for a change of policy in the future.[11] Following the 1962 Sino–Indian war and the Chinese atomic test in 1964, arguments for countering the growth of the Chinese nuclear-weapon capability were strong. China's ultimatum to India during the 1965 Indo–Pakistani war strengthened the claims at the time of the pro-bomb lobby in India, then mainly led by the right-wing pro-Hindu party, the Jan Sangh. But as the Chinese threat receded in the late 1960s, and the hostility of both the Soviet Union and the United States toward China was apparent, the need for embarking on a nuclear-weapon program was considered unnecessary. At that stage an Indian nuclear-weapon program might have aggravated the Chinese threat without providing India with a credible nuclear deterrent. While China was capable of hitting major Indian cities from New Delhi to Calcutta with aircraft taking off from Tibetan bases, India was a long way from possessing a delivery system capable of reaching China's major cities of Beijing and Shanghai or its industrial bases elsewhere.

There were also serious problems seen in the text of the NPT. Thus, while India took part in the negotiations that drew up the draft of the NPT, it subsequently refused to sign the treaty.[12] From the Indian standpoint, the treaty was not only discriminatory, but it formalized the existing groups of nuclear haves and have-nots indefinitely. Article III, which called for supervision and inspection of all nuclear and ancillary facilities by the International Atomic Energy Agency, was seen further as a violation of the sovereignty of nations, a condition that the existing nuclear powers until recently were unwilling to accept.[13] Article VI, which called on the five nuclear powers to negotiate disarmament in "good faith," has appeared to be a dead letter—the nuclear arms race has continued unabated as newer and more sophisticated weapons of mass destruction are periodically introduced into the stockpiles of the nuclear states. Meanwhile, little progress has been made in reaching an agreement on a comprehensive test ban treaty.

India has argued repeatedly that the growth and complexity of newer forms of nuclear weapons among the haves (vertical proliferation) pose as great, if not greater, a danger to international security as the potential spread of nuclear weapons among the have-nots (horizontal proliferation). Yet there is insufficient attention being paid to this problem. And surely, if more, and more complex, nuclear weapons are perceived by the nuclear powers to be the only antidote to perceptions of nuclear threats from the other NWSs, then the same argument must apply to the nonnuclear-weapon states (NNWSs) that may face nuclear threats from across their borders in the future. Such is the case of the nuclear threat to India from China, a state that has not signed the NPT or the Limited Test Ban Treaty of 1963, and with whom India fought an unexpected war in 1962. The best that India could do under the circumstances was voluntarily to refrain from acquiring nuclear weapons, but also to keep its option to do so if the situation became intolerable in the future.

The problem of proliferation, according to India, may only be resolved globally. India cannot give up its nuclear-weapon option unless China gets rid of its nuclear stockpile. However, China will not give up its nuclear weapons unless the Soviet Union does so; and the Soviet Union will not do so unless the three Western nuclear powers disarm. Nuclear proliferation did not begin with the Indian atomic test of 1974 but much earlier, when the Soviet Union undertook its first atomic test in 1949 to counter the American atomic weapon capability which, in turn, had begun with the first U.S. test at Alamogordo in 1945.[14] Stemming the forward advance of the nuclear proliferation chain—real or potential—thus calls for unraveling the chain backwards all the way to the Soviet Union and the United States.

The NPT was seen as an unsatisfactory document for other legal and technical reasons. Articles I and II, on the one hand, and Articles IV and V, on the other, are perceived to be in contradiction to each other. According to the first two articles, NWSs should not provide assistance or encouragement to NNWSs to acquire nuclear weapons, while the NNWSs should make no efforts, domestic or international, to acquire such weapons. On the other hand, the fourth and fifth articles encourage the sharing and transfer of peaceful nuclear technology between the haves and have-nots, including the "peaceful applications of nuclear explosions." A basic problem with the aims of these provisions is the difficulty of distinguishing nuclear programs that are intended for civilian purposes from those which are intended for, or which may be diverted to, military purposes.

Such problems are further compounded by Article X, which allows any signatory to the NPT to withdraw giving only three-months notice if it perceives that "extraordinary events . . . have jeopardized the supreme interests" of that country. Theoretically, a signatory state may embark upon an IAEA-supervised nuclear energy program, allowing it to acquire enrichment and reprocessing facilities more readily, and subsequently may withdraw on the grounds of "extraordinary" changes in its strategic environment.

Hence, the government of India has followed a policy of strategic ambiguity by maintaining its nuclear-weapon option. Under this policy, India will not make nuclear weapons but will constantly threaten to do so, and, indeed, carried out the threat once in 1974. Such a posture carries a dual purpose: first, by serving notice to the nuclear powers that it needed adequate security guarantees against regional nuclear threats to itself; and second, by pressuring the nuclear powers into reducing and eventually eliminating their stockpiles, thereby reducing the dangers of a global nuclear holocaust in which nonnuclear states would also be engulfed.

A BOLD STEP FORWARD

Arguments that India should acquire nuclear weapons have been made periodically since the Chinese atomic test of October 1964. These pressures intensified during the East Pakistani revolt against West Pakistan and the ensuing civil war that began in March 1971. That crisis ended with the Indo–Pakistani war of December 1971 and the creation of the new state of Bangladesh. During this prolonged crisis that kept India and Pakistan on the brink of war, efforts by President Richard Nixon and Secretary of State Henry Kissinger to seek the normalization of U.S. relations with China suddenly raised doubts about the credibility of external nuclear "guarantees" against China. The signing of the Indo–Soviet Treaty of Peace and Friendship in August 1971 may be interpreted as the immediate Indian reaction to these global realignments among the major powers.[15] The treaty was intended to paralyze Chinese threats to intervene in the looming Indo–Pakistani conflict by formalizing Indo–Soviet ties, thereby increasing the risk of Soviet military intervention against China on behalf of India.

However, in spite of the treaty, doubts remained about the long-term effects of the new Sino–American relationship on India's nuclear security. The nuclear insurance provided by the hostility of both superpowers toward China before 1971 now seems to have been reduced to a more dubious Soviet nuclear guarantee alone. Because the United States and the Soviet Union were perceived to neutralize each other with their retaliatory strike capabilities, potential Chinese nuclear threats in the future have appeared to be more credible.

The intrusion of the American nuclear-powered aircraft carrier *Enterprise* into the Bay of Bengal in a show of force against India during the Indo–Pakistani war of December 1971 further strengthened the case for the acquisition of nuclear weapons by India. An Indian decision, therefore, was made in 1972 to go for the bomb, and the 1974 atomic test may be seen as the delayed response by Prime Minister Indira Gandhi to evolving global realignments. Note also, however, that the decision to detonate in May 1974 may have been directed primarily at a domestic Indian audience to shore up the prime minister's sagging prestige.

Pakistan's military defeat and its dismemberment produced a similar decision in 1972 on the part of Prime Minister Zulfikar Ali Bhutto to acquire nuclear weapons. This policy was accelerated after the Indian atomic test in 1974. While the Western outcry against India's "peaceful nuclear explosion" immediately reduced the Indian stockpile from one to zero and appeared to have ended the prospect of an Indian nuclear-weapon program, Pakistan proceeded headlong into various avenues for acquiring a nuclear-weapon capability. It first sought to acquire a reprocessing plant from France to provide it with plutonium but was frustrated by pressures from President Carter to prevent the sale; it then sought more successfully to put together a uranium enrichment plant through the clandestine transfer of various sensitive machines and parts from Western Europe, the United States, and Canada.[16] Other Indian reports in the late 1970s and early 1980s indicated that the Pakistani nuclear bomb was being developed with uranium supplies from Niger and with indirect Libyan and Saudi financing.[17] As suggested, these developments climaxed in 1988 and 1989 when Indian reports claimed that Pakistan had produced a few bombs based on the uranium enrichment process or, at least, had acquired the capability to assemble the bomb at short notice.

Herein lies the case for the bomb in India.[18] While it was one thing to accept the risk of a Chinese nuclear threat all these years without an Indian counter-response, it was quite another to expect India to ignore a nuclear China as well as a Pakistan with "bombs-in-the-basement," Israeli style. With further allegations that India's two traditional adversaries colluded in the design and development of the Pakistani nuclear-weapon program, the present situation now appears to be intolerable.

If the overwhelming Indian assessment is that Pakistan is covertly stockpiling nuclear weapons, whether untested or secretly tested at China's Lop Nor site, then India has little choice but to embark on an overt nuclear-weapon program. At this point, merely maintaining a nuclear-weapon option has no significant deterrent or defense value since the concept of defense mobilization carries little meaning in a nuclear confrontation. Although it was possible for India to mobilize during and immediately after the 1962 Sino–Indian war, in the future a nuclear threat from Pakistan or China, or both, would force India to capitulate, unless it possessed nuclear weapons as well.

To be sure, the acquisition of nuclear weapons in itself would provide no security value unless India could establish and manage a stable two-way nuclear deterrent relationship with China and Pakistan. This too was perceived to be a feasible proposition. The "Indo–Chinese" and "Indo–Pakistani" nuclear relationships would resemble that between the Soviet Union and the United States on the one hand, and the Soviet Union and China on the other. In the Indo–Chinese case, the relationship would be one of mutual assured destruction, especially because India has the capability to produce intermediate-range ballistic missiles immediately, and intercontinental ballistic missiles by the late 1990s through technologies being obtained from its civilian space program. In the Indo–Pakistani case, the relationship would be one of dominance and control on the assumption that India's larger resource capability and more advanced nuclear know-how would enable it to maintain an overwhelming nuclear superiority at all times. Pakistan dare not attack, while India need not attack because it could inflict a massive and unacceptable retaliatory blow.

The argument for a nuclear-weapon program in India rests also on the assumption that Indian and Pakistani decision-makers are no less rational and responsible than American, Soviet, or Chinese decision-makers.[19] Indeed, the development of nuclear weapons by both India and Pakistan might eliminate direct wars, both nuclear and conventional, between the two sides altogether. The parallel here would be the absence of direct conventional wars between the United States and the Soviet Union because of the fear of escalation to nuclear levels. Evidence of India's and Pakistan's ability to act cautiously and rationally may be seen in the agreement not to attack each other's nuclear installations signed by Prime Ministers Rajiv Gandhi and Benazir Bhutto in Islamabad in December 1988. Nuclear weapons will introduce further restraint.

Would not disavowals of nuclear-weapon intentions by a democratic Pakistan under Prime Minister Benazir Bhutto weaken the case for the Indian bomb? The pro-bomb lobby's argument here is that Prime Minister Bhutto is still weak. The military is still in charge on all military matters, including the nature and type of defense allocations, especially for the nuclear-weapon program; this was the price of a return to civilian leadership, especially under a woman prime minister whose following is largely in the Sind and not in the Punjab, which provides 80 percent of the Pakistani armed forces. In any case, a Pakistani nuclear-weapon capability will not disappear, regardless of whether a military or civilian government is in control.

A case could also be made for a covert Indian nuclear-weapon program to match the Pakistani program—a case of going for the bomb while denying it—

resulting in a mutual bombs-in-the-basement strategic posture. Instead of officially and abruptly declaring itself a nuclear-weapon state, the government of India could simply let the present situation drift and slide into the next stage. There are problems, however, with engaging in a covert nuclear arms race. Apart from the ethical arguments that could be advanced against such a policy, and the constant international accusations of deceit that India would face, such a relationship faces a great danger of breakdown. Bombs on either side are not supposed to exist, but because both sides are aware that they do, and are also uncertain about the extent of each other's capabilities, there will be a greater temptation to launch preemptive attacks. Such an Indo–Pakistani nuclear relationship would establish a climate of paranoia and constant recrimination on the subcontinent and would be highly unstable. While it would be one thing to have failures in communication between the two sides leading to armed border skirmishes and conventional wars as in 1965, such a failure at the nuclear level would be disastrous. Moreover, no nuclear arms control talks may be conducted in the region on arms that are officially nonexistent. Hence, if India is to manage a two-way nuclear arms race with Pakistan and China successfully, going for the bomb should be a clear and explicit policy.

Considerations of international and domestic prestige may also play a part in arguments for the bomb in India, although they are not as important as they would be in the case of Brazil. If they were, then in combination with security arguments, India would have gone nuclear long ago. Many of the arguments for the bomb based on prestige arise from anger at the United States for its treatment of India on the same level as Pakistan instead of, more appropriately, China. While the United States has shown a great deal of sensitivity about providing arms to Taiwan in order not to alienate China, India has constantly alleged that various U.S. administrations have attempted to maintain a military balance between India and Pakistan, a nation once a fourth of India's size, and now only an eighth. India has always felt that it has never received much respect from the West compared to China, although in population, size, and economic potential, India and China are comparable.

To be sure, going nuclear in India would provoke a similar decision in Pakistan. But as with the present trend in the conventional military balance, India's superior economic resources and technological manpower would simply overwhelm Pakistan's nuclear capability and match that of China, whose nuclear technology is considered to be less sophisticated than that of India. On the other hand, the nuclearization of the subcontinent, at least in the perception of some advocates of the bomb, would bring greater international attention that would benefit all the states of the region.[20]

A BOLD STEP BACKWARD

Despite the arguments that may be advanced in support of maintaining a nuclear-weapon option or becoming a nuclear-weapon power, on balance India is best served by adhering to the nonproliferation treaty. There are a variety of arguments for signing the NPT. First, unlike going for the bomb, which may lock India into a permanent two-way nuclear arms race with Pakistan and China, signing the NPT is a reversible step. If the policy proves to be unsatisfactory—that is, if it does not halt and reverse a covert Pakistani nuclear-weapon program—India could withdraw from the NPT in the future as permitted under Article X. But the value and effectiveness of the NPT ought to be tested before the irreversible step forward is taken. Such a step backward would not constitute a radical change from the earlier policy because India has not embarked on a nuclear-weapon program as yet. On the other hand, in the present circumstances of an ambiguous Pakistani nuclear posture, India does not obtain the advantages of being either a nuclear-weapon power or of being a party to the NPT.

With the exception of the 1974 atomic test, India has behaved as though it had already signed the NPT. To be sure, India has not allowed inspection of its indigenously built nuclear power plants by the IAEA. There are occasional allegations that weapon-usable plutonium derived from the Kalapakam atomic power plant (KAPP) at Madras is being stored and is ready for nuclear-weapon use if necessary.[21] Unlike the Canadian-assisted Rajasthan atomic power plants and the American-supplied Tarapur atomic power plants, KAPP is not under IAEA safeguards. And there is the exception in India's behavior when the Canadian-supplied Cirus research reactor was alleged to have been used to obtain the plutonium for the 1974 atomic test. For the rest, India has voluntarily adhered to most of the terms of the NPT, especially those pertaining to the construction of bombs and the transfer of sensitive technology to other potential proliferators. The Indian rejection of Libya's request for nuclear assistance in 1974 is a case in point. If India plans to go on doing this, then it might as well sign the NPT and avoid the periodic pressures and harassment from some members of the international community, especially the Western powers.

Second, signing the NPT and relying on a large conventional military force may be a more cost-effective way of dealing with the threats posed by China and Pakistan than going for the bomb. The argument advanced by General De Gaulle at one time that the acquisition of nuclear weapons by France would reduce its overall military costs by allowing for heavy reductions in conventional forces has not yet been apparent among any of the existing nuclear powers, including France. No doubt, the relative cost of strategic nuclear forces are much less than the maintenance of large-scale conventional forces, but the former has not usually displaced the latter. Again, it is possible to argue that the size and cost of conventional forces might have been even larger if it were not for nuclear forces. However, the lesson of China is particularly significant for India, because Chinese conventional forces have remained the same or even increased as China continued to build up its nuclear forces. Nuclear forces have been rarely treated as a substitute for conventional forces, but more often as a supplement.

One basic criterion in India for the allocation of resources to the armed services and their military programs is the degree to which their claims tend to be labor-intensive or capital-intensive.[22] Thus, the Indian Army has always been able to muster the bulk of the resource allocations for defense because it emphasizes the employment of manpower on a larger scale, and relatively smaller and cheaper weapon systems produced in bulk, than either the Indian Air Force or the Indian

Navy. In a country with an abundance of cheap labor, it makes more economic sense to emphasize army programs, even if this may sometimes distort the essential military strategy that needs to be adopted to deal with the external strategic environment. In this context, programs in India for nuclear weapons and associated delivery systems would be highly capital-intensive even if the total costs of such programs are relatively smaller than the total costs of conventional military programs. And as suggested above, a nuclear-weapon program in India is not likely to reduce the size and cost of conventional forces.[23] Going nuclear would be an additional cost, a cost that may constantly accelerate as both Pakistan and China respond in the familiar action–reaction process that sends arms spiralling. Eventually this could lead to less Indian security at a much higher price.

Third, offering to sign the NPT would be a means of testing Pakistan's sincerity. Pakistan has repeatedly indicated its willingness to sign the treaty or to establish South Asia as a nuclear-weapon-free zone if India reciprocates. Pakistani diplomatic strategy has been to blame India for increasing the threat of proliferation in South Asia. However, Pakistan may have stronger reasons for not signing the NPT, because nuclear weapons may be perceived as the ultimate option to negate the growing Indian conventional military superiority on the subcontinent. By offering to sign the NPT, India would shift the burden of demonstrating good faith to Pakistan. Failure on the part of Pakistan to reciprocate would give India a form of diplomatic victory, because the blame, unlike in the past, would fall on Pakistan.

As observed earlier, much of the Indian fear about a covert Pakistani nuclear-weapon program may be deliberately fed by Islamabad in order to provoke India into jumping the gun toward the bomb, thus generating the preferred Pakistani position of a nuclear military balance on the subcontinent based on mutual retaliatory strike capabilities. Under these conditions, India's conventional military superiority will have been rendered less relevant while, say, 10 Pakistani bombs would sufficiently deter 100 Indian bombs as well as conventional Indian military forces. In contrast, signing the NPT, according to one State Department official, would leave India as the "winner of the conventional arms race" in South Asia and the dominant power in the region.

Fourth, signing the treaty will allow India to obtain peaceful technological know-how more readily, for both its nuclear energy as well as its space programs. There would be a greater willingness on the part of international suppliers to provide spares, parts, and new technologies for the Indian nuclear energy program without the constant tensions and delays that India has had to cope with in the past. Japan, South Korea, and Taiwan are all parties to the NPT, and they have relatively larger nuclear energy programs than India. Membership in the NPT has given them more easy and ready access to the best and most advanced peaceful technologies available in the field. On the other hand, maintaining the nuclear option merely gives India the worst of all possible technological worlds, military and civilian.

A somewhat Machiavellian argument could perhaps be advanced that by signing the treaty, India could obtain substantial technology from the West for its civilian program and thereby also increase its potential military capabilities for future use. Nuclear and space technologies, after all, have dual uses in both the civilian and military sectors. Subsequently, India could pull out of the NPT under Article X on the grounds that strategic circumstances had substantially changed.

This may seem like a rather cynical observation, but it applies to all states that have signed the treaty. Israeli suspicions of the ultimate nuclear intentions of Iraq and Libya—both signatories to the NPT—may not be entirely groundless, although these two cases could be the exception to the rule among the present adherents to the treaty. In general, although Article X may be perceived as a loophole for would-be horizontal proliferators, the purpose is also to make all signatories feel comfortable with a decision to accede to the treaty, and not feel trapped for all time to come. More likely, Article X would place a moral obligation on a would-be signatory to adhere to the spirit of the treaty in good faith. No signatory state has as yet considered invoking Article X—not even Iraq, whose Osirak nuclear reactor was attacked by Israel in June 1981. There is no reason to believe that India would behave differently than the other signatory states unless the circumstances were grave. An exception to this commitment could be made in the circumstances described below in order to strengthen the global nonproliferation regime.

Fifth, in spite of the preceding observation, the threat (as well as willingness) to withdraw from the NPT under Article X could be used to pressure the nuclear "haves" into implementing Article VI, which calls on them to negotiate the reduction and eventual elimination of all nuclear weapons.[24] The past neglect and failure to implement Article VI has been one of the major grievances of the have-nots within and outside the treaty. Indeed, India's adherence to the treaty should be made conditional on the implementation of this provision by the nuclear powers on a stricter schedule. Such an approach would carry greater moral weight and effectiveness than the earlier Indian policy of putting pressure on the vertical proliferators to reduce their nuclear stockpiles by refusing to sign the treaty.

Ultimately, the question boils down to whether a nuclear India facing both a nuclear China and a nuclear Pakistan is the preferred security position to a non-nuclear India having to live in the shadow of a nuclear China with whom India's relations have been improving in recent years. If India could live with the Chinese nuclear threat for twenty-five years under worse circumstances, then it may be worth continuing with this policy indefinitely, especially if the potential Pakistani nuclear threat could be checkmated through mutual adherence to the NPT.

CONCLUSIONS AND PROSPECTS

Each of these three policy options are viable and minimally reasonable for a country such as India to pursue, but each option also carries potential risks. In the case of continuing the present Indian policy of maintaining a nuclear option, there is some danger that the existing posture of mutual nuclear brinksmanship between India and Pakistan could irretrievably slide into a covert and unstable nuclear arms race that may tempt one or both sides to preempt the other under conditions of paranoia. Nuclear secrecy and uncertainty are unlikely to contribute to political confidence on the subcontinent, a problem that is already evident in the case of the clandestine Pakistani nuclear-weapon program.

It seems unlikely also that the Indo–Pakistani agreement of 1988 not to attack each other's nuclear installations will prevent attacks on such targets if war did occur, or lessen the probability of a nuclear war if nuclear weapons have been stockpiled covertly by both sides. This may appear to be a worst-case scenario, but surely contingency plans based on such fears and eventualities must exist in both countries. After all, nuclear installations on either side—the source of much fear and mistrust—are the most logical targets for preemptive strikes under conditions of paranoia and subsequent war, as already demonstrated by the Israeli attack on Iraq's Osirak nuclear reactor. Chasma and Kahuta on the Pakistani side, and Kota and Trombay on the Indian side, may not be spared in an intense crisis leading to armed hostilities.

In the case of going for the bomb, a similar risk exists that the projected two-way stable relationship with Pakistan and China may break down in practice, especially in relation to Pakistan. There are problems of intensity and proximity. The fact that crisis management has been successfully conducted among the existing nuclear powers over the last forty years may not apply to the same degree to two countries that have already fought three major wars. Issues between India and Pakistan carry a religious intensity that could be more emotional than the ideological differences among the United States, the Soviet Union, and China. The major cities and populations of India and Pakistan have greater proximity than those of the existing three rival nuclear powers, which increases the level of mutual anxiety on the subcontinent. Moreover, the addition of India and Pakistan to the nuclear club would almost certainly tempt other countries such as Iran, Iraq, Israel, Syria, and Libya to eventually embark on nuclear-weapon programs as well. This will not improve the broader security environment of India, where the level of nuclear uncertainty will have spread and considerably increased.

In the case of India along with Pakistan signing the NPT, the Chinese nuclear threat, as well as the threat of Pakistani bombs that may have already been stockpiled secretly, will remain. The risk from China, which has been tested for twenty-five years under far more adverse security conditions than those which prevail today, has been proven relatively low. Indeed, if India is threatened in the future by China or any other nuclear power, that would be sufficient reason for India to withdraw from the NPT and subsequently to go for the bomb. Although such a postcrisis decision will not resolve the immediate problem arising from that particular nuclear threat, neither will the strategy of merely maintaining a nuclear-weapon option. As regards the second risk, Pakistan has denied that it has produced and stockpiled nuclear weapons, and for the time being this declaration will have to be accepted until further evidence surfaces. Besides, Pakistan may have similar fears of India as well.

In determining which of the three policy options optimizes India's security needs, there are certain pitfalls that India should avoid. The first pitfall is that of attempting to teach the vertical proliferators a lesson. India has repeatedly questioned the moral right of the nuclear haves to lay down restrictive guidelines for the nuclear have-nots. And, indeed, it makes no sense for the real nuclear proliferators to ask those states on the brink of a nuclear-weapon capability, but who have voluntarily shown restraint, not to proliferate. Part of India's resistance to the NPT arises from this attitude of indignation. However, the relevant question for India is the more simple one: "Under what policy option is India most secure?" Threatening to imitate the five foolish nuclear nations caught up in an inextricable and senseless nuclear arms race, or resisting their demands to sign the NPT because of their double standards, will not maximize India's security.

The second pitfall may be found in making demands that essentially defeat those very demands. India's demand that the proliferation issue should, and can only, be resolved globally, is a self-defeating objective. If India's ultimate objective is to eliminate all nuclear weapons, then however remote the success of this objective at present, this demand makes India's objective even more difficult to achieve. With several nations on the brink of a nuclear-weapon capability or the motivation to acquire such a capability, and with the existing nuclear powers nowhere near the goal of complete nuclear disarmament, the actual result of the Indian demand would be to push even more nations into nuclear arms races and to eliminate the prospect of global nuclear disarmament for all time to come. Horizontal proliferation will not resolve vertical proliferation.

The other perplexing aspect of India's demand for the global resolution of the proliferation issue is that in the past India has usually sought regional solutions to the problems of the subcontinent. Why, then, is there an exception in this particular case, when a regional solution within the subcontinent has a greater chance of success than a global solution? Indeed, achieving a regional solution to the proliferation issue on the subcontinent through the NPT will increase the pressure on Israel, South Africa, Brazil, and Argentina to do the same. That, in turn, will put greater pressure on the nuclear haves to carry out in good faith Article VI of the NPT calling for global nuclear disarmament.

The third pitfall is one of political and bureaucratic inertia under changing strategic conditions. There have been several landmark events that mark a significant change in India's nuclear strategic environment: the 1964 Chinese atomic test; the introduction of the NPT in 1968; the seeds of Sino–American rapprochement in 1971–72; Pakistan's nuclear responses to its defeat in the 1971 Indo–Pakistani war and the Indian atomic test of 1974; the first major reports of the clandestine Pakistani acquisition of a uranium enrichment capability in 1980–81; and the most recent reports in early 1989 that the U.S. government may find itself unable to certify that Pakistan has not already acquired nuclear weapons. Throughout these changes, a nuclear-weapon option has been maintained by the government of India.

Policy persistence is not unique to the Indian governmental bureaucracy. But in India the bureaucratic decision-making process is larger and more complex, and party control and leadership of the central government have shown relatively few changes since independence in 1947. The Congress party has ruled except for the period of 1977–79, when the Janata party displaced it. Apart from the brief interim prime ministership of Gulzarilal Nanda in 1964 and 1966, there have been only five Indian prime ministers, of which two, Lal Bahadur Shastri and Morarji Desai, were in office for fewer than three years. The rest of India's independent history has been dominated by the Nehru family: Jawaharlal Nehru, and Indira and Rajiv Gandhi. This may not entirely explain the persistence of Indian policy on the nuclear question— and, in any case, the issue became relevant only after Nehru's death in May 1964— but it is interesting to note that an attempt to change the policy to one of unilateral nuclear renunciation was attempted for the first time under Prime Minister Desai of the Janata government. Again, in early 1985, there were reports that Rajiv Gandhi, newly elected as prime minister in December 1984, raised the possibility of signing the NPT but was dissuaded by the civilian bureaucracy in the Ministry of Defense and the Ministry of External Affairs.[25] This would suggest that only a radical change in the external strategic circumstances, such as an overt Pakistani nuclear-weapon program or a change of government at the center through the defeat (though unlikely) of the Congress party in the 1989 national elections, would be more likely to bring about a change in India's nuclear policy toward the bomb or the NPT.

The fourth pitfall is the tendency to treat the NPT as an issue unrelated to or separate from India's broader strategic nuclear interests, and then to resist the NPT for its own sake.[26] For India, the questions of whether to sign the NPT or to go for the bomb are seemingly posed separately. The fact that signing the NPT may partially resolve India's nuclear dilemma in South Asia does not appear to be taken seriously. India's resistance to the NPT makes even less sense when one considers that over 135 nonnuclear states have signed the NPT. While their strategic concerns are probably less critical than that of India, their overriding concern and goal is that global security cannot possibly be enhanced if more states became nuclear powers. Thus, while regional security goals may provide compelling reasons for India to become a nuclear-weapon state, global security concerns provide compelling reasons for India to sign the NPT.

Given all the weaknesses of the NPT, it may be the best possible document under the worst of circumstances. To be sure, when the NPT comes up for renewal in 1995, the lessons derived from the twenty-five years of the treaty's formal existence since 1970 must be incorporated. However, in the immediate future, there may be no alternative to the perpetuation of nuclear haves and have-nots. Clearly, Article VI, which calls for negotiations to reduce and eliminate nuclear weapons, will need to be pushed more forcefully. The outrageous situation of five nuclear powers continuing to accumulate sophisticated weapons of mass destruction—more than twenty years after the NPT was finalized—cannot be allowed to go on indefinitely. Perhaps a deadline should be set for reaching a comprehensive test ban treaty when the NPT is renegotiated, with the clause that failure to keep the deadline by the nuclear haves should allow have-not signatories to the NPT to withdraw.

Other problems with the NPT will also remain. So long as a technological "fix" that would eliminate the intrinsic relation between nuclear energy programs and nuclear-weapon development cannot be found, the contradiction between clauses that attempt to prevent the transfer of nuclear weapons, and those which attempt to encourage peaceful nuclear cooperation among the haves and have-nots, will continue to pose problems. India will need to live with such weaknesses in the NPT.

If nothing else, India should open the domestic debate once again on its nuclear policy. When doing this, India should remember that in the twenty-first century the international prestige of nations is going to be determined by the "economic prosperity race" and not by the "nuclear arms race." It is going to be countries such as Japan, South Korea, and Taiwan that will be recognized as national success stories, and not a nuclear Pakistan, Israel, or Libya. Under such circumstances, it may be in India's interest to get the nuclear issue behind it by signing the NPT, and to concentrate on the more important business of rapid economic advancement.

NOTES AND REFERENCES

1. Two earlier studies in India of Pakistan's efforts to acquire the bomb may be found in P. K. S. Namboodiri, "Pakistan's Nuclear Future," in K. Subrahmanyam, ed., *Nuclear Myths and Realities: India's Dilemma* (New Delhi: ABC Publishers, 1981), pp. 139–94; and in P. B. Sinha and R. R. Sinha, *Nuclear Pakistan: Atomic Threat to South Asia* (New Delhi: Vision Books, 1980).
2. *Hindustan Times*, January 29, 1989; and *Times of India*, January 29, 1989. See also Leonard S. Spector, *The Undeclared Bomb* (Cambridge, Mass.: Ballinger, 1988), pp. 128–43.
3. *Times of India*, January 13, 1989.
4. Two detailed studies have been undertaken by an Indian analyst demonstrating Pakistan's path toward nuclear weapons. See S. R. Sreedhar, *Pakistan's Bomb: A Documentary Study* (New Delhi: ABC Publishers, 1987); and his *Dr. A. Q. Khan on the Pakistan Bomb* (New Delhi: ABC Publishers, 1987).
5. This proposal was made by Brigadier (ret.) A. Bannerji during my presentation on the NPT at the Institute for Defense Studies and Analyses in New Delhi, January 12, 1989.
6. In the introductory chapter of K. Subrahmanyam, ed., *India and the Nuclear Challenge* (New Delhi: Lancer International, 1987), p. 10.
7. See T. T. Poulose, "Nuclear Proliferation and the Second NPT Review Conference," in Subrahmanyam, *Nuclear Myths and Realities*, pp. 21–37.
8. Arguments against the bomb may be seen in a study by the Centre for Policy Research put together by one of the leading opponents of the bomb in India, Bhabani Sen Gupta, *Nuclear Weapons: Policy Options for India* (New Delhi: Sage Publications, 1983).
9. K. Subrahmanyam made this remark in response to a comment by me deploring the lack of diverse positions on the issue at a conference on Indo–American relations at the India International Centre in New Delhi, January 31, 1989.
10. See S. P. Seth, "The Indo–Pak Nuclear Duet and the United States," *Asian Survey* 28, no. 7 (July 1988), pp. 719–22; and Shrikant Paranjpe, *U.S. Nonproliferation Policy in Action: South Asia* (New York: Envoy Press, 1987), pp. 89–90.
11. For a more detailed discussion of this policy, see Raju G. C. Thomas, *Indian Security Policy* (Princeton, N.J.: Princeton University Press, 1986), pp. 28–30 and 44–50.
12. This observation was made by Ratakonda Dayakar, the Press Counselor of the Embassy of India, Washington, D.C., in a letter to the editor entitled, "India Believes in Global Path to Nonproliferation," *New York Times*, February 8, 1989.
13. The mutual on-site inspection and verification clauses agreed to in the INF treaty by the superpowers was the first departure from this attitude.
14. See Raju G. C. Thomas, "India's Nuclear Programs and the Nuclear Nonproliferation Treaty," *Wisconsin International Law Journal* (1986), pp. 111–17.
15. See Thomas, *Indian Security Policy*, p. 45.
16. Reported in the *Statesman*, June 23 and 24, 1984. See also earlier reports in the *New York Times*, April 28 and 30, 1981.
17. See the *Hindustan Times*, December 21, 1980.
18. The strongest case for an Indian bomb may be found in the collection of articles in K. Sub-

rahmanyam, ed., *India and the Nuclear Challenge* (New Delhi: Lancer International, 1987). Here K. Subrahmanyam, Jasjit Singh, P. K. S. Namboodiri, C. Raja Mohan, R. R. Subramaniam, and Rikhi Jaipal point out the several problems underlying threats from the nuclear superpowers, China and Pakistan, failures of perceptions and deterrence theories, fears of nuclear terrorism, and the failings of nuclear-free zones and verification proposals, as justifications for India to abandon the nonproliferation regime and to embark on a nuclear-weapon program. Subrahmanyam concludes by arguing that the only way for India to avoid going nuclear would be the total elimination of nuclear weapons everywhere.

19. This observation has been made on several occasions by leading Indian analysts. See, for instance, Subrahmanyam, *India and the Nuclear Challenge*, pp. 7 9; and T. T. Poulose, *Nuclear Proliferation and the Third World* (New Delhi: ABC Publishers, 1982), pp. 6–19.

20. See note 23 below.

21. See Leonard Spector, *The Undeclared Bomb*, pp. 84–93.

22. See Raju G. C. Thomas, "The Armed Services and the Indian Defense Budget," *Asian Survey* 20, no. 3 (March 1980), pp. 280–97.

23. K. Subrahmanyam has argued in the particular case of Pakistan, that going nuclear would please the generals on one of their pet objectives and enable Prime Minister Benazir Bhutto to cut down on Pakistan's conventional military spending. See K. Subrahmanyam, "Dialogue With Benazir-I," *Hindustan Times*, January 12, 1989.

24. See Raju G. C. Thomas, "Banning the Bomb in India," *New York Times*, December 29, 1988.

25. This information was obtained from the author's discussions with members of the Ministry of External Affairs and defense analysts in India.

26. This point was made by Ravi Shastri, a doctoral candidate at Jawaharlal Nehru University, during my presentation on the NPT at the Institute for Defense Studies and Analyses in New Delhi, January 12, 1989. Although the observation was from only one member of the audience, it has since occurred to me that the point indeed reflected the Indian approach to the NPT and nuclear-weapon issues.

13

A World without the NPT?[1]

Joseph F. Pilat

The world we have experienced since the NPT came into force in 1970 has not been the best of all possible worlds; the world without the NPT would undoubtedly not be the worst of all possible worlds. But is a world without the NPT possible or probable? How might it come about? In principle, several paths might be possible. First, it is extremely difficult but not impossible to imagine a catastrophic failure of the NPT in 1995, following the conference convened in accordance with Article X.2, "to decide whether the treaty shall continue in force indefinitely, or shall be extended for an additional fixed period or periods." A fundamental transformation of East–West or North–South relations could undermine the foundations of the treaty, or the dynamics of a controversial extension conference could result in chaos. While such developments are unlikely, if a collapse of the treaty does not occur, it will not be a consequence of language that would appear to make the legal termination of the NPT in 1995 unlikely, if not unthinkable. Rather, it will be a result of political forces favoring the extension of the treaty for a majority of its parties. Second, blatant noncompliance by any party, overt moves by the holdout states to demonstrate their nuclear capabilities (including nuclear testing), or other dramatic nuclear events (including nuclear theft, sabotage, or terrorism) could indicate to parties that the NPT was irrelevant, at best a hollow shell, and that its survival was of no interest to them. The occurrence of any such events, however, seems unlikely before 1995. Third, the NPT could be undermined by the withdrawal of a large number of member states or, to prevent such a massive withdrawal, amendments or compromises which would have to diminish the authority, credibility, and effectiveness of the treaty. Even this prospect is not probable, but it is all too easily imagined, particularly because efforts to obtain universal ad-

Joseph F. Pilat • Staff Member, Center for National Security Studies, Los Alamos National Laboratory, Los Alamos, New Mexico.

herence for the treaty have brought in parties who may not receive, or may not understand they are participating in, the full benefits of the treaty.

In the aftermath of one or another of these different possibilities, all of which would probably be equally destructive to the international nonproliferation regime during the course of a decade, the resultant world would undoubtedly be worse than one in which a solid and strengthened NPT were in place as the twenty-first century begins. Without predicting the worst (for this is clearly not the most probable outcome) and to demonstrate concretely the importance of a treaty that is praised rather routinely in vague and general terms, this chapter will attempt to delineate the contours of a world in which the NPT was no longer in force or no longer effective. In this effort, we shall not assume any one of the paths for the decline or demise of the NPT we have put forward, on the already stated assumption that despite very different immediate impacts, within ten years any weakening of the treaty by external events, withdrawals, or amendments would probably create conditions equivalent to its total collapse. Such speculations, which presumably have some scholarly value, are all the more justified since it is frequently stated that this treaty does not by itself constitute the nonproliferation regime. In this context, it is often argued that the interest in nonproliferation shown by NPT states parties would survive the erosion or collapse of the treaty, that IAEA safeguards would continue to apply with continued effectiveness, and that the world would not fundamentally change. This view is not without some degree of validity, particularly in the immediate aftermath of an unsuccessful extension conference in 1995. However, it assumes a homogeneity and strength of interest among the parties to the treaty that would be belied by its collapse, and a less than full realization of how much the regime and all of its elements have been tied to the NPT during the twenty years the treaty has been in force. As well, it assumes that those regime structures and principles that survive the collapse of the treaty could endure indefinitely without the NPT as a buttress. In contrast, it is argued in the following pages that possible or probable effects of the loss of the NPT on the international regime, international security, and international relations would be considerable, and largely unwelcome to parties and nonparties alike.

EFFECTS ON THE INTERNATIONAL REGIME, ITS PURPOSES, PRINCIPLES, AND INSTITUTIONS

In the absence of the NPT, the prospect for the nuclear "democracy"—the reduction or removal of differences between nuclear-weapon states (NWSs) and nonnuclear-weapon states (NNWs), between nuclear "haves" and "have-nots"—suggested, if not explicitly demanded, by Articles IV and VI of the treaty would become even more distant than it is at present. The universal and inalienable rights embodied in Article IV would become irrelevant, and reception of nuclear assistance or exports would depend on the greed, good will, or grand strategy of the suppliers, without whom indigenous development of a nuclear energy program would be slow, inefficient, difficult, and costly in terms of human and material resources. Obstacles to cooperation could be erected haphazardly, and efforts to reduce existing obstacles undermined. On the other hand, experimental efforts by the NWSs to assume obligations agreed to by the NNWSs, exemplified by acceptance of voluntary safeguards, would effectively end.

With respect to obligations and expectations associated with Article VI, one of the most likely causes of the treaty's collapse would be efforts by NNWSs parties to the treaty to use the NPT in an attempt to force the pace of arms control and disarmament. It is clear that the NPT has not been successful in creating a world without nuclear weapons. While this objective was envisioned by many states at the time of the treaty's conclusion in 1968 and represents current expectations of the great majority of NNWSs, the NPT was not originally burdened with being the international instrument to bring about such a sea change. Nevertheless, the NPT is an arms control treaty, and without its existence or effective functioning, hopes for arms control would be diminished, as the uncertainties created by the existence or prospect of new nuclear states could be expected to inhibit any further movement among established NWSs to reduce their nuclear arsenals. It remains true today, as it was at the time that the NPT was concluded, that effective efforts to manage or prevent horizontal proliferation are necessary but not sufficient conditions for progress in arms control.

If the vision embodied in the NPT would diminish if not altogether disappear with its decline or demise, the underlying interest in the principle of nonproliferation would not necessarily share this fate. It is undoubtedly true that the NPT has reflected and furthered the objective of nonproliferation as a globally respected principle, has enhanced the predisposition of the vast majority of states to forgo nuclear weaponry, and has affected the attitudes as well as the behavior of non-NPT as well as NPT states in this sphere. A demonstration that nonproliferation is irrelevant, either through noncompliance of parties or overt moves by nonparties to go nuclear, would almost certainly lead to the collapse of the treaty. But, absent such dramatic events, a collapse of the NPT, perhaps due to the dynamics of international diplomacy or the conflict of ideologies, would not immediately or necessarily be followed by a decline of nonproliferation as a principle and a predisposition. Undoubtedly, voices would be heard denouncing nonproliferation in the wake of the treaty's demise, but this message is heard today. Indeed, we might perhaps expect that the cries of support for nonproliferation would be far louder in the event of the treaty's decline or demise, at least for such time as the issue would be in the forefront of international attention. For, the power of the nonproliferation principle has depended on its practical service to security and perceptions of security. But, with no evident and certainly no adequate means of affecting the reality or perceptions of security, which were primarily derived from the confidence-building effects of the NPT, nonproliferation could begin more and more to fade as a vital national and international value.

Just as the value of nonproliferation would not immediately disappear in the event of the collapse of the treaty that has furthered it, neither would the primary organizational structure supporting the treaty's objectives, the International Atomic Energy Agency (IAEA), immediately decline. A pillar of the nonproliferation regime, the IAEA was established long before the NPT entered into force, and it is rightly assumed that the IAEA would likely continue in existence if the NPT should fail. Yet, it is difficult to believe that the agency would not be profoundly affected by the problems of the treaty to which it has been so intimately bound for so long.

The agency's safeguards activities would certainly be adversely affected. The obligations of NNWSs parties to the NPT under Article III.1 and III.2 would be terminated along with all safeguards agreements entered into under the treaty. The view that materials and facilities currently under safeguards would remain under safeguards, and subsequent generations of special nuclear materials derived from or produced in safeguarded items would be placed under safeguards, is a legal interpretation that may not be generally understood or accepted and which could be challenged. Only with respect to non-NPT safeguards (INFCIRC/66/Rev. 2) has the issue of their continuation been resolved. Even if legal ambiguities were removed for NPT safeguards (INFCIRC/153) by 1995 to assure a recognized, formal requirement for their continuation, or if no legal challenges were forthcoming in 1995 or subsequent years, we might still expect important politically derived challenges to emerge.

Because IAEA safeguards have become so closely bound to the NPT, the credibility of these safeguards would be undermined by the treaty's collapse, perhaps fatally, for parties and nonparties alike. Indeed, it is difficult to imagine, even in the best of circumstances, viable IAEA safeguards a decade after the collapse of the NPT. It is not clear that states would be willing to endow post-NPT safeguards with the role and importance safeguards now have, because these technical–political–legal creations would be burdened with the absence of the NPT's more expansive political commitments, including its formal "no-weapons" pledge, and because the IAEA as the implementing agency would itself be weakened. Presumably, those fall-back safeguards that have been provided for (both bilateral and trilateral) would come into play in this situation, but such arrangements are not in place for the nuclear exports of the majority of suppliers. Even where they are provided for, however, fall-back safeguards may be useless if we assume that the willingness to accept safeguards at all will disappear with the decline or demise of the NPT. Without such an assumption, these arrangements are preferable to no safeguards at all, but they are no substitute for comprehensive safeguards administered by an international agency, and they would pose considerable administrative and financial problems for suppliers and recipients alike.

Without a viable NPT, some states would undoubtedly attempt to shore up the IAEA and, lacking real alternatives, strive to maintain existing IAEA safeguards, extend them to new items, and expand their scope. It will undoubtedly be argued by the governments of the United States, the Soviet Union, Sweden, and other staunch supporters of nonproliferation that if the agency and its safeguards system were given greater responsibilities and had behind them greater political (and perhaps military) authority, they could fulfill the functions that had formerly been the preserve of the NPT. In practice, however, this would be extremely difficult. Once the IAEA became burdened by the trappings of the NPT, whether this occurred formally or informally, it could begin to lose its broad appeal. And, this appeal is not universal even today. It must be recognized that the critics of the NPT do not vent their spleen only on the treaty or the Nuclear Suppliers' Group (NSG); they have also frequently castigated the IAEA and, in particular, its excessive concern over its regulatory as opposed to promotional functions, which critics attribute to the predominance of the major suppliers in IAEA councils.

Exacerbating these difficulties, there could be public and parliamentary challenges to efforts to strengthen the IAEA in the event of the NPT's collapse. The Congress of the United States, for example, might balk at dependence on international institutional solutions in such a situation and mandate unilateral actions to restrict and perhaps even effectively end U.S. involvement in international nuclear trade, to end U.S. approvals for reprocessing and plutonium use, and the like. We might expect considerable support for such a stance from public interest groups and the public at large in the United States, with perhaps emulative action by other Western parliaments and the sanction of public opinion around the world. Whatever the justification for, and the concrete effects of, such moves, they can be expected to create an atmosphere in which states seeking to burden the IAEA and the agency's safeguards with additional responsibilities would undoubtedly find their actions to be less than fully effective and perhaps even futile. Perhaps immediately, but certainly over time, confidence in IAEA and other safeguards would decline to a level so low that they would offer few benefits and be as likely to arouse as to allay suspicions of nuclear-weapon development among states that are not recognized to possess these weapons. And, as suggested, there is no way that the only obvious and practicable alternative—new or renewed bilateral or trilateral safeguards arrangements—could ever fulfill the function of IAEA safeguards backed by the political–legal commitments of the NPT.

Any problems with the IAEA and its safeguards system would reverberate through other structures of the nonproliferation regime, all of which depend to greater or lesser extent upon IAEA safeguards. The Latin American Nuclear-Weapon-Free Zone established by the Treaty of Tlatelolco, if it is fully in effect in the mid-1990s, would be confronted with difficult choices and challenges if the IAEA safeguards that are so central to its operation were not perceived as credible. And, it may be difficult to create nuclear-weapon-free zones in other regions— which is viewed by many states as highly desirable to buttress NPT commitments or, in some cases, to avoid sanctioning the NPT while undertaking equivalent commitments—without the existence of IAEA safeguards as a common and acceptable standard for their functioning. This is probably true even in such regions as the Middle East, where at least some prospective parties have declared they would require additional, bilateral or regional, safeguards measures.

So too would the Zangger Committee's and NSG's activities be adversely affected by any loss of confidence in IAEA safeguards. Unlike Tlatelolco, however, the committee as well as the group would also be directly affected by the loss of the commitments established by the NPT itself. In this situation, the committee would probably be disbanded. And, in the absence of the NPT, especially if IAEA safeguards were no longer credible, the "gentleman's agreement" embodied in the NSG could become a mockery, and those formal arrangements which serve the suppliers and have thus far received their support would probably be effectively ended. Without established rules, the confidence of supplier states that others were not using "sweeteners" to capitalize on those sales opportunities which presented themselves would deteriorate rapidly, exacerbating existing differences among the suppliers. Public criticism of nuclear trade by the supplier states, and possible action by the U.S. Congress and perhaps other legislative bodies, would further this process. Battered on every side, the current NSG could collapse, although there might be an effort to revive and strengthen it to fulfill functions the NPT and the Zangger Committee once fulfilled. While the French, among others, would today oppose such a move because of concern about Third World reactions, such perceptions might change in the aftermath of the NPT's failure. Unfortunately, given the limits of the NSG consensus and its underpinning in the NPT/IAEA regime, the NSG would be ill-suited for this function. As a consequence, the logical step of formalizing through a treaty the commitments and the "organizational structures" of the NSG, perhaps broadened to include the emerging suppliers, in the hopes of creating a body to fulfill the role of the NPT/IAEA regime, would probably be stillborn.

EFFECTS ON INTERNATIONAL SECURITY

It has been the NPT, the IAEA safeguards specified by the treaty, and the passage of time that have served to dispel doubts that we are moving toward life in a nuclear-armed crowd. Without the treaty and the safeguards obligations it required, in time this perception could, and probably would, reemerge. However, unless the collapse of the NPT were brought about by the nuclearization of nonparties or even parties, the world without the NPT would not necessarily bristle with new nuclear states. We would not necessarily find ourselves in the midst of a nuclear crowd. If we did, this new situation would undoubtedly create serious concerns, but it would not necessarily be a disaster.

Whatever the importance of the international nonproliferation regime, a decision by a state to acquire nuclear weapons ultimately is based on internal assessments of national interests, with priority given to whether or not national security would be served by the possession of nuclear weapons. For the great majority of states, such considerations have driven decisions to forgo nuclear weapons, and this situation is unlikely to change immediately should the NPT be undermined or even destroyed in 1995.

The collapse of the NPT would eventually affect security perceptions across the globe. But it would not be likely in the near-term to damage perceptions of security in any regional contexts, except in Europe and the Far East, primarily because the obvious countries of concern elsewhere are nonparties. Yet, certain Arab states parties to the NPT, the Koreas, Indonesia, Vietnam, and other countries might immediately cause concern for their neighbors if they were suddenly released from the obligations that the NPT requires. This concern might be diminished by such considerations as the high cost of nuclear weapons in these countries (some of which are burdened by stagnant economies and exorbitant international debts), anticipated superpower pressures, and the like. But such considerations would probably be secondary if the nuclear capability of a regional adversary were demonstrated. Even where this was not the case, there is little doubt that the regional security situation would deteriorate, as confidence among nonnuclear states that regional adversaries were not undertaking weapon programs, never absolute under the NPT, would decline without this most impressive of confidence-building measures. (It is, of course, true that IAEA safeguards embody political commitments and do themselves serve as confidence-building measures. But, as we have suggested, it is difficult to imagine them remaining credible in the event of the NPT's collapse, let alone serving to substitute for the NPT's wider commitments.) The prospect of armed attacks on other states' nuclear facilities could increase, with disastrous consequences for nuclear power programs within the region and, possibly, an adverse effect on global nuclear energy development.

As for the general political stability within any region, or around the world, it could deteriorate relatively rapidly if states were unsure of their neighbors' nuclear intentions. Whether or not preemptive military actions were undertaken, the shifting security situation could result in reassessments by all parties of their need to develop nuclear arms or perhaps more readily attainable chemical and biological weapons with which they might attempt to deter the perceived existing or imminent nuclear threat. Military contingency plans would have to be adopted to take the new situation into account, with the possibility that preparations, including new weapon acquisitions, changes in operational doctrine, and the like, could appear so threatening to an adversary as to impel it to realize the capability that was originally feared. There could be a self-fulfilling threat–response interaction of a troubling but virtually inevitable kind.

If the number of nuclear powers should increase, grave concern is warranted but dire predictions of nuclear disaster do not necessarily follow. Arguments about the establishment and stabilizing effect of regional deterrence situations as a result of proliferation are frequently ethnocentric and ahistorical, but there is no reason to believe that proliferation of nuclear weapons would dramatically increase the risk of nuclear war. Unless the collapse of the NPT were preceded or accompanied by the immediate nuclearization of some states, there is no obvious reason why it would inevitably decrease stability on a regional or global scale.

Regionally, the presence of nuclear weapons in and of itself is unlikely to precipitate a conflict—although there may be grounds for concern about the political instability of a nuclear-armed country; less effective command, control, communications, and intelligence mechanisms than those utilized in current NWSs; and the like. Moreover, should conflict occur, whether or not it is the result of miscalculation or accidental or unauthorized use, these weapons could be used if they were available. The use of chemical weaponry in the Gulf War may help reduce glibly expressed certainties that nuclear weapons, if acquired, would be unusable.

On the global stage, some of the least compelling scenarios of nuclear war between the United States and the Soviet Union are those which involve deliberate escalation from, or miscalculated reactions to, "nth country" nuclear explosions or exchanges. However, such perceptions would follow perhaps all too rapidly after ambiguity was spawned by the treaty's collapse, and they could develop a life of their own. Clearly, it is likely that some contingency measures would be undertaken by the United States or the Soviet Union in the new security situation, in order to assure that they could preserve their interests and influence, and particularly their ability to project power in potential nuclear environments. Perhaps some of these measures would actually increase the danger of precipitating a nuclear war, although this is by no means clear, due to difficulties in anticipating superpower moves. However, the prospect of new nuclear states fundamentally altering the superpowers' strategic relationship is highly unlikely without a significant increase in the arsenals of the French, British, or Chinese spurred by perceived security requirements in a proliferated world, or a perceived or actual movement toward nuclear weapons by certain states or groups of states with strong industrial bases, for example, Japan or the Federal Republic of Germany.

EFFECTS ON INTERNATIONAL RELATIONS

Not only would the decline or demise of the treaty affect international security, both regionally and globally, but it would profoundly affect international relations. It would effectively limit or eliminate the influence of international fora created to deal with this vital issue, and perhaps decrease the prospect of effectively considering nonproliferation in other international fora. The decline or demise of the NPT would force the issue to an ever greater extent into bilateral and other multilateral channels, thereby creating or exacerbating tensions and divergent interests along East–West, West–West, and North–South lines.

Without the international regime, the superpowers could in principle reestablish an effective control system based upon their common interests and the prospect of common action. In practice, however, such a superpower condominium may not be fully effective, if the erosion of the "blocs" provides any indication of the declining political–military influence of the United States and the Soviet Union on the global stage. More importantly, perhaps, there is no reason to believe that interests are so common as is frequently assumed. While superpower cooperation in this sphere has persisted through chills and thaws in East–West relations, the most effective and enduring cooperation has involved technical matters within the purview of the IAEA. Political issues, in particular those involving the nuclear weapon aspirations of allies or friendly countries, have, with few exceptions, been contentious.

In the absence of the NPT, and assuming a diminished and diminishing confidence in the IAEA and its safeguards, the activities of allies and client states regarded as potential proliferants would remain bones of contention and so politically sensitive that they would be largely outside the scope of U.S.–Soviet cooperation. Indeed, the more controversial issues would probably come to dominate bilateral superpower relations in this sphere. As proliferation issues become more politicized, traditional U.S.–Soviet differences may be exacerbated as either the Soviets or the United States seeks political advantage, especially because the very different geopolitical situations of the superpowers suggest that a threat to one superpower is not necessarily a threat to the other, although it might very well be a threat to the other's interests. For example, if U.S. nonproliferation efforts in its traditional spheres of influence (e.g., Latin America) appear ineffective to the Soviets, or if proliferation appears inevitable (e.g., South Asia), the Soviets might attempt to take advantage of the situation either to increase nuclear trade or to weaken the United States geopolitically. To the extent that it can do so while minimizing risks to itself, it may pursue this path, the more so because the benefits provided by the international nonproliferation regime would not continue as a powerful countervailing influence.

While trade questions per se might not provoke excessive friction in U.S.– Soviet relations, we have indicated they will not be without problems, particularly if the Soviets should decide, either to obtain hard currency or to extend political influence, to enter the international market more aggressively in the late 1990s and into the next century. This scenario, of course, assumes that there is a revival of the market, and that the Soviets can develop an efficient, competitive line of nuclear goods and services that effectively erases memories of the Chernobyl disaster.

Such shifts in U.S.–Soviet relations would not be likely to affect relations within the Eastern bloc on the issues of nuclear trade and nonproliferation. Barring even more dramatic shifts in the Soviet Union's position in the world than we have witnessed in the early Gorbachev years, the Eastern bloc will most likely continue to follow the Soviet lead in this area. The prospects for harmonious relations among the Western states on the issues of nuclear trade and nonproliferation are far less likely. West–West relations could be adversely affected by the demise or decline of the NPT. Relations between the United States, Australia, Canada, and some others who fully share nonproliferation interests, perspectives, and policies would presumably be unchanged. But their relations with other Western states could very well worsen.

In the last decade, real differences have emerged among the Western states on nuclear cooperation and nonproliferation issues. Supply consensus has been challenged and questions of nuclear supply, and of supplier-state policy, have often appeared at the forefront of the debate over proliferation concerns and nonproliferation policy. The guidelines of the NSG have been extremely controversial, as has been the very existence of the group. Both recipient and supplier states have on occasion criticized the group, its provisions, or its perceived operations. Nevertheless, along with the NPT, the NSG guidelines reflect such supplier consensus as exists, and they are essential for the survival of the supply regime. However, there are differences in the manner in which these states implement their nuclear supply undertakings, and even more important differences between their implementation of supply policy and that of the United States. Their requirements for licensing nuclear exports and the nature of their nuclear export licensing review processes, along with their provisions for post-export controls, vary widely and reflect differing political and legal systems, policy perspectives, economic and political pressures, and industry–government relationships. And, even with a robust NPT, the limited NSG consensus would continue to be challenged by commercial competition, differing perspectives on trade with non-NPT states, adoption of comprehensive safeguards as a condition of significant nuclear trade, and what can and should be done to regulate crucial dual-use exports.

These divergent policies and perspectives are deeply rooted and are likely to widen in the event of the NPT's collapse. They not only reflect the specific nuclear-trading interests of the major suppliers, but also their views of international trade. All of these states have a greater reliance on international trade than the United States. The European and Japanese suppliers tend to see it in terms of political and strategic, as well as economic, benefits. They hold the interdependencies created by international commerce to be crucial instruments in managing their relations with other states. Of particular relevance to nuclear supply and nonproliferation policy are the special strategic trade relationships between each of these states and various countries and regions in the Third World. In the same vein, the approach of all these states to nuclear supply is also shaped by their differing attitudes toward the proliferation danger, which reflect their unique national security, economic, and political interests and perspectives. Nonproliferation is a declared objective of all of these states. Nevertheless, while the European and Japanese suppliers now hold nonproliferation to be in their national interests, some of them have perceived themselves to be "victims" of the nonproliferation policies of the United States and are unlikely to develop a perspective upon nonproliferation identical to that of the United States. Most of the major suppliers are not nuclear states, and their direct military–strategic interest in proliferation is largely limited to potential effects of a proliferated world on the American nuclear umbrella. France and the United Kingdom, as nuclear states, do have strategic interests in proliferation, but they are scarcely identical to those of the United States.

These profound differences among the established nuclear supplier states have often been minimized. It is frequently argued that international market conditions do not portend troubling nuclear trade issues in the next decade. The situation since the late 1970s has been characterized by a decline in orders for nuclear power stations (both domestically and internationally) and a slowing of the spread of nuclear equipment, technologies, and materials as well as of movement toward a plutonium economy. It may be argued with some validity that if the world nuclear market continues to stagnate and nuclear trade recedes to a trickle in coming decades, supply problems may become less and less important, or even disappear altogether. And, it appears that the nuclear market slump, as well as the existence of established "rules of the game" enshrined in the NPT/IAEA regime and the NSG guidelines, has served to reduce possible pressures and ameliorate potential problems of nuclear trade for over a decade. However, with increasing underutilization of nuclear reactor production and uranium enrichment capacity, there will be increasing economic pressures to export, even to states with questionable nonproliferation credentials, if they can pay. A collapse of the NPT, and with it credible IAEA safeguards, would increase the dangers of the proliferation of nuclear-weapon capabilities, and concern about this prospect could once again throw nuclear trade relations into disarray. This situation could easily be complicated by actions within the United States, where the traditional congressional preference for unilateral actions in this sphere might result in legislation to restrict or terminate U.S. nuclear trade, and to attempt to exert more stringent controls over U.S.-origin nuclear materials, equipment, and technology.

Although the decline or demise of the NPT would have significant effects on East–West and West–West relations, the most profound effects could appear in North–South relations, with the reemergence of the politicized nuclear trade issues of the 1970s, and the removal of regime restraints on the behavior and attitudes of holdout states and emerging suppliers. Despite pessimistic market projections, it does seem likely that we will continue to be confronted with contentious supply issues in the foreseeable future, especially since the ideological dimensions of nuclear trade have by no means been resolved. The war of words on international trade in nuclear material, equipment, and technology has been waged for two decades between North and South—between nuclear haves and have-nots. It reveals differences that go beyond trade itself and permeate the full range of relations between these states. Obviously, should North–South relations deteriorate, it would portend acute difficulties for the 1990 and 1995 review conferences. But the differences which create this prospect illustrate the extent to which fundamental differences exist at the very root of the international system, differences which could result in open controversy in the nuclear-trading arena with the NPT firmly in place, but which would be far more likely to do so after the treaty collapsed and IAEA safeguards became less and less credible.

If the worst occurred, the most worrisome consequences could involve changes in the behavior of the NPT holdouts and the emerging suppliers. Even though the NPT does not now have universal adherence, and is unlikely to have it in the foreseeable future, it has exerted an influence on the behavior of holdout states, effectively constraining their actions by its effects on nuclear exports, and perhaps also by its moral suasion. In the absence of the NPT, the treaty obligation for states parties to require IAEA safeguards on all of their nuclear exports would, as indicated, be terminated, and in time the moral and political principles once upheld by the "supply regime" might be seen to be increasingly irrelevant. Should this occur, one set of restraints upon the behavior of the holdout states might disappear. Those concrete interests of holdout states that currently foster behavior supportive of the regime could be expected to change, however gradually, and ideologically derived repugnance for the perceived "technological imperialism" of the regime could more freely sway behavior. Moreover, this situation would be seen to justify the rationalizations of the holdouts for their abstention from adherence to the treaty, and strengthen their influence, particularly because the influence of the supporters of the NPT could be expected to diminish in international nuclear councils in the wake of the treaty's decline or demise.

It is true that the emerging suppliers have proffered support for some elements of the existing supply regime, but many have refused to accept either the NPT or the Treaty of Tlatelolco. Without the formal and informal supply structures that depend to a greater or lesser extent on the NPT and the IAEA, it is not clear how the behavior of the emerging suppliers could be channeled in ways conducive to nonproliferation. Moreover, these states will inevitably perceive the proliferation danger differently than either the United States or the other major suppliers. Their view of themselves as the victims of the proliferation policies of the nuclear supplier states is especially vivid, and they have bitterly denounced the "nuclear colonialism" of the "Caucasian Club," and the existence of "atomic apartheid." For states like India and Argentina, the opposition to the existing nonproliferation regime has been ideological, and all of these states have expressed a principled opposition to restrictions on the transfer of all types of technology. For all emerging suppliers, with the exception of those with robust domestic power programs heavily dependent upon imported technology, equipment, and material (e.g., South Korea, Taiwan), the preservation of the existing regime may not be a matter of concrete economic or commercial interest. Indeed, some of these states might welcome its collapse, hoping to prosper amid conditions in which nuclear commerce, at least to certain states and regions, was perceived as extremely dangerous and avoided by the major nuclear suppliers. Even the more moderate states among them could be expected to become radicalized if the United States or other major suppliers undertook executive or legislative actions that intensified differences and increased feelings of discrimination.

Most of the emerging suppliers have no military–strategic interests beyond the region in which they are located, although states like China, which is a nuclear state, as well as Brazil and India, which are viewed as "near-nuclear" states, aspire to the status of global powers. Essentially, this means that if such countries perceive a proliferation danger at all, they do so only in regional terms. Although the emerging suppliers can be expected to pursue responsible policies toward their own regions, with or without the influence of the NPT/IAEA regime, there would be few concrete inhibitions to irresponsible trade with extra-regional states if this regime were to collapse. It is true that these states could be influenced by the political reactions of the nuclear states and other advanced nuclear countries, with whom they might also have military, diplomatic, and trade relations. Yet, it is unclear whether the great powers would actively intervene to prevent nuclear trade they deemed dangerous and irresponsible. The record of the past is not especially reassuring, and the situation could worsen in the absence of the NPT. Further, most emerging suppliers have ties to international groups of states (e.g., Islamic, neutral and nonaligned), which could influence their behavior either through expectations of disapproval and possible sanctions or because of an unwillingness to diminish their preponderance in the bloc by trading away an area of clear superiority. However, membership in these groups might facilitate some irresponsible types of nuclear transfer, as is suggested by perhaps exaggerated fears of Pakistani assistance to the nuclear ambitions of other Islamic states.

CONCLUSIONS

Clearly, the principal lesson of the 1985 NPT review conference, as recognized by many participants and analysts, is that the parties to the treaty held the NPT to be in their national interest and were not prepared to see it destroyed or undermined by an acrimonious review conference that replayed the tragedy of 1980. While this common interest produced a fragile consensus in 1985, there are no guarantees that this consensus will endure until (or perhaps reappear in) 1995. Nonetheless, the vision of a world without the NPT should demonstrate that the decline or demise of the treaty would pose problems for holdouts or wavering parties, no less than for fully committed parties. To the extent that it does so, it reveals foundations on which to base a firmer consensus in the future and thereby provides an impetus for preserving this essential treaty regime intact.

NOTES AND REFERENCES

1. A version of this chapter appeared in John Simpson, ed., *Nuclear Non-Proliferation: An Agenda for the 1990s* (New York: Cambridge University Press, 1987). Reprinted by permission of Cambridge University Press.

Conclusions

Joseph F. Pilat and Robert E. Pendley

What are the prospects, then, for the NPT beyond 1995? Will it survive or succumb? Advocates as well as critics of the treaty recognize that it is the center-piece of the nonproliferation regime, has promoted confidence by helping to assure states that their neighbors are not developing nuclear weapons, and has furthered the nonproliferation norm. And while none of the authors hold that the NPT is more important than security considerations in national decisions on whether or not to go nuclear, the treaty is viewed as nonetheless vital by the majority of the contributors. According to Lawrence Scheinman, "It cannot be said, nor should it be expected, that the NPT alone can or does prevent proliferation. The single most important factor in nonproliferation is a decision by national political authorities that acquiring nuclear weapons or retaining an option to do so is not in the national interest. That decision is based on a presumably reasoned calculation of political and security requirements and national interests. . . . Where the NPT becomes relevant is in its contribution to the shaping of political and security perceptions and to the calcula tion of whether the national interest is better served by forswearing or by maintain-ing a weapon option, or even by actually acquiring nuclear weapons." Yet, despite this widespread perception of the value of the NPT, virtually every contributor recognized that in 1995 the treaty will not go unchallenged by parties and nonparties alike, and a struggle for its extension can be anticipated. Although most of the contributors believe that the treaty will survive, a catastrophic failure of the NPT was recognized as all too possible.

A fundamental shift in East–West or North–South relations, noncompliance by NPT parties, a demonstration of nuclear-weapon capabilities by nonparties, other dramatic nuclear events such as theft or terrorism, or massive withdrawals from the treaty to protest inadequate arms control progress could all herald the end of an effective NPT regime. None of these events now appear probable, and the success of the 1985 review conference is viewed as a hopeful portent for the continued viability of the treaty. However, it must be remembered that we have no

Joseph F. Pilat and Robert E. Pendley • Staff Members, Center for National Security Studies, Los Alamos National Laboratory, Los Alamos, New Mexico.

Delphic oracle capable of discerning the shape of things to come, and that the 1985 review conference may not be a good indicator for gauging success in 1990 and 1995. In 1985, unique conditions prevailed, including a reluctance on the part of the Group of 77 (G-77) to rock the boat after the failed conference of 1980; a resumption of U.S.–Soviet arms control talks after a year's hiatus; and a coming U.S.–Soviet summit that no state was eager to jeopardize.

The case against the treaty in 1990 and 1995 will be made from within (e.g., Iran) and without (e.g., India, Argentina). India has already suggested an alternative to the NPT which involves the disarmament of the nuclear powers by the year 2010, and several contributors have spoken of the desirability of an alternative treaty structure or a successor regime. According to Antonio Carrea, "We should look to a nonproliferation regime in the twenty-first century in which emphasis will be put not on stopping horizontal proliferation, but on the cessation of the arms race and on nuclear disarmament." And, in the view of Ambassador Richard Butler, "Despite widespread support for the NPT, the two central issues—the atom and development—need to be addressed anew if the goals of the treaty are to be fulfilled, or indeed, if the treaty is to survive. First, nuclear weapons must be progressively eliminated . . . . Second, there are continuing claims upon the world's attention of the demand for development in the South . . . . True vision recognizes that the challenges now confronting humanity demand a rethinking, and a reworking, of the solutions conceived in the period from 1945 to 1970. . . . A successor to the NPT is necessary to resolve the problems of the atom and development that are now before us."

While the treaty has ardent advocates, and is the most widely adhered to arms control treaty in history, a large number of states have no genuine interest in nuclear power and do not perceive themselves as directly threatened by existing or emerging nuclear powers. Accordingly, these states may have no strong commitment to the NPT and could be susceptible to the arguments of those who would alter or replace the treaty. But the states that might possibly defect because they have no genuine interest in the treaty's broad nonproliferation or nuclear power promotion objectives, as well as those that have rejected the treaty because they have wished to keep a nuclear-weapon option open, may nonetheless have national interests at stake in regional confrontations that have a nuclear overhang. Several contributors suggested that finding better ways to deal with regional confrontations and conflicts in the future is a critical factor for continued viability of the NPT's multilateral approach to nuclear control. A number of possibilities were discussed, ranging from the better promulgation of peaceful nuclear technologies to regional security guarantees, confidence-building measures, and economic development in an enlarged vision of a future nonproliferation regime.

While the connections between arms control and nonproliferation implicit and explicit in Article VI of the NPT were discussed in the volume, and it was argued by some contributors that the connections were historically and substantively unfounded, it was widely recognized that widespread perceptions among the G-77 would make the arms control record of the United States and the Soviet Union as central an issue in 1990 and 1995 as it had been at the first three NPT review conferences. In this context, it was suggested that with the conclusion of the Intermediate-Range Nuclear Forces (INF) Treaty and the negotiations on strategic arms reductions and nuclear testing, arms control may be perceived as moving in the right direction. As Ambassador Mohamed Shaker states, "In the 1990s the most powerful guarantee for successful reviews and extension of the NPT beyond its initial duration of twenty-five years would be the conclusion of concrete agreements on disarmament. The Intermediate Nuclear Forces agreement of 1987 is an important step in the right direction." However, as Lewis Dunn warns, "Prudent planning should assume that in the absence of significant reductions of U.S. and Soviet nuclear weapons between now and 1995, going beyond the INF Treaty, supporters of the NPT will face an uphill fight for its renewal. Faced with the need to choose between renewal of the NPT on the grounds that it serves their security interests even without effective implementation of Article VI and nonrenewal (or renewal for a short period with conditions for further extension), the majority of developing countries that hold the balance might choose the latter." All in all, then, the way Article VI plays out in 1990 and 1995 will depend on the expectations and perceptions of the neutral and nonaligned states, and the G-77 reaction to any of these developments cannot now be calculated. In this vein, the ongoing negotiations in the conventional and chemical arms control arenas may result in a reconsideration of the U.S.–Soviet arms control process among thoughtful critics. The possibility is real that by 1990 or 1995 substantial progress will have been made in negotiations to reduce armed forces in Europe and to ban chemical arms, and that an actual reduction of troops and of chemical and conventional weapons may have begun as well. In the context of improved relations between, and continued negotiations on nuclear weapons by, the United States and the Soviet Union, such developments should provide a powerful counter to the two-decade-long argument that the superpowers were only interested in maintaining their nuclear hegemony through the NPT, and have not adequately fulfilled their own obligations to engage in negotiations to reduce nuclear weapons. They could help to refocus the Article VI debate on all arms, as the language of the article seems to require.

While it is anticipated that the major confrontations in 1990 and 1995 will probably center on arms control issues, a number of contributors urged the nonproliferation community not to forget the rights and obligations embodied in Article IV of the treaty. As the superpower relationship becomes potentially less confrontational, and less centered on questions involving nuclear weapons and European security, other regional and global questions will become increasingly important to global stability. In this light, continued and increasing attention to questions of the environment and of economic development in key regions and around the world, including the potential benefits of greater access to nuclear technology by the developing world, was argued to be supportive of the nonproliferation regime in the long haul.

The battle to save the treaty from being undermined or ended should be a high priority, many authors suggested, because there is no good prospect for a viable alternative to the treaty—the obligations it creates could not be duplicated today— and efforts to amend it could ultimately unravel the treaty entirely. As Benjamin

Sanders, looking at the history of the negotiations that led to the NPT, argued: "The text that resulted from the negotiations was the most that could be achieved under the circumstances. Those circumstances have changed somewhat since the late 1960s, but the political priorities of the protagonists in the protracted discussion have remained basically the same. There is no reason to believe that an attempt at amending or replacing the NPT would yield a more satisfactory instrument. There is every likelihood that such attempts would destroy the treaty, or at best greatly weaken it. . . . By endangering the partial solutions that are in place, such attempts inevitably aggravate the problems they are meant to solve."

With such considerations in mind, those contributors who sought to salvage and to strengthen the NPT suggested, each in his own way, that a viable strategy for 1990 and 1995 necessarily involves engaging other states parties to the treaty to show them how it has benefited them, in particular by continued emphasis on the contribution of the treaty to regional and global security, and thus to all states; continued support for peaceful nuclear cooperation, with a strong preference for NPT parties; and continued serious negotiations on the reduction of nuclear, chemical, and conventional arms. Extensive consultations among the Western and Eastern states will be essential, along with engaging key moderate nonaligned states in a dialogue, in particular to avoid the collapse of the NPT through G-77 miscalculations. And, while there are dangers in this approach, it is important to begin to think about fall-back scenarios to be sure we are prepared if, for instance, there should be a vote proposed in 1995 to extend the treaty for a finite period until various disarmament and other demands, or conditions, are met.

For the majority of authors, the decline or demise of the NPT would appear as a tragedy for nonproliferation and arms control efforts and would have consequences for regional and global security. According to David Fischer, "One must not see the loss of the NPT only through the narrow lens of safeguards. In the worst case, its demise might affect the prospects for peace in the twenty-first century . . . . The loss of the NPT would be a major international setback, perhaps a political disaster. It might gravely damage the prospects for arms control. It might destroy one of the few enduring bases of superpower cooperation. It might revive suspicions of the nuclear intentions of the most dynamic nations of Western Europe and the Far East. The confidence and security of all states might be weakened, even for those who still formally reject the nonproliferation regime."

APPENDIX

Toward 1995
United Nations Documents Relating to the Establishment and Functioning of the NPT, 1959–1988

GENERAL ASSEMBLY RESOLUTION 1380 (XIV): PREVENTION OF THE WIDER DISSEMINATION OF NUCLEAR WEAPONS, NOVEMBER 20, 1959[1]

The General Assembly,

Recognizing that the danger now exists that an increase in the number of States possessing nuclear weapons may occur, aggravating international tension and the difficulty of maintaining world peace, and thus rendering more difficult the attainment of general disarmament agreement,

Convinced therefore that consideration of this danger is appropriate within the framework of deliberations on disarmament,

Noting the resolution of the United Nations Disarmament Commission of 10 September 1959,

Desiring to bring to the attention of the ten-nation disarmament committee its conviction that consideration should be given to this problem,

1. *Suggests* that the ten-nation disarmament committee, in the course of its deliberations, should consider appropriate means whereby this danger may be averted, including the feasibility of an international agreement, subject to inspection and control, whereby the Powers producing nuclear weapons would refrain from handing over the control of such weapons to any nation not possessing them and whereby the Powers not possessing such weapons would refrain from manufacturing them;

2. *Invites* the committee to include the results of its deliberations on these matters in its report to the Disarmament Commission.

---

[1]U.N. doc A/RES/1380 (XIV), November 23, 1959, in Department of State, *Documents on Disarmament, 1945–1959*, vol. II (Washington, D.C.: U.S. Government Printing Office, 1960), p. 1547.

GENERAL ASSEMBLY RESOLUTION 1576 (XV): PREVENTION OF THE WIDER DISSEMINATION OF NUCLEAR WEAPONS, DECEMBER 20, 1960[1]

The General Assembly,

Recalling its resolution 1380 (XIV) of 20 November 1959,

Recognizing the urgent danger that now exists that an increase in the number of States possessing nuclear weapons may occur, aggravating international tension and the difficulty of maintaining world peace, and thus rendering more difficult the attainment of general disarmament agreement,

Noting with regret that the Ten-Nation Committee on Disarmament did not find it possible to consider this problem, which was referred to it by General Assembly resolution 1380 (XIV),

Believing in the necessity of an international agreement, subject to inspection and control, whereby the Powers producing nuclear weapons would refrain from relinquishing control of such weapons to any nation not possessing them and whereby Powers not possessing such weapons would refrain from manufacturing them,

Believing further that, pending the conclusion of such an international agreement, it is desirable that temporary and voluntary measures be taken to avoid the aggravation of this danger,

1. *Calls upon* all Governments to make every effort to achieve permanent agreement on the prevention of the wider dissemination of nuclear weapons;

2. *Calls upon* Powers producing such weapons, as a temporary and voluntary measure pending the negotiation of such a permanent agreement, to refrain from relinquishing control of such weapons to any nation not possessing them and from transmitting to it the information necessary for their manufacture;

3. *Calls upon* Powers not possessing such weapons, on a similar temporary and voluntary basis, to refrain from manufacturing these weapons and from otherwise attempting to acquire them.

GENERAL ASSEMBLY RESOLUTION 1664 (XVI): QUESTION OF DISARMAMENT, DECEMBER 4, 1961[2]

The General Assembly,

Convinced that all measures should be taken that could halt further nuclear weapons tests and prevent the further spread of nuclear weapons,

Recognizing that the countries not possessing nuclear weapons have a grave interest, and an important part to fulfil, in the preparation and implementation of such measures,

Believing that action taken by those countries will facilitate agreement by the nuclear Powers to discontinue all nuclear tests and to prevent any increase in the number of nuclear Powers,

Taking note of the suggestion that an inquiry be made into the conditions under which

---

[1]U.N. doc. A/RES/1576 (XV), December 27, 1960, in Department of State, *Documents on Disarmament, 1960*, p. 373.

[2]U.N. doc. A/RES/1664 (XVI), December 5, 1961, in United States Arms Control and Disarmament Agency, *Documents on Disarmament, 1961*, p. 693.

countries not possessing nuclear weapons might be willing to enter into specific undertakings to refrain from manufacturing or otherwise acquiring such weapons and to refuse to receive, in the future, nuclear weapons in their territories on behalf of any other country,

1. *Requests* the Secretary-General to make such an inquiry as soon as possible and to submit a report on its results to the Disarmament Commission not later than 1 April 1962;

2. *Requests* the Disarmament Commission to take such further measures as appear to be warranted in the light of that report;

3. *Calls upon* the nuclear Powers to extend their fullest co-operation and assistance with regard to the implementation of the present resolution.

GENERAL ASSEMBLY RESOLUTION 1665 (XVI): PREVENTION OF THE WIDER DISSEMINATION OF NUCLEAR WEAPONS, DECEMBER 4, 1961 (Proposed by Ireland)[1]

The General Assembly,

Recalling its resolutions 1380 (XIV) of 20 November 1959 and 1576 (XV) of 20 December 1960,

Convinced that an increase in the number of States possessing nuclear weapons is growing more imminent and threatens to extend and intensify the arms race and to increase the difficulties of avoiding war and of establishing international peace and security based on the rule of law,

Believing in the necessity of an international agreement, subject to inspection and control, whereby the states producing nuclear weapons would refrain from relinquishing control of such weapons to any nation not possessing them and whereby states not possessing such weapons would refrain from manufacturing them,

1. *Calls upon* all States, and in particular upon the States at present possessing nuclear weapons, to use their best endeavours to secure the conclusion of an international agreement containing provisions under which the nuclear States would undertake to refrain from relinquishing control of nuclear weapons and from transmitting the information necessary for their manufacture to States not possessing such weapons, and provisions under which States not possessing nuclear weapons would undertake not to manufacture or otherwise acquire control of such weapons;

2. *Urges* all States to co-operate to those ends.

GENERAL ASSEMBLY RESOLUTION 2028 (XX): NON-PROLIFERATION OF NUCLEAR WEAPONS, NOVEMBER 19, 1965[2]

The General Assembly,

Conscious of its responsibility under the Charter of the United Nations for disarmament and the consolidation of peace,

Mindful of its responsibility in accordance with Article 11, paragraph 1, of the *Charter*,

---

[1]U.N. doc. A/RES/1665 (XVI), December 5, 1961, in *Documents on Disarmament, 1961*, p. 694.

[2]U.N. doc. A/RES/2028 (XX), November 23, 1965, in *Documents on Disarmament, 1965*, pp. 532–34.

which stipulates that the General Assembly may consider the general principles of co-operation in the maintenance of international peace and security, including the principles governing disarmament and the regulation of armaments, and may make recommendations with regard to such principles to the Members or to the Security Council or to both,

Recalling its resolutions 1665 (XVI) of 4 December 1961 and 1908 (XVIII) of 27 November 1963,

Recognizing the urgency and great importance of the question of preventing the proliferation of nuclear weapons,

Noting with satisfaction the efforts of Brazil, Burma, Ethiopia, India, Mexico, Nigeria, Sweden and the United Arab Republic to achieve the solution of the problem of non-proliferation of nuclear weapons, as contained in their joint memorandum of 15 September 1965,

Convinced that the proliferation of nuclear weapons would endanger the security of all States and make more difficult the achievement of general and complete disarmament under effective international control,

Noting the declaration adopted by the Assembly of Heads of State and Government of the Organization of African Unity at its first regular session, held at Cairo in July 1964, and the Declaration entitled "Programme for Peace and International Co-operation" adopted by the Second Conference of Heads of State or Government of Non-Aligned Countries, held at Cairo in October 1964,

Noting also the draft treaties to prevent the proliferation of nuclear weapons submitted by the United States of America and the Union of Soviet Socialist Republics, respectively,

Noting further that a draft unilateral non-acquisition declaration has been submitted by Italy,

Convinced that General Assembly resolutions 1652 (XVI) of 24 November 1961 and 1911 (XVIII) of 27 November 1963 aim at preventing the proliferation of nuclear weapons,

Believing that it is imperative to exert further efforts to conclude a treaty to prevent the proliferation of nuclear weapons,

1. *Urges* all States to take all steps necessary for the early conclusion of a treaty to prevent the proliferation of nuclear weapons;

2. *Calls upon* the Conference of the Eighteen-Nation Committee on Disarmament to give urgent consideration to the question of non-proliferation of nuclear weapons and, to that end, to reconvene as early as possible with a view to negotiating an international treaty to prevent the proliferation of nuclear weapons, based on the following main principles:

(*a*) The treaty should be void of any loop-holes which might permit nuclear or non-nuclear Powers to proliferate, directly or indirectly, nuclear weapons in any form;

(*b*) The treaty should embody an acceptable balance of mutual responsibilities and obligations of the nuclear and non-nuclear Powers;

(*c*) The treaty should be a step towards the achievement of general and complete disarmament and, more particularly, nuclear disarmament;

(*d*) There should be acceptable and workable provisions to ensure the effectiveness of the treaty;

(*e*) Nothing in the treaty should adversely affect the right of any group of States to conclude regional treaties in order to ensure the total absence of nuclear weapons in their respective territories;

3. *Transmits* the records of the First Committee relating to the discussion of the item entitled "Non-proliferation of nuclear weapons", together with all other relevant documents, to the Eighteen-Nation Committee for its consideration;

4. *Requests* the Eighteen-Nation Committee to submit to the General Assembly at an

early date a report on the results of its work on a treaty to prevent the proliferation of nuclear weapons.

GENERAL ASSEMBLY RESOLUTION 2149 (XXI): RENUNCIATION BY STATES OF ACTIONS HAMPERING THE CONCLUSION OF AN AGREEMENT ON THE NON-PROLIFERATION OF NUCLEAR WEAPONS, NOVEMBER 4, 1966[1]

The General Assembly,

Reaffirming its resolution 2028 (XX) of 19 November 1965,

Convinced that the proliferation of nuclear weapons would endanger the security of all States and hamper the achievement of general and complete disarmament,

Considering that international negotiations are now under way with a view to the preparation of a treaty on the non-proliferation of nuclear weapons, and wishing to create an atmosphere conducive to the successful conclusion of those negotiations,

Urgently appeals to all States, pending the conclusion of such a treaty:

(*a*) To take all the necessary steps to facilitate and achieve at the earliest possible time the conclusion of a treaty on the non-proliferation of nuclear weapons in accordance with the principles laid down in General Assembly resolution 2028 (XX),

(*b*) To refrain from any actions conducive to the proliferation of nuclear weapons or which might hamper the conclusion of an agreement on the non-proliferation of nuclear weapons.

GENERAL ASSEMBLY RESOLUTION 2153 (XXI): NON-PROLIFERATION OF NUCLEAR WEAPONS, NOVEMBER 17, 1966[2]

A

The General Assembly,

Having discussed the report of the Conference of the Eighteen-Nation Committee on Disarmament on the non-proliferation of nuclear weapons,

Noting that it has not yet been possible to reach agreement on an international treaty to prevent the proliferation of nuclear weapons,

Viewing with apprehension the possibility that such a situation may lead not only to an increase of nuclear arsenals and to a spread of nuclear weapons over the world but also to an increase in the number of nuclear-weapon Powers,

Believing that if such a situation persists it may lead to the aggravation of tensions between States and the risk of a nuclear war,

Believing further that the remaining differences between all concerned should be re-

---

[1]U.N. doc. A/RES/2149 (XXI), November 7, 1966, in *Documents on Disarmament, 1966*, pp. 686–87.

[2]U.N. doc. A/RES/2153 (XXI)/Rev. 1, January 5, 1967, in *Documents on Disarmament, 1966*, pp. 748–50.

solved quickly so as to prevent any further delay in the conclusion of an international treaty on the non-proliferation of nuclear weapons,

Convinced, therefore, that it is imperative to make further efforts to bring to a conclusion a treaty which reflects the mandate given by the General Assembly in its resolution 2028 (XX) of 19 November 1965 and which is acceptable to all concerned and satisfactory to the international community,

1. *Reaffirms* its resolution 2028 (XX);

2. *Urges* all States to take all the necessary steps conducive to the earliest conclusion of a treaty on the non-proliferation of nuclear weapons;

3. *Calls upon* all nuclear-weapon Powers to refrain from the use, or the threat of use, of nuclear weapons against States which may conclude treaties of the nature defined in paragraph 2 (*e*) of General Assembly resolution 2028 (XX);

4. *Requests* the Conference of the Eighteen-Nation Committee on Disarmament to consider urgently the proposal that the nuclear-weapon Powers should give an assurance that they will not use, or threaten to use, nuclear weapons against non-nuclear-weapon States without nuclear weapons on their territories, and any other proposals that have been or may be made for the solution of this problem;

5. *Calls upon* all States to adhere strictly to the principles laid down in its resolution 2028 (XX) for the negotiation of the above-mentioned treaty;

6. *Calls* upon the Conference of the Eighteen-Nation Committee on Disarmament to give high priority to the question of the non-proliferation of nuclear weapons in accordance with the mandate contained in General Assembly resolution 2028 (XX);

7. *Transmits* the records of the First Committee relating to the discussion of the item entitled "Non-proliferation of nuclear weapons", together with all other relevant documents, to the Conference of the Eighteen-Nation Committee on Disarmament;

8. *Requests* the Conference of the Eighteen-Nation Committee on Disarmament to submit to the General Assembly at an early date a report on the results of its work on the question of the non-proliferation of nuclear weapons.

B

The General Assembly,

Recalling previous resolutions on the non-proliferation of nuclear weapons,

Considering that the further spread of nuclear weapons would endanger the peace and security of all States,

Convinced that the emergence of additional nuclear-weapon Powers would provoke an uncontrollable nuclear arms race,

Reiterating that the prevention of further proliferation of nuclear weapons is a matter of the highest priority demanding the unceasing attention of both nuclear-weapon and non-nuclear-weapon Powers,

Believing that a conference of non-nuclear-weapon Powers would contribute to the conclusion of arrangements designed to safeguard the security of those States,

1. *Decides* to convene a conference of non-nuclear-weapon States to meet not later than July 1968 to consider the following and other related questions:

"(*a*) How can the security of the non-nuclear States best be assured?

"(*b*) How may non-nuclear Powers co-operate among themselves in preventing the proliferation of nuclear weapons?

"(*c*) How can nuclear devices be used for exclusively peaceful purposes?";

2. *Requests* the President of the General Assembly immediately to set up a preparatory committee, widely representative of the non-nuclear-weapon States, to make appropriate arrangements for convening the conference and to consider the question of the association of nuclear States with the work of the conference and report thereon to the General Assembly at its twenty-second session.

GENERAL ASSEMBLY RESOLUTION 2346 (XXII): NON-PROLIFERATION OF NUCLEAR WEAPONS, DECEMBER 19, 1967[1]

A

The General Assembly,

Having received the interim report of the Conference of the Eighteen-Nation Committee on Disarmament,

Noting the progress that the Conference of the Eighteen-Nation Committee on Disarmament has made towards preparing a draft international treaty to prevent the proliferation of nuclear weapons,

Noting further that it has not been possible to complete the text of an international treaty to prevent the proliferation of nuclear weapons,

Reaffirming that it is imperative to make further efforts to conclude such a treaty at the earliest possible date,

Expressing the hope that the remaining differences between all the States concerned can be quickly resolved,

Taking into account the fact that the Conference of the Eighteen-Nation Committee on Disarmament is continuing its work with a view to negotiating a draft treaty on the non-proliferation of nuclear weapons and intends to submit a full report for the consideration of the General Assembly as soon as possible,

1. *Reaffirms* its resolutions 2028 (XX) of 19 November 1965, 2149 (XXI) of 4 November 1966 and 2153 A (XXI) of 17 November 1966;

2. *Calls upon* the Conference of the Eighteen-Nation Committee on Disarmament urgently to continue its work; giving all due consideration to all proposals submitted to the Committee and to the views expressed by Member States during the twenty-second session of the General Assembly;

3. *Requests* the Conference of the Eighteen-Nation Committee on Disarmament to submit to the General Assembly, on or before 15 March 1968, a full report on the negotiations regarding a draft treaty on the non-proliferation of nuclear weapons, together with the pertinent documents and records;

4. *Recommends* that upon the receipt of that report appropriate consultations should be initiated, in accordance with the rules of procedure of the General Assembly, on the setting of an early date after 15 March 1968 for the resumption of the twenty-second session of the General Assembly to consider agenda item 28 (a) entitled "Non-proliferation of nuclear weapons: report of the Conference of the Eighteen-Nation Committee on Disarmament".

---

[1]U.N. doc. A/RES/2346 (XXII), January 5, 1968, in *Documents on Disarmament, 1967*, pp. 732–33.

B

The General Assembly,

Recalling its resolution 2153 B (XXI) of 17 November 1966, by which it decided that a conference of non-nuclear-weapon States should be convened not later than July 1968,

Having considered with appreciation the report of the Preparatory Committee for the Conference of Non-Nuclear Weapon States,

1. *Approves* the recommendations of the Preparatory Committee for the Conference of Non-Nuclear-Weapon States, subject to paragraph 2 below;

2. *Decides* to convene the Conference of Non-Nuclear-Weapon States at Geneva from 29 August to 28 September 1968;

3. *Decides* to invite to the Conference non-nuclear-weapon States members of the United Nations and members of the specialized agencies and of the International Atomic Energy Agency;

4. *Requests* the Secretary-General to make appropriate arrangements for convening the Conference in accordance with the recommendations of the Preparatory Committee.

GENERAL ASSEMBLY RESOLUTION 2373 (XXII): TREATY ON THE NON-PROLIFERATION OF NUCLEAR WEAPONS, JUNE 12, 1968[1]

The General Assembly,

Recalling its resolutions 2346 A (XXII) of 19 December 1967, 2153 A (XXI) of 17 November 1966, 2149 (XXI) of 4 November 1966, 2028 (XX) of 19 November 1965 and 1665 (XVI) of 4 December 1961,

Convinced of the urgency and great importance of preventing the spread of nuclear weapons and of intensifying international co-operation in the development of peaceful applications of atomic energy,

Having considered the report of the Conference of the Eighteen-Nation Committee on Disarmament, dated 14 March 1968, and appreciative of the work of the Committee on the elaboration of the draft non-proliferation treaty, which is attached to that report,

Convinced that, pursuant to the provisions of the treaty, all signatories have the right to engage in research, production and use of nuclear energy for peaceful purposes and will be able to acquire source and special fissionable materials, as well as equipment for the processing, use and production of nuclear material for peaceful purposes,

Convinced further that an agreement to prevent the further proliferation of nuclear weapons must be followed as soon as possible by effective measures on the cessation of the nuclear arms race and on nuclear disarmament, and that the non-proliferation treaty will contribute to this aim,

Affirming that in the interest of international peace and security both nuclear-weapon and non-nuclear-weapon States carry the responsibility of acting in accordance with the principles of the Charter of the United Nations that the sovereign equality of all States shall be respected, that the threat or use of force in international relations shall be refrained from and that international disputes shall be settled by peaceful means,

1. *Commends* the Treaty on the Non-Proliferation of Nuclear Weapons, the text of which is annexed to the present resolution;

---

[1]U.N. doc. A/RES/2373 (XXII), June 18, 1968, in *Documents on Disarmament, 1968*, pp. 431–32.

2. *Requests* the Depositary Governments to open the Treaty for signature and ratification at the earliest possible date;

3. *Expresses the hope* for the widest possible adherence to the Treaty by both nuclear-weapon and non-nuclear-weapon States;

4. *Requests* the Conference of the Eighteen-Nation Committee on Disarmament and the nuclear-weapon States urgently to pursue negotiations on effective measures relating to the cessation of the nuclear arms race at an early date and to nuclear disarmament, and on a treaty on general and complete disarmament under strict and effective international control;

5. *Requests* the Conference of the Eighteen-Nation Committee on Disarmament to report on the progress of its work to the General Assembly at its twenty-third session.

TREATY ON THE NON-PROLIFERATION OF NUCLEAR WEAPONS*

**Opened for Signature at London, Moscow and Washington: 1 July 1968
Entered into Force: 5 March 1970
Depositary Governments: Union of Soviet Socialist Republics, United Kingdom of Great Britain and Northern Ireland and United States of America**

The States concluding this Treaty, hereinafter referred to as the "Parties to the Treaty",

Considering the devastation that would be visited upon all mankind by a nuclear war and the consequent need to make every effort to avert the danger of such a war and to take measures to safeguard the security of peoples,

Believing that the proliferation of nuclear weapons would seriously enhance the danger of nuclear war,

In conformity with resolutions of the United Nations General Assembly calling for the conclusion of an agreement on the prevention of wider dissemination of nuclear weapons,

Undertaking to co-operate in facilitating the application of International Atomic Energy Agency safeguards on peaceful nuclear activities,

Expressing their support for research, development and other efforts to further the application, within the framework of the International Atomic Energy Agency safeguards system, of the principle of safeguarding effectively the flow of source and special fissionable materials by use of instruments and other techniques at certain strategic points,

Affirming the principle that the benefits of peaceful applications of nuclear technology, including any technological by-products which may be derived by nuclear-weapon States from the development of nuclear explosive devices, should be available for peaceful purposes to all Parties to the Treaty, whether nuclear-weapon or non-nuclear-weapon States,

Convinced that, in furtherance of this principle, all Parties to the Treaty are entitled to participate in the fullest possible exchange of scientific information for, and to contribute alone or in co-operation with other States to, the further development of the applications of atomic energy for peaceful purposes,

Declaring their intention to achieve at the earliest possible date the cessation of the nuclear arms race and to undertake effective measures in the direction of nuclear disarmament,

---

Status of Multilateral Arms Regulation and Disarmament Agreements, 3d ed., 1987 (New York: United Nations, 1988), pp. 71–99.

Urging the co-operation of all States in the attainment of this objective,

Recalling the determination expressed by the Parties to the 1963 Treaty banning nuclear weapons tests in the atmosphere, in outer space and under water in its Preamble to seek to achieve the discontinuance of all test explosions of nuclear weapons for all time and to continue negotiations to this end,

Desiring to further the easing of international tension and the strengthening of trust between States in order to facilitate the cessation of the manufacture of nuclear weapons, the liquidation of all their existing stockpiles, and the elimination from national arsenals of nuclear weapons and the means of their delivery pursuant to a Treaty on general and complete disarmament under strict and effective international control,

Recalling that, in accordance with the Charter of the United Nations, States must refrain in their international relations from the threat or use of force against the territorial integrity or political independence of any State, or in any other manner inconsistent with the Purposes of the United Nations, and that the establishment and maintenance of international peace and security are to be promoted with the least diversion for armaments of the world's human and economic resources,

Have agreed as follows:

Article I

Each nuclear-weapon State Party to the Treaty undertakes not to transfer to any recipient whatsoever nuclear weapons or other nuclear explosive devices or control over such weapons or explosive devices directly, or indirectly; and not in any way to assist, encourage, or induce any non-nuclear weapon State to manufacture or otherwise acquire nuclear weapons or other nuclear explosive devices, or control over such weapons or explosive devices.

Article II

Each non-nuclear-weapon State Party to the Treaty undertakes not to receive the transfer from any transferor whatsoever of nuclear weapons or other nuclear explosive devices or of control over such weapons or explosive devices directly, or indirectly; not to manufacture or otherwise acquire nuclear weapons or other nuclear explosive devices; and not to seek or receive any assistance in the manufacture of nuclear weapons or other nuclear explosive devices.

Article III

1. Each non-nuclear-weapon State Party to the Treaty undertakes to accept safeguards, as set forth in an agreement to be negotiated and concluded with the International Atomic Energy Agency in accordance with the Statute of the International Atomic Energy Agency and the Agency's safeguards system, for the exclusive purpose of verification of the fulfilment of its obligations assumed under this Treaty with a view to preventing diversion of nuclear energy from peaceful uses to nuclear weapons or other nuclear explosive devices. Procedures for the safeguards required by this Article shall be followed with respect to source or special fissionable material whether it is being produced, processed or used in any principal nuclear facility or is outside any such facility. The safeguards required by this Article shall be applied on all source or special fissionable material in all peaceful nuclear activities

within the territory of such State, under its jurisdiction, or carried out under its control anywhere.

2. Each State Party to the Treaty undertakes not to provide: (a) source or special fissionable material, or (b) equipment or material especially designed or prepared for the processing, use or production of special fissionable material, to any non-nuclear-weapon State for peaceful purposes, unless the source or special fissionable material shall be subject to the safeguards required by this Article.

3. The safeguards required by this Article shall be implemented in a manner designed to comply with Article IV of this Treaty, and to avoid hampering the economic or technological development of the Parties or international co-operation in the field of peaceful nuclear activities, including the international exchange of nuclear material and equipment for the processing, use or production of nuclear material for peaceful purposes in accordance with the provisions of this Article and the principle of safeguarding set forth in the Preamble of the Treaty.

4. Non-nuclear-weapon States Party to the Treaty shall conclude agreements with the International Atomic Energy Agency to meet the requirements of this Article either individually or together with other States in accordance with the Statute of the International Atomic Energy Agency. Negotiation of such agreements shall commence within 180 days from the original entry into force of this Treaty. For States depositing their instruments of ratification or accession after the 180-day period, negotiation of such agreements shall commence not later than the date of such deposit. Such agreements shall enter into force not later than eighteen months after the date of initiation of negotiations.

Article IV

1. Nothing in this Treaty shall be interpreted as affecting the inalienable right of all the Parties to the Treaty to develop research, production and use of nuclear energy for peaceful purposes without discrimination and in conformity with Articles I and II of this Treaty.

2. All the Parties to the Treaty undertake to facilitate, and have the right to participate in, the fullest possible exchange of equipment, materials and scientific and technological information for the peaceful uses of nuclear energy. Parties to the Treaty in a position to do so shall also co-operate in contributing alone or together with other States or international organizations to the further development of the applications of nuclear energy for peaceful purposes, especially in the territories of non-nuclear-weapon States Party to the Treaty, with due consideration for the needs of the developing areas of the world.

Article V

Each Party to the Treaty undertakes to take appropriate measures to ensure that, in accordance with this Treaty, under appropriate international observation and through appropriate international procedures, potential benefits from any peaceful applications of nuclear explosions will be made available to non-nuclear-weapon States Party to the Treaty on a non-discriminatory basis and that the charge to such Parties for the explosive devices used will be as low as possible and exclude any charge for research and development. Non-nuclear-weapon States Party to the Treaty shall be able to obtain such benefits, pursuant to a special international agreement or agreements, through an appropriate international body with adequate representation of non-nuclear-weapon States. Negotiations on this subject shall commence as soon as possible after the Treaty enters into force. Non-nuclear-weapon States Party to the Treaty so desiring may also obtain such benefits pursuant to bilateral agreements.

Article VI

Each of the Parties to the Treaty undertakes to pursue negotiations in good faith on effective measures relating to cessation of the nuclear arms race at an early date and to nuclear disarmament, and on a treaty on general and complete disarmament under strict and effective international control.

Article VII

Nothing in this Treaty affects the right of any group of States to conclude regional treaties in order to assure the total absence of nuclear weapons in their respective territories.

Article VIII

1. Any Party to the Treaty may propose amendments to this Treaty. The text of any proposed amendment shall be submitted to the Depositary Governments which shall circulate it to all Parties to the Treaty. Thereupon, if requested to do so by one-third or more of the Parties to the Treaty, the Depositary Governments shall convene a conference, to which they shall invite all the Parties to the Treaty, to consider such an amendment.

2. Any amendment to this Treaty must be approved by a majority of the votes of all the Parties to the Treaty, including the votes of all nuclear-weapon States Party to the Treaty and all other Parties which, on the date the amendment is circulated, are members of the Board of Governors of the International Atomic Energy Agency. The amendment shall enter into force for each Party that deposits its instrument of ratification of the amendment upon the deposit of such instruments of ratification by a majority of all the Parties, including the instruments of ratification of all nuclear-weapon States Party to the Treaty and all other Parties which, on the date the amendment is circulated, are members of the Board of Governors of the International Atomic Energy Agency. Thereafter, it shall enter into force for any other Party upon the deposit of its instrument of ratification of the amendment.

3. Five years after the entry into force of this Treaty, a conference of Parties to the Treaty shall be held in Geneva, Switzerland, in order to review the operation of this Treaty with a view to assuring that the purposes of the Preamble and the provisions of the Treaty are being realised. At intervals of five years thereafter, a majority of the Parties to the Treaty may obtain, by submitting a proposal to this effect to the Depositary Governments, the convening of further conferences with the same objective of reviewing the operation of the Treaty.

Article IX

1. This Treaty shall be open to all States for signature. Any State which does not sign the Treaty before its entry into force in accordance with paragraph 3 of this Article may accede to it at any time.

2. This Treaty shall be subject to ratification by signatory States. Instruments of ratification and instruments of accession shall be deposited with the Governments of the United

Kingdom of Great Britain and Northern Ireland, the Union of Soviet Socialist Republics and the United States of America, which are hereby designated the Depositary Governments.

3. This Treaty shall enter into force after its ratification by the States, the Governments of which are designated Depositaries of the Treaty, and forty other States signatory to this Treaty and the deposit of their instruments of ratification. For the purposes of this Treaty, a nuclear-weapon State is one which has manufactured and exploded a nuclear weapon or other nuclear explosive device prior to 1 January 1967.

4. For States whose instruments of ratification or accession are deposited subsequent to the entry into force of this Treaty, it shall enter into force on the date of the deposit of their instruments of ratification or accession.

5. The Depositary Governments shall promptly inform all signatory and acceding States of the date of each signature, the date of deposit of each instrument of ratification or of accession, the date of the entry into force of this Treaty, and the date of receipt of any requests for convening a conference or other notices.

6. This Treaty shall be registered by the Depositary Governments pursuant to Article 102 of the Charter of the United Nations.

Article X

1. Each Party shall in exercising its national sovereignty have the right to withdraw from the Treaty if it decides that extraordinary events, related to the subject matter of this Treaty, have jeopardized the supreme interests of its country. It shall give notice of such withdrawal to all other Parties to the Treaty and to the United Nations Security Council three months in advance. Such notice shall include a statement of the extraordinary events it regards as having jeopardized its supreme interests.

2. Twenty-five years after the entry into force of the Treaty, a conference shall be convened to decide whether the Treaty shall continue in force indefinitely, or shall be extended for an additional fixed period or periods. This decision shall be taken by a majority of the Parties to the Treaty.

Article XI

This Treaty, the English, Russian, French, Spanish and Chinese texts of which are equally authentic, shall be deposited in the archives of the Depositary Governments. Duly certified copies of this Treaty shall be transmitted by the Depositary Governments to the Governments of the signatory and acceding States.

IN WITNESS WHEREOF the undersigned, duly authorized, have signed this Treaty.

Done in triplicate, at the cities of London, Moscow and Washington, the first day of July, one thousand nine hundred and sixty-eight.

List of Signatories and Parties

(i)   Signatures affixed on the original of the Treaty deposited with the Governments of the: Union of Soviet Socialist Republics (M), United Kingdom of Great Britain and Northern Ireland (L), and United States of America (W).

(ii) Instruments of ratification, accession (a) or succession (s) deposited with the Governments of the: Union of Soviet Socialist Republics (M), United Kingdom of Great Britain and Northern Ireland (L), and United States of America (W).

Signatory or party reported		(i) Signature	(ii) Deposit
Afghanistan	(M)	1 July 1968	5 February 1970
	(L)	1 July 1968	5 March 1970
	(W)	1 July 1968	4 February 1970
Antigua and Barbuda	(M)	—	*
	(L)	—	17 June 1985(s)
	(W)	—	*
Australia	(M)	27 February 1970[1]	23 January 1973
	(L)	27 February 1970[1,2]	23 January 1973
	(W)	27 February 1970[1]	23 January 1973
Austria	(M)	1 July 1968	27 June 1969
	(L)	1 July 1968	27 June 1969
	(W)	1 July 1968	27 June 1969
Bahamas	(M)	—	30 August 1976(s)
	(L)	—	11 August 1976(s)
	(W)	—	13 August 1976(s)[3]
Bahrein	(M)	—	—
	(L)	—	—
	(W)	—	3 October 1988(a)
Bangladesh	(M)	—	31 August 1979(a)
	(L)	—	31 August 1979(a)
	(W)	—	27 September 1979(a)
Barbados	(M)	*	*
	(L)	*	*
	(W)	1 July 1968	21 February 1980
Belgium	(M)	20 August 1968	4 May 1975
	(L)	20 August 1968	2 May 1975
	(W)	20 August 1968	2 May 1975
Belize	(M)	—	*
	(L)	—	9 August 1985(s)
	(W)	—	*
Benin (Dahomey)	(M)	*	*
	(L)	*	*
	(W)	1 July 1968	31 October 1972
Bhutan	(M)	—	*
	(L)	—	*
	(W)	—	23 May 1985(a)
Bolivia	(M)	—	*
	(L)	—	26 May 1970
	(W)	1 July 1968	
Botswana	(M)	—	*
	(L)	—	28 April 1969
	(W)	1 July 1968	*

Signatory or party reported		(i) Signature	(ii) Deposit
Brunei Darussalam	(M)	—	*
	(L)	—	*
	(W)	—	26 March 1985(a)
Bulgaria	(M)	1 July 1968	18 September 1969
	(L)	1 July 1968	3 November 1969
	(W)	1 July 1968	5 September 1969
Burkina Faso (Upper Volta)	(M)	11 August 1969	*
	(L)	*	*
	(W)	25 November 1968	3 March 1970
Burundi	(M)	—	19 March 1971(a)
	(L)	—	*
	(W)	—	*
Cameroon (United Republic of Cameroon)	(M)	18 July 1968	*
	(L)	*	*
	(W)	17 July 1968	8 January 1969
Canada	(M)	29 July 1968	8 January 1969
	(L)	23 July 1968	8 January 1969
	(W)	23 July 1968	8 January 1969
Cape Verde	(M)	—	24 October 1979(a)
	(L)	—	*
	(W)	—	*
Central African Republic (Central African Empire)	(M)	—	*
	(L)	—	*
	(W)	—	25 October 1970(a)
Chad	(M)	1 July 1968	11 March 1971
	(L)	*	23 March 1971
	(W)	*	10 March 1971
Colombia	(M)	*	20 April 1986(a)
	(L)	*	30 April 1986(a)
	(W)	1 July 1968	8 April 1986(a)
Congo	(M)	—	*
	(L)	—	*
	(W)	—	23 October 1978(a)
Costa Rica	(M)	*	*
	(L)	*	*
	(W)	1 July 1968	3 March 1970
Cote d'Ivoire (Ivory Coast)	(M)	*	*
	(L)	*	*
	(W)	1 July 1968	6 March 1973

(continued)

Signatory or party reported		(i) Signature	(ii) Deposit
Cyprus	(M)	1 July 1968	10 February 1970
	(L)	1 July 1968	5 March 1970
	(W)	1 July 1968	16 February 1970
Czechoslovakia	(M)	1 July 1968	22 July 1969
	(L)	1 July 1968	22 July 1969
	(W)	1 July 1968	22 July 1969
Democratic Kampuchea	(M)	—	*
	(L)	—	*
	(W)	—	2 June 1972(a)
Democratic People's Republic of Korea	(M)	—	12 December 1985(a)
	(L)	—	*
	(W)	—	*
Democratic Yemen	(M)	14 November 1968	1 June 1979
	(L)	*	*
	(W)	*	*
Denmark	(M)	1 July 1968	3 January 1969
	(L)	1 July 1968	3 January 1969
	(W)	1 July 1968	3 January 1969
Dominica	(M)	—	*
	(L)	—	10 August 1984(s)
	(W)	—	*
Dominican Republic	(M)	*	*
	(L)	*	*
	(W)	1 July 1968	24 July 1971
Ecuador	(M)	*	*
	(L)	*	*
	(W)	9 July 1968	7 March 1969
Egypt	(M)	1 July 1968	*
	(L)	1 July 1968	26 February 1981
	(W)	—	*
El Salvador	(M)	*	*
	(L)	*	*
	(W)	1 July 1968	11 July 1972
Equatorial Guinea	(M)	—	*
	(L)	—	*
	(W)	—	1 November 1984(a)
Ethiopia	(M)	5 September 1968	5 February 1970
	(L)	5 September 1968	5 March 1970
	(W)	5 September 1968	5 March 1970
Fiji	(M)	—	29 August 1972(s)
	(L)	—	14 July 1972(s)
	(W)	—	21 July 1972(s)

Signatory or party reported		(i) Signature	(ii) Deposit
Finland	(M)	1 July 1968	5 February 1969
	(L)	1 July 1968	5 February 1969
	(W)	1 July 1968	5 February 1969
Gabon	(M)	—	*
	(L)	—	*
	(W)	—	19 February 1974(a)
Gambia	(M)	24 September 1968	*
	(L)	4 September 1968	*
	(W)	20 September 1968	12 May 1975
German Democratic Republic	(M)	1 July 1968	31 October 1969
	(L)	*	*
	(W)	*	*
Germany, Federal Republic of	(M)	28 November 1969	*
	(L)	29 November 1969[4]	2 May 1975[5]
	(W)	28 November 1969[4]	2 May 1975[5]
Ghana	(M)	1 July 1968	11 May 1970
	(L)	24 July 1968	4 May 1970
	(W)	1 July 1968	5 May 1970
Greece	(M)	1 July 1968	*
	(L)	*	*
	(W)	1 July 1968	11 March 1970
Grenada	(M)	—	2 September 1975(s)[3]
	(L)	—	3 December 1975(s)[3]
	(W)	—	
Guatemala	(M)	*	*
	(L)	*	*
	(W)	26 July 1968	22 September 1970
Guinea	(M)	—	29 April 1985(a)
	(L)	—	*
	(W)	—	*
Guinea-Bissau	(M)	—	*
	(L)	—	*
	(W)	—	*
Haiti	(M)	*	*
	(L)	*	*
	(W)	1 July 1968	2 June 1970
Holy See	(M)	—	25 February 1971(a)[6]
	(L)	—	25 February 1971(a)[6]
	(W)	—	25 February 1971(a)[6]
Honduras	(M)	*	*
	(L)	*	*
	(W)	1 July 1968	16 May 1973

(continued)

Signatory or party reported		*(i) Signature*	*(ii) Deposit*
Hungary	(M)	1 July 1968	27 May 1969
	(L)	1 July 1968	27 May 1969
	(W)	1 July 1968	27 May 1969
Iceland	(M)	1 July 1968	18 July 1969
	(L)	1 July 1968	18 July 1969
	(W)	1 July 1968	18 July 1969
Indonesia	(M)	2 March 1970[7]	12 July 1979
	(L)	2 March 1970[7]	12 July 1979
	(W)	2 March 1970[7]	12 July 1979
Iran (Islamic Republic of) (Iran)	(M)	1 July 1968	10 February 1970
	(L)	1 July 1968	5 March 1970
	(W)	1 July 1968	2 February 1970
Iraq	(M)	1 July 1968	29 October 1969
	(L)	*	*
	(W)	*	*
Ireland	(M)	1 July 1968	2 July 1968
	(L)	4 July 1968	4 July 1968
	(W)	1 July 1968	1 July 1968
Italy	(M)	28 January 1969	4 May 1975
	(L)	28 January 1969[8]	2 May 1975[9]
	(W)	28 January 1969	2 May 1975
Jamaica	(M)	14 April 1969	5 March 1970
	(L)	14 April 1969	5 March 1970
	(W)	14 April 1969	5 March 1970
Japan	(M)	3 February 1970[10]	8 June 1976[11]
	(L)	3 February 1970[10]	8 June 1976[11]
	(W)	3 February 1970[10]	8 June 1976[11]
Jordan	(M)	*	*
	(L)	*	*
	(W)	10 July 1968	11 February 1970
Kenya	(M)	*	11 June 1970
	(L)	*	*
	(W)	1 July 1968	*
Kiribati	(M)	—	*
	(L)	—	18 April 1985(s)
	(W)	—	*
Kuwait	(M)	15 August 1968	—
	(L)	22 August 1968	—
	(W)	15 August 1968	—
Lao People's Democratic Republic (Laos)	(M)	1 July 1968	20 February 1970
	(L)	1 July 1968	5 March 1970
	(W)	1 July 1968	5 March 1970

Signatory or party reported		(i) Signature	(ii) Deposit
Lebanon	(M)	1 July 1968	15 July 1970
	(L)	1 July 1968	15 July 1970
	(W)	1 July 1968	20 November 1970
Lesotho	(M)	*	*
	(L)	*	*
	(W)	9 July 1968	20 May 1970
Liberia	(M)	*	*
	(L)	*	*
	(W)	1 July 1968	5 March 1970
Libyan Arab Jamahiriya (Libya)	(M)	23 July 1968	26 May 1975
	(L)	18 July 1968	26 May 1975
	(W)	19 July 1968	26 May 1975
Liechtenstein	(M)	—	20 April 1978(a)
	(L)	—	20 April 1978(a)
	(W)	—	20 April 1978(a)
Luxembourg	(M)	14 August 1968	4 May 1975
	(L)	14 August 1968	2 May 1975
	(W)	14 August 1968	2 May 1975
Madagascar	(M)	*	*
	(L)	*	*
	(W)	22 August 1968	8 October 1970
Malawi	(M)	—	4 March 1986(a)
	(L)	—	18 February 1986(a)
	(W)	—	19 February 1986(a)
Malaysia	(M)	1 July 1968	5 March 1970
	(L)	1 July 1968	5 March 1970
	(W)	1 July 1968	5 March 1970
Maldives	(M)	*	*
	(L)	*	*
	(W)	11 September 1968	7 April 1970
Mali	(M)	15 July 1969	10 February 1970
	(L)	*	*
	(W)	14 July 1969	5 March 1970
Malta	(M)	*	*
	(L)	*	*
	(W)	17 April 1969	6 February 1970
Mauritius	(M)	*	25 April 1969
	(L)	*	14 April 1969
	(W)	1 July 1968	8 April 1969
Mexico	(M)	26 July 1968	21 January 1969
	(L)	26 July 1968[12]	21 January 1969
	(W)	26 July 1968[12]	21 January 1969

(continued)

Signatory or party reported		*(i) Signature*	*(ii) Deposit*
Mongolia	(M)	1 July 1968	14 May 1969
	(L)	—	*
	(W)	—	*
Morocco	(M)	1 July 1968	27 November 1970
	(L)	1 July 1968	30 November 1970
	(W)	1 July 1968	16 December 1970
Nauru	(M)	—	*
	(L)	—	7 June 1982(a)
	(W)	—	*
Nepal	(M)	1 July 1968	9 January 1970
	(L)	1 July 1968	3 February 1970
	(W)	1 July 1968	5 January 1970
Netherlands	(M)	20 August 1968	2 May 1975
	(L)	20 August 1968	2 May 1975[13,14]
	(W)	20 August 1968	2 May 1975[13]
New Zealand	(M)	1 July 1968	10 September 1969
	(L)	1 July 1968	10 September 1969
	(W)	1 July 1968	10 September 1969
Nicaragua	(M)	*	*
	(L)	1 July 1968	*
	(W)	1 July 1968	6 March 1973
Nigeria	(M)	1 July 1968	14 October 1968
	(L)	1 July 1968	27 September 1968
	(W)	1 July 1968	7 October 1968
Norway	(M)	1 July 1968	5 February 1969
	(L)	1 July 1968	5 February 1969
	(W)	1 July 1968	5 February 1969
Panama	(M)	*	*
	(L)	*	*
	(W)	1 July 1968	13 January 1977
Papua New Guinea	(M)	—	16 February 1982(a)
	(L)	—	13 January 1982(a)
	(W)	—	25 January 1982(a)
Paraguay	(M)	*	*
	(L)	*	5 March 1970
	(W)	1 July 1968	4 February 1970
People's Republic of Kampuchea	(M)	—	25 September 1987(a)
	(L)	—	*
	(W)	—	*
Peru	(M)	*	*
	(L)	*	*
	(W)	1 July 1968	3 March 1970
Philippines	(M)	18 July 1968	20 October 1972
	(L)	*	16 October 1972
	(W)	1 July 1968	5 October 1972

Signatory or party reported		(i) Signature	(ii) Deposit
Poland	(M)	1 July 1968	12 June 1969
	(L)	1 July 1968	12 June 1969
	(W)	1 July 1968	12 June 1969
Portugal	(M)	—	15 December 1977(a)
	(L)	—	15 December 1977(a)
	(W)	—	15 December 1977(a)
Republic of Korea	(M)	*	*
	(L)	*	*
	(W)	1 July 1968[15]	23 April 1975
Romania	(M)	1 July 1968	4 February 1970
	(L)	1 July 1968	4 February 1970
	(W)	1 July 1968	4 February 1970
Rwanda	(M)	—	20 May 1975(a)
	(L)	—	20 May 1975(a)
	(W)	—	20 May 1975(a)
Saint Kitts and Nevis (Saint Christopher and Nevis)[16]	(M)		
	(L)		
	(W)		
Saint Lucia	(M)	—	*
	(L)	—	28 December 1979(s)[3]
	(W)	—	*
Saint Vincent and the Grenadines	(M)	—	*
	(L)	—	6 November 1984(s)[17]
	(W)	—	*
Samoa (Western Samoa)	(M)	—	17 March 1975(a)
	(L)	—	26 March 1975(a)
	(W)	—	18 March 1975(a)
San Marino[18]	(M)	21 November 1968	20 August 1970
	(L)	29 November 1968	10 August 1970
	(W)	21 July 1968	31 August 1970
Sao Tome and Principe	(M)	—	20 July 1983(a)
	(L)	—	*
	(W)	—	*
Saudi Arabia	(M)	—	*
	(L)	—	*
	(W)	—	3 October 1988(a)
Senegal	(M)	1 July 1968	17 December 1970
	(L)	26 July 1968	15 January 1971
	(W)	1 July 1968	22 December 1970
Seychelles	(M)	—	14 March 1985(a)
	(L)	—	12 March 1985(a)
	(W)	—	8 April 1985(a)

(continued)

Signatory or party reported		(i) Signature	(ii) Deposit
Sierra Leone	(M)	—	26 February 1975(a)
	(L)	—	26 February 1975(a)
	(W)	—	26 February 1975(a)
Singapore	(M)	5 February 1970	10 March 1976
	(L)	5 February 1970	10 March 1976
	(W)	5 February 1970	10 March 1976
Solomon Islands	(M)	—	17 June 1981(s)[2]
	(L)	—	*
	(W)	—	*
Somalia	(M)	1 July 1968	*
	(L)	1 July 1968	5 March 1970
	(W)	1 July 1968	12 November 1970
Spain	(M)	—	5 November 1987(a)
	(L)	—	5 November 1987(a)
	(W)	—	5 November 1987(a)
Sri Lanka (Ceylon)	(M)	1 July 1968	5 March 1979
	(L)	1 July 1968	5 March 1979
	(W)	1 July 1968	5 March 1979
Sudan	(M)	24 December 1968	22 November 1973
	(L)	—	10 December 1973
	(W)	—	31 October 1973
Suriname	(M)	—	*
	(L)	—	*
	(W)	—	30 June 1976(s)[19]
Swaziland	(M)	*	12 January 1970
	(L)	24 June 1969	11 December 1969
	(W)	*	16 December 1969
Sweden	(M)	19 August 1968	9 January 1970
	(L)	19 August 1968	9 January 1970
	(W)	19 August 1968	9 January 1970
Switzerland	(M)	27 November 1969[20]	9 March 1977[21]
	(L)	27 November 1969[20]	9 March 1977[21]
	(W)	27 November 1969[20]	9 March 1977[21]
Syrian Arab Republic	(M)	1 July 1968	24 September 1968[22]
	(L)	*	*
	(W)	*	*
Thailand	(M)	—	*
	(L)	—	7 December 1972(a)
	(W)	—	*
Togo	(M)	*	*
	(L)	*	*
	(W)	1 July 1968	26 February 1970

Signatory or party reported		(i) Signature	(ii) Deposit
Tonga	(M)	—	24 August 1971(s)
	(L)	—	7 July 1971(s)
	(W)	—	15 July 1971(s)[3]
Trinidad and Tobago	(M)	*	—
	(L)	22 August 1968	30 October 1986
	(W)	20 August 1968	30 October 1986
Tunisia	(M)	1 July 1968	26 February 1970
	(L)	1 July 1968	26 February 1970
	(W)	1 July 1968	26 February 1970
Turkey	(M)	28 January 1969	17 April 1980
	(L)	28 January 1969	17 April 1980
	(W)	28 January 1969	17 April 1980[23]
Tuvalu	(M)	—	*
	(L)	—	19 January 1979(s)[3]
	(W)	—	*
Uganda	(M)	—	*
	(L)	—	*
	(W)	—	20 October 1982(a)
Union of Soviet Socialist Republics	(M)	1 July 1968	5 March 1970
	(L)	1 July 1968	5 March 1970
	(W)	1 July 1968	5 March 1970
United Kingdom of Great Britain and Northern Ireland[24]	(M)	1 July 1968	29 November 1968
	(L)	1 July 1968	27 November 1968[25]
	(W)	1 July 1968	27 November 1968[25]
United States of America	(M)	1 July 1968	5 March 1970
	(L)	1 July 1968	5 March 1970
	(W)	1 July 1968	5 March 1970
Uruguay	(M)	*	*
	(L)	*	*
	(W)	1 July 1968	31 August 1970
Venezuela	(M)	*	3 October 1975
	(L)	*	25 September 1975
	(W)	1 July 1968	26 September 1975
Viet Nam	(M)	—	14 June 1982(a)
	(L)	—	*
	(W)	—	*
Yemen	(M)	23 September 1968	*
	(L)	*	14 May 1986
	(W)	*	*

(continued)

Signatory or party reported		(i) Signature	(ii) Deposit
Yugoslavia	(M)	10 July 1968	5 March 1970
	(L)	10 July 1968	5 March 1970
	(W)	10 July 1968	4 March 1970[26]
Zaire (Congo, Democratic Republic of the)	(M)	26 July 1968	*
	(L)	17 September 1968	*
	(W)	22 July 1968	4 August 1970

A dash (—) after the name of a country or party reported indicates that the action has not been taken.

*The action has not been taken with this depositary.

[1]With the following declaration:

"The Government of Australia:

"Supports effective international measures to counter the spread of nuclear weapons and weapons of mass destruction. In April 1968 when the Treaty to prevent the further spread of nuclear weapons was introduced in the United Nations General Assembly, Australia supported the resolution commending the Treaty for the consideration of Governments.

"Is conscious of the fact that in the long run the security of the world as a whole will depend upon effective measures to control the nuclear arms race and to bring about general and complete disarmament. The Government therefore welcomes the call in Article VI of the Treaty for negotiations to achieve these ends.

"Hopes that the Treaty will be effective in its operation and will lead to improved relationships and enhanced co-operation between the nations of the world, and in particular between the nations of the Asian and Pacific region.

"Believes that a condition of an effective Treaty is that it should attract a necessary degree of support. Some progress in this direction has been made but the Government will nevertheless want to be assured that there is a sufficient degree of support for the Treaty.

"Regards it as essential that the Treaty should not affect continuing security commitments under existing treaties of mutual security.

"Attaches weight to the statements by the Governments of the United States, United Kingdom and the Soviet Union declaring their intention to seek immediate Security Council action to provide help to any non-nuclear weapons state party to the Treaty that is subject to aggression or the threat of aggression with nuclear weapons. At the same time the Government reaffirms its adherence to the principle, contained in Article 51 of the Charter of the United Nations, of the right of individual or collective self-defence if an armed attack occurs against a member of the United Nations, until the Security Council has taken measures necessary to maintain international peace and security.

"Notes that Article 10 of the Treaty provides that any party has the right to withdraw in circumstances that jeopardised its supreme interests.

"Notes that the Treaty will in no way inhibit and is in fact designed to assist non-nuclear weapon states in their research, development and use of nuclear energy and nuclear explosions for peaceful purposes either individually or collectively; nor must it discriminate against any state or states in their peaceful pursuits in nuclear activities.

"Considers that the safeguards agreement to be concluded by Australia with the International Atomic Energy Agency in accordance with Treaty Article III must in no way subject

Australia to treatment less favourable than is accorded to other states which, individually or collectively, conclude safeguards agreements with that agency.

"Considers it essential that the inspection and safeguards arrangements should not burden research, development, production and use of nuclear energy for peaceful purposes; that they should not constitute an obstacle to a nation's economic development, commercial interests and trade; and that they should be effective in ensuring that any breaches of the Treaty would be detected.

"Attaches importance to a review of the IAEA safeguards system and procedures to clarify those issues of importance to Australia.

"Welcomes the fact that the Treaty in Articles 4 and 5 provides for international co-operation for the development of the peaceful uses of nuclear energy and the peaceful applications of nuclear explosions; notes the assurances that under the Treaty the supply of knowledge, materials and equipment would not be denied to any party; and considers it important that no nuclear development should be prohibited except when such activities would have no other purposes than the manufacture of nuclear weapons or other nuclear explosive devices.

"Will co-operate closely with other governments in seeking clarifications and understandings in relation to those matters which must be resolved before Australia could proceed to ratification, being convinced that a Treaty which was truly effective in preventing the further proliferation of nuclear weapons would be a major contribution to the security of the world as a whole."

[2]In a note of 29 August 1985 the Government of Australia informed the Government of the United Kingdom that certain parts of the declaration made by Australia at the time of its signature of the Treaty on the Non-Proliferation of Nuclear Weapons no longer accurately reflect Australian policy: the said Declaration was not intended to have any further application after Australia's ratification of the Treaty on 23 January 1973.

[3]Succeeded to the Treaty by virtue of the ratification of the United Kingdom of Great Britain and Northern Ireland.

[4]With the following declaration:

"The Government of the Federal Republic of Germany, on the occasion of and in formal conjunction with its signature today of the Treaty on the Non-Proliferation of Nuclear Weapons, has the honour to expound to the Government of the United Kingdom of Great Britain and Northern Ireland [and the Government of the United States] the following understandings on which it signs the Treaty.

"I

"The Federal Government understands that

"the provisions of the Treaty shall be interpreted and applied in relation to the Federal Republic of Germany in the same way as in relation to the other Parties to the Treaty;

"the security of the Federal Republic of Germany and its allies shall continue to be ensured by NATO or an equivalent security system;

"Resolution No. 255 adopted by the United Nations Security Council, as well as the Declaration of Intent of the United States, the Soviet Union and Great Britain upon which that Resolution is based, shall also apply without any restriction to the Federal Republic of Germany;

"the Treaty shall not hamper the unification of the European States;

"the Parties to the Treaty will commence without delay the negotiations on disarmament envisaged under the Treaty, especially with regard to nuclear weapons.

"II

"The Federal Government declares that signature of this Treaty does not imply recognition of the German Democratic Republic under international law;

"therefore, no relations under international law with the German Democratic Republic shall arise out of this Treaty for the Federal Republic of Germany.

"III

"With respect to the peaceful use of nuclear energy and to the verification agreement to be concluded with the IAEA, the Federal Government starts from the following assumptions:

"*(a) Limitation to the purpose of the Treaty*

"It is the purpose of the Treaty to prevent the present non-nuclear-weapon States from manufacturing or otherwise acquiring nuclear weapons or other nuclear explosive devices. The provisions of the Treaty are therefore solely designed to attain this objective. In no case shall they lead to restricting the use of nuclear energy for other purposes by non-nuclear-weapon States.

"*(b) Research and Development*

"Freedom of research and development is essential in the advancement of the peaceful uses of nuclear energy, and to the Federal Republic of Germany it is beyond all doubt that the Treaty may never be interpreted or applied in such a way as to hamper or inhibit research and development in this sphere. The Federal Government has taken note of the statement made by the US Permanent Representative to the United Nations on 15 May 1968, and, in particular, of the following remarks:

"'. . .there is no basis for any concern that this Treaty would impose inhibitions or restrictions on the opportunity for non-nuclear-weapon States to develop their capabilities in nuclear science and technology';

"'This Treaty does not ask any country to accept a status of technological dependency or to be deprived of developments in nuclear research';

"'The whole field of nuclear science associated with electric power production . . . will become more accessible under the Treaty, to all who seek to exploit it. This includes not only the present generation of nuclear power reactors but also that advanced technology, which is still developing, of fast breeder power reactors which, in producing energy, also produce more fissionable material than they consume'; and

"'Many nations are now engaged in research in an even more advanced field of science, that of controlled thermonuclear fusion. The future developments of this science and technology may well lead to the nuclear reactor of the future, in which the fission process of uranium or plutonium is replaced by the fusion reactions of hydrogen isotopes as the source of energy. Controlled thermonuclear fusion technology will not be affected by the Treaty. . .'

"*(c) Onus of proof*

"In connection with paragraph 3 of Article III and with Article IV of the Treaty no nuclear activities in the fields of research, development, manufacture or use for peaceful purposes are prohibited nor can the transfer of information, materials and equipment be denied to non-nuclear-weapon States merely on the basis of allegations that such activities or transfers could be used for the manufacture of nuclear weapons or other nuclear explosive devices.

"*(d) Exchange of Information*

"Article IV requires those Parties to the Treaty in a position to do so to co-operate in contributing to the further development of the applications of nuclear energy for peaceful purposes. The Federal Government therefore expects that any measures restricting the un-hampered flow of scientific and technological information will be re-examined with a view to facilitating the fullest possible exchange of scientific and technological information for peaceful purposes.

"*(e) Other nuclear explosive devices*

"At the present stage of technology nuclear explosive devices are those designed to release in microseconds in an uncontrolled manner a large amount of nuclear energy accompanied by shock waves, i.e., devices that can be used as nuclear weapons.

"At the same time the Federal Government holds the view that the Non-Proliferation Treaty must not hamper progress in the field of developing and applying the technology of using nuclear explosives for peaceful purposes.

"(f) Safeguards and Verification Agreements

"There is no incompatibility between the aims of the Non-Proliferation Treaty and those of the Treaty establishing EURATOM. As to the safeguards provided for in its Article III, the Non-Proliferation Treaty limits itself to referring to agreements to be concluded with the IAEA, the contents of which have therefore not yet been laid down.

"The safeguards agreements with the IAEA, as described in paragraphs 1 and 4 of Article III, can be concluded by Parties to the Treaty not only 'individually' but also 'together with other States'. States being members of an organization the work of which is related to that of the IAEA comply with their obligation to conclude the agreement by the organization concerned concluding it with the IAEA, as also provided in Article XVI of the Statute of the IAEA and in the Agency's safeguards system.

"The obligation of a non-nuclear-weapon State Party to the Treaty under paragraph 1 of Article III to accept safeguards outside its own territory prevails only if such Party has dominant and effective control over a nuclear facility.

"In order to avoid incompatibility between the implementation of the Non-Proliferation Treaty and compliance with the provisions of the Treaty establishing EURATOM, the verification procedures must be so defined that the rights and obligations of member States and the Community remain unaffected, in accordance with the opinion rendered by the Commission under Article 103 of the Treaty establishing EURATOM.

"To this end, the Commission of the European Communities will have to enter into negotiations with the IAEA.

"The Government of the Federal Republic of Germany intends to postpone the ratification procedure of the Non-Proliferation Treaty until negotiations between the Commission and the IAEA have led to agreement.

"IV

"The Government of the Federal Republic of Germany reaffirms the attached Statement made by it on signing the Non-Proliferation Treaty.

"'London, 28 November 1969.

"'STATEMENT BY THE GOVERNMENT OF THE FEDERAL REPUBLIC OF GERMANY ON SIGNING THE TREATY ON THE NON-PROLIFERATION OF NUCLEAR WEAPONS

"'The Government of the Federal Republic of Germany

"'(1) welcomes the fact that the principle of non-proliferation of nuclear weapons has now been consolidated world-wide by treaty and points out that the Federal Republic of Germany has as early as October 1954, in the Brussels Treaty, renounced the manufacture of nuclear, biological and chemical weapons and accepted relevant controls;

"'(2) reaffirms its expectation that the Treaty will be a milestone on the way towards disarmament, international detente, and peace, and that it will render an important contribution towards the creation of an international community based on the security of independent nations and on the progress of mankind;

"'(3) understands that the provisions of the Treaty shall be interpreted and applied in relation to the Federal Republic of Germany in the same way as in relation to the other Parties of the Treaty;

"'(4) understands that the security of the Federal Republic of Germany shall continue to be ensured by NATO; the Federal Republic of Germany for its part shall remain unrestrictedly committed to the collective security arrangements of NATO;

" '(5) understands that Resolution No. 255 adopted by the United Nations Security Council, as well as the Declarations of Intent of the United States, Great Britain and the Soviet Union upon which that Resolution is based, shall also apply without any restriction to the Federal Republic of Germany;

" '(6) states that the principles contained in the Preamble to the Treaty, and the principles of international law laid down in Article 2 of the United Nations Charter which preclude any threat or use of force directed against the territorial integrity or the political independence of a State, are the indispensable prerequisite to the Treaty itself and shall apply without any restriction also in relation to the Federal Republic of Germany;

" '(7) signs the Treaty in the expectation that it will encourage further agreements on the prohibition of the use and threat of force, which will serve to stabilize peace in Europe;

" '(8) states that the Federal Republic of Germany, in a situation in which it considers its supreme interests in jeopardy, will remain free by invoking the principle of international law laid down in Article 51 of the United Nations Charter to take the measures required to safeguard these interests;

" '(9) signs the Treaty convinced that it will not hamper European unification;

" '(10) regards the Treaty not as an end but rather a starting point for the negotiations, provided for the Treaty itself as its natural supplement and to ensure its effective implementation, concerning disarmament, the peaceful uses of nuclear energy, and the benefits arising for the peaceful applications of nuclear energy;

" '(11) stresses that the research, development and use of nuclear energy for peaceful purposes and the international or multinational co-operation in this field must not be hampered but should even be furthered by the Treaty, especially as regards non-nuclear-weapon States;

" '(12) notes that no incompatibility exists between the aims of the Non-Proliferation Treaty and those of the Treaty establishing EURATOM;

" '(13) understands that the agreements between the IAEA and EURATOM, as described in Article III of the Non-Proliferation Treaty, shall be concluded on the basis of the principle of verification, and that verification shall take place in a way that does not affect the tasks of the European Atomic Energy Community in the political, scientific, economic and technical fields;

" '(14) insists that, in accordance with the letter and the spirit of the Treaty, the safeguards shall only be applied to source and special fissionable material and in conformity with the principle of safeguarding effectively the flow of source and special fissionable materials at certain strategic points. It understands that the words 'source material' and 'special fissionable material' used in the Treaty shall have—subject to amendments expressly accepted by the Federal Republic of Germany—the meaning laid down in the present wording of Article XX of the Statute of the IAEA;

" '(15) understands that each Party to the Treaty shall decide for itself which 'equipment or material' shall fall under the export provision of paragraph 2 of Article III. In so doing the Federal Republic of Germany will accept only those interpretations and definitions of the terms 'equipment or material' which it has expressly approved.

" '(16) reaffirms the necessity of settling the question of the costs of safeguards in a way that does not place unfair burdens on non-nuclear-weapon States;

" '(17) declares that the Federal Republic of Germany does not intend to ratify the Non-Proliferation Treaty before an agreement in accordance with Article III of that Treaty has been concluded between EURATOM and the IAEA which both in form and substance meets the requirements of paragraphs 13, 14, 15 and 16 of this Statement and compatibility with the Treaty instituting the European Atomic energy Community has been established;

"'(18) stresses the vital importance it attaches, with a view to ensuring equal opportunities in the economic and scientific fields, to the fulfilment of the assurance given by the United States and Great Britain concerning the application of safeguards to their peaceful nuclear facilities, and hopes that other nuclear-weapon States as well will give similar assurances;

"'(19) reaffirms its view that, until the conclusion of the agreement between the IAEA and EURATOM, the supply contracts concluded between EURATOM and the Parties to the Non-Proliferation Treaty shall remain in force, and that, after the entry into force of the Non-Proliferation Treaty, supply contracts should, in the interest of an unhampered exchange of information, equipment and materials for peaceful purposes, be freed from any additional political or administrative restrictions'.

"The Government of the Federal Republic of Germany signs today in Washington, London and Moscow, the capitals of the three Depositary Governments, the Treaty on the Non-Proliferation of Nuclear Weapons.

"On this same day, the Government of the Federal Republic of Germany hands to the Depositary Governments—informing simultaneously the Governments of all States with which the Federal Republic of Germany maintains diplomatic relations—the text of a Note bringing the above Statement to the attention of these Governments. The Note also contains the known German interpretations of the Non-Proliferation Treaty which are designed to preserve the sphere of peaceful activities and to ensure the conclusion of the verification agreement between the IAEA and EURATOM in accordance with Article III of the Non-Proliferation Treaty."

[5]With the following declaration:

"In connection with the deposit today of the instruments of ratification of the Federal Republic of Germany to the Treaty of 1 July 1968 on the Non-Proliferation of Nuclear Weapons, the Government of the Federal Republic of Germany sets out below in summary form the understanding on which the Federal Republic of Germany becomes a Party to the Treaty and on which it commented in its Note and in its Statement of 28 November 1969 on the occasion of signing the Treaty.

"The Government of the Federal Republic of Germany

"1. reaffirms its expectation that the Treaty will be a milestone on the way towards disarmament, international detente, and peace, and that in particular the nuclear-weapon States will intensify their efforts in accordance with the undertaking and aims embodied in Article VI of the Treaty;

"2. understands that the security of the Federal Republic of Germany continues to be ensured by NATO; the Federal Republic of Germany will for its part remain committed to the collective security arrangements of NATO;

"3. states that no provision of the Treaty may be interpreted in such a way as to hamper the further development of European unification, especially the creation of a European Union with appropriate competence;

"4. understands that research, development and use of nuclear energy for peaceful purposes as well as international and multinational co-operation in this field, must not be prejudiced by the Treaty;

"5. understands that the application of the Treaty, including the implementation of safeguards, will not lead to discrimination of the nuclear industry of the Federal Republic of Germany in international competition;

"6. stresses once again in this connection the vital importance it attaches to the undertaking given by the Government of the United States and by the Government of the United Kingdom of Great Britain and Northern Ireland concerning the application of safeguards to their peaceful nuclear facilities, and hopes that other nuclear-weapon States will assume similar obligations.

"In connexion with the deposit of the instrument of ratification the Government of the Federal Republic of Germany also stated '. . . with effect from the day on which the Treaty enters into force for the Federal Republic of Germany it will also apply to Berlin (West) without affecting Allied rights and responsibilities, including those relating to demilitarization'. Concerning this statement the Government of the Union of Soviet Socialist Republics expressed the following view:

"'The statement by the Federal Republic of Germany concerning the extension of the Treaty on the Non-Proliferation of Nuclear Weapons to Berlin (West) is a violation of the Quadripartite Agreement of 3 September 1971 and can therefore have no legal force. The Quadripartite Agreement, as is generally known, does not permit the Federal Republic of Germany to represent the interests of Berlin (West) on questions relating to status and security in the international field. The Treaty on the Non-Proliferation of Nuclear Weapons relates directly to questions of status and security. It follows therefore that the Federal Republic of Germany cannot arrogate to itself rights and obligations in connexion with the observance in Berlin (West) of the provisions of the Treaty on the Non-Proliferation of Nuclear Weapons."

[6]With the following declaration:

"1. This accession by the Holy See to the Treaty on the Non-Proliferation of Nuclear Weapons is inspired by its constant desire, illuminated by the teaching of universal brotherhood and of justice and peace between man and peoples contained in the Gospel message, to make its contribution to undertakings which; through disarmament as well as by other means, promote security, mutual trust and peaceful co-operation in relations between peoples.

"In that perspective, the Holy See judges—as is said in the official document of accession—that the aims of disarmament and easing of international tension by which the Treaty is inspired correspond with its own mission of peace, and that the Treaty, although it has its intrinsic limitations, constitutes a noteworthy step forward on the road to disarmament. In fact, in so far as the Treaty proposes to stop the dissemination of nuclear weapons—while awaiting the achievement of the cessation of the nuclear arms race and the undertaking of effective measures in the direction of complete nuclear disarmament—it has the aim of lessening the danger of terrible and total devastation which threatens all mankind, and it wishes to constitute a premise for wider agreements in the future for the promotion of a system of general and complete disarmament under effective international control.

"2. In the first place, therefore, the Holy See appreciates and shares the following considerations and intentions which the States Party to the Treaty have expressed or declared in the Preamble of the Treaty:

"(1) The awareness of the devastation 'that would be visited upon all mankind by a nuclear war and the consequent need to make every effort to avert the danger of such a war and to take measures to safeguard the security of peoples';

"(2) The reaffirmation of the principle that 'in accordance with the Charter of the United Nations, States must refrain in their international relations from the threat or use of force against the territorial integrity or political independence of any State, or in any other manner inconsistent with the Purposes of the United Nations, and that the establishment and maintenance of international peace and security are to be promoted';

"(3) The intention 'to achieve at the earliest possible date the cessation of the nuclear arms race and to undertake effective measures in the direction of nuclear disarmament';

"(4) The intention 'to further the easing of international tension and the strengthening of trust between States in order to facilitate the cessation of the manufacture of nuclear weapons, the liquidation of all their existing stockpiles, and the elimination from national arsenals of nuclear weapons and the means of their delivery pursuant to a Treaty on general and complete disarmament under strict and effective international control'.

"3. The Holy See is furthermore convinced that the Treaty on the Non-Proliferation of Nuclear Weapons will be able to attain in full the noble objectives of security and peace which constitute the reasons for contracting it and justify the limitations to which the States Party to the Treaty submit only if it is fully executed in every clause and with all its implications.

"In the Holy See's view, that actuation concerns not only the obligations to be applied immediately but also those which envisage a process of ulterior commitments. Among the latter, the Holy See considers it suitable to point out the following:

"(a) The adoption of appropriate measures to ensure, on a basis of equality, that all non-nuclear-weapon States Party to the Treaty will have available to them the benefits deriving from peaceful applications of nuclear technology, in the spirit of paragraphs 4, 5, 6 and 7 of the Preamble, and in conformity with articles IV and V of the Treaty;

"(b) The pursuit of negotiations in good faith 'on effective measures relating to cessation of the nuclear arms race at an early date and to nuclear disarmament, and on a treaty on general and complete disarmament under strict and effective international control', in accordance with the commitment foreseen in article VI.

"The Holy See, therefore, expresses the sincere wish that these undertakings will be executed by all the Parties. In particular it declares its special interest and expresses its earnest desire:

"(1) That the current talks between the United States of America and the Union of Soviet Socialist Republics on the limitation of strategic armaments may soon lead to a satisfactory agreement which will make possible the cessation in an effective and lasting manner of the preoccupying arms race in that costly and murderous sector of warlike preparations, both offensive and defensive;

"(2) That the proposals and drafts of agreements which have been put forward for some time past by various sources, especially within the Conference of the United Nations Committee for Disarmament, and which concern complete nuclear disarmament, the prohibition of bacteriological and chemical weapons and the limitation and control of conventional armaments, as well as the draft treaty on general and complete disarmament under strict and effective international control, may attain speedy and concrete results, in conformity with the repeated resolutions of the United Nations Organization and in fulfilment of the justified and anxious expectations of men and peoples of every continent.

"4. In the spirit of the considerations expressed above, which gave rise to and which accompany this accession to the Treaty, the Holy See is convinced that the attainment of the Treaty's aims of security and peace will be all the more complete and effective according as the extent of its application is the wider and more universal."

7With the following declaration:

"The Government of Indonesia has decided to sign the Treaty on the Non-Proliferation of Nuclear Weapons in the conviction that it will serve as an important step towards effective measures on the cessation of the nuclear arms race and nuclear disarmament.

"Together with the Non-Aligned Countries, it is the consistent policy of the Government of Indonesia to support all efforts to achieve a comprehensive Test Ban Treaty and to direct all endeavours towards the exclusive peaceful applications of nuclear energy. The Indonesian Government is already party to the Partial Test Ban Treaty of 1963, and it has always supported draft proposals designed to limit the spread of nuclear weapons.

"There is no doubt that the present Treaty could be effective only if all countries, nuclear-weapon as well as non-nuclear-weapon States, could become party to this Treaty.

"The Indonesian Government takes special note of Article III, paragraph 3, stating that the safeguards required by the Treaty shall be implemented in such a manner as to avoid hampering the economic or technological development of the parties, or international co-operation in the field of peaceful nuclear activities. It is therefore the common task of all parties to this Treaty to make the relevant safeguards agreement acceptable to all.

"The Government of Indonesia, further, attaches great importance to the declarations of the United States of America, the United Kingdom and the Soviet Union, affirming their intention to seek Security Council action in order to provide or support immediate assistance to any non-nuclear-weapon State, party to the Treaty, that is a victim of an act of aggression or an object of a threat of aggression in which nuclear weapons are used.

"Of utmost importance, however, is not the action after a nuclear attack has been committed but the guarantees to prevent such an attack. The Indonesian Government trusts that the nuclear-weapon States will study further this question of effective measures to ensure the security of the non-nuclear-weapon States.

"It is in this context that the Indonesian Government feels obliged to state, further, that its decision to sign the Treaty is not to be taken in any way as a decision to ratify the Treaty. Its ratification will be considered after matters of national security, which are of deep concern to the Government and people of Indonesia, have been clarified to their satisfaction."

[8]With the following declaration:

"The Italian Government, in signing the Treaty on the Non-Proliferation of Nuclear Weapons, wish to confirm the statements made on the Treaty in various international fora and approved by the Italian Parliament in the debate that took place during the second half of July and at the end of August, 1968.

"On the basis of the above mentioned statements the Italian Government:

"(1) re-affirm their firm belief that the Treaty—for which the Italian Government have made for years all possible efforts with a view to its early conclusion—is a milestone on the road to disarmament, international detente and peace, and represents a fundamental contribution for the establishment of a new international society, based on security of peoples and on the progress of humanity;

"(2) stress their persuasion that the principles set forth in the clauses of the Preamble to the Treaty on the engagement of the signatories, in accordance with the U.N. Charter, to refrain in their international relations from the threat or use of force against the territorial integrity or the political independence of any State, are an intransgressible presupposition of the Treaty itself, and that a scrupulous and general respect for such principles constitutes a supreme interest for all;

"(3) consider the Treaty not as a point of arrival, but only as a point of departure towards negotiations on disarmament, on peaceful use of nuclear energy and on benefits deriving from the peaceful use of nuclear energy which the Treaty itself takes into consideration for its natural completion and for its effective execution;

"(4) sign the Treaty in the firm belief that nothing in it is an obstacle to the unification of the Countries of Western Europe and to the justified expectations that the peoples of this area have in the developments and progress towards unity with a view to the creation of a European entity;

"(5) are convinced that the purposes of the Treaty on the Non-Proliferation of Nuclear Weapons are consistent with the provisions of the Treaty of Rome on EURATOM;

"(6) note the full compatibility of the Treaty with the existing security agreements;

"(7) note that the needs of freedom of scientific and technological research—that cannot be derogated from—are in no way hindered by the Treaty;

"(8) note that the prohibitions in Articles I and II of the Treaty—also in the general spirit of the Treaty on Non-Proliferation—refer only to nuclear explosive devices that cannot be differentiated from nuclear weapons; and consequently that when technological progress will allow the development of peaceful explosive devices differentiated from nuclear weapons, the prohibition relating to their manufacture and use shall no longer apply;

"(9) with reference to the provisions of Article III, para. 4, of the Treaty, express the hope that the agreements in the matter of controls foreseen in it will be reached between IAEA and EURATOM on the basis of the concept of verification. Pending the conclusion of the Agreement between IAEA and EURATOM, the understandings reached on the matter of supplies between EURATOM and the Governments which have signed the Treaty will remain in force;

"(10) note that in the letter and in the spirit of the Treaty the controls provided for in Article III of the Treaty are applicable only to source and special fissionable material. Consider that the words 'source' and 'special fissionable material' used in the Treaty should be understood—unless modifications are expressly accepted by Italy—in the meaning defined in the present text of Article XX of the Statute of IAEA;

"(11) interpret the provisions of Article IX, para. 3, of the Treaty, relating to the definition of a nuclear-weapon State, in the sense that it refers only to the five Countries that have manufactured or exploded a nuclear weapon or another nuclear explosive device before 1st January, 1967. Any claim to belong to this category, and for any title, shall not be recognized by the Italian Government to other States, whether or not they have signed the Treaty;

"(12) state here and now that the signature and ratification of the Treaty by the Government of a Union of States covers the signature and ratification that might be carried out by Governments of States members of the said Union: the Italian Government therefore would not recognize legal effects to the latter signature and ratification.

"To integrate the above mentioned statements the Italian Government attach to the present Note the texts of the 'ordini del giorno' on the Treaty on the Non-Proliferation of Nuclear Weapons, approved by the Italian Senate and the Italian Chamber of Deputies on the 19th and 26th July, 1968."

[9]With the following declaration:

"The Italian Government—empowered by Parliament to ratify the Non-Proliferation Treaty on Nuclear Weapons—in depositing the Instrument of Ratification, confirm the Statement brought to the knowledge of Her Majesty's Government on the 28th of January, 1969, on the occasion of the signing of the Treaty itself, being Great Britain a depositary country. The contents of such Statement are given herebelow:

"The Italian Government, in proceeding to the signature of the Non-Proliferation Treaty On Nuclear Weapons, wish to renew the statements concerning the Treaty they have already made at several international fora, and which were approved by the Italian Parliament during the debate which took place in the second half of July and at the end of August, last.

"On the basis of such statements the Italian Government:

"1. Reaffirm their deep conviction that the Treaty—for the speedy conclusion of which all possible efforts have for years been made by the Italian Government—represents a milestone on the way to disarmament, to international detente and peace and is a fundamental contribution to the establishment of a new international society based upon the security of nations and the progress of mankind.

"2. Deem it important to underline their conviction that the principles, stated in the clauses of the Treaty's preface and regarding the signatories' commitment, in accordance with the UN Charter, to refrain, in their international relations, from threatening to use or from using force against the territorial integrity or the political independence of any other country, are an essential condition to the Treaty itself and that their thorough and general observances will be in the supreme interest of all those concerned.

"3. Consider the Treaty not as a point of arrival, but only as a starting point for those negotiations on disarmament, on peaceful use of nuclear power and the benefits deriving therefrom which are contemplated by the Treaty for its natural completion and its effective enforcement.

"4. Sign the Treaty in the conviction that nothing in it is of hindrance to the aspirations of the Western European countries to unification and to the rightful expectations of the peoples of this area in the development and progress of the unification process, in view of the establishment of a European entity.

"5. Express the belief that the aims of the Non-Proliferation Treaty are compatible with the rules of the EURATOM Treaty of Rome.

"6. Take note of the full compatibility of the Treaty with existing security commitments.

"7. Take note that the Treaty is in no way an obstacle to the essential need for freedom in scientific and technological research.

"8. Take note that the bans mentioned in Articles I and II of the Treaty—also in consideration of the general spirit of the Non-Proliferation Treaty—only refer to those nuclear explosive devices which are not different from nuclear armaments, and that, therefore, should technological progress eventually enable the development of peaceful nuclear devices different from nuclear weapons, the bans on their manufacture and use will no longer apply.

"9. Trust, with reference to the provisions of Article III, para. 4, of the Treaty, that the agreements on the matter of controls therein contained will be concluded between IAEA and EURATOM on the basis of the concept of verification. Whilst awaiting the conclusion of the Agreement between EURATOM and IAEA, existing agreements on supplies between EU-RATOM and signatory Governments of the Treaty will remain in force.

"10. Take note that according to the letter and spirit of the Treaty the controls referred to in Article III of the Treaty itself are intended to apply to 'source material' and to 'special fissile material' only, and believe that the meaning of the words 'source material' and 'special fissile material' used in the Treaty should be interpreted—with the exception of amendments explicitly accepted by Italy—in accordance with the definition in the present text of article XX of the IAEA Charter.

"11. Interpret the provisions of Article IX, para. 3 of the Treaty, concerning the definition of a militarily nuclear state, in the sense that it refers exclusively to the five countries who have manufactured and exploded a nuclear weapon or other nuclear explosive device prior to the 11th of January, 1967. Under no circumstance, a claim pertaining to such category will be recognised by the Italian Government to any other State, whether signatory or non signatory of the Treaty.

"12. Declare as of now, in the event that Governments of States at present members of Unions of States should sign or ratify the Treaty in addition to the Government of the Union itself, that they will be unable to recognise juridical validity to such signature and ratification, as such Governments are already covered by the signature and ratification of the Government of the Union."

In a note, dated 30 June 1976, addressed to the Italian Embassy, the Government of the United Kingdom expresses the following view:

"The Government of the United Kingdom, as a state party to the Non-Proliferation Treaty, take the view that the obligations in Articles I and II of the Treaty apply without any distinction to all nuclear explosive devices. They are accordingly unable to agree with the interpretation of the Treaty, and of those Articles in particular, contained in paragraph 8 of the Note of the Italian Embassy."

[10]With the following declaration:

"The Government of Japan, believing that the proliferation of nuclear weapons would increase the danger of nuclear war, has always been in favour of the spirit underlying this Treaty, since the prevention of the proliferation of nuclear weapons is in accord with its policy with regard to the maintenance of world peace.

"The Government of Japan is signing this Treaty on the basis of its fundamental position which is stated below.

"The Government of Japan is convinced that this Treaty will serve as a first step towards nuclear disarmament and hopes that as many States as possible will adhere to this Treaty to make it effective. The Government of Japan hopes, especially, that the Government of the Republic of France and the People's Republic of China which possess nuclear weapons but have yet to express their intention of adhering to this Treaty will become parties thereto at an early date and pursue negotiations in good faith on nuclear disarmament and that they will refrain, even before that, from taking such actions as are contrary to the purposes of this Treaty.

"This Treaty permits only the present nuclear-weapon States to possess nuclear weapons. This discrimination should ultimately be made to disappear through the elimination of nuclear weapons by all the nuclear-weapon States from their national arsenals. Until such time the nuclear-weapon States should be conscious of the fact that they have special responsibilities as a consequence of this special status.

"The prohibition under this Treaty applies solely to the acquisition of nuclear weapons and other nuclear explosive devices and of control over them. Therefore, this Treaty must in no way restrict non-nuclear-weapon States in their research, development, or implementation of the peaceful use of nuclear energy, or in their international co-operation in these fields, nor must it subject them to discriminatory treatment in any aspect of such activities.

"The Government of Japan wishes to state that it has a deep interest in the following matters in the list of its basic position stated above.

"The Government stresses that it will also concern itself most vigorously with these matters when it decides to ratify the Treaty as well as when it participates in the review of its operation in the future as a party to the Treaty.

"*I. Disarmament and security*

"1. Under Article VI of the Treaty each State Party 'undertakes to pursue negotiations in good faith on effective measures relating to cessation of the nuclear arms race at an early date and to nuclear disarmament, and on a treaty on general and complete disarmament under strict and effective international control'. The Government of Japan believes it essential for the attainment of the purposes of this Treaty that, above all, the nuclear-weapon States should take concrete nuclear disarmament measures in pursuance of this undertaking. As a member of the Committee on Disarmament, Japan is also prepared to co-operate in the furtherance of disarmament.

"2. The Government of Japan deems it important that in the preamble to the Treaty there is a provision stating that 'in accordance with the Charter of the United Nations, States must refrain in their international relations from the threat or use of force against the territorial integrity or political independence of any State, or in any other manner inconsistent with the Purpose of the United Nations'. It also wishes to emphasise that the nuclear-weapon States must not have recourse to the use of nuclear weapons or threaten to use such weapons against non-nuclear-weapon States.

"3. The Government of Japan also attaches great importance to the declarations of the United States, the United Kingdom, and the Soviet Union affirming their intention to seek immediate Security Council action to provide assistance, in accordance with the Charter of the United Nations, to any non-nuclear-weapon State, party to the Treaty, that is a victim of an act of aggression or an object of a threat of aggression in which nuclear weapons are used, and hopes that the nuclear-weapon States will continue their studies with regard to effective measures to ensure the security of non-nuclear-weapon States.

"4. The Government of Japan, pending its ratifications of this Treaty, will pay particular attention to developments in disarmament negotiations and progress in the implementation of the Security Council Resolution on the security of non-nuclear-weapon States and continue to make a close study of other problems which require consideration for the safeguarding of her national interests.

"5. The Government of Japan takes note of the fact that Article X of the Treaty provides that: 'each Party shall in exercising its national sovereignty have the right to withdraw from the Treaty if it decides that extraordinary events, related to the subject matter of this Treaty, have jeopardised the supreme interests of its country'.

"*II. Peaceful uses of nuclear energy*

"1. The safeguards agreement to be concluded by Japan with the International Atomic Energy Agency in accordance with Article III of the Treaty must not be such as would subject her to disadvantageous treatment as compared with the safeguards agreements which other States Parties conclude with the same Agency, either individually or together with other States. The Government of Japan intends to give full consideration to this matter before taking steps to ratify the Treaty.

"2. The Government of Japan greatly appreciates as a measure supplementing this Treaty, the declarations of the Governments of the United States and the United Kingdom, which are both nuclear-weapon States, that they will accept the application of safeguards of the International Atomic Energy Agency to all their nuclear activities, excluding only those directly related to their national security, and earnestly hopes that these assurances will be faithfully implemented. It also hopes most earnestly that the other nuclear-weapon States will take similar action.

"3. Safeguards should be subject to the principle that they should be applied at certain strategic points of the nuclear fuel cycle, and the procedure for their application must be rational when considered from the point of view of cost-effectiveness and made as simple as possible by making the maximum use of material control systems of the respective countries. Furthermore, adequate measures must be taken to ensure that the application of safeguards does not cause the leakage of industrial secrets or otherwise hinder industrial activities. The Government of Japan hopes that the International Atomic Energy Agency will make constant efforts to improve safeguards in the light of technological developments with the above aims in mind. This Government is prepared to co-operate in such efforts and hopes that the States concerned will also co-operate to achieve this end.

"4. The Government of Japan understands that no unfair burden in connection with the cost of applying safeguards will be imposed on the non-nuclear-weapon States to which such safeguards are to be applied.

"5. The Government of Japan considers that, when safeguards are applied in accordance with the safeguards agreement to be concluded by Japan with the International Atomic Energy Agency under Article III of this Treaty, steps should be taken to arrange that such safeguards supersede the existing safeguards which are being applied in connection with

Japan's co-operation with the United States, the United Kingdom, and Canada in the peaceful use of nuclear energy.

"6. Concrete measures should be taken to promote the implementation of the provisions of Articles IV and V of the Treaty relating to International Co-operation for the Peaceful Use of Nuclear Energy and for the Peaceful Application of Nuclear Explosions. In particular, no peaceful nuclear activities in non-nuclear-weapon States shall be prohibited or restricted, nor shall the transfer of information, nuclear materials, equipment or other material relating to the peaceful use of nuclear energy be denied to non-nuclear-weapon States, merely on the grounds that such activities or transfers could be used also for the manufacture of nuclear weapons or other nuclear explosive devices."

[11]With the following declaration:

"Today the Government of Japan is depositing its Instruments of Ratification of the Treaty on the Non-Proliferation of Nuclear Weapons with the Governments of the United Kingdom, the Soviet Union and the United States, and Japan becomes a party to this Treaty.

"Japan, as the only nation to have suffered atomic bombing, has consistently followed a fundamental policy of forsaking nuclear armament and has steadfastly pursued the foreign policy of a nation committed to peace under its peace constitution. On the occasion of the depositing of its Instruments of Ratification of this Treaty, the Government of Japan declares anew to the world this fundamental policy. It firmly believes that Japan's adherence to this Treaty will contribute to stability in international relations, and, in particular, to peace and stability in Asia.

"Japan, as a party to this Treaty, is determined hereafter to intensify its efforts to prevent the proliferation of nuclear weapons and to contribute to international cooperation with respect to the peaceful uses of nuclear energy.

"This Treaty permits only the 'nuclear-weapon states' to possess nuclear weapons and allows them a special status. The Government of Japan holds the belief that the nuclear-weapon states must rectify this discrimination in the future by totally abolishing their nuclear weapons. To achieve this end, the Government of Japan is determined to make special efforts for the furthering of nuclear disarmament.

"On the basis of these fundamental considerations, the Government of Japan stresses especially the following points:

"1. The Government of Japan hopes that as many states as possible, whether possessing a nuclear explosive capability or not, will become parties to this Treaty in order to make it truly effective. In particular, it strongly hopes that the Republic of France and the People's Republic of China, which possess nuclear weapons but are not parties to this Treaty, will accede thereto.

"2. The Government of Japan urges the nuclear-weapon states, which have special responsibilities for nuclear disarmament, to take concrete nuclear disarmament measures such as the reduction of nuclear arms and the realization of a comprehensive nuclear test ban, in accordance with Article VI of this Treaty. It urges the nuclear-weapon states not party to this Treaty also to take nuclear disarmament measures.

"3. The Government of Japan takes particular note of the Declarations in June 1968 of the United Kingdom, the Soviet Union and the United States concerning the security of non-nuclear-weapon states, as well as of Security Council Resolution 255 (1968), and hopes that the nuclear-weapon states will make further efforts towards effective measures for the security of non-nuclear-weapon states. It further urges all states, both nuclear-weapon states and non-nuclear-weapon states, to refrain, in accordance with the Charter of the United Nations, from the threat or use of force in their international relations involving either nuclear or non-nuclear weapons.

"4. The Government of Japan is convinced that, for the well-being of all mankind, international co-operation with respect to the peaceful uses of nuclear energy and the peaceful applications of nuclear explosions should be vigorously promoted in accordance with the provisions of this Treaty. It considers that peaceful nuclear activities in non-nuclear-weapon states party to the Treaty should in no way be hampered by this Treaty and also that Japan should not be discriminated against in favour of other states party to the Treaty in any aspect of such activities.

"5. The Government of Japan appreciates the Declarations of the United Kingdom and the United States, both nuclear-weapon states, that they will accept the application of safeguards of the International Atomic Energy Agency to their peaceful nuclear activities. It urges the other nuclear-weapon states to take similar actions.

"6. The Government of Japan hopes that Review Conferences, as provided for in this Treaty, will continue to be held at regular intervals in order to ensure the appropriate operation of this Treaty."

[12]With the following declaration:

"1. In accordance with what is laid down in Article VII of the Treaty, none of the provisions of the said Treaty shall be interpreted as affecting in any way whatsoever the rights and obligations of Mexico as a State Party to the Treaty for the Prohibition of Nuclear Weapons in Latin America (Treaty of Tlatelolco), opened for signature on 14 February 1967, and concerning which the United Nations General Assembly adopted Resolution 2286 (XXII) of 5 December 1967;

"2. At the present time any nuclear explosive (device) is capable of being used as a nuclear weapon and there is no indication that in the near future it will be possible to manufacture nuclear explosive (devices) which are not potentially nuclear weapons. However, if technological advances succeeded in modifying this situation, it would be necessary to amend the relevant provisions of the Treaty in accordance with the procedure established therein."

[13]Ratification by the Netherlands is in respect of the Kingdom in Europe, Suriname and the Netherlands Antilles. (On 25 November 1975 Suriname became a foreign State.)

[14]On 20 December 1985, the Netherlands informed the depositary Government that as the island of Aruba, which on that date was still part of the Netherlands Antilles, would obtain internal autonomy as a country within the Kingdom of the Netherlands as of 1 January 1986, the Treaty would, as of 1 January 1986, as concerns the Kingdom of the Netherlands apply to the Netherlands Antilles (without Aruba), and Aruba.

[15]With the following statement:

"The signing by the Government of the Republic of Korea of the present Treaty does not in any way mean or imply the recognition of any territory or regime which has not been recognized by the Government of the Republic of Korea as a State or Government."

[16]Considered to be a party by the United Kingdom of Great Britain and Northern Ireland on the basis of declarations made to the United Nations prior to its independence.

[17]In a letter dated 30 September 1983 to the Secretary-General of the United Nations, the Government of Saint Vincent and the Grenadines declared that, with regard to multilateral treaties applied or extended to the former British Associated State of St. Vincent, it would continue to apply the terms of each such treaty provisionally and on the basis of reciprocity until such time as it notifies the depositary authority of its decision in respect thereof.

On 22 October 1984, the Government of Saint Vincent and the Grenadines informed the Government of the United Kingdom of Great Britain and Northern Ireland that, "having examined the text of the said Treaty, [it] hereby declares that it considers itself a party to the said Treaty by virtue of the ratification of the said Treaty by the Government of the United Kingdom of Great Britain and Northern Ireland. . . ."

[18]In a note dated 9 September 1968 the Secretariat of State for Foreign Affairs of the Republic of San Marino stated the following position of the Government of San Marino:

". . .in the event that no act of recognition as prescribed by international law has taken place between the Republic of San Marino and another State, the signing of the Treaty on Non-Proliferation of Nuclear Weapons by such other State or Government, or the deposit by it of its instrument of ratification, or the notification of such acts by a depositary State, does not imply recognition of that State or of that Government by the Government of San Marino."

[19]Succeeded to the Treaty by virtue of the ratification of the Netherlands.

[20]With the following declaration:

"On the occasion of the signature today of the Treaty for the Non-Proliferation of Nuclear Weapons, the Swiss Government expressly declare that they will not submit the Treaty to Parliament for its approval until such time as they consider that a sufficient measure of universal support has been obtained by the Treaty.

"The Swiss Government also reserve the right to make such declarations as they shall deem necessary at the time of the deposit of their instrument of ratification."

[21]With the following declaration:

"Recalling that the aim of the Treaty is to prevent those States which do not possess nuclear weapons from manufacturing or acquiring such arms and other nuclear explosive devices, Switzerland ratifies the Treaty in the belief that its provisions are directed solely towards the attainment of that aim and will not have the effects of limiting the use of nuclear energy for other purposes.

"Availing itself of the opportunity afforded by the deposit of its instruments of ratification, Switzerland makes the following declaration:

"1. Switzerland recalls that, according to Article IV, research, production and use for peaceful purposes in the nuclear sector do not come within the scope of the prohibitions in Articles I and II. Such activities include in particular the whole field of energy production and allied operations, research and technology in the sector of future generations of nuclear fission or fusion reactors and the production of isotopes.

"2. Switzerland defines the expression 'source and special fissionable material', used in Article III, in accordance with the present Article XX of the Statute of the IAEA. Any modification of this interpretation requires Switzerland's formal approval.

"It will, furthermore, accept only those interpretations and definitions of the concepts 'equipment or material specially designed or prepared for the processing, use or production of special fissionable material', mentioned in Article III, para. 2, which it has expressly approved.

"3. Switzerland understands that the application of the Treaty and in particular the control measures will not lead to any discrimination against Swiss industry in international competition."

[22]With the following declaration:

"The acceptance of this Treaty by the Syrian Arab Republic and the ratification thereof by the Government of the Syrian Arab Republic shall in no way signify recognition of Israel or entail entry into relations with Israel thereunder."

[23]With the following statement:

"The Government of the Republic of Turkey decided to deposit today the instrument of ratification of the Treaty on the Non-Proliferation of Nuclear Weapons.

"In voting in favour of the Treaty on 12 June 1968 at the twenty-second session of the

United Nations General Assembly and in signing the Treaty on 28 January 1969, the Turkish Government indicated its intention for eventual ratification.

"The Turkish Government is convinced that the Treaty is the most important multilateral arms control agreement yet concluded. By reducing the danger of a nuclear war, it greatly contributed to the process of detente, international security and disarmament.

"Turkey believes that her adherence would further the universality of the Treaty and strengthen the international nuclear non-proliferation system. It is however evident that cessation of the continuing arms race and preventing the war technology from reaching dangerous dimensions for the whole of mankind can only be realised through the conclusion of a treaty on general and complete disarmament under strict and effective international control. Furthermore, Turkey would like to underline the non-proliferation obligations of the nuclear-weapon States under relevant paragraphs of the Preamble and Article VI of the Treaty. Proliferation of all kinds must be halted and measures must be taken to meet adequately the security requirements of non-nuclear weapon States. Continuing absence of such assurances might have such consequences that may undermine the objectives and the provisions of the Treaty.

"Having included nuclear energy in its development plan as one of the sources of electricity production, Turkey is prepared, as stipulated in Article IV of the Treaty, to cooperate further with the technologically advanced States, on a non-discriminatory basis, in the field of nuclear research and development as well as in nuclear energy production. Measures developed or to be developed at national and international levels to ensure the non-proliferation of nuclear weapons should in no case restrict the non-nuclear-weapon States in their options for the application of nuclear energy for peaceful purposes."

[24]Statement communicated on 3 July 1968 to all States recognized by the United Kingdom:

"The Government of the United Kingdom wish to recall their view that if a regime is not recognized by the Government of a State, neither signature nor the deposit of any instrument by it, nor notification of any of those acts will bring about recognition of that regime by any other state."

[25]With the following declaration:

"In respect of the United Kingdom of Great Britain and Northern Ireland, the Associated States (Antigua, Dominica, Grenada, St. Kitts-Nevis-Anguilla and St. Lucia), and territories under the territorial sovereignty of the United Kingdom, as well as the State of Brunei, the Kingdom of Tonga and the British Solomon Islands Protectorate. With a declaration that the provisions of the Treaty shall not apply in regard to Southern Rhodesia unless and until the Government of the United Kingdom informs the other depositary Governments that it is in a position to ensure that the obligations imposed by the Treaty in respect of that territory can be fully implemented."

The Embassy of the Federal Republic of Cameroon informed the United States Department of State by a note dated April 24, 1969 that "The Government of the Federal Republic of Cameroon is unable to accept the reservation made by the Government of the United Kingdom . . . regarding its dependent territory of Southern Rhodesia. It is . . . the position of the Government of the Federal Republic of Cameroon that the Government of the United Kingdom, being the lawful Government of Rhodesia, remains responsible for the implementation of the obligations imposed by this Treaty as well as other International Treaties and conventions until that territory is granted independence in accordance with the United Nations Resolution 2379 (XXIII)."

Concerning the above declaration the Government of the Union of Soviet Socialist Republics expressed the following view:

"The Soviet Government supports the view that the United Kingdom, as has also been repeatedly noted in decisions of the General Assembly of the United Nations, bears full responsibility with regard to Southern Rhodesia until the people of that Territory obtain genuine independence. This fully applies also to the aforementioned Treaty."

26With the following declaration:

"In connection with the adoption by the Federal Assembly of the Socialist Federal Republic of Yugoslavia of the Law on the ratification of the Treaty on the Non-Proliferation of Nuclear Weapons, the Government of Yugoslavia wishes to reaffirm its conviction that the Treaty will contribute to the cessation of the nuclear arms race, facilitate the setting in motion of the process of nuclear disarmament and stimulate the trend towards general and complete disarmament.

"The Government of Yugoslavia attaches great importance to further efforts by all countries to create a universal system of international security that would ensure a lasting peace and create conditions for an accelerated development in the whole world. Although the realization of this objective necessarily calls for an essential change in the existing practices in international relations, which are so often characterized by inequality, interference in internal affairs of other countries and the power policy, the Government of Yugoslavia considers that the Non-Proliferation Treaty, and similar collateral measures, can constitute a beneficial contribution to the search for peace and international security.

"On this occasion the Government of Yugoslavia wishes to recall that prior to the signing of the Non-Proliferation Treaty the Socialist Federal Republic of Yugoslavia had been exerting efforts, together with other countries, to eliminate some of its deficiencies in order to make it more acceptable to the non-nuclear-weapon states. These efforts have produced definite results. Many of these positions are contained in the Memorandum of the Government of Yugoslavia to the United Nations Commission on Disarmament dated May 3, 1965 and in the Communiqué of April 11, 1968 issued by the Government of Yugoslavia relating to the problem of non-proliferation of nuclear weapons.

"In this connection the Government of Yugoslavia wishes to set forth the motives and expectations which it has in proposing to the Federal Assembly to ratify the Treaty on the Non-Proliferation of Nuclear Weapons.

"The Government of Yugoslavia, viewing this Treaty against the background of the search for peace, general and complete disarmament, international security and development:

"1. considers the ban on the development, manufacture and use of nuclear weapons and the destruction of all stockpiles of them to be indispensable for the maintenance of a stable peace and international security, and expects the nuclear-weapon powers to display, with this objective in mind, their willingness to conclude a convention on the general renunciation of the threat or use of nuclear weapons,

"2. holds the view that the chief responsibility for the progress in this direction rests with the nuclear-weapon powers and expects them to show maximum goodwill and determination to embark upon that road, a matter made obligatory upon them also by the fact that non-nuclear-weapon states party to the treaty have voluntarily renounced to manufacture or otherwise acquire nuclear weapons or other nuclear explosive devices,

"3. expects that the already initiated talks between the superpowers relating to containment and cessation of the race in the development and production of the strategic nuclear arms will be expanded also to the so-called tactical nuclear weapons and lead to the prohibition of the stationing of these arms in the areas free thereof to the withdrawal from alien territories within one's own state borders and to the discontinuance of the training of the non-nuclear-weapon states' armed forces in the use of nuclear weapons, creating thereby favourable conditions for even more far-reaching measures in the field of nuclear disarmament,

"4. lends its support to every action aimed at creating nuclear-weapon-free zones and the thinned armament zones, as significant measures for the easing of tensions and strengthening of international security,

"5. notes that the continuance of nuclear weapons tests is inconsistent with the spirit of letter of the Non-Proliferation Treaty and considers it indispensable for the nuclear-weapon powers to initiate, at an early date, negotiations for the completion of the Moscow Agreement,

"6. attaches special importance to finding a satisfactory solution to the problem of safeguarding the security of non-nuclear-weapon states and expects nuclear-weapon powers, on the one hand, to undertake not to use nuclear weapons against the countries having renounced them as well as against non-nuclear-weapon states in general, and to refrain from the threat to use them, and, on the other hand, expects that in the event of such a threat, United Nations will act in a manner as shall ensure effective protection of the non-nuclear-weapon states.

"7. considers that the Non-Proliferation Treaty makes all the states parties entitled to full and unhampered utilization, on a non-discriminatory basis, of all the achievements of nuclear activities for peaceful purposes, including nuclear explosions, through appropriate international procedures yet to be established,

"8. believes that all countries will be ensured the same treatment with regard to the contents and modalities of control of the use of nuclear energy for peaceful purposes and that the expenditure for the system of control will be regulated in a way not burdening the non-nuclear-weapon states and, in particular, the developing countries,

"9. requests the nuclear-weapon states party to the Non-Proliferation Treaty to render all the appropriate assistance to the non-nuclear-weapon states in the application of nuclear energy for peaceful purposes and expects the International Atomic Energy Agency to adjust itself more fully to the current needs of the international community, particularly to those of the developing countries.

"The Government of Yugoslavia emphasizes once again the great significance it attaches to the universality of the efforts relating to the realization of the Non-Proliferation Treaty, in the belief that all the states parties will make their greatest possible contribution to have the spirit and letter of the Non-Proliferation Treaty fully and constructively applied, in order to facilitate, inter alia, the accession of all countries to the Treaty."

[27] With the following declaration:

"The accession by the State of Bahrein to the Treaty on the Non-Proliferation of Nuclear Weapons, 1968, shall in no way constitute recognition of Israel or be a cause for the establishment of any relations of any kind therewith."

GENERAL ASSEMBLY RESOLUTION 3184 (XXVIII): GENERAL AND COMPLETE DISARMAMENT, DECEMBER 18, 1973[1]

B

The General Assembly,

Recalling its resolution 2373 (XXII) of 12 June 1968, in which it commended the Treaty on the Non-Proliferation of Nuclear Weapons, annexed thereto, and expressed the hope for the widest possible adherence to that Treaty,

---

[1]U.N. doc. A/RES/3184 (XXVIII), February 11, 1974, in *Documents on Disarmament, 1973*, pp. 902–3.

Noting that article VIII, paragraph 3, of the Treaty provides, *inter alia*, that:

Five years after the entry into force of this Treaty, a conference of Parties to the Treaty shall be held in Geneva, Switzerland, in order to review the operation of this Treaty with a view to assuring that the purposes of the Preamble and the provisions of the Treaty are being realized.

Bearing in mind that the Treaty will have been in force for five years on 5 March 1975 and expecting that the review conference called for in the Treaty will take place soon after that date,

1. *Notes* that, following appropriate consultation, a preparatory committee has been formed of parties to the Treaty on the Non-Proliferation of Nuclear Weapons serving on the Board of Governors of the International Atomic Energy Agency or represented at the Conference of the Committee on Disarmament;

2. *Requests* the Secretary-General to render the necessary assistance and to provide such services, including summary records, as may be required for the review conference and its preparation.

GENERAL ASSEMBLY RESOLUTION 3261 (XXIX): GENERAL AND COMPLETE DISARMAMENT, DECEMBER 9, 1974[1]

D

The General Assembly,

Recalling its resolutions on the urgent need for prevention of nuclear proliferation,

Recalling also its resolution 2829 (XXVI) of 16 December 1971,

Recognizing that the acceleration of the nuclear arms race and the proliferation of nuclear weapons endanger the security of all States,

Convinced that recent international developments have underlined the urgent necessity for all States, in particular nuclear-weapon States, to take effective measures to reverse the momentum of the nuclear arms race and to prevent further proliferation of nuclear weapons,

Further convinced that the achievement of these goals would be advanced by an effective comprehensive test ban,

Bearing in mind that it has not yet proved possible to differentiate between the technology for nuclear weapons and that for nuclear explosive devices for peaceful purposes,

Noting with concern that, during the current year, six States have engaged in nuclear testing,

Recognizing that even those States which renounce the possession of nuclear weapons may wish to be able to enjoy any benefits which may materialize from nuclear explosions for peaceful purposes,

Noting with great concern that, as a result of the wider dissemination of nuclear technology and nuclear materials, the possible diversion of nuclear energy from peaceful to military uses would present a serious danger for world peace and security,

Considering, therefore, that the planning and conducting of peaceful nuclear explosions should be carried out under agreed and non-discriminatory international arrangements, such as those envisaged in the Treaty on the Non-Proliferation of Nuclear Weapons, which are designed to help prevent the proliferation of nuclear explosive devices and the intensification of the nuclear arms race,

---

[1]U.N. doc. A/RES/3261 (XXIX), January 6, 1975, in *Documents on Disarmament, 1974*, pp. 803–6.

Recalling the statements made at the 1577th meeting of the First Committee, on 31 May 1968, by the representatives of the Union of Soviet Socialist Republics and the United States of America concerning the provisions of article V of the Treaty on the Non-Proliferation of Nuclear Weapons which relate to the conclusion of a special international agreement on nuclear explosions for peaceful purposes,

Noting that the Review Conference of the Parties to the Treaty on the Non-Proliferation of Nuclear Weapons will be held at Geneva in May 1975,

Noting further that, in the introduction to his report on the work of the Organization dated 30 August 1974, the Secretary-General pointed out the possible danger of peaceful nuclear explosions leading to the proliferation of nuclear weapons and suggested that the question of peaceful nuclear explosions in all its aspects should now be a subject for international consideration,

1. *Appeals* to all States, in particular nuclear-weapon States, to exert concerted efforts in all the appropriate international forums with a view to working out promptly effective measures for the cessation of the nuclear arms race and for the prevention of the further proliferation of nuclear weapons;

2. *Requests* the International Atomic Energy Agency to continue its studies on the peaceful applications of nuclear explosions, their utility and feasibility, including legal, health and safety aspects, and to report on these questions to the General Assembly at its thirtieth session;

3. *Calls upon* the Conference of the Committee on Disarmament, in submitting its report to the General Assembly at its thirtieth session on the elaboration of a treaty designed to achieve a comprehensive test ban, to include a section on its consideration of the arms control implications of peaceful nuclear explosions and, in so doing, to take account of the views of the International Atomic Energy Agency as requested in paragraph 2 above;

4. *Expresses the hope* that the Review Conference of the Parties to the Treaty on the Non-Proliferation of Nuclear Weapons, to be held at Geneva in May 1975, will also give consideration to the role of peaceful nuclear explosions as provided for in that Treaty and will inform the General Assembly at its thirtieth session of the results of its deliberations;

5. *Invites*, in this connexion, the Union of Soviet Socialist Republics and the United States of America to provide the Review Conference of the Parties to the Treaty on the Non-Proliferation of Nuclear Weapons with information concerning such steps as they have taken since the entry into force of the Treaty, or intend to take, for the conclusion of the special basic international agreement on nuclear explosions for peaceful purposes which is envisaged in article V of the Treaty;

6. *Invites* the Secretary-General, should he deem it appropriate, to submit further comments on this matter, taking into account the reports referred to in paragraphs 2, 3 and 4 above.

FINAL DECLARATION OF THE REVIEW CONFERENCE OF THE PARTIES TO THE TREATY ON THE NON-PROLIFERATION OF NUCLEAR WEAPONS, MAY 30, 1975[1]

Preamble

The States Party to the Treaty on the Non-Proliferation of Nuclear Weapons which met in Geneva in May 1975, in accordance with the Treaty, to review the operation of the Treaty

---

[1]U.N. doc. NPT/CONF/30/Rev. 1, Annex 1, May 30, 1975, in *Documents on Disarmament, 1975*, pp. 146–56.

with a view to assuring that the purposes of the Preamble and the provisions of the Treaty are being realized,

Recognizing the continuing importance of the objectives of the Treaty,

Affirming the belief that universal adherence to the Treaty would greatly strengthen international peace and enhance the security of all States,

Firmly convinced that, in order to achieve this aim, it is essential to maintain, in the implementation of the Treaty, an acceptable balance of mutual responsibilities and obligations of all States Party to the Treaty, nuclear-weapon and non-nuclear-weapon States,

Recognizing that the danger of nuclear warfare remains a grave threat to the survival of mankind,

Convinced that the prevention of any further proliferation of nuclear weapons or other nuclear explosive devices remains a vital element in efforts to avert nuclear warfare, and that the promotion of this objective will be furthered by more rapid progress towards the cessation of the nuclear arms race and the limitation and reduction of existing nuclear weapons, with a view to the eventual elimination from national arsenals of nuclear weapons, pursuant to a Treaty on general and complete disarmament under strict and effective international control,

Recalling the determination expressed by the Parties to seek to achieve the discontinuance of all test explosions of nuclear weapons for all time,

Considering that the trend towards détente in relations between States provides a favourable climate within which more significant progress should be possible towards the cessation of the nuclear arms race,

Noting the important role which nuclear energy can, particularly in changing economic circumstances, play in power production and in contributing to the progressive elimination of the economic and technological gap between developing and developed States,

Recognizing that the accelerated spread and development of peaceful applications of nuclear energy will, in the absence of effective safeguards, contribute to further proliferation of nuclear explosive capability,

Recognizing the continuing necessity of full co-operation in the application and improvement of International Atomic Energy Agency (IAEA) safeguards on peaceful nuclear activities,

Recalling that all Parties to the Treaty are entitled to participate in the fullest possible exchange of scientific information for, and to contribute alone or in co-operation with other States to, the further development of the applications of atomic energy for peaceful purposes,

Reaffirming the principle that the benefits of peaceful applications of nuclear technology, including any technological by-products which may be derived by nuclear-weapon States from the development of nuclear explosive devices, should be available for peaceful purposes to all Parties to the Treaty, and

Recognizing that all States Parties have a duty to strive for the adoption of tangible and effective measures to attain the objectives of the Treaty,

Declares as follows:

Purposes

The States Party to the Treaty reaffirm their strong common interest in averting the further proliferation of nuclear weapons. They reaffirm their strong support for the Treaty, their continued dedication to its principles and objectives, and their commitment to implement fully and more effectively its provisions.

They reaffirm the vital role of the Treaty in international efforts

- to avert further proliferation of nuclear weapons,
- to achieve the cessation of the nuclear arms race and to undertake effective measures in the direction of nuclear disarmament, and
- to promote co-operation in the peaceful uses of nuclear energy under adequate safeguards.

Review of Articles I and II

The review undertaken by the Conference confirms that the obligations undertaken under Articles I and II of the Treaty have been faithfully observed by all Parties. The Conference is convinced that the continued strict observance of these Articles remains central to the shared objective of averting the further proliferation of nuclear weapons.

Review of Article III

The Conference notes that the verification activities of the IAEA under Article III of the Treaty respect the sovereign rights of States and do not hamper the economic, scientific or technological development of the Parties to the Treaty or international co-operation in peaceful nuclear activities. It urges that this situation be maintained. The Conference attaches considerable importance to the continued application of safeguards under Article III, 1, on a non-discriminatory basis, for the equal benefit of all States Party to the Treaty.

The Conference notes the importance of systems of accounting for and control of nuclear material, from the standpoints both of the responsibilities of States Party to the Treaty and of co-operation with the IAEA in order to facilitate the implementation of the safeguards provided for in Article III, 1. The Conference expresses the hope that all States having peaceful nuclear activities will establish and maintain effective accounting and control systems and welcomes the readiness of the IAEA to assist States in so doing.

The Conference expresses its strong support for effective IAEA safeguards. In this context it recommends that intensified efforts be made towards the standardization and the universality of application of IAEA safeguards, while ensuring that safeguards agreements with non-nuclear-weapon States not Party to the Treaty are of adequate duration, preclude diversion to any nuclear explosive devices and contain appropriate provisions for the continuance of the application of safeguards upon re-export.

The Conference recommends that more attention and fuller support be given to the improvement of safeguards techniques, instrumentation, data-handling and implementation in order, among other things, to ensure optimum cost-effectiveness. It notes with satisfaction the establishment by the Director General of the IAEA of a standing advisory group on safeguards implementation.

The Conference emphasises the necessity for the States Party to the Treaty that have not yet done so to conclude as soon as possible safeguards agreements with the IAEA.

With regard to the implementation of Article III, 2, of the Treaty, the Conference notes that a number of States suppliers of nuclear material or equipment have adopted certain minimum, standard requirements for IAEA safeguards in connexion with their exports of certain such items to non-nuclear-weapon States not Party to the Treaty (IAEA document INFCIRC/209 and Addenda). The Conference attaches particular importance to the condition, established by those States, of an undertaking of non-diversion to nuclear weapons or other nuclear explosive devices, as included in the said requirements.

The Conference urges that:

(*a*) in all achievable ways, common export requirements relating to safeguards be strengthened, in particular by extending the application of safeguards to all peaceful nuclear activities in importing States not Party to the Treaty;

(*b*) such common requirements be accorded the widest possible measure of acceptance among all suppliers and recipients;

(*c*) all Parties to the Treaty should actively pursue their efforts to these ends.

The Conference takes note of:

(*a*) the considered view of many Parties to the Treaty that the safeguards required under Article III, 2, should extend to all peaceful nuclear activities in importing States;

(*b*) (*i*) the suggestion that it is desirable to arrange for common safeguards requirements in respect of nuclear material processed, used or produced by the use of scientific and technological information transferred in tangible form to non-nuclear-weapon States not Party to the Treaty; (*ii*) the hope that this aspect of safeguards could be further examined.

The Conference recommends that, during the review of the arrangements relating to the financing of safeguards in the IAEA which is to be undertaken by its Board of Governors at an appropriate time after 1975, the less favourable financial situation of the developing countries be fully taken into account. It recommends further that, on that occasion, the Parties to the Treaty concerned seek measures that would restrict within appropriate limits the respective shares of developing countries in safeguards costs.

The Conference attaches considerable importance, so far as safeguards inspectors are concerned, to adherence by the IAEA to Article VII.D of its Statute, prescribing, among other things, that "due regard shall be paid . . . to the importance of recruiting the staff on as wide a geographical basis as possible"; it also recommends that safeguards training be made available to personnel from all geographic regions.

The Conference, convinced that nuclear materials should be effectively protected at all times, urges that action be pursued to elaborate further, within the IAEA, concrete recommendations for the physical protection of nuclear material in use, storage and transit, including principles relating to the responsibility of States, with a view to ensuring a uniform, minimum level of effective protection for such material.

It calls upon all States engaging in peaceful nuclear activities (*i*) to enter into such international agreements and arrangements as may be necessary to ensure such protection; and (*ii*) in the framework of their respective physical protection systems, to give the earliest possible effective application to the IAEA's recommendations.

Review of Article IV

The Conference reaffirms, in the framework of Article IV, 1, that nothing in the Treaty shall be interpreted as affecting, and notes with satisfaction that nothing in the Treaty has been identified as affecting, the inalienable right of all the Parties to the Treaty to develop research, production and use of nuclear energy for peaceful purposes without discrimination and in conformity with Articles I and II of the Treaty.

The Conference reaffirms, in the framework of Article IV, 2, the undertaking by all Parties to the Treaty to facilitate the fullest possible exchange of equipment, materials and scientific and technological information for the peaceful uses of nuclear energy and the right of all Parties to the Treaty to participate in such exchange and welcomes the efforts made towards that end. Noting that the Treaty constitutes a favourable framework for broadening international co-operation in the peaceful uses of nuclear energy, the Conference is convinced that on this basis, and in conformity with the Treaty, further efforts should be made to ensure that the benefits of peaceful applications of nuclear technology should be available to all Parties to the Treaty.

The Conference recognizes that there continues to be a need for the fullest possible exchange of nuclear materials, equipment and technology, including up-to-date developments, consistent with the objectives and safeguards requirements of the Treaty. The Conference reaffirms the undertaking of the Parties to the Treaty in a position to do so to co-operate in contributing, alone or together with other States or international organizations, to the further development of the applications of nuclear energy for peaceful purposes, especially in the territories of non-nuclear-weapon States Party to the Treaty, with due consideration for the needs of the developing areas of the world. Recognizing, in the context of Article IV, 2, those growing needs of developing States the Conference considers it necessary to continue and increase assistance to them in this field bilaterally and through such multilateral channels as the IAEA and the United Nations Development Programme.

The Conference is of the view that, in order to implement as fully as possible Article IV of the Treaty, developed States Party to the Treaty should consider taking measures, making contributions and establishing programmes, as soon as possible, for the provision of special assistance in the peaceful uses of nuclear energy for developing States Party to the Treaty.

The Conference recommends that, in reaching decisions on the provision of equipment, materials, services and scientific and technological information for the peaceful uses of nuclear energy, on concessional and other appropriate financial arrangements and on the furnishing of technical assistance in the nuclear field, including co-operation related to the continuous operation of peaceful nuclear facilities, States Party to the Treaty should give weight to adherence to the Treaty by recipient States. The Conference recommends, in this connexion, that any special measures of co-operation to meet the growing needs of developing States Party to the Treaty might include increased and supplemental voluntary aid provided bilaterally or through multilateral channels such as the IAEA's facilities for administering funds-in-trust and gifts-in-kind.

The Conference further recommends that States Party to the Treaty in a position to do so, meet, to the fullest extent possible, "technically sound" requests for technical assistance, submitted to the IAEA by developing States Party to the Treaty, which the IAEA is unable to finance from its own resources, as well as such "technically sound" requests as may be made by developing States Party to the Treaty which are not Members of the IAEA.

The Conference recognizes that regional or multinational nuclear fuel cycle centres may be an advantageous way to satisfy, safely and economically, the needs of many States in the course of initiating or expanding nuclear power programmes, while at the same time facilitating physical protection and the application of IAEA safeguards, and contributing to the goals of the Treaty.

The Conference welcomes the IAEA's studies in this area, and recommends that they be continued as expeditiously as possible. It considers that such studies should include, among other aspects, identification of the complex practical and organizational difficulties which will need to be dealt with in connexion with such projects.

The Conference urges all Parties to the Treaty in a position to do so to co-operate in these studies, particularly by providing to the IAEA where possible economic data concerning construction and operation of facilities such as chemical reprocessing plants, plutonium fuel fabrication plants, waste management installations, and longer-term spent fuel storage, and by assistance to the IAEA to enable it to undertake feasibility studies concerning the establishment of regional nuclear fuel cycle centres in specific geographic regions.

The Conference hopes that, if these studies lead to positive findings, and if the establishment of regional or multinational nuclear fuel cycle centres is undertaken, Parties to the Treaty in a position to do so will co-operate in, and provide assistance for, the elaboration and realization of such projects.

Review of Article V

The Conference reaffirms the obligation of Parties to the Treaty to take appropriate measures to ensure that potential benefits from any peaceful applications of nuclear explosions are made available to non-nuclear-weapon States Party to the Treaty in full accordance with the provisions of Article V and other applicable international obligations. In this connexion, the Conference also reaffirms that such services should be provided to non-nuclear-weapon States Party to the Treaty on a non-discriminatory basis and that the charge to such Parties for the explosive devices used should be as low as possible and exclude any charge for research and development.

The Conference notes that any potential benefits could be made available to non-nuclear-weapon States not Party to the Treaty by way of nuclear explosion services provided by nuclear-weapon States, as defined by the Treaty, and conducted under the appropriate international observation and international procedures called for in Article V and in accordance with other applicable international obligations. The Conference considers it imperative that access to potential benefits of nuclear explosions for peaceful purposes not lead to any proliferation of nuclear explosive capability.

The Conference considers the IAEA to be the appropriate international body, referred to in Article V of the Treaty, through which potential benefits from peaceful applications of nuclear explosions could be made available to any non-nuclear-weapon State. Accordingly, the Conference urges the IAEA to expedite work on identifying and examining the important legal issues involved in, and to commence consideration of, the structure and content of the special international agreement or agreements contemplated in Article V of the Treaty, taking into account the views of the Conference of the Committee on Disarmament (CCD) and the United Nations General Assembly and enabling States Party to the Treaty but not Members of the IAEA which would wish to do so to participate in such work.

The Conference notes that the technology of nuclear explosions for peaceful purposes is still at the stage of development and study and that there are a number of interrelated international legal and other aspects of such explosions which still need to be investigated.

The Conference commends the work in this field that has been carried out within the IAEA and looks forward to the continuance of such work pursuant to United Nations General Assembly resolution 3261 D (XXIX). It emphasizes that the IAEA should play the central role in matters relating to the provision of services for the application of nuclear explosions for peaceful purposes. It believes that the IAEA should broaden its consideration of this subject to encompass, within its area of competence, all aspects and implications of the practical applications of nuclear explosions for peaceful purposes. To this end it urges the IAEA to set up appropriate machinery within which intergovernmental discussion can take place and through which advice can be given on the Agency's work in this field.

The Conference attaches considerable importance to the consideration by the CCD, pursuant to United Nations General Assembly resolution 3261 D (XXIX) and taking due account of the views of the IAEA, of the arms control implications of nuclear explosions for peaceful purposes.

The Conference notes that the thirtieth session of the United Nations General Assembly will receive reports pursuant to United Nations General Assembly resolution 3261 D (XXIX) and will provide an opportunity for States to discuss questions related to the application of nuclear explosions for peaceful purposes. The Conference further notes that the results of discussion in the United Nations General Assembly at its thirtieth session will be available to be taken into account by the IAEA and the CCD for their further consideration.

Review of Article VI

The Conference recalls the provisions of Article VI of the Treaty under which all Parties undertook to pursue negotiations in good faith on effective measures relating

- to the cessation of the nuclear arms race at an early date and
- to nuclear disarmament and
- to a treaty on general and complete disarmament under strict and effective international control.

While welcoming the various agreements on arms limitation and disarmament elaborated and concluded over the last few years as steps contributing to the implementation of Article VI of the Treaty, the Conference expresses its serious concern that the arms race, in particular the nuclear arms race, is continuing unabated.

The Conference therefore urges constant and resolute efforts by each of the Parties to the Treaty, in particular by the nuclear-weapon States, to achieve an early and effective implementation of Article VI of the Treaty.

The Conference affirms the determination expressed in the preamble to the 1963 Partial Test Ban Treaty and reiterated in the preamble to the Non-Proliferation Treaty to achieve the discontinuance of all test explosions of nuclear weapons for all time. The Conference expresses the view that the conclusion of a treaty banning all nuclear weapons tests is one of the most important measures to halt the nuclear arms race. It expresses the hope that the nuclear-weapon States Party to the Treaty will take the lead in reaching an early solution of the technical and political difficulties on this issue. It appeals to these States to make every effort to reach agreement on the conclusion of an effective comprehensive test ban. To this end, the desire was expressed by a considerable number of delegations at the Conference that the nuclear-weapon States Party to the Treaty should as soon as possible enter into an agreement, open to all States and containing appropriate provisions to ensure its effectiveness, to halt all nuclear weapons tests of adhering States for a specified time, whereupon the terms of such an agreement would be reviewed in the light of the opportunity, at that time, to achieve a universal and permanent cessation of all nuclear weapons tests. The Conference calls upon the nuclear-weapon States signatories of the Treaty on the limitation of underground nuclear weapons tests, meanwhile, to limit the number of their underground nuclear weapons tests to a minimum. The Conference believes that such steps would constitute an incentive of particular value to negotiations for the conclusion of a treaty banning all nuclear weapons test explosions for all time.

The Conference appeals to the nuclear-weapon States Parties to the negotiations on the limitation of strategic arms to endeavour to conclude at the earliest possible date the new agreement that was outlined by their leaders in November 1974. The Conference looks forward to the commencement of follow-on negotiations on further limitations of, and significant reductions in, their nuclear weapons systems as soon as possible following the conclusion of such an agreement.

The Conference notes that, notwithstanding earlier progress, the CCD has recently been unable to reach agreement on new substantive measures to advance the objectives of Article VI of the Treaty. It urges, therefore, all members of the CCD Party to the Treaty, in particular the nuclear-weapon States Party, to increase their efforts to achieve effective disarmament agreements on all subjects on the agenda of the CCD.

The Conference expresses the hope that all States Party to the Treaty, through the United Nations and the CCD and other negotiations in which they participate, will work with determination towards the conclusion of arms limitation and disarmament agreements which will contribute to the goal of general and complete disarmament under strict and effective international control.

The Conference expresses the view that, disarmament being a matter of general concern, the provision of information to all governments and peoples on the situation in the field of the arms race and disarmament is of great importance for the attainment of the aims of Article VI. The Conference therefore invites the United Nations to consider ways and means of improving its existing facilities for collection, compilation and dissemination of information on disarmament issues, in order to keep all governments as well as world public opinion properly informed on progress achieved in the realization of the provisions of Article VI of the Treaty.

Review of Article VII and the Security of Non-Nuclear-Weapon States

Recognizing that all States have need to ensure their independence, territorial integrity and sovereignty, the Conference emphasizes the particular importance of assuring and strengthening the security of non-nuclear-weapon States Parties which have renounced the acquisition of nuclear weapons. It acknowledges that States Parties find themselves in different security situations and therefore that various appropriate means are necessary to meet the security concerns of States Parties.

The Conference underlines the importance of adherence to the Treaty by non-nuclear-weapon States as the best means of reassuring one another of their renunciation of nuclear weapons and as one of the effective means of strengthening their mutual security.

The Conference takes note of the continued determination of the Depositary States to honour their statements, which were welcomed by the United Nations Security Council in resolution 255 (1968), that, to ensure the security of the non-nuclear-weapon States Party to the Treaty, they will provide or support immediate assistance, in accordance with the Charter, to any non-nuclear-weapon State Party to the Treaty which is a victim of an act or an object of a threat of aggression in which nuclear weapons are used.

The Conference, bearing in mind Article VII of the Treaty, considers that the establishment of internationally recognized nuclear-weapon-free zones on the initiative and with the agreement of the directly concerned States of the zone, represents an effective means of curbing the spread of nuclear weapons, and could contribute significantly to the security of those States. It welcomes the steps which have been taken toward the establishment of such zones.

The Conference recognizes that for the maximum effectiveness of any Treaty arrangements for establishing a nuclear-weapon-free zone the co-operation of the nuclear-weapon States is necessary. At the Conference it was urged by a considerable number of delegations that nuclear-weapon States should provide, in an appropriate manner, binding security assurances to those States which become fully bound by the provisions of such regional arrangements.

At the Conference it was also urged that determined efforts must be made especially by the nuclear-weapon States Party to the Treaty, to ensure the security of all non-nuclear-weapon States Parties. To this end the Conference urges all States, both nuclear-weapon States and non-nuclear-weapon States to refrain, in accordance with the Charter of the United

Nations, from the threat or the use of force in relations between States, involving either nuclear or non-nuclear weapons. Additionally, it stresses the responsibility of all Parties to the Treaty and especially the nuclear-weapon States, to take effective steps to strengthen the security of non-nuclear-weapon States and to promote in all appropriate fora the consideration of all practical means to this end, taking into account the views expressed at this Conference.

Review of Article VIII

The Conference invites States Party to the Treaty which are Members of the United Nations to request the Secretary-General of the United Nations to include the following item in the provisional agenda of the thirty-first session of the General Assembly: "Implementation of the conclusions of the first Review Conference of the Parties to the Treaty on the Non-Proliferation of Nuclear Weapons".

The States Party to the Treaty participating in the Conference propose to the Depositary Governments that a second Conference to review the operation of the Treaty be convened in 1980.

The Conference accordingly invites States Party to the Treaty which are Members of the United Nations to request the Secretary-General of the United Nations to include the following item in the provisional agenda of the thirty-third session of the General Assembly: "Implementation of the conclusions of the first Review Conference of the Parties to the Treaty on the Non-Proliferation of Nuclear Weapons and establishment of a preparatory committee for the second Conference".

Review of Article X

The five years that have passed since the entry into force of the Treaty have demonstrated its wide international acceptance. The Conference welcomes the recent progress towards achieving wider adherence. At the same time, the Conference notes with concern that the Treaty has not as yet achieved universal adherence. Therefore, the Conference expresses the hope that States that have not already joined the Treaty should do so at the earliest possible date.

GENERAL ASSEMBLY RESOLUTION 3484 (XXX): GENERAL AND COMPLETE DISARMAMENT, DECEMBER 12, 1975[1]

A

The General Assembly,

Recalling its resolutions 3261 D (XXIX) of 9 December 1974 and 3386 (XXX) of 12 November 1975,

Convinced of the urgent necessity that all States, in particular nuclear-weapon States, take effective measures to reverse the momentum of the nuclear arms race,

Recalling also its resolutions on the urgent need for the prevention of nuclear proliferation and for an effective comprehensive nuclear weapon test ban,

Bearing in mind that it has not yet proved possible to differentiate between the technolo-

---

[1]U.N. doc. A/RES/3484 (XXX), January 6, 1976, in *Documents on Disarmament, 1975*, pp. 803–6.

gy for nuclear weapons and that for nuclear explosive devices for peaceful purposes and that, consequently, it is not possible at present to develop nuclear explosive devices for peaceful purposes without at the same time acquiring a nuclear weapon capability,

Conscious of the fact that the testing and application of nuclear explosions for peaceful purposes can have significant arms control implications both for the spread of nuclear weapons and their technology to States which do not already have them and, in the context of limitations of nuclear weapon testing, for the refinement of the arsenals of existing nuclear-weapon States,

Desirous of ensuring the fullest possible exchange of nuclear technology and nuclear materials for the economic and social benefit of mankind without increasing the risk of diversion to military purposes and the consequent danger to world peace and security,

Noting that non-nuclear-weapon States parties to the Treaty on the Non-Proliferation of Nuclear Weapons have the right to obtain the potential benefits from any applications of nuclear explosions for peaceful purposes, under appropriate international observation and through appropriate international procedures, pursuant to a special international agreement, through an appropriate international body with adequate representation of non-nuclear-weapon States, as contemplated in article V of the Treaty,

Noting further that the potential benefits from any applications of nuclear explosions for peaceful purposes could be made available to non-nuclear-weapon States not parties to the Treaty on the Non-Proliferation of Nuclear Weapons by way of nuclear explosion services provided by nuclear-weapon States, as defined by the Treaty, and conducted under the appropriate international observation and appropriate international procedures called for in article V of the Treaty and in accordance with other applicable international obligations,

Recalling once again the statements made at the 1577th meeting of the First Committee, on 31 May 1968, by the representatives of the Union of Soviet Socialist Republics and the United States of America concerning the provisions of article V of the Treaty on the Non-Proliferation of Nuclear Weapons which relate to the conclusion of a special international agreement on nuclear explosions for peaceful purposes,

Convinced of the need for the special international agreement or agreements contemplated in article V of the Treaty on the Non-Proliferation of Nuclear Weapons in respect of the peaceful application of nuclear explosions,

1. *Appeals once again* to all States, in particular nuclear-weapon States, to exert concerted efforts in all the appropriate international forums with a view to working out promptly effective measures for the cessation of the nuclear arms race and for the prevention of the further proliferation of nuclear weapons;

2. *Notes with appreciation*:

(*a*) The report of the International Atomic Energy Agency concerning its studies of the peaceful applications of nuclear explosions, their utility and feasibility, including legal, health and safety aspects, which comprises information regarding the establishment by the Agency of the *Ad Hoc* Advisory Group on Nuclear Explosions for Peaceful Purposes;

(*b*) The section of the report of the Conference of the Committee on Disarmament with respect to the arms control implications of peaceful nuclear explosions within the framework of a comprehensive test ban;

(*c*) The consideration given by the Review Conference of the Parties to the Treaty on the Non-Proliferation of Nuclear Weapons to the role of nuclear explosions for peaceful purposes as provided for in that Treaty;

(*d*) The observations of the Secretary-General in the introduction to his annual report submitted to the General Assembly at its thirtieth session;

3. *Notes* the conclusions of the Review Conference of the Parties to the Treaty on the Non-Proliferation of Nuclear Weapons with respect to article V of the Treaty, contained in the Final Declaration of the Conference, adopted by consensus on 30 May 1975;

4. *Notes also* that the final documentation of the Conference included a draft resolution submitted by eight States which attended the Conference, which urged the Depositary Governments of the Treaty on the Non-Proliferation of Nuclear Weapons to initiate immediate consultations with all of the other States parties to the Treaty in order to reach agreement on the most appropriate place and date for holding a meeting of the parties in order to conclude the special basic international agreement contemplated in article V of the Treaty;

5. *Notes* in this connexion that, according to information provided by the Union of Soviet Socialist Republics and the United States of America to the Review Conference of the Parties to the Treaty on the Non-Proliferation of Nuclear Weapons in response to the invitation addressed to them in General Assembly resolution 3261 D (XXIX), no consultations have yet taken place for the conclusion of the special basic international agreement on nuclear explosions for peaceful purposes as envisaged in article V of that Treaty;

6. *Invites* the Union of Soviet Socialist Republics and the United States of America to provide information on such consultations as they may have entered into or may intend to enter into for the conclusion of the special basic international agreement on nuclear explosions for peaceful purposes, as envisaged in article V of the Treaty on the Non-Proliferation of Nuclear Weapons, to the General Assembly at its thirty-first session through the Secretary-General;

7. *Requests* the International Atomic Energy Agency, within its sphere of competence, to continue its present examination of the aspects of the peaceful application of nuclear explosions, which the Board of Governors of the Agency has authorized under its resolution adopted on 11 June 1975, and to report on progress in all these areas to the General Assembly at its thirty-first session;

8. *Requests* the Conference of the Committee on Disarmament to keep under review, in its consideration of an elaboration of a comprehensive test ban treaty, the arms control implications of nuclear explosions for peaceful purposes, including the possibility that such explosions could be misused to circumvent any ban on the testing of nuclear weapons;

9. *Stresses* the need to ensure, particularly in the context of a comprehensive test ban, that any testing or application of nuclear explosions for peaceful purposes does not contribute to the testing or refinement of the nuclear weapon arsenals of nuclear-weapon States or to the acquisition of nuclear explosive capability by other States;

10. *Calls upon* all Member States to support and assist in the fulfilment of these tasks.

GENERAL ASSEMBLY RESOLUTION 31/75: IMPLEMENTATION OF THE CONCLUSIONS OF THE FIRST REVIEW CONFERENCE OF THE PARTIES TO THE TREATY ON THE NON-PROLIFERATION OF NUCLEAR WEAPONS, DECEMBER 10, 1976[1]

The General Assembly,

Recognizing that the danger of nuclear warfare remains a grave threat to the survival of mankind,

---

[1]U.N. doc. A/RES/31/75, January 11, 1977, in *Documents on Disarmament, 1976*, pp. 933–35.

Convinced that the prevention of any further proliferation of nuclear weapons or other nuclear explosive devices remains a vital element in efforts to avert nuclear warfare,

Convinced that the promotion of this objective will be furthered by more rapid progress towards the cessation of the nuclear arms race and the initiation of effective measures of nuclear disarmament,

Further convinced that the discontinuance of all test explosions of nuclear weapons for all time would constitute an important step in these efforts,

Noting that the Treaty on the Non-Proliferation of Nuclear Weapons, to which about one hundred States are parties, implies a balance of mutual responsibilities and obligations of all States parties to the Treaty, nuclear-weapon as well as non-nuclear-weapon States,

Recalling that the States parties to the Treaty on the Non-Proliferation of Nuclear Weapons met at Geneva from 5 to 30 May 1975 to review the operation of the Treaty with a view to assuring that the purposes of the preamble and the provisions of the Treaty were being realized,

Further recalling that the Final Document of the Review Conference of the Parties to the Treaty on the Non-Proliferation of Nuclear Weapons includes, *inter alia*, a Final Declaration and a number of interpretative statements in connexion with the Final Declaration,

Noting that the Conference has called for universal adherence to the Treaty on the Non-Proliferation of Nuclear Weapons,

Recognizing the necessity of effective international safeguards in order to ensure that the peaceful applications of nuclear energy will not lead to further proliferation of nuclear weapons or other nuclear explosive devices,

Underlining the important role of the International Atomic Energy Agency in implementing international non-proliferation policies in connexion with the peaceful uses of nuclear energy,

Concerned that the nuclear arms race continues unabated,

Recognizing that various appropriate means are necessary to meet the security concerns of non-nuclear-weapon States,

1. *Urgently calls* for determined efforts by all nuclear-weapon States:

(*a*) To bring about the cessation of the nuclear arms race;

(*b*) To undertake effective measures in the direction of nuclear disarmament;

(*c*) To find an early solution to the difficulties in reaching agreement to discontinue all test explosions of nuclear weapons for all time as a step towards the realization of these objectives;

2. *Emphasizes* the particular responsibility of the two major nuclear-weapon States in this regard;

3. *Stresses* the urgency of international co-operative efforts in appropriate forums to prevent the further proliferation of nuclear weapons or other nuclear explosive devices;

4. *Recognizes* that States accepting effective non-proliferation restraints have a right to full access to the peaceful uses of nuclear energy and underlines the importance of all efforts to increase the availability of energy, particularly for the needs of the developing countries of the world;

5. *Requests* the International Atomic Energy Agency to accord high priority to its programme of work in these areas;

6. *Decides* to include in the provisional agenda of its thirty-third session an item entitled "Implementation of the conclusions of the first Review Conference of the Parties to the Treaty on the Non-Proliferation of Nuclear Weapons and establishment of a preparatory committee for the second Conference".

GENERAL ASSEMBLY RESOLUTION 33/57: IMPLEMENTATION OF THE CONCLUSIONS OF THE FIRST REVIEW CONFERENCE OF THE PARTIES TO THE TREATY ON THE NON-PROLIFERATION OF NUCLEAR WEAPONS AND ESTABLISHMENT OF A PREPARATORY COMMITTEE FOR THE SECOND CONFERENCE, DECEMBER 14, 1978[1]

The General Assembly,

Recalling its resolution 2373 (XXII) of 12 June 1968, the annex of which contains the Treaty on the Non-Proliferation of Nuclear Weapons,

Noting the provisions of article VIII, paragraph 3, of that Treaty concerning the holding of successive review conferences,

Noting that in the Final Document of the first Review Conference of the Parties to the Treaty on the Non-Proliferation of Nuclear Weapons, held at Geneva from 5 to 30 May 1975, a majority of the States parties to the Treaty proposed to the depositary Governments that a second conference should be convened in 1980,

Recalling its resolution 31/75 of 10 December 1976, in which it decided to include in the provisional agenda of its thirty-third session an item entitled "Implementation of the conclusions of the first Review Conference of the Parties to the Treaty on the Non-Proliferation of Nuclear Weapons and establishment of a preparatory committee for the second Conference",

1. *Notes* that, following appropriate consultations, a preparatory committee has been formed of parties to the Treaty on the Non-Proliferation of Nuclear Weapons serving on the Board of Governors of the International Atomic Energy Agency or represented on the Committee on Disarmament;

2. *Requests* the Secretary-General to render the necessary assistance and to provide such services, including summary records, as may be required for the Review Conference of the Parties to the Treaty on the Non-Proliferation of Nuclear Weapons and its preparation.

THE SECOND REVIEW CONFERENCE OF THE PARTIES TO THE TREATY ON THE NON-PROLIFERATION OF NUCLEAR WEAPONS, 1980[2]

The Second Review Conference of the Parties to the Treaty on the Non-proliferation of Nuclear Weapons could not agree on an agreed final declaration, primarily because of fundamental differences on Articles IV and VI of the treaty; it did recommend that a third review conference be convened in 1985, stating:

At its final plenary meeting, on 7 September, the Conference proposed to the Depositary Governments that a third conference to review the operation of the Treaty be convened in 1985. The Conference accordingly invited States Parties to the Treaty which are Members of the United Nations to request the Secretary-General of the United Nations to include the following item in the provisional agenda of the thirty-eighth session of the General Assembly: "Implementation of the conclusions of the Second Review Conference of the Parties to the Treaty on the Non-Proliferation of Nuclear Weapons and Establishment of a Preparatory Committee for the Third Conference."

---

[1]U.N. doc. A/RES/33/57, January 10, 1979, in *Documents on Disarmament, 1978*, p. 717.
[2]United Nations Department for Disarmament Affairs, U.N. doc. NPT/CONF. II/22/I., 1980.

GENERAL ASSEMBLY RESOLUTION 38/74: IMPLEMENTATION OF THE CONCLUSIONS OF THE SECOND REVIEW CONFERENCE OF THE PARTIES TO THE TREATY ON THE NON-PROLIFERATION OF NUCLEAR WEAPONS AND ESTABLISHMENT OF THE PREPARATORY COMMITTEE FOR THE THIRD REVIEW CONFERENCE OF THE PARTIES TO THE TREATY, DECEMBER 15, 1983[1]

The General Assembly,

Recalling its resolution 2373 (XXII) of 12 June 1968, the annex to which contains the Treaty on the Non-Proliferation of Nuclear Weapons,

Noting the provisions of article VIII, paragraph 3, of that Treaty concerning the holding of successive review conferences,

Noting that in the Final Document of the Second Review Conference of the Parties to the Treaty on the Non-Proliferation of Nuclear Weapons, held at Geneva from 11 August to 7 September 1980, the Conference proposed to the Depositary Governments that a third conference to review the operation of the Treaty be convened in 1985 and noting that there appears to be a consensus among the parties that the Third Review Conference should be held at Geneva in August/September of that year,

1. *Notes* that, following appropriate consultations, an open-ended Preparatory Committee for the Third Review Conference of the Parties to the Treaty on the Non-Proliferation of Nuclear Weapons was formed of parties to the Treaty serving on the Board of Governors of the International Atomic Energy Agency or represented on the Committee on Disarmament as well as any party to the Treaty which may express its interest in participating in the work of the Preparatory Committee;

2. *Requests* the Secretary-General to render the necessary assistance and to provide such services, including summary records, as may be required for the Third Review Conference of the Parties to the Treaty on the Non-Proliferation of Nuclear Weapons and its preparation.

THE THIRD REVIEW CONFERENCE OF THE PARTIES TO THE TREATY ON THE NON-PROLIFERATION OF NUCLEAR WEAPONS, 1985, FINAL DECLARATION[2]

The States Party to the Treaty on the Non-proliferation of Nuclear Weapons which met in Geneva from 27 August to 21 September 1985 to review the operation of the treaty solemnly declare:

- their conviction that the Treaty is essential to international peace and security,
- their continued support for the objectives of the Treaty which are:
  - the prevention of proliferation of nuclear weapons or other nuclear explosive devices;
  - the cessation of the nuclear arms race, nuclear disarmament and a Treaty on general and complete disarmament;
  - the promotion of co-operation between States Parties in the field of the peaceful uses of nuclear energy,

---

[1]United Nations Department for Disarmament Affairs, U.N. doc. A/RES/38/74, December 15, 1983.
[2]United Nations Department for Disarmament Affairs, U.N. doc. NPT/CONF. III/64/I, Annex I, 1985.

- the reaffirmation of their firm commitment to the purposes of the Preamble and the provisions of the Treaty,
- their determination to enhance the implementation of the Treaty and to further strengthen its authority.

Review of the Operation of the Treaty and Recommendations

Articles I and II and preambular paragraphs 1–3

The Conference noted the concerns and convictions expressed in preambular paragraphs 1 to 3 and agreed that they remain valid. The States Party to the Treaty remain resolved in their belief in the need to avoid the devastation that a nuclear war would bring. The Conference remains convinced that any proliferation of nuclear weapons would seriously increase the danger of a nuclear war.

The Conference agreed that the strict observance of the terms of Articles I and II remains central to achieving the shared objectives of preventing under any circumstances the further proliferation of nuclear weapons and preserving the Treaty's vital contribution to peace and security, including to the peace and security of non-Parties.

The Conference acknowledged the declarations by nuclear-weapons States Party to the Treaty that they had fulfilled their obligations under Article I. The Conference further acknowledged the declarations that non-nuclear-weapons States Party to the Treaty had fulfilled their obligations under Article II. The Conference was of the view therefore that one of the primary objectives of the Treaty had been achieved in the period under review.

The Conference also expressed deep concern that the national nuclear programmes of some States non-Party to the Treaty may lead them to obtain a nuclear weapon capability. States Party to the Treaty stated that any further detonation of a nuclear explosive device by any non-nuclear-weapon State would constitute a most serious breach of the non-proliferation objective.

The Conference noted the great and serious concerns expressed about the nuclear capability of South Africa and Israel. The Conference further noted the calls on all States for the total and complete prohibition of the transfer of all nuclear facilities, resources or devices to South Africa and Israel and to stop all exploitation of Namibian uranium, natural or enriched, until the attainment of Namibian independence.

Article III and preambular paragraphs 4 and 5

1. The Conference affirms its determination to strengthen further the barriers against the proliferation of nuclear weapons and other nuclear explosive devices to additional States. The spread of nuclear explosive capabilities would add immeasurably to regional and international tensions and suspicions. It would increase the risk of nuclear war and lessen the security of all States. The Parties remain convinced that universal adherence to the Non-Proliferation Treaty is the best way to strengthen the barriers against proliferation and they urge all States not party to the Treaty to accede to it. The Treaty and the régime of non-proliferation it supports play a central role in promoting regional and international peace and security, *inter alia*, by helping to prevent the spread of nuclear explosives. The non-proliferation and safeguards commitments in the Treaty are essential also for peaceful nuclear commerce and co-operation.

2. The Conference expresses the conviction that IAEA safeguards provide assurance that

States are complying with their undertakings and assist States in demonstrating this compliance. They thereby promote further confidence among States and, being a fundamental element of the Treaty, help to strengthen their collective security. IAEA safeguards play a key role in preventing the proliferation of nuclear weapons and other nuclear explosive devices. Unsafeguarded nuclear activities in non-nuclear-weapon States pose serious proliferation dangers.

3. The Conference declares that the commitment to non-proliferation by nuclear-weapon States Party to the Treaty pursuant to Article I, by non-nuclear-weapon States Party to the Treaty pursuant to Article II, and by the acceptance of IAEA safeguards on all peaceful nuclear activities within non-nuclear-weapon States Party to the Treaty pursuant to Article III is a major contribution by those States to regional and international security. The Conference notes with satisfaction that the commitments in Articles I–III have been met and have greatly helped prevent the spread of nuclear explosives.

4. The Conference therefore specifically urges all non-nuclear-weapon States not party to the Treaty to make an international legally-binding commitment not to acquire nuclear weapons or other nuclear explosive devices and to accept IAEA safeguards on all their peaceful nuclear activities, both current and future, to verify that commitment. The Conference further urges all States in their international nuclear co-operation and in their nuclear export policies and, specifically as a necessary basis for the transfer of relevant nuclear supplies to non-nuclear-weapon States, to take effective steps towards achieving such a commitment to non-proliferation and acceptance of such safeguards by those States. The Conference expresses its view that accession to the Non-Proliferation Treaty is the best way to achieve that objective.

5. The Conference expresses its satisfaction that four of the five nuclear-weapon States have voluntarily concluded safeguards agreements with the IAEA, covering all or part of their peaceful nuclear activities. The Conference regards those agreements as further strengthening the non-proliferation régime and increasing the authority of IAEA and the effectiveness of its safeguards system. The Conference calls on the nuclear-weapon States to continue to co-operate fully with the IAEA in the implementation of these agreements and calls on IAEA to take full advantage of this co-operation. The Conference urges the People's Republic of China similarly to conclude a safeguards agreement with IAEA. The Conference recommends the continued pursuit of the principle of universal application of IAEA safeguards to all peaceful nuclear activities in all States. To this end, the Conference recognizes the value of voluntary offers and recommends further evaluation of the economic and practical possibility of extending application of safeguards to additional civil facilities in the nuclear-weapon States as and when IAEA resources permit and consideration of separation of the civil and military facilities in the nuclear-weapon States. Such an extending of safeguards will enable the further development and application of an effective régime in both nuclear-weapon States and non-nuclear-weapon States.

6. The Conference also affirms the great value to the non-proliferation régime of commitments by the nuclear-weapon States that nuclear supplies provided for peaceful use will not be used for nuclear weapons or other nuclear explosive purposes. Safeguards in nuclear-weapon States pursuant to their safeguards agreements with IAEA can verify observance of those commitments.

7. The Conference notes with satisfaction the adherence of further Parties to the Treaty and the conclusion of further safeguards agreements in compliance with the undertaking of the Treaty and recommends that:

(a) The non-nuclear-weapon States Party to the Treaty that have not concluded the agreements required under Article III (4) conclude such agreements with IAEA as soon as possible;

(b) The Director-General of IAEA intensify his initiative of submitting to States concerned draft agreements to facilitate the conclusion of corresponding safeguards agreements, and that Parties to the Treaty, in particular Depositary Parties, should actively support these initiatives;

(c) All States Party to the Treaty make strenuous individual and collective efforts to make the Treaty truly universal.

8. The Conference notes with satisfaction that IAEA in carrying out its safeguards activities has not detected any diversion of a significant amount of safeguarded material to the production of nuclear weapons, other nuclear explosive devices or to purposes unknown.

9. The Conference notes that IAEA safeguards activities have not hampered the economic, scientific or technological development of the Parties to the Treaty, or international co-operation in peaceful nuclear activities and it urges that this situation be maintained.

10. The Conference commends IAEA on its implementation of safeguards pursuant to this Treaty and urges it to continue to ensure the maximum technical and cost effectiveness and efficiency of its operations, while maintaining consistency with the economic and safe conduct of nuclear activities.

11. The Conference notes with satisfaction the improvement of IAEA safeguards which has enabled it to continue to apply safeguards effectively during a period of rapid growth in the number of safeguarded facilities. It also notes that IAEA safeguards approaches are capable of adequately dealing with facilities under safeguards. In this regard, the recent conclusion of the project to design a safeguards régime for centrifuge enrichment plants and its implementation is welcomed. This project allows the application of an effective régime to all plants of this type in the territories both of nuclear-weapon States and non-nuclear-weapon States Parties to the Treaty.

12. The Conference emphasizes the importance of continued improvements in the effectiveness and efficiency of IAEA safeguards, for example, but not limited to:

(a) Uniform and non-discriminatory implementation of safeguards;

(b) The expeditious implementation of new instruments and techniques;

(c) The further development of methods for evaluation of safeguards effectiveness in combination with safeguards information;

(d) Continued increases in the efficiency of the use of human and financial resources and of equipment.

13. The Conference believes that further improvement of the list of materials and equipment which, in accordance with Article III (2) of the Treaty, calls for the application of IAEA safeguards should take account of advances in technology.

14. The Conference recommends that IAEA establish an internationally agreed effective system of international plutonium storage in accordance with Article XII(A)5 of its statute.

15. The Conference welcomes the significant contributions made by States Parties in facilitating the application of IAEA safeguards and in supporting research, development and other supports to further the application of effective and efficient safeguards. The Conference urges that such co-operation and support be continued and that other States Parties provide similar support.

16. The Conference calls upon all States to take IAEA safeguards requirements fully into account while planning, designing and constructing new nuclear fuel cycle facilities and while modifying existing nuclear fuel cycle facilities.

17. The Conference also calls on States Parties to the Treaty to assist IAEA in applying its safeguards, *inter alia*, through the efficient operation of State systems of accounting for and control of nuclear material, and including compliance with all notification requirements in accordance with safeguards agreements.

18. The Conference welcomes the Agency's endeavours to recruit and train staff of the highest professional standards for safeguards implementation with due regard to the widest possible geographical distribution, in accordance with Article VII D of the IAEA Statute. It calls upon States to exercise their right regarding proposals of designation of IAEA inspectors in such a way as to facilitate the most effective use of safeguards manpower.

19. The Conference also commends to all States Parties the merits of establishment of international fuel cycle facilities, including multinational participation, as a positive contribution to reassurance of the peaceful use and non-diversion of nuclear materials. While primarily a national responsibility, the Conference sees advantages in international co-operation concerning spent fuel storage and nuclear waste storage.

20. The Conference calls upon States Parties to continue their political, technical and financial support of the IAEA safeguards system.

21. The Conference underlines the need for IAEA to be provided with the necessary financial and human resources to ensure that the Agency is able to continue to meet effectively its safeguards responsibilities.

22. The Conference urges all States that have not done so to adhere to the Convention on the physical protection of nuclear material at the earliest possible date.

Article IV and preambular paragraphs 6 and 7

1. The Conference affirms that the NPT fosters the world-wide peaceful use of nuclear energy and reaffirms that nothing in the Treaty shall be interpreted as affecting the inalienable right of any Party to the Treaty to develop research, production and use of nuclear energy for peaceful purposes without discrimination and in conformity with Articles I and II.

2. The Conference reaffirms the undertaking by all Parties to the Treaty, in accordance with Article IV and preambular paragraphs 6 and 7, to facilitate the fullest possible exchange of equipment, materials and scientific and technological information for the peaceful uses of nuclear energy and the right of all Parties to the Treaty to participate in such exchange. In this context, the Conference recognizes the importance of services. This can contribute to progress in general and to the elimination of technological and economic gaps between the developed and developing countries.

3. The Conference reaffirms the undertaking of the Parties to the Treaty in a position to do so to co-operate in contributing, alone or together with other States or international organizations, to the further development of the applications of nuclear energy for peaceful purposes, especially in the territories of the non-nuclear-weapon States Party to the Treaty, with due consideration for the needs of the developing areas of the world. In this context the Conference recognizes the particular needs of the least developed countries.

4. The Conference requests that States Parties consider possible bilateral co-operation measures to further improve the implementation of Article IV. To this end, States Parties are requested to give in written form their experiences in this area in the form of national contributions to be presented in a report to the next Review Conference.

5. The Conference recognizes the need for more predictable long-term supply assurances with effective assurances of non-proliferation.

6. The Conference commends the recent progress which the IAEA's Committee on Assurances of Supply (CAS) has made towards agreeing on a set of principles related to this matter, and expresses the hope that the Committee will complete this work soon. The Conference further notes with satisfaction the measures which CAS has recommended to the IAEA Board of Governors for alleviating technical and administrative problems in international shipments of nuclear items, emergency and back-up mechanisms, and mechanisms for

the revision of international nuclear co-operation agreements and calls for the early completion of the work of CAS and the implementation of its recommendations.

7. The Conference reaffirms that in accordance with international law and applicable treaty obligations, States should fulfill their obligations under agreements in the nuclear field, and any modification of such agreements, if required, should be made only by mutual consent of the parties concerned.

8. The Conference confirms that each country's choices and decisions in the field of peaceful uses of nuclear energy should be respected without jeopardizing their respective fuel cycle policies. International co-operation in this area, including international transfer and subsequent operations should be governed by effective assurances of non-proliferation and predictable long-term supply assurances. The issuance of related licences and authorization involved should take place in a timely fashion.

9. While recognizing that the operation and management of the back-end of the fuel cycle including nuclear waste storage are primarily a national responsibility, the Conference acknowledges the importance for the peaceful uses of nuclear energy of international and multilateral collaboration for arrangements in this area.

10. The Conference expresses its profound concern about the Israeli military attack on Iraq's safeguarded nuclear reactor on 7 June 1981. The Conference recalls Security Council Resolution 487 of 1981, strongly condemning the military attack by Israel which was unanimously adopted by the Council and which considered that the said attack constituted a serious threat to the entire IAEA safeguards régime which is the foundation of the Non-Proliferation Treaty. The Conference also takes note of the decisions and resolutions adopted by the United Nations General Assembly and the International Atomic Energy Agency on this attack, including Resolution 425 of 1984 adopted by the General Conference of the IAEA.

11. The Conference recognizes that an armed attack on a safeguarded nuclear facility, or threat of attack, would create a situation in which the Security Council would have to act immediately in accordance with provisions of the United Nations Charter. The Conference further emphasizes the responsibilities of the Depositaries of NPT in their capacity as permanent members of the Security Council to endeavour, in consultation with the other members of the Security Council, to give full consideration to all appropriate measures to be undertaken by the Security Council to deal with the situation, including measures under Chapter VII of the United Nations Charter.

12. The Conference encourages Parties to be ready to provide immediate peaceful assistance in accordance with international law to any Party to the NPT, if it so requests, whose safeguarded nuclear facilities have been subject to an armed attack, and calls upon all States to abide by any decisions taken by the Security Council in accordance with the United Nations Charter in relation to the attacking State.

13. The Conference considers that such attacks could involve grave dangers due to the release of radioactivity and that such attacks or threats of attack jeopardize the development of the peaceful uses of nuclear energy. The Conference also acknowledges that the matter is under consideration by the Conference on Disarmament and urges co-operation of all States for its speedy conclusion.

14. The Conference acknowledges the importance of the work of the International Atomic Energy Agency (IAEA) as the principal agent for technology transfer amongst the international organizations referred to in Article IV (2) and welcomes the successful operation of the Agency's technical assistance and co-operation programmes. The Conference records with appreciation that projects supported from these programmes covered a wide spectrum of applications, related both to power and non-power uses of nuclear energy notably in agriculture, medicine, industry and hydrology. The Conference notes that the Agency's

assistance to the developing States Party to the Treaty has been chiefly in the non-power uses of nuclear energy.

15. The Conference welcomes the establishment by the IAEA, following a recommendation of the First Review Conference of the Parties to the Treaty, of a mechanism to permit the channelling of extra-budgetary funds to projects additional to those financed from the IAEA Technical Assistance and Co-operation Fund. The Conference notes that this channel has been used to make additional resources available for a wide variety of projects in developing States Party to the Treaty.

16. In this context, the Conference proposes the following measures for consideration by the IAEA:

(i) IAEA assistance to developing countries in siting, construction, operation and safety of nuclear power projects and the associated trained manpower provision to be strengthened.

(ii) To provide, upon request, assistance in securing financing from outside sources for nuclear power projects in developing countries, and in particular the least developed countries.

(iii) IAEA assistance in nuclear planning systems for developing countries to be strengthened in order to help such countries draw up their own nuclear development plans.

(iv) IAEA assistance on country-specific nuclear development strategies to be further developed, with a view to identifying the application of nuclear technology that can be expected to contribute most to the development both of individual sectors and developing economies as a whole.

(v) Greater support for regional co-operative agreements, promoting regional projects based on regionally agreed priorities and using inputs from regional countries.

(vi) Exploration of the scope for multi-year, multi-donor projects financed from the extra-budgetary resources of the IAEA.

(vii) The IAEA's technical co-operation evaluation activity to be further developed, so as to enhance the Agency's effectiveness in providing technical assistance.

17. The Conference underlines the need for the provision to the IAEA of the necessary financial and human resources to ensure that the Agency is able to continue to meet effectively its responsibilities.

18. The Conference notes the appreciable level of bilateral co-operation in the peaceful uses of nuclear energy, and urges that States in a position to do so should continue and where possible increase the level of their co-operation in these fields.

19. The Conference urges that preferential treatment should be given to the non-nuclear-weapon States Party to the Treaty in access to or transfer of equipment, materials, services and scientific and technological information for the peaceful uses of nuclear energy, taking particularly into account needs of developing countries.

20. Great and serious concerns were expressed at the Conference about the nuclear capability of South Africa and Israel and that the development of such a capability by South Africa and Israel would undermine the credibility and stability of the non-proliferation Treaty régime. The Conference noted the demands made on all States to suspend any co-operation which would contribute to the nuclear programme of South Africa and Israel. The Conference further noted the demands made on South Africa and Israel to accede to the NPT, to accept IAEA safeguards on all their nuclear facilities and to pledge themselves not to manufacture or acquire nuclear weapons or other nuclear explosive devices.

21. The Conference recognizes the growing nuclear energy needs of the developing countries as well as the difficulties which the developing countries face in this regard, particularly with respect to financing their nuclear power programmes. The Conference calls upon States Party to the Treaty to promote the establishment of favourable conditions in national, regional and international financial institutions for financing of nuclear energy

projects including nuclear power programmes in developing countries. Furthermore, the Conference calls upon the IAEA to initiate and the Parties to the Treaty to support the work of an expert group study on mechanisms to assist developing countries in the promotion of their nuclear power programmes, including the establishment of a Financial Assistance Fund.

22. The Conference recognizes that further IAEA assistance in the preparation of feasibility studies and infrastructure development might enhance the prospects for developing countries for obtaining finance, and recommends such countries as are members of the Agency to apply for such help under the Agency's technical assistance and co-operation programmes. The Conference also acknowledges that further support for the IAEA's Small and Medium Power Reactor (SMPR) Study could help the development of nuclear reactors more suited to the needs of some of the developing countries.

23. The Conference expresses its satisfaction at the progress in the preparations for the United Nations Conference for the Promotion of International Co-operation in the Peaceful Uses of Nuclear Energy (UNCPICPUNE) and its conviction that UNCPICPUNE will fully realize its goals in accordance with the objectives of resolution 32/50 and relevant subsequent resolutions of the General Assembly for the development of national programmes of peaceful uses of nuclear energy for economic and social development, especially in the developing countries.

24. The Conference considers that all proposals related to the promotion and strengthening of international co-operation in the peaceful uses of nuclear energy which have been produced by the Third Review Conference of the NPT, be transmitted to the Preparatory Committee of the UNCPICPUNE.

Article V

1. The Conference reaffirms the obligation of Parties to the Treaty to take appropriate measures to ensure that potential benefits from any peaceful applications of nuclear explosions are made available to non-nuclear weapon States Party to the Treaty in full accordance with the provisions of article V and other applicable international obligations, that such services should be provided to non-nuclear weapon States Party to the Treaty on a non-discriminatory basis and that the charge to such Parties for the explosive devices used should be as low as possible and exclude any charge for research and development.

2. The Conference confirms that the IAEA would be the appropriate international body through which any potential benefits of the peaceful applications of nuclear explosions could be made available to non-nuclear weapon States under the terms of article V of the Treaty.

3. The Conference notes that the potential benefits of the peaceful applications of nuclear explosions have not been demonstrated and that no requests for services related to the peaceful applications of nuclear explosions have been received by the IAEA since the Second NPT Review Conference.

Article VI and preambular paragraphs 8–12

A.

1. The Conference recalled that under the provisions of article VI all parties have undertaken to pursue negotiations in good faith:

- on effective measures relating to cessation of the nuclear arms race at an early date;
- on effective measures relating to nuclear disarmament;
- on a Treaty on general and complete disarmament under strict and effective international control.

2. The Conference undertook an evaluation of the achievements in respect of each aspect of the article in the period under review, and paragraphs 8 to 12 of the preamble, and in particular with regard to the goals set out in preambular paragraph 10 which recalls the determination expressed by the parties to the Partial Test Ban Treaty to:

- continue negotiations to achieve the discontinuance of all test explosions of nuclear weapons for all time.

3. The Conference recalled the declared intention of the parties to the Treaty to achieve at the earliest possible date the cessation of the nuclear arms race and to undertake effective measures in the direction of nuclear disarmament and their urging made to all States parties to co-operate in the attainment of this objective. The Conference also recalled the determination expressed by the parties to the 1963 Treaty banning nuclear weapons tests in the atmosphere, in outer space and under water in its preamble to seek to achieve the discontinuance of all test explosions on nuclear weapons for all time and the desire to further the easing of international tension and the strengthening of trust between States in order to facilitate the cessation of the manufacture of nuclear weapons, the liquidation of all existing stockpiles, and the elimination from national arsenals of nuclear weapons and the means of their delivery.

4. The Conference notes that the Tenth Special Session of the General Assembly of the United Nations concluded, in paragraph 50 of its Final Document, that the achievement of nuclear disarmament will require urgent negotiations of agreements at appropriate stages and with adequate measures of verification satisfactory to the States concerned for:

(a) Cessation of the qualitative improvement and development of nuclear-weapon systems;

(b) Cessation of the production of all types of nuclear weapons and their means of delivery, and of the production of fissionable material for weapons purposes;

(c) A comprehensive, phased programme with agreed time tables whenever feasible, for progressive and balanced reduction of stockpiles of nuclear weapons and their means of delivery, leading to their ultimate and complete elimination at the earliest possible time.

5. The Conference also recalled that in the Final Declaration of the First Review Conference, the parties expressed the view that the conclusion of a treaty banning all nuclear-weapon tests was one of the most important measures to halt the nuclear arms race and expressed the hope that the nuclear-weapon States party to the Treaty would take the lead in reaching an early solution of the technical and political difficulties of this issue.

6. The Conference examined developments relating to the cessation of the nuclear arms race, in the period under review and noted in particular that the destructive potentials of the nuclear arsenals of nuclear-weapon States parties, were undergoing continuing development, including a growing research and development component in military spending, continued nuclear testing, development of new delivery systems and their deployment.

7. The Conference noted the concerns expressed regarding developments with far reaching implications and the potential of a new environment, space, being drawn into the arms race. In that regard the Conference also noted the fact that the United States of America and the Union of Soviet Socialist Republics are pursuing bilateral negotiations on a broad complex of questions concerning space and nuclear arms, with a view to achieving effective agreements aimed at preventing an arms race in space and terminating it on Earth.

8. The Conference noted with regret that the development and deployment of nuclear weapon systems had continued during the period of review.

9. The Conference also took note of numerous proposals and actions, multilateral and unilateral, advanced during the period under review by many States with the aim of making progress towards the cessation of the nuclear arms race and nuclear disarmament.

10. The Conference examined the existing situation in the light of the undertaking assumed by the parties in Article VI to pursue negotiations in good faith on effective measures relating to cessation of the nuclear arms race at an early date and to nuclear disarmament. The Conference recalled that a stage of negotiations on the Strategic Arms Limitations Talks (SALT II) had been concluded in 1979, by the signing of the Treaty which had remained unratified. The Conference noted that both the Union of Soviet Socialist Republics and the United States of America have declared that they are abiding by the provisions of SALT II.

11. The Conference recalled that the bilateral negotiations between the Union of Soviet Socialist Republics and the United States of America which were held between 1981 and 1983 were discontinued without any concrete results.

12. The Conference noted that bilateral negotiations between the Union of Soviet Socialist Republics and the United States of America had been held in 1985 to consider questions concerning space and nuclear arms, both strategic and intermediate-range, with all the questions considered and resolved in their interrelationship. No agreement has emerged so far. These negotiations are continuing.

13. The Conference evaluated the progress made in multilateral nuclear disarmament negotiations in the period of the Review.

14. The Conference recalled that the trilateral negotiations on a comprehensive test ban treaty, begun in 1977 between the Union of Soviet Socialist Republics, the United Kingdom of Great Britain and Northern Ireland and the United States of America, had not continued after 1980, that the Committee on Disarmament and later the Conference on Disarmament had been called upon by the General Assembly of the United Nations in successive years to begin negotiations on such a Treaty, and noted that such negotiations had not been initiated, despite the submission of draft treaties and different proposals to the Conference on Disarmament in this regard.

15. The Conference noted the lack of progress on relevant items of the agenda of the Conference on Disarmament, in particular those relating to the cessation of the nuclear arms race and nuclear disarmament, the prevention of nuclear war including all related matters and effective international arrangements to assure non-nuclear-weapon States against the use or threat of use of nuclear weapons.

16. The Conference noted that two Review Conferences had taken place since 1980, one on the Sea-bed Treaty and one on the Environmental Modification Treaty and three General Conferences of the Agency for the Prohibition of Nuclear Weapons in Latin America. In 1982, a Special United Nations General Assembly Session on Disarmament took place without any results in matters directly linked to nuclear disarmament.

17. The Conference also noted the last five years had thus not given any results concerning negotiations on effective measures relating to cessation of the nuclear arms race and to nuclear disarmament.

B.

1. The Conference concluded that, since no agreements had been reached in the period under review on effective measures relating to the cessation of an arms race at an early date, on nuclear disarmament and on a Treaty on general and complete disarmament under strict and effective international control, the aspirations contained in preambular paragraphs 8 to 12 had still not been met, and the objectives under Article VI had not yet been achieved.

2. The Conference reiterated that the implementation of Article VI is essential to the maintenance and strengthening of the Treaty, reaffirmed the commitment of all States Parties to the implementation of this Article and called upon the States Parties to intensify their

efforts to achieve fully the objectives of the Article. The Conference addressed a call to the nuclear-weapon States Parties in particular to demonstrate this commitment.

3. The Conference welcomes the fact that the United States of America and the Union of Soviet Socialist Republics are conducting bilateral negotiations on a complex of questions concerning space and nuclear arms—both strategic and intermediate-range—with all these questions considered and resolved in their interrelationship. It hopes that these negotiations will lead to early and effective agreements aimed at preventing an arms race in space and terminating it on Earth, at limiting and reducing nuclear arms, and at strengthening strategic stability. Such agreements will complement and ensure the positive outcome of multilateral negotiations on disarmament, and would lead to the reduction of international tensions and the promotion of international peace and security. The Conference recalls that the two sides believe that ultimately the bilateral negotiations, just as efforts in general to limit and reduce arms, should lead to the complete elimination of nuclear arms everywhere.

4. The Conference urges the Conference on Disarmament, as appropriate, to proceed to early multilateral negotiations on nuclear disarmament in pursuance of paragraph 50 of the Final Document of the First Special Session of the General Assembly of the United Nations devoted to disarmament.

5. The Conference reaffirms the determination expressed in the preamble of the 1963 Partial Test Ban Treaty, confirmed in Article I(b) of the said Treaty and reiterated in preambular paragraph 10 of the Non-Proliferation Treaty, to achieve the discontinuance of all test explosions of nuclear weapons for all time.

6. The Conference also recalls that in the Final Document of the First Review Conference, the Parties expressed the view that the conclusion of a Treaty banning all nuclear weapons tests was one of the most important measures to halt the nuclear arms race. The Conference stresses the important contribution that such a treaty would make toward strengthening and extending the international barriers against the proliferation of nuclear weapons; it further stresses that adherence to such a treaty by all States would contribute substantially to the full achievement of the non-proliferation objective.

7. The Conference also took note of the appeals contained in five successive United Nations General Assembly resolutions since 1981 for a moratorium on nuclear weapons testing pending the conclusion of a comprehensive test ban Treaty, and of similar calls made at this Conference. It also took note of the measure announced by the Union of Soviet Socialist Republics for a unilateral moratorium on all nuclear explosions from 6 August 1985 until 1 January 1986, which would continue beyond that date if the United States of America, for its part, refrained from carrying out nuclear explosions. The Union of Soviet Socialist Republics suggested that this would provide an example for other nuclear-weapon States and would create favourable conditions for the conclusion of a Comprehensive Test Ban Treaty and the promotion of the fuller implementation of the Non-Proliferation Treaty.

8. The Conference took note of the unconditional invitation extended by the United States of America to the Union of Soviet Socialist Republics to send observers, who may bring any equipment they deem necessary, to measure a United States of America nuclear test in order to begin a process which in the view of the United States of America would help to ensure effective verification of limitations on under-ground nuclear testing.

9. The Conference also took note of the appeals contained in five United Nations General Assembly resolutions since 1982 for a freeze on all nuclear weapons in quantitative and qualitative terms, which should be taken by all nuclear-weapon States or, in the first instance and simultaneously, by the Union of Soviet Socialist Republics and the United States of America on the understanding that the other nuclear-weapon States would follow their example, and of similar calls made at this Conference.

10. The Conference took note of proposals by the Union of Soviet Socialist Republics and the United States of America for the reduction of nuclear weapons.

11. The Conference took note of proposals submitted by States Parties on a number of related issues relevant to achieving the purposes of Article VI and set out in Annex I to this document and in the statements made in the General Debate of the Conference.

12. The Conference reiterated its conviction that the objectives of Article VI remained unfulfilled and concluded that the nuclear-weapon States should make greater efforts to ensure effective measures for the cessation of the nuclear arms race at an early date, for nuclear disarmament and for a Treaty on general and complete disarmament under strict and effective international control.

The Conference expressed the hope for rapid progress in the United States–USSR bilateral negotiations.

The Conference except for certain States whose views are reflected in the following subparagraph deeply regretted that a comprehensive multilateral Nuclear Test Ban Treaty banning all nuclear tests by all States in all environments for all time had not been concluded so far and, therefore, called on the nuclear-weapon States Party to the Treaty to resume trilateral negotiations in 1985 and called on all the nuclear-weapon States to participate in the urgent negotiation and conclusion of such a Treaty as a matter of the highest priority in the Conference on Disarmament.

At the same time, the Conference noted that certain States Party to the Treaty, while committed to the goal of an effectively verifiable comprehensive Nuclear Test Ban Treaty, considered deep and verifiable reductions in existing arsenals of nuclear weapons as the highest priority in the process of pursuing the objectives of Article VI.

The Conference also noted the statement of the USSR, as one of the nuclear-weapon States Party to the Treaty, recalling its repeatedly expressed readiness to proceed forthwith to negotiations, trilateral and multilateral, with the aim of concluding a comprehensive Nuclear Test Ban Treaty and the submission by it of a draft Treaty proposal to this end.

Article VII and the Security of Non-Nuclear-Weapon States

1. The Conference observes the growing interest in utilizing the provisions of Article VII of the Non-Proliferation Treaty, which recognizes the right of any group of States to conclude regional treaties in order to assure the absence of nuclear weapons in their respective territories.

2. The Conference considers that the establishment of nuclear-weapon-free zones on the basis of arrangements freely arrived at among the States of the region concerned constitutes an important disarmament measure and therefore the process of establishing such zones in different parts of the world should be encouraged with the ultimate objective of achieving a world entirely free of nuclear weapons. In the process of establishing such zones, the characteristics of each region should be taken into account.

3. The Conference emphasizes the importance of concluding nuclear-weapon-free zone arrangements in harmony with internationally recognized principles, as stated in the Final Document of the First Special Session of the United Nations devoted to disarmament.

4. The Conference holds the view that, under appropriate conditions, progress towards the establishment of nuclear-weapon-free zones will create conditions more conducive to the establishment of zones of peace in certain regions of the world.

5. The Conference expresses its belief that concrete measures of nuclear disarmament

would significantly contribute to creating favourable conditions for the establishment of nuclear-weapon-free zones.

6. The Conference expresses its satisfaction at the continued successful operation of the Treaty for the Prohibition of Nuclear Weapons in Latin America (Treaty of Tlatelolco). It reaffirms the repeated exhortations of the General Assembly to France, which is already a signatory of Additional Protocol I, to ratify it, and calls upon the Latin American States that are eligible to become parties to the treaty to do so. The Conference welcomes the signature and ratification of Additional Protocol II to this Treaty by all nuclear-weapon States.

7. The Conference also notes the continued existence of the Antarctic Treaty.

8. The Conference notes the endorsement of the South Pacific Nuclear Free Zone Treaty by the South Pacific Forum on 6 August 1985 at Rarotonga and welcomes this achievement as consistent with Article VII of the Non-Proliferation Treaty. The Conference also takes note of the draft Protocols to the South Pacific Nuclear Free Zone Treaty and further notes the agreement at the South Pacific Forum that consultations on the Protocols should be held between members of the Forum and the nuclear-weapon States eligible to sign them.

9. The Conference takes note of the existing proposals and the ongoing regional efforts to achieve nuclear-weapon-free zones in different areas of the world.

10. The Conference recognizes that for the maximum effectiveness of any treaty arrangements for establishing a nuclear-weapon-free zone the co-operation of the nuclear-weapon States is necessary. In this connection, the nuclear-weapon States are invited to assist the efforts of States to create nuclear-weapon-free zones, and to enter into binding undertakings to respect strictly the status of such a zone and to refrain from the use or threat of use of nuclear weapons against the States of the zone.

11. The Conference welcomes the consensus reached by the United Nations General Assembly at its thirty-fifth session that the establishment of a nuclear-weapon-free zone in the region of the Middle East would greatly enhance international peace and security, and urges all parties directly concerned to consider seriously taking the practical and urgent steps required for the implementation of the proposal to establish a nuclear-weapon-free zone in the region of the Middle East.

12. The Conference also invites the nuclear-weapon States and all other States to render their assistance in the establishment of the zone and at the same time to refrain from any action that runs counter to the letter and spirit of United Nations General Assembly resolution 39/54.

13. The Conference considers that acceding to the Non-Proliferation Treaty and acceptance of IAEA safeguards by all States in the region of the Middle East will greatly facilitate the creation of a nuclear-weapon-free zone in the region and will enhance the credibility of the Treaty.

14. The Conference considers that the development of a nuclear weapon capability by South Africa at any time frustrates the implementation of the Declaration on the Denuclearization of Africa and that collaboration with South Africa in this area would undermine the credibility and the stability of the Non-Proliferation Treaty régime. South Africa is called upon to submit all its nuclear installations and facilities to IAEA safeguards and to accede to the Non-Proliferation Treaty. All States Parties directly concerned are urged to consider seriously taking the practical and urgent steps required for the implementation of the proposal to establish a nuclear-weapon-free zone in Africa. The nuclear-weapon States are invited to assist the efforts of States to create a nuclear-weapon-free zone in Africa, and to enter into binding undertakings to respect strictly the status of such a zone and to refrain from the use or threat of use of nuclear weapons against the States of the zone.

15. The Conference considers that the most effective guarantee against the possible use

of nuclear weapons and the danger of nuclear war is nuclear disarmament and the complete elimination of nuclear weapons. Pending the achievement of this goal on a universal basis and recognizing the need for all States to ensure their independence, territorial integrity and sovereignty, the Conference reaffirms the particular importance of assuring and strengthening the security of non-nuclear-weapon States Parties which have renounced the acquisition of nuclear weapons. The Conference recognizes that different approaches may be required to strengthen the security of non-nuclear-weapon States Parties to the Treaty.

16. The Conference underlines again the importance of adherence to the Treaty by non-nuclear-weapon States as the best means of reassuring one another of their renunciation of nuclear weapons and as one of the effective means of strengthening their mutual security.

17. The Conference takes note of the continued determination of the Depositary States to honour their statements, which were welcomed by the United Nations Security Council in resolution 255 (1968), that, to ensure the security of the non-nuclear-weapon States Parties to the Treaty, they will provide or support immediate assistance, in accordance with the Charter, to any non-nuclear-weapon State Party to the Treaty which is a victim of an act or an object of a threat of aggression in which nuclear weapons are used.

18. The Conference reiterates its conviction that, in the interest of promoting the objectives of the Treaty, including the strengthening of the security of non-nuclear-weapon States Parties, all States, both nuclear-weapon and non-nuclear-weapon States, should refrain, in accordance with the Charter of the United Nations, from the threat or the use of force in relations between States, involving either nuclear or non-nuclear weapons.

19. The Conference recalls that the Tenth Special Session of the General Assembly in paragraph 59 of the Final Document took note of the declarations made by the nuclear-weapon States regarding the assurance of non-nuclear-weapon States against the use or threat of use of nuclear weapons and urged them to pursue efforts to conclude, as appropriate, effective arrangements to assure non-nuclear-weapon States against the use or threat of use of nuclear weapons.

20. Being aware of the consultations and negotiations on effective international arrangements to assure non-nuclear-weapon States against the use or threat of use of nuclear weapons, which have been under way in the Conference on Disarmament for several years, the Conference regrets that the search for a common approach which could be included in an international legally binding instrument, has been unsuccessful. The Conference takes note of the repeatedly expressed intention of the Conference on Disarmament to continue to explore ways and means to overcome the difficulties encountered in its work and to carry out negotiations on the question of effective international arrangements to assure non-nuclear-weapon States against the use or threat of use of nuclear weapons. In this connection, the Conference calls upon all States, particularly the nuclear-weapon States, to continue the negotiations in the Conference on Disarmament devoted to the search for a common approach acceptable to all, which could be included in an international instrument of a legally binding character.

Article VIII

The States Party to the Treaty participating in the Conference propose to the Depositary Governments that a fourth Conference to review the operation of the Treaty be convened in 1990.

The Conference accordingly invites States Party to the Treaty which are Members of the United Nations to request the Secretary-General of the United Nations to include the following item in the provisional agenda of the forty-third session of the General Assembly:

Implementation of the conclusions of the third Review Conference of the Parties to the Treaty on the Non-Proliferation of Nuclear Weapons and establishment of a Preparatory Committee for the fourth Conference.

Article IX

The Conference, having expressed great satisfaction that the overwhelming majority of States have acceded to the Treaty on the Non-Proliferation of Nuclear Weapons and having recognized the urgent need for further ensuring the universality of the Treaty, appeals to all States, particularly the nuclear-weapon States and other States advanced in nuclear technology, which have not yet done so, to adhere to the Treaty at the earliest possible date.

GENERAL ASSEMBLY RESOLUTION 40/94 M: THIRD REVIEW CONFERENCE OF THE PARTIES TO THE TREATY ON THE NON-PROLIFERATION OF NUCLEAR WEAPONS, DECEMBER 12, 1985[1]

The General Assembly,

Recalling its resolution 38/74 of 15 December 1983, in which, *inter alia*, it noted that in the Final Document of the Second Review Conference of the Parties to the Treaty on the Non-Proliferation of Nuclear Weapons, held at Geneva from 11 August to 7 September 1980, the Conference had proposed to the depositary Governments that a third conference to review the operation of the Treaty be convened in 1985 and that there appeared to be a consensus among the parties that the Third Review Conference should be held at Geneva in August/September of that year,

Recalling that States parties to the Treaty met at Geneva from 27 August to 21 September 1985 to review the operation of the Treaty with a view to assuring that the purposes of the preamble and the provisions of the Treaty were being realized,

Notes with satisfaction that on 21 September 1985, the Third Review Conference of the Parties to the Treaty on the Non-Proliferation of Nuclear Weapons adopted by consensus a Final Declaration.

GENERAL ASSEMBLY RESOLUTION 43/82: IMPLEMENTATION OF THE CONCLUSIONS OF THE THIRD REVIEW CONFERENCE OF THE PARTIES TO THE TREATY ON THE NON-PROLIFERATION OF NUCLEAR WEAPONS AND ESTABLISHMENT OF A PREPARATORY COMMITTEE FOR THE FOURTH REVIEW CONFERENCE, DECEMBER 7, 1988[2]

The General Assembly,

Recalling its resolution 2373 (XXII) of 12 June 1968, the annex to which contains the Treaty on the Non-Proliferation of Nuclear Weapons,

Noting the provisions of article VIII, paragraph 3, of that Treaty concerning the holding of successive review conferences,

---

[1]United Nations Department for Disarmament Affairs, U.N. doc. A/RES/40/94, December 12, 1985.
[2]United Nations Department for Disarmament Affairs, U.N. doc. A/RES/43/82, December 7, 1988.

Noting that, in the Final Declaration of the Third Review Conference of the Parties to the Treaty on the Non-Proliferation of Nuclear Weapons held at Geneva from 27 August to 21 September 1985, the Conference proposed to the Depositary Governments that a fourth conference to review the operation of the Treaty be convened in 1990, and also noting that there appears to be a consensus among the parties that the Fourth Review Conference should be held at Geneva in August/September of that year,

1. *Notes* that, following appropriate consultations, an open-ended preparatory committee has been formed of parties to the Treaty on the Non-Proliferation of Nuclear Weapons serving on the Board of Governors of the International Atomic Energy Agency or represented in the Conference on Disarmament, as well as any party to the Treaty that may express its interest in participating in the work of the preparatory committee;

2. *Requests* the Secretary-General to render the necessary assistance and to provide such services, including summary records, as may be required for the Fourth Review Conference of the Parties to the Treaty on the Non-Proliferation of Nuclear Weapons and its preparation.

SELECTED NATIONAL STATEMENTS ON THE TWENTIETH ANNIVERSARY OF THE OPENING FOR SIGNATURE OF THE NPT[1]

Secretary-General Commends Effective Performance of Nuclear Non-Proliferation Treaty

The following statement, regarding the Nuclear Non-Proliferation Treaty, is attributable to the Spokesman for Secretary-General Javier Perez de Cuellar:

Twenty years ago today the Treaty on the Non-Proliferation of Nuclear Weapons was opened for signature. Since that time no new nuclear-weapon State has emerged and 133 non-nuclear-weapon parties have committed themselves not to acquire nuclear weapons.

The Treaty has thus so far effectively performed its function as a barrier against the acquisition of nuclear weapons.

The need remains to strengthen the regime still further, both by encouraging wider adherence to the Treaty and by the achievement of early and significant reductions in the number of existing nuclear weapons, so that the Treaty may continue to play its valuable role in contributing to international peace and security. In this context the Secretary-General hopes that further steps shall be taken towards the implementation of all the provisions of the Treaty.

Efforts to halt and prevent the proliferation of nuclear weapons, in all its aspects, are of utmost importance and the Secretary-General urges that all States should make every endeavour to pursue these objectives.

Statement by the Honourable R. J. L. Hawke, AC, Prime Minister of Australia, on the Occasion of the Twentieth Anniversary of the Opening for Signature of the Treaty on the Non-Proliferation of Nuclear Weapons

Today marks the Twentieth Anniversary of the opening for signature of the Treaty on the Non-Proliferation of Nuclear Weapons (NPT).

The NPT is the basis of international efforts to prevent the spread of nuclear weapons. The Treaty makes a major contribution to international peace and security and is generally

---

[1]United Nations Department of Public Information, July 1, 1988

recognized as the single most effective and widely adhered to nuclear arms control agreement in existence. Australia ratified the Treaty on 23 January 1973.

Membership of the Treaty provides reassurance to the international community and neighbouring States of a nation's peaceful nuclear intentions and has become the standard for responsible international nuclear behaviour.

Australia continues to urge universal adherence to the NPT. It is my hope that the Twentieth Anniversary of its opening for signature will act as a spur to those countries which have yet to commit themselves to the Treaty.

Statement by the Ministry of Foreign Affairs of the Arab Republic of Egypt on the Occasion of the Twentieth Anniversary of the Opening for Signature of the Treaty on the Non-Proliferation of Nuclear Weapons

1 July 1988 is the twentieth anniversary of the opening for signature of the Treaty on the Non-Proliferation of Nuclear Weapons, the purpose of which was to save the world from the calamities of nuclear war and the dangers of proliferation and escalation in the production of nuclear weapons. Accordingly, the Treaty constitutes one of the principal achievements of the United Nations and the international community in the field of nuclear disarmament and, as such, takes pride of place in this field with other achievements at the multilateral and bilateral levels. The Treaty on the Non-Proliferation of Nuclear Weapons has also given greater impetus to efforts aimed at establishing nuclear-weapon-free zones, particularly in the Middle Eastern and African regions.

In celebrating this anniversary, the Ministry of Foreign Affairs of the Arab Republic of Egypt wishes to express Egypt's firm belief in the need to achieve complete disarmament, and particularly nuclear disarmament, so that the world can enjoy undisturbed peace and reassuring security in which friendly relations among States will flourish, in which resources and energies will be directed towards the development and welfare of peoples and in which the use of nuclear energy will be restricted to peaceful purposes, in keeping with the provisions of article IV of the Treaty on the Non-Proliferation of Nuclear Weapons.

Egypt made a considerable effort to ensure the adoption of the Non-Proliferation Treaty, and was eager to be among the first States to sign it. Accordingly, Egypt realizes the vital importance of extending the scope of application of the Treaty to all States, and is therefore making a strong appeal to all countries of the world, and particularly those in the Middle Eastern and African regions, that have not yet acceded to the Treaty, to rapidly accede thereto and to comply with the provisions of the Treaty and subject all their nuclear installations to the system of safeguards of the International Atomic Energy Agency in order to confirm their good intentions and contribute to the confidence-building measures, particularly in these two vital regions to which Egypt belongs.

In conclusion, the Egyptian Ministry of Foreign Affairs wishes to commend the diligent and positive endeavours that are being made by the International Atomic Energy Agency in its task of ensuring the application of the system of safeguards to the States parties to the Treaty and co-operating with them in the field of the peaceful uses of nuclear energy.

Declaration by the Foreign Affairs Committee of the Parliament of the Hungarian People's Republic on the Twentieth Anniversary of the Opening for Signature of the Treaty on the Non-Proliferation of Nuclear Weapons

Twenty years ago, on 1 July 1968 the Treaty on the Non-Proliferation of Nuclear Weapons was opened for signature and signed on the very first day by not less than 61 States including the Hungarian People's Republic. During the past two decades the number of States Parties has increased to 136 which has made the Treaty on the Non-Proliferation of Nuclear Weapons an arms control agreement with the widest adherence and contributed to averting the danger of nuclear catastrophes threatening the destruction of the entire world.

The Foreign Affairs Committee is convinced that it is expressing the unanimous view of the Hungarian public opinion by reaffirming—after two decades of its operation—continued commitment of Hungary towards the objectives, obligations and measures set forth in the Treaty. It would have a beneficial effect if all the States which for whatever reason have not yet signed or ratified the Treaty would take that step without delay, which is rightly expected from them by the international community. The reality of the nuclear age is that every country of the world has a share of responsibility to discharge in promoting the cause of peace and security, the reduction of international tension, the limitation of armaments and disarmament.

A special responsibility is placed upon the States possessing nuclear weapons. They are expected by the peoples of the world to set an example and to take the lead in the limitation, reduction and elimination of nuclear weapons. The Foreign Affairs Committee therefore welcomes with profound appreciation the ratification of the agreement concluded by the Union of Soviet Socialist Republics and the United States of America on the elimination of the medium and shorter range missiles as well as the beginning of its implementation. It attaches also great importance to the efforts of the two States aimed at reaching an agreement on the 50 per cent reduction of their strategic offensive armaments. The agreements that may lead to a large-scale reduction in the number and yield of the test explosions by the two States can be welcomed as important intermediate steps on the way to halting the nuclear arms race.

The Treaty on the Non-Proliferation of Nuclear Weapons lays emphasis on the promotion of research and use for peaceful purposes of the nuclear energy and on the international co-operation in this field. The Hungarian People's Republic is particularly interested that various forms of such co-operation should develop unhindered.

In this connection the Foreign Affairs Committee attaches paramount importance to the activity of the International Atomic Energy Agency whose task is to verify compliance with the Treaty, to prevent the misuse of nuclear materials, and to provide for the international co-ordination of measures relating to the peaceful uses of nuclear energy.

The security of peaceful applications would be greatly enhanced by the early conclusion of an international agreement on the prohibition of any attack against nuclear power stations and other nuclear facilities. The Foreign Affairs Committee wishes to stress that the Conference on Disarmament is an appropriate forum for bringing the negotiations to a successful end, which in its turn requires constructive efforts and readiness to come to an agreement from all the participants of the negotiations.

Joint Statement by the Nordic Foreign Ministers on the Twentieth Anniversary of the Non-Proliferation Treaty
1 July 1988

The Treaty on the Non-Proliferation of Nuclear Weapons was opened for signature 20 years ago today. The five Nordic countries, Denmark, Finland, Iceland, Norway and Sweden were among the first to sign and to ratify the Treaty.

The Nordic Governments consider the Non-Proliferation Treaty a vital instrument to prevent the proliferation of nuclear weapons and to ensure that nuclear energy is only developed for peaceful purposes. In our view, the Treaty remains the most important arms control agreement reached multilaterally so far. The Treaty has made a significant contribution to international stability and security.

The strong commitment of the five Nordic countries to further strengthening the non-proliferation régime is reflected in joint Nordic initiatives and working documents submitted to the United Nations and to the NPT Review Conferences. Universal adherence to the NPT and full compliance with the letter and spirit of its obligations are the best approach to achieving the primary goals of the Treaty: to avert the spread of nuclear weapons, to promote international co-operation in the field of peaceful uses of nuclear energy and to limit and reduce nuclear weapons.

The vast majority of States are already parties to the NPT. Close to 140 States have now ratified and adhered to the Treaty. It is regrettable, however, that some important States have not yet done so. Since its entry into force, no State party to the Treaty has acquired nuclear weapons. In the view of the Nordic Governments, the constantly increasing membership as well as the successful conclusion of the Third Review Conference testify to the great significance of the Treaty and are an encouraging development in efforts to prevent the spread of nuclear weapons.

In celebrating the twentieth anniversary of the Treaty, the Nordic Governments urge all States which have not already done so to accede to the Non-Proliferation Treaty.

Twentieth Anniversary of the Non-Proliferation Treaty: Statement by the Secretary of State for Foreign and Commonwealth Affairs, Sir Geoffrey Howe, 1 July 1988

We celebrate today the 20th anniversary of the Treaty on the Non-Proliferation of Nuclear Weapons. The United Kingdom, one of the Treaty's three depositary powers, is proud to have been closely involved in this Treaty enterprise from the very start.

The Treaty has made an inestimable contribution to peace in the world today by containing the spread of nuclear weapons while at the same time encouraging the peaceful uses of nuclear energy. It is therefore central to the security of each and every one of us. The Treaty is the most widely supported arms control agreement in existence with 136 parties—four-fifths of the total membership of the United Nations. I welcome the recent accession of Spain and Trinidad and Tobago as well as the decision by Saudi Arabia announced earlier this year to accede. On this 20th anniversary, I applaud their example and appeal to all countries who have not yet signed the Non-Proliferation Treaty to do so. It is vital that, at a time when there is significant progress in arms control, all governments should play their part in discouraging nuclear proliferation.

Statement by the Government of Mexico on the Occasion of the Twentieth Anniversary of the Opening for Signature of the Treaty on the Non-Proliferation of Nuclear Weapons

The Government of Mexico welcomes the celebration of the twentieth anniversary of the opening for signature of the Treaty on the Non-Proliferation of Nuclear Weapons. During the last two decades, the existence of this important international instrument has helped to create a safer world, promoting the principle that nuclear energy should be used above all for peaceful purposes.

The Treaty on Non-Proliferation (NPT) established the legal framework for preventing the destructive power of the atom from spreading out of control and threatening the very survival of mankind. At the same time, in order to give effect to its provisions, the International Atomic Energy Agency was set up, a body which has kept careful watch on the way different countries have used atomic energy for peaceful purposes. By preventing the proliferation of States possessing nuclear weapons and regulating the peaceful uses of nuclear energy, the NPT has strengthened international peace and security and opened up new development possibilities for all nations.

The Treaty establishes binding obligations of great importance for all States Parties, and in particular those that possess nuclear weapons. Thus the Parties to the Treaty undertake to pursue negotiations in good faith on effective measures relating to cessation of the nuclear arms race and to nuclear disarmament. Prominent among these negotiations are those relating to the complete prohibition of nuclear weapon tests, a priority objective of Mexico's disarmament policy.

The Government of Mexico welcomes the progress made in negotiations on nuclear weapons between the United States and the Soviet Union and expresses the hope that it will lead to the adoption of new measures to promote general and complete disarmament, to which they committed themselves under the Non-Proliferation Treaty. At the same time, the Government of Mexico expresses its concern at the possibility of the two Powers concluding an agreement which by legitimizing the carrying out of nuclear tests would depart from the original spirit of the Treaty.

The celebration of the twentieth anniversary of the opening for signature of the Treaty on the Non-Proliferation of Nuclear Weapons is a proper occasion to reiterate that only faithful fulfilment of their obligations by all States Parties will create the necessary conditions to ensure its success and universal application. In the same way, this is an appropriate moment to appeal to States which are not yet Parties to the Treaty to make their contribution to strengthening the nuclear non-proliferation system in the near future.

Answers Given by Mr. N. I. Ryzhkov, Chairman of the Council of Ministers of the USSR, in Reply to Questions from a TASS Correspondent

Question: On 1 July 1988 we celebrate the twentieth anniversary of the opening for signature of the Treaty on the Non-Proliferation of Nuclear Weapons. The Soviet Government is, of course, one of the depositaries of this Treaty, together with the Governments of the United Kingdom and the United States. What do you see as the basic results of the Treaty over the past twenty years and what is its place in the present system of international relations?

Answer: The Treaty on the Non-Proliferation of Nuclear Weapons was one of the very first international agreements on nuclear arms limitation. It has been an important factor in ensuring international security and strategic stability.

Above all, the conclusion of the Treaty erected a powerful barrier of international law in the way of a very serious potential danger—the acquisition of nuclear weapons by a wide range of States, which would undoubtedly have carried with it a threat of putting excessive strain on the whole structure of international relations and increasing the number of different kinds of crisis situations and incidents, and indeed simply of fatal accidents. Not to mention the fact that the spread of nuclear weapons could be compared to the chain reaction which is the basis for the operation of the weapon itself. And this in circumstances where a large number of countries had reached a level of scientific and technological development enabling them to produce the bomb if they wished.

Mankind recognized that the spread of nuclear weapons was a general threat to everyone and that an adequate collective response had to be found to that threat.

For many countries, this meant weighing on the political scales, with all due serious-ness, considerations of national prestige, their strategic interests and ideas and the task of ensuring security.

In his article "Reality and the guarantees of a secure world", Mr. M. S. Gorbachev, General Secretary of the Central Committee of the Communist Party of the Soviet Union, called the Treaty on the Non-Proliferation of Nuclear Weapons "a unique example of a high sense of responsibility on the part of States".

A high sense of responsibility for the fate of our planet was shown both by the nuclear and by the non-nuclear States; the former by binding themselves not to contribute in any way to the spread of nuclear weapons and to pursue negotiations on nuclear disarmament in good faith; the latter by voluntarily renouncing the acquisition of nuclear weapons by any means. The signature of the Treaty containing these commitments was a display of great political realism.

Today the non-proliferation principles established by the Treaty enjoy wide recog-nition, they have become an integral part of the fundamentals of modern international law. It is no accident that the Treaty on the Non-Proliferation of Nuclear Weapons has the widest range of parties—136 States—of any international legal instrument in the field of arms limitation.

The history of the Treaty on the Non-Proliferation of Nuclear Weapons confirms its effectiveness. The international régime of non-proliferation of nuclear weapons established on the basis of the Treaty, including a system of safeguards (verification) by the International Atomic Energy Agency, agreements on the principles governing nuclear exports, and the practice that has grown up of bilateral and multilateral consultations between parties to the Treaty, is convincing evidence of the international community's sincere interest in supporting and strengthening its foundation. The Soviet Union makes a weighty contribution to the process of establishing the non-proliferation régime, strictly fulfilling its obligations under the Treaty and vigorously complying with the relevant rules on nuclear exports.

Particular recognition should be given to the role of IAEA, which is entrusted with verification functions under the Treaty and has developed a system of safeguards for effec-tively and reliably ensuring that nuclear materials are not diverted from peaceful uses to the production of nuclear weapons. This verification is carried out with full respect for States' sovereign rights and without detriment to the development of their peaceful nuclear activities or international co-operation in the field of the peaceful uses of atomic energy.

The wide international recognition of the ideas involved in the non-proliferation of nuclear weapons is reflected in the fact that countries that are not parties to the Treaty itself do not as a rule object to the principles established in it, but in essence conform with them in their policies and commercial and economic activities. It is thus possible to speak of these principles as being universal in their application.

Admittedly, among those who are not parties to the Treaty on the Non-Proliferation of Nuclear Weapons, there are also some States which have no particular scruples about openly displaying their nuclear ambitions. These include above all Israel and South Africa, whose position on the matter undoubtedly complicates the already complicated situations in the Middle East and southern Africa. It is high time the Israeli and South African authorities recognized that their countries' welfare does not lie in a nuclear future and that acceding to the Treaty on the Non-Proliferation of Nuclear Weapons is the only choice dictated by reason and morality, by any feeling of responsibility to their peoples.

Question: How do you now see the future of the Treaty, particularly in connection with the task of freeing the world completely from nuclear weapons?

Answer: The Treaty already symbolizes for most States the reality of a peaceful alternative to the military use of nuclear energy. What we see as the ultimate aim is that this should become the rule for everyone. Incidentally, one of the arguments often put forward against nuclear disarmament is this: once having invented nuclear weapons, mankind will not be able to forget how to make them. That may be true enough, but after all the Treaty has a whole set of machinery to ensure that nuclear technology does not take practical form in the production of weapons. In particular, we consider that there is every reason to use the experience of the IAEA safeguards to develop a system of verification for future nuclear disarmament measures.

The twentieth anniversary of the Treaty comes at a time of highly important events in the life of the international community. New political thinking reflecting the pressing demands and imperatives of today's world has found specific expression in the programme put forward by the Soviet Union for the stage-by-stage elimination of nuclear weapons. Today we are witnessing the first actual results of its practical implementation. I have in mind first and foremost the conclusion of the INF Treaty, substantial progress in the drafting of an agreement on a 50 per cent reduction in the strategic strike weapons of the USA and the USSR, and Soviet–United States talks on the limitation and ultimate prohibition of nuclear tests. Positive changes have become evident in many other spheres of international life. And there is a highly contemporary ring now to the commitment entered into by every party to the Treaty on the Non-Proliferation of Nuclear Weapons to pursue negotiations in good faith on effective measures relating to cessation of the nuclear arms race and to nuclear disarmament under strict and effective international control.

One of the prerequisites for a steady and unceasing process of nuclear disarmament such as is now just beginning is without doubt the preservation and strengthening of the Non-Proliferation Treaty. The Soviet Union will continue to come out firmly in support of the Treaty, which should remain in force until such time as a non-nuclear and non-violent peace becomes a reality on earth. The only thing that can replace it is a comprehensive international treaty on the non-resurrection of nuclear weapons after their complete and final elimination. ·

Statement of the President of the United States, Ronald Reagan, Commemorating the Twentieth Anniversary of the Signing of the Treaty on the Non-Proliferation of Nuclear Weapons

The Non-Proliferation Treaty is one of the international community's most vital instruments for preventing the spread of nuclear weapons and strengthening international peace and stability.

I firmly believe that nuclear war can never be won and must never be fought. If we are to succeed in halting the spread of nuclear weapons, the nations of the world must continue to work together. I call on all countries that have not yet adhered to the Non-Proliferation Treaty to do so to demonstrate their commitment to preventing the spread of nuclear weapons and to strengthening the foundations of peace. I also urge all parties to the Treaty to rededicate themselves to achieving its objective.

About the Authors

MOHAMED I. SHAKER is Ambassador of the Arab Republic of Egypt to the United Kingdom. He was president of the 1987 U. N. Conference to Promote International Cooperation in the Peaceful Uses of Nuclear Energy. Previously, he served as president of the 1985 Third Review Conference of the Parties to the NPT. He has also served as representative of the director-general of the International Atomic Energy Agency to the United Nations in New York. He is the author of *The Nuclear Non-Proliferation Treaty: Origin and Implementation, 1957–1979* (Oceana Publications, 1980).

BENJAMIN SANDERS is Coordinator, Programme for Promoting Nuclear Non-Proliferation, an international, nongovernmental project operating under the aegis of the University of Southhampton. He was secretary-general of the 1985 Third Review Conference of Parties to the NPT and deputy secretary-general of the 1980 Second Review Conference. He has also served as Director, Information and Studies Branch, U. N. Department for Disarmament Affairs. In the International Atomic Energy Agency, he held the positions of senior officer and, later, chief, Executive Section, in the Safeguards Department. He was the author of the first Stockholm International Peace Research Institute monograph on nuclear safeguards.

LEWIS A. DUNN is assistant vice president and manager of the Negotiations and Planning Division, Science Applications International Corporation. He has served as assistant director of the U. S. Arms Control and Disarmament Agency and as U. S. ambassador to the 1985 Third Review Conference of Parties to the NPT. He is the author of *Controlling the Bomb* (Yale University Press, 1982), and is the coeditor of *On-Site Inspection for Arms Control Verification* (forthcoming).

DAVID FISCHER is a consultant to the International Atomic Energy Agency. He has been the agency's assistant director general for external affairs and a consultant to IAEA Director General Hans Blix. He is the author of *Safeguarding the Atom* (Stockholm International Peace Research Institute, 1985), *The International Nuclear Non-Proliferation Regime* (United Nations, 1987), and *The Future of Non-Proliferation* (forthcoming).

247

LAWRENCE SCHEINMAN is professor of international law and relations at Cornell University, where he is currently Acting Director, Peace Studies Program. He served as a special advisor to the Director General, International Atomic Energy Agency. He has also been the head of the Office of International Policy Planning in the Energy Research and Development Administration and principal deputy to the Deputy Undersecretary of State for Security Assistance, Science, and Technology. His most recent book is *The International Atomic Energy Agency and World Nuclear Order* (Resources for the Future, 1987).

RICHARD BUTLER is Ambassador of Australia to Thailand. Previously, he served as the first Australian Ambassador for Disarmament. He was the Australian representative to the 1985 Third Review Conference of the Parties to the NPT. His diplomatic career has seen him posted to the Australian embassies at the United Nations, New York, Singapore, Bonn, Paris (OECD), and Geneva. He has also been deputy representative of Australia at the International Atomic Energy Agency. In 1988 he was made a Member of the Order of Australia "for services to international peace and disarmament."

ANTONIO CARREA is the Counselor on Nuclear Affairs for the Embassy of Argentina in Austria. He is also Alternate Permanent Representative and Alternate Governor for Argentina to the International Atomic Energy Agency. Previously, he held several different posts in the Argentine National Atomic Energy Commission, and he was the Argentine coordinator for and cochairman of the Spent Fuel Management Group of the International Nuclear Fuel Cycle Evaluation.

MUNIR AHMAD KHAN is Chairman of the Pakistan Atomic Energy Commission. He has been a member of the Board of Governors of the International Atomic Energy Agency and, in addition, has served as its chairman. He has also served in the Nuclear Power and Reactors Division of the IAEA. He has participated in numerous panels and groups related to international cooperation in the nuclear field sponsored by the Royal Institute of International Affairs, the Rockefeller Foundation, the American Nuclear Society, and the Japan Atomic Industrial Forum.

HARALD MÜLLER is Senior Fellow and Director of International Programs with the Peace Research Institute, Frankfurt and serves on the institute's executive board. He is also Visiting Professor, Johns Hopkins University, Center for International Relations, Bologna, Italy. Previously, he was a senior fellow at the Center for European Policy Studies, Brussels. He has also been visiting lecturer at the University of Southern California in Frankfurt.

RYUKICHI IMAI is Ambassador of Japan to Mexico. He has served as Permanent Representative of Japan to the Conference on Disarmament from 1982, and he represented Japan at the 1985 Third Review Conference of the Parties to the NPT. In addition, he is a member of the United Nations Advisory Board on Disarmament.

He is coauthor of *Nuclear Energy and Nuclear Proliferation: Japanese and American Views* (Westview Press, 1980).

ASHOK KAPUR is professor of political science at the University of Waterloo, Ontario. He has served as a member of the United Nations committee that reported on Israeli Nuclear Armament. He is the author of *India's Nuclear Option: Atomic Diplomacy and Decision Making* (Praeger, 1976), *International Nuclear Proliferation* (Praeger, 1979), and *Pakistan's Nuclear Development* (Croom Helm, 1987).

RAJU G. C. THOMAS is professor of political science at Marquette University. He has been a visiting scholar at Harvard, the University of California, Los Angeles, and the Massachusetts Institute of Technology. He is the author of *Indian Security Policy* (Princeton University Press, 1986), the editor of *The Great Power Triangle and Asian Security* (Lexington Books, 1983), and the coauthor of *Energy and Security in the Industrializing States* (University of Kentucky Press, 1989).

JOSEPH F. PILAT is on the staff of the Center for National Security Studies. He was a special adviser to the Department of Energy's representative at the 1985 Third Review Conference of the Parties to the NPT, and he also served as the representative of the office of the Secretary of Defense to the first and second meetings of the preparatory committee to the 1990 NPT review conference. He has been Special Assistant to the Principal Director and Assistant for Nonproliferation Policy in the Office of the Deputy Assistant Secretary of Defense for Negotiations Policy. He has taught at Georgetown University, where he was a Philip E. Mosely Fellow at the Center for Strategic and International Studies. He is the editor of *The Nonproliferation Predicament* (Transaction Books, 1985) and coeditor of *Atoms for Peace: An Analysis after Thirty Years* (Westview Press, 1985) and *The Nuclear Suppliers and Nonproliferation: International Policy Choices* (Lexington Books, 1985).

ROBERT E. PENDLEY is on the staff of the Center for National Security Studies. He holds a Ph.D. in political science from Northwestern University, as well as degrees in physics from the University of California at Berkeley and the University of Oregon. At Los Alamos he has held staff and program management positions in arms control, verification, and international security policy and has interacted extensively with U. S. government agencies and governments and institutes abroad. His Center responsibilites include formulation and execution of a number of the Center's programs of analysis and policy research. He is coeditor of *Atoms for Peace: An Analysis after Thirty Years* (Westview Press, 1985).

Index